華人情境下的基督宗教與社會關懷

王成勉◎主編

中央大學出版中心｜遠流

目次

作者簡介 （依論文順序排列）

Edmund Ryden SJ（雷敦龢）

Edmund Ryden SJ holds a PhD in Chinese Philosophy from the School of Oriental and African Studies, London University. He has published and translated in the field of sinology and is also active in the area of human rights. He lectures in the Law Department of Fu Jen Catholic University and in the Human Rights Programme of Soochow University, Taipei. He is a member of the Chinese Province of the Society of Jesus and resides among the indigenous peoples of Xinzhu County, Taiwan.

郭承天（Cheng-tian Kuo）

美國芝加哥大學政治學博士，國立政治大學政治系特聘教授、宗教所合聘教授。主要著作有：《政教的分立與制衡：從聖經看政教關係》、《國族神學的民主化：臺灣與中國大陸》、*Religion and Democracy in Taiwan*。

李向平

歷史學博士，華東師範大學二級教授、社會學系系主任、宗教與社會研究中心主任，中國社會學會宗教社會學專業委員會主任，上海市宗教學會副會長。主要論著有：《救世與救心》、《信仰、革命與權力秩序》、《信仰但不認同》、《中國信仰社會學論集》等。

李宜涯

中國文化大學中文研究所博士，曾任中原大學人文與教育學院通識教育中心主任，現為中原大學通識教育中心教授兼圖書館館長。主要著作：《聖壇前的創作——20年代基督教文學研究》、《晚唐詠史詩與平話演義之關係》。

劉義章

美國加州大學（Santa Barbara）哲學博士（歷史學），建道神學院基督教與中國文化研究中心學術總監。著有：《中國現代化的起步》、《盼望之灣——靈實建基50年》等，主編有《香港客家》等。

Philip L. Wickeri（魏克利）

Philip L. Wickeri is Advisor to the Archbishop on Theological and Historical Studies, the Hong Kong Sheng Kung Hui (Anglican-Episcopal), and Provincial Archivist for the HKSKH. He teaches at Ming Hua Theological College, and is a frequent speaker at universities, social science academies and seminaries.

His most recent book is *Christian Encounters with Chinese Culture: Essays on Anglican and Episcopal History in China* (2015). He is the author of the award-winning *Reconstructing Christianity in China: K. H. Ting and the Chinese Church* (2007). The Chinese version of this book will be published in 2017.

Rolf Gerhard Tiedemann（狄德滿）

Ph. D., School of Oriental and African Studies, University of London. Professor, Center for Boxer Movement Studies, Shandong University, China. Major Publications: *Reference Guide to Christian Missionary Societies in China: From the 16th to the 20th Century; Handbook of Christianity in China*, Vol. II.

張勤瑩

成功大學歷史所博士，世新大學舍我紀念館協同研究員。曾執行科技部「補

助赴國外從事博士後研究」，赴英國倫敦大學亞非學院歷史系進行訪問研究（2015.09-2016.09）。著有《被遺忘的中國童年——芝罘學校與內地會傳教士子女》（2014）。

皮國立

國立臺灣師範大學歷史學博士，現為中原大學通識教育中心助理教授。主要著作有：《國族、國醫與病人：近代中國的醫療和身體》、《「氣」與「細菌」的近代中國醫療史——外感熱病的知識轉型與日常生活》等書。

王成勉

美國亞利桑那大學東方研究博士，國立中央大學歷史研究所特聘教授。主要著作有：《文社的盛衰——二〇年代基督徒本色化之個案研究》、《教會、文化與國家》，主編 Contextualization of Christianity in China: An Evaluation in Modern Perspective。

陳睿文

香港中文大學宗教研究哲學博士，香港明華神學院講師。主要研究方向為中國基督教史。作品包括 Fragrant Flowers Bloom: T. C. Chao, Bliss Wiant and the Contextualization of Hymns in Twentieth Century China (Leipzig: Evangelische Verlagsanstalt, 2015)、《萬代要稱妳有福：香港聖公會聖馬利亞堂史（1912-2012）》（香港：基督教中國宗教文化研究社，2014，與 Philip. L. Wickeri 合著）等。

吳蕙芳

國立政治大學歷史學博士，國立臺灣海洋大學海洋文化研究所教授。代表著作有：《民初直魯豫盜匪之研究（1912-1928）》、《萬寶全書：明清時期的民間生活實錄》、《明清以來民間生活知識的建構與傳遞》、《基隆中元祭：史實、記憶與傳說》。

蘇友瑞

國立中正大學心理學研究所博士，中原大學通識教育中心助理教授。主要著作散見心靈小憩網站（http://life.fhl.net）的各類藝文欣賞相關文章，如《舒伯特的音樂心靈世界》、《古典音樂欣賞的科學精神與實踐》等。

潘秋郎

Trinity International University, Ph. D.（宣教神學）。曾任中原大學宗教研究所，現任中華基督教基層宣教訓練學院專任教師與門諾會信仰與生活委員會委員。

陳能治

國立成功大學歷史學博士，南臺科技大學通識教育中心專任副教授。主要著作有：《戰前十年中國的大學教育（1927-1937）》、《續修台南市志教育行政、教育設施與活動篇》、〈早期的孔祥熙：一位基督徒的教會歷練與公共參與（1890-1922）〉等論文。

劉家峰

山東大學歷史文化學院特聘教授。主要著作有：《抗戰時期的中國基督教大學》（與劉天路合著）、《中國基督教鄉村建設研究》等。

胡衛清

華東師範大學歷史學博士，山東大學歷史文化學院教授。著作有：《普遍主義的挑戰：近代中國基督教教育研究》、《教育與福音》、《苦難與信仰：近代潮汕基督徒的宗教經驗》。

序

　　基督宗教一方面是要信徒仰望神，追求天國，另一方面則是具有積極入世的精神，除要信徒潔身自愛外，還要關懷弱勢，依公義而行。如舊約有：「你們要洗濯、自潔，從我眼前除掉你們的惡行，要止住作惡，學習行善，尋求公平，解救受欺壓的；給孤兒伸冤，為寡婦辨屈。」（《以賽亞書》1: 16-17）在《彌迦書》則更清楚的講到上帝對信徒的要求為「只要你行公義，好憐憫，存謙卑的心，與你的上帝同行。」（6: 8）在新約中要求基督徒「行善」，更是一個經常出現的命令，如「我們原是他的工作，在基督耶穌裡造成的，為要叫我們行善，就是上帝所預備叫我們行的。」（《以弗所書》2: 10）「你們的光也當這樣照在人前，叫他們看見你們的好行為，便將榮耀歸給你們在天上的父。」（《馬太福音》5: 16）

　　是以「社會關懷」是基督宗教的重要教義，亦為所有信徒奉為圭臬。舉凡基督宗教所到之地，無不顯示教會（包括傳教士、信徒與教會機構）對於當地社會之關懷，形成教會與社會密切的互動關係。而自基督宗教入華以來，「社會關懷」更是引起極大的反響，一方面是有著各種慈善、愛心的活動，進而延伸到促進社會與政治的改革；另一方面則是因為教會介入許多事物，衝擊到社會的許多層面，在地方或國家引起不同的感受，甚至是排斥。這個有趣又複雜的現象，是一個非常值得重視與探討的課題。

　　雖然基督徒都同意「社會關懷」的基本意義，但是應用到社會時，卻會因宗派、領袖、過去經歷的不同，而有不同的見解與做法。是以「社會關懷」的光譜極大，從醫療、教育、救災、孤兒院等慈善活動，以迄戒毒、反纏足、提升婦女地位、改善工人農民生活等社會改革都有。顯示出「社會關懷」工作上有極大的差異性與多元性。到

十九、二十世紀之交,「現代派」神學思想的興起與「社會福音」的流行,也讓「社會關懷」的思想被廣泛的應用在許多教會的活動上。

過去極少以「社會關懷」作為探討主題的著作,同時坊間往往以慈善的角度來看待基督宗教的「社會關懷」,造成各界對於基督宗教「社會關懷」的了解有所侷限,而教會界也未有共識。然而,如果未能知悉基督宗教「社會關懷」的意涵,不惟不夠了解教會與社區互動的情形,更無法正確解讀教會發展、教會立場,以及教會的歷史。是以本書邀集對於基督宗教「社會關懷」卓有研究的中外學者,針對理論與案例撰文,而後經過審核,選編論文成為專輯,藉以呈現基督宗教在華發展的豐富面向,盼能提升認識,嘉惠學界。

此書共分為五部分來開展,每一部分的文章都是依據探討主題時間的先後來排列。第一部分是「解經與應用」,包括三篇文章。首先是 Edmund Ryden(雷敦龢)教授的 "Modalities and Changes in Christian Social Concern"。此文係以天主教的歷史脈絡來分析其中所演化的五種社會關懷模式,以大歷史的角度,提供讀者一個思考與比較的架構。接著是郭承天教授的論文 "In the Beginning, There Were Hermeneutical Mistakes of Church-State Relations in Modern China" 則是一個很有挑戰性的論文。他認為由於在中文《聖經》翻譯上的誤差,導致華人長期以來把「政教分立」當作「政教分離」,影響教會的社會參與,更影響到政權對待教會的立場與態度。相信這個背景,也一定影響到基督宗教「社會關懷」的層面。此部分最後一篇文章,則是李向平教授的〈私人信仰方式與基督教的社會關懷:以改革開放後的江浙城市為例〉。這篇文章基於在江浙一帶的田野調查,指出中國當代基督教的基本信仰方式已經呈現了一種私人化的信仰方式,產生對內優先、肢體互助的特性,也影響到社會關懷的態度與做法,但這情況是否能存續與繼續發展,則有待觀察主客觀的環境與互動。

第二部分為「關懷機構」之研究,主要在介紹「中華基督教青年會」、「基督教靈實協會」與「愛德基金會」三個單位。第一篇是李宜涯教授的〈中華基督教青年會的「全人關懷」:以《青年進步》

（1917-1920）為中心的探討〉。基督教青年會是常被注意到的教會團體，但是過去的研究卻沒有將其放在「全人關懷」的角度來檢視。根據作者對於該會機關報《青年進步》的研究，青年會所提出「德智體群」之論說與活動，相當符合今日「全人教育」的理念，也就是在塑造出一個有人格、有學識、健全體魄又具有公民意識的現代青年。第二篇文章是劉義章教授的〈「尊重生命・改變生命」：基督教靈實協會的服侍理念及其實踐（1953-2013）〉。「基督教靈實協會」誕生於香港1950年代初期的調景嶺難民營，自始就是懷著福音與救濟的目的來服務流離失所者。而後隨著時間的發展，該協會產生很有意義的演化，從醫藥宣教士到本土醫護人員接棒，從個人救濟到社區健康，建立起「尊重生命・改變生命」的核心價值與優良傳統。第三篇的作者是 Philip L. Wickeri（魏克利）教授，他是撰寫「愛德基金會」最理想的人選，不但曾經是該基金會在香港最早的代表，並且是實際推動工作的人士，與當時中國教會領袖交往甚深。而他這篇 "The Amity Foundation: Social Responsibility and Social Development in the Chinese Context"，就是在探討「愛德基金會」成立的經過，其與中國教會領袖的互動，以及如何度過這段磨合期。

　　第三部分的主題為「醫療事工」。這是社會上廣為人知、最受大眾稱道的教會關懷行動。第一篇是 R. G. Tiedemann（狄德滿）教授的文章 "Catholic Missions & the Ministry of Healing in China: With Special Reference to Health Care in Shandong"，主要在探討十九世紀末和二十世紀初，天主教在山東的醫療事工。他檢視在現代專業醫療制度以前，天主教修女在地方上所經營醫院和診所的特色與問題。第二篇文章〈二十世紀前期《使信月刊》中的臺灣：以英國長老教會傳教士的事工為中心〉，作者是張勤瑩博士，是藉傳教士辦的《使信月刊》來呈現英國長老教會傳教士的醫療關懷與福音事工。《使信月刊》是英國長老教會的機關報，自十九至二十世紀中葉報導不少有關臺灣的報導，不但向英國基督徒讀者介紹臺灣社會的生活與福音事工，亦圖激起基督徒讀者支持海外的宣教事業。第三篇是皮國立教授的文章〈民

國時期農村的醫療與衛生：以基督教人士之相關言論為主的分析〉。此文先論述1920年代末起基督教對中國農村社會的觀察，特別著眼於環境衛生與醫療方面的論述和作為。文章中很微妙的展現基督宗教的鄉村衛生論述與工作，及其在民國史上的特色與地位。

　　第四部分的主題為「特殊事工」，即是著眼於一些有別以往的新型社會關懷。第一篇文章是李宜涯、王成勉兩位教授所著的〈一戰時期「華工基督教青年會」的再評估〉。鑒於一些學界人士貶抑或忽視該青年會的成就與宗教性，兩位作者對一戰的「華工基督教青年會」進行辯證。他們檢視美國基督教青年會檔案館的史料與《華工週報》，探討「華工青年會」推展「德育」（spiritual education）的構想與作為，並呈現「華工基督教青年會」在基督教社會關懷上的意義。第二篇論文〈一種歌唱的關懷：以《民眾聖歌集》（1931）為例〉，則是注意到聖樂方面的社會關懷。中文的聖樂是研究過去教會史上較缺乏的地方，主要是需要在聖樂上專門的素養。作者陳睿文教授本身就有多年的音樂造詣，此處她分析趙紫宸與范天祥（Bliss Wiant）合作編撰《民眾聖歌集》中處境化及關懷民眾的特色，以及其中上帝與救贖的觀念，顯示這本讚美詩與基督教社會關懷之關聯。第三篇論文是吳蕙芳教授的〈天主教聖言會的社會服務事業：以新店大坪林德華女子公寓為例（1968-1988）〉。這項特殊的關懷起自聖言會的萬德華（Edward J. Wojniak）神父對於社會的回應。他在1960年代觀察到新店地區工廠林立，有大量受雇女工沒有適當的安頓之處，遂多方籌資，建成「德華女子公寓」。這公寓不只是提供住宿之用，更顧及到住宿女子的休閒活動與才藝學習，成為一項極具特色與時代意義的社會關懷。第四篇文章是蘇友瑞、潘秋郎兩位教授的論文〈深度休閒的實踐：真善美全人關懷協會的「為成人說故事」系列〉，主題是在論述一群基督徒在現代社會的一種新型的關懷方式。他們設計「為成人說故事」的社區事工，藉由社區讀書會及帶領人培訓為核心方向，並輔以網站企劃及有聲書的發行，使得參與讀書會的成員獲得支持團體的協助與聆聽，達到社會正向支持的力量與轉化，

並讓參與者從故事中重新找回人的意義。

　　第五部分為「時代考驗」，即是在討論在某一重大變動的時代，教會或基督徒如何去應付時代的考驗。基督徒並非必然是聖賢，他們都有人性，遇到試探、誘惑、動盪時代的考驗時，有些人會軟弱，扭曲了本應關懷社會的使命。此部分的第一篇文章是陳能治教授所撰的〈歐柏林學院與從政前的孔祥熙〉。孔祥熙是民國時期在金融與政治上的聞人。但是陳能治教授藉由歐柏林學院檔案館的史料，指出孔祥熙早年有很深的基督教淵源與信仰。其留學歐柏林學院返國後，投身山西銘賢中學的工作，並肩負許多教會界的工作，此皆顯示受到歐柏林精神之影響。第二篇文章〈從協進會幹事到國府專員：張福良與鄉村建設（1927-1939）〉，是劉家峰教授對於張福良身分轉化的探討。張福良在美國受過林業、園藝和鄉村教育的訓練，回國後有心就鄉村建設來振興國家。然而他本為協進會的農村幹事，卻在抗戰時期應聘擔任國民政府專員，在江西創辦農村服務區。這篇文章指出，張福良對於鄉村的關懷與建設是一致的，但是手段卻從「基督化鄉村社會」轉為「運用政治」來推動鄉村建設。然而社會關懷是否是使人皈依基督教的目的和手段，可能是更大一個問題，有待更多學者的研究與討論。最後一篇文章是胡衛清教授的〈大米與信仰：戰後中華基督教會汕頭區會的重建及困境（1945-1949）〉，主要在探討教會在抗戰勝利後的現實面。中華基督教會嶺東大會汕頭區會在二戰結束後過於依賴海外的救濟，不但失去自立的精神，更出現為爭利而勾心鬥角，不擇手段的情況。許多會堂濫用國外教會關懷之心，在利字之前失足，失去基督徒的見證，顯現人性的軟弱。

　　這五部分的十六篇論文，建構出基督宗教「社會關懷」的多元面向，研究內容從理論到實務、從機構到個人，而研究的案例則從正面肯定到負面批評都有包括。作者們包括歷史學、文學、政治學、社會學、宗教學、神學等不同領域，在觀點與視野的面相上相當廣闊。而提供論文的學者，有好幾位是此領域的資深學者，也有少數是甫獲博士學位的新秀，觀點與論述上可以說是互相輝映。少數幾篇論文的作

者因有需在學報發表之考量，曾先行發表於學報。現均取得各學報之授權收於本書。同時此論文集所收文章皆通過嚴格的外審，有些文稿甚至是經過兩次審核，使這本論文集達到學術的高水準，相信對於學術界會有很好的貢獻，這也是所有作者共同的心願。

王成勉 謹識於中大歷史所

2016.9.16

【解經與應用】

Modalities and Changes in Christian Social Concern

Edmund Ryden SJ

Abstract

This paper sets out how the Christian church, in particular the Catholic church, has shown its concern for human society. Five challenges are addressed: the collapse of the Roman empire, pilgrimage and travel, the discovery of the New World, the industrial revolution and the digital age. The paper first analyses five different modes by which the church has exercised social concern from early monastic communities to current charitable networks that rely on the internet. The paper argues that the church is not limited to one particular form of social engagement, even if that form is taken by all as the sole expected model. The vast institutions spawned by the nineteenth century charitable works and missions may be on the wane, but the networking and commitment of new bodies shows that social action lives with a new format in a new age.

Keywords: Catholic social teaching, Henry Manning, monastery, Jesuit Reductions, Sant'Egidio, William Wilberforce

基督宗教社會關懷模式及其變動歷程

雷敦龢

摘要

　　本文在闡述基督宗教（特別是天主教）如何關懷社會，展現在教會所面對的五種挑戰，分別為：羅馬帝國的崩潰、中世紀的朝聖、發現美洲、工業革命，以及數位時代。本文第一部分在分析教會從早期修道院到今日網路慈善機構所應用過的五種不同關懷社會的模式。第二部分則是從思想脈絡來檢視社會思想的演變與發展。

　　今日人權概念可以追溯到中世紀的教會法典，而後經歷過維護美洲原住民族，以及反對奴隸買賣，一直演進到十九世紀末天主教社會思想的正式出現。本文指出，教會的社會關懷並不限於某種特殊方式，也不見得就落於某個久已成為大家期待的範例。雖然十九世紀教會所發展出慈善事工的龐大機構或許會衰退，但新組織的網路模式及個人參與，則顯示社會關懷事業在新時代日新又新的一面。

關鍵詞：天主教社會思想、亨利‧曼寧、修道院、耶穌會美洲原住民部落、聖艾智德團體、威爾伯福斯

Introduction

The present paper will not only not focus exclusively on social concern in a Chinese context, it will also not address the whole range of social responses by all Christian bodies. It is thus a selective account of Christian social concern, which, given my own background, is necessarily based more on the Catholic Church's work. I apologise in advance for thus narrowing the subject. At the same time, I think it will be helpful to situate Christian social concern within a wider sociological framework. By doing so I hope that we will be able to take a broader view of aspects that will be covered in more detail during the Conference.

The paper takes an historical perspective, examining some of the major shifts in the way Christian Churches have lived out the command to love one's neighbour. In the Chinese context the dominant modality is that developed in the nineteenth century, according to which Churches ran schools, hospitals and other charitable institutions. At the present time many of these are either closing or being turned over to secular bodies, thus losing their ecclesiastical identity. We can lament this fact or seek to place it within a broader view and examine if it is the only possible way of putting into practice the works of mercy. It is for this reason that I seek to draw on a broader historical perspective, since this may give us room for hope. Besides looking at practice I will also consider the evolution of theory that has informed social work. This is particularly noticeable in the social doctrine of the Catholic Church. Whilst formed in a Catholic context it is in fact open to all Christian bodies and can be profitably used by all.

1 The Jewish Roots of Christian Social Work

Besides the assertion of monotheism contained in the Ten Words

(Commandments), there is another remarkable feature of Judaism: the intimate relationship established between worship of God and concern for one's neighbour. The Commandments are not only a statement of dogmatic belief; they are also a programme of ethical living. Already in *Leviticus* we find this formulated in terms of loving one's neighbour (*Lev.* 19: 18) and showing concern for the wayfarer and orphan (*Dt.* 24: 20-22). Whether or not it was actually implemented in practice, the institution of the Jubilee with its call to restore relationships to their state of pristine equality is a sign that Jewish ethics was concerned about right relationships in human society, as a reflection of the right relationship with God (*Lev.* 25: 8-17). The prophets, with their castigation of wealth and oppression of the poor, the praise of a man like Boaz (*Ruth*) who is kind to the gleaners in his field and to the outsider, Ruth, is testimony to this social concern. In the *Book of Tobit* we meet a man who will not even sit down to eat if a corpse is left unattended in the street. Burial of the dead is a work of mercy, just as much as care for the poor.

Christianity remains faithful to its Jewish roots. In Matthew's parable of the Last Judgment, Jesus describes the just as those who feed the hungry, clothe the naked, visit the prisoners and the sick (*Mt.* 25: 31-46). Paul insists on making a collection to help the needy church in Jerusalem and praises the generous giver (2 *Cor.* 8-9). In *Acts* the apostles call for deacons to serve the Greek-speaking Christians and take care of them, since there was a tendency to neglect their material needs (*Acts* 6: 1-2). Tertullian notes that Christians stand out because they do not, like the pagans, leave new-born babies out to die. These various works were summarised as the seven corporal works of mercy by the medieval church.[1] The number 'seven' here should be read

---

1 To feed the hungry, give drink to the thirsty, clothe the naked, shelter the homeless, visit the sick, visit the imprisoned and bury the dead.

according to its Hebrew sense as all-embracing and not as an exclusive restriction.

2 Challenges to the Implementation of the Works of Mercy

The Church does not exist in a social vacuum. Changes in society necessitate new ways of living out the works of mercy. For the present purposes I will simply consider a few major sociological challenges and describe the Church's response to them. The first will be the collapse of the Roman empire; the second the challenge of pilgrimage and travel; the third the discovery of the New World, the fourth the industrial revolution and the fifth the digital age. My purpose is not to present a comprehensive history of Christian social work but to look at the way the Church developed new institutions or modes to deal with major shifts in society.

2.1 The footprint of the monastery

The Roman empire had been 'idolatrous' and even persecuted Christianity. Although it later changed its religious identity, nonetheless its political power rapidly declined, becoming reduced to a rump state centred on Byzantium. European unity was shattered by the emergence of small disconnected statelets. These gradually formed some sort of cooperation especially when faced with, what at the time, was a more monolithic Islamic world. The positive values of the Roman empire were retained in three ways. First of all Christianity adopted the Roman system of government, with leaders of towns (ie. bishops), provinces (ie. dioceses) and one legal system (ie. canon law). This provided a framework for administration which combined elements of unity with regional government. The second force for continuity lay in the remarkable development of Judaism as the vehicle for trade and commerce, from the construction of inns to brewing (beer being required in the inns), to management of finance (Jewish knowledge and use of mathematics meant that Jews were far more reliable bankers than Christians, who did all their calculations in Roman numerals or by physically pilling up coins on a bench [banca=bank]). Kings built their castles, bishops their cathedrals and abbots their monasteries with the help of Jewish bankers. Trade routes were kept open despite the decline in the old Roman roads thanks to the Jewish hostelries and ability to use a language which transcended national boundaries.[2] Thirdly, the Benedictine Order and its offshoots (Cluny, Cîteau) gave rise to a new institution which upheld education and agriculture.

It is this third development which is particularly relevant to our topic. Monasteries brought together groups of educated men and women in semi-autonomous communities that needed to be self-supporting. St Benedict's simple formula *ora et labora* (prayer and work) ensured that life was regulated according to a natural rhythm in which no-one was made idle. It also brought about a distinction between educated 'choir monks' and illiterate 'lay-brothers', but this distinction should not be exaggerated as the monastery was at least in theory open to social mobility. While most monasteries ran separate male and female establishments, some, such as Vadstena in Sweden, were founded for both men and women (with the abbess as the person in overall charge).[3] A monastery had a significant social footprint. By its economy of scale it could develop a water-mill and thus provide flour; its herb garden provided medicines; its sheep provided wool. While the Cistercians are famous for developing agriculture and sheep-farming in wastelands, other monasteries, such as Bury St Edmund's or Canterbury, took care of shrines

---

2 See Paul Kriwaczek, *Yiddish Civilisation: The rise and fall of a forgotten nation* (London: Weidenfeld & Nicolson, 2005).

3 The impact of Vadstena was felt throughout the Nordic lands. It had foundations in Nådendal (now Finland), Danzig (now Poland). The monasteries not only served economic and social needs, they also promoted writing and culture. St Birgitta composed music and even designed the church herself.

and became centres for pilgrimage. They provided hostels and hospitals for the sick.[4] The monastery can thus be viewed as a centre for the overall network of social help, including religious and psychological help, in a given locality. It was school, hospital, institute for agricultural development, smithy, miller, and hostel for the local area. As part of a family of monasteries (Birgittine, Augustinian, Benedictine and the like), it had links to other such institutions and was thus able to develop an international network of knowledge and social assistance.

2.2 The time of the cathedrals

As the period we now disparagingly called the Middle Ages developed into its familiar form – the age of cathedrals[5] – two of the typical functions of a monastery began to gain a new independent form: the university and the hospital. Turning to universities first, we note that when Frederick I Barbarossa promulgated a *Constitutio Habita* in admiration of four law professors from the university of Bologna he did so to ensure that universities would not be subject to the whims of local town councils.[6] Graduates from the university would be allowed to teach anywhere within the realm of Christendom. Scholarship was independent of local politics and granted a freedom that enabled St Thomas Aquinas to draw on Arabic thought and Aristotle, while his teacher St Albert developped scientific experiments and scientific method. This led to a network of European universities from St Andrew's to Rome, Cambridge to Vienna. Graduates were international persons sharing a common international culture.

---

4 The words hostel, hospital, hotel etc. all have a common origin.

5 "Il est venu le temp des cathédrales, le monde est entré dans un nouveau millénaire; l'homme a voulu monter sur les étoiles, écrire son histoire dans le verre ou dans la pierre." (*Notre Dame de Paris*)

6 See University of Bologna website: http://www.unibo.it/en/university/who-we-are/our-history/university-from-12th-to-18th-century

The hospital developed in response to travel. By the eleventh century, before the Crusades began, pilgrims were pouring into Jerusalem. The roads of Europe, neglected since Roman times, heard the tramp of footsteps to Compostella, Canterbury, Rome, Jerusalem, Walsingham and countless smaller shrines. It was especially in the context of pilgrimages to the Holy Land, that hostels were required. The long distances travelled on foot or in rickety boats brought about a need for medical care at the point of destination. Furthermore, the dangers of robbers and pirates and, of Islamic armies, meant that military protection was required. Although disparaged nowadays, the military Orders – Hospitallers, Templars, the Order of St Ladre (for lepers), the Teutonic Knights – were groups of, largely illiterate, laymen bound together under vows of poverty, chastity and obedience to protect pilgrims and keep the sea-routes open. Their closest equivalent in the modern world are the United Nations peacekeeping forces, with perhaps this exception that the members of military orders were bound to stricter codes of conduct, lifelong celibacy for instance, than any which the United Nations could dare to ask of men and women today. Malta's renowned hospital continued in operation until closed by Napoleon; the area of Prussia-Lithuania-Poland ruled by the Teutonic knights was said to be the best governed in all Europe, with the most contended peasantry.[7]

The new international organisations (universities and military orders) existed alongside the monasteries which provided the basic local system of social security. At the same time, other institutions formed. We may note, for instance, the Mercedarians, who were prepared to exchange positions with persons taken hostage by Muslims, an extraordinary feat of self-giving that is unparalleled today. At the local level, though, parish structures were the focus

---

7 See Desmond Seward, *The Monks of War: The military orders* (London: Folio, 2000 [1972]). I wrote an essay based on this book: "Reassessing the Crusades and Military Orders," *Universitas* 359 (April 2004), pp. 97-116.

for pious groups of all kinds. These provided upkeep of the local sanctuary, ensured a proper burial for their members and the blessing of the local fields. Wills often reflect how the testator desires that a certain sum of money be given to poor people to enable them to pray for the repose of his soul and yet have enough to eat without having to go to work for that day. The complexity of social care was woven into the fabric of medieval life, which was not yet infected by the dichotomy between religion and daily life that grew up after the Reformation.[8]

The corporal works of mercy were written into the fabric of the church itself. Looking up above the altar the people would see the Rood (Cross with Mary and John) and behind it the painting of the Last Judgment (the Doom). This was based on the parable of *Mt*. 25: 31-46 mentioned above. The same theme recurred at the climax of the Corpus Christi plays. Funerals were important occasions for giving to the poor because without care for the poor one risked being swallowed up by the gape of hell, painted so realistically in the doom scene.[9]

2.3 Utopia on earth

The end of the Middle Ages is marked by the rise of the absolute nation-state. Monasteries declined and the international cooperative venture we call the crusades faded away. Even more dramatic, in Protestant countries such as England, the parish structure with its guilds and lay organisations was destroyed; the paintings and plays disappeared and the local social networks were disbanded. New groups had to provide for education and medical care. In England local persons or organisations opened schools, often using old monastic premises such as the London Charterhouse. The universities of

8 On medieval parish life, see Eamon Duffy, *The Stripping of the Altars: Traditional religion in England 1400-1580* (New Haven & London: Yale University Press, 2nd ed. 2005 [1992]), especially pp. 131-368.
9 See Duffy, *The Stripping of the Altars*, pp. 357-359.

Oxford and Cambridge quickly lost their international standing and became backward clubs of provincial gentlemen. In Catholic lands, education fell, remarkably, into the hands of the Society of Jesus. St Ignatius Loyola founded the Society of Jesus to be at the universal service of the universal church. It very soon emerged that one of the concrete forms this had to take was that of the local college. Jesuits replaced Benedictines as the schoolmasters of Europe whilst various women's congregations such as the Ursulines took on the education of girls.

Yet this period is also marked by the discovery of the Americas and the creation by both Catholic and Protestant groups of a new form of social service. The iniquities of old Europe and its colonial practices led idealists to seek new forms of governance away from society. Anabaptists tried to establish semi-independent entities that would mirror the kingdom of heaven. The Pilgrim Fathers took to sea and founded a new, supposedly perfect community, in Maryland. The Quakers rejected the warfare of the nation-state, practised non-violence and eschewed military service. With William Penn they established a new state (Pennsylvania) founded on a treaty with the Delaware Indians. Meanwhile southwards in Paraguay the Jesuits formed the indigenous people into villages ('reductions') where they learnt the craft of building, the skills of agriculture as well as the beauties of polyphony. Escape here was from the cruelty of Spanish and Portuguese colonialism, providing a safe haven for the indigenous people. Compared with the old monasteries of Europe, these new forms of political-social-religious life are characterised by a complete absence of any other form of social structure. A monastery could be a celibate male community only because it was surrounded by, to put it crudely, breeding farming families. In the Reductions or the new colonies the families formed the nucleus of the community, with church leaders either few in number (in the case of the Jesuits) or being members of those same families.

The problem with these new forms of ideal life is that they could only hold out so long against the surrounding political reality. The various idealist Protestant groups were faced either with a diminution of their fervour when they met the harsh realities of life, such as when the American Quakers were challenged by the war of independence from the crown, or by a retreat into an archaic way of life such as that of the Amish. The Reductions too met a similar fate when the Society of Jesus was suppressed. Thus these island kingdoms of God were either engulfed by the surrounding land or left as insignificant, quaint groupings of little social significance.

2.4 The industrial revolution

With the industrial revolution new forms of social awareness came into being. Within the Catholic Church there was a massive expansion in the number of religious congregations, many of them directly engaged in particular works of mercy, principally in the fields of education and medicine, but also in the area of agriculture (eg. the Scheut Fathers in Inner Mongolia). Protestant Churches were no less active sending missionaries to many lands, partly in competition and rivalry with their Catholic counterparts. We now take this endeavour so much for granted that we are perhaps no longer struck by its strangeness. How is it that vast groups of people could enter religious life or go abroad as missionaries and bring the institutions of European Christianity to the most remote islands and hinterlands of the globe?

The eighteenth century had seen advances in hygiene and control of waste water combined with increased agricultural yields. In response to industrialisation, urban conglomerates developed and population exploded as the death rate for new-born babies fell and longevity rose.[10] At the same time

---

10 The classic study of this issue is by Buer: M. C. Buer, *Health, Wealth and Population in the Early Days of the Industrial Revolution* (Oxford: Routledge, *reprint* 2006 [1926]): "The almost total absence of all hygienic and medical knowledge had been another factor in the high death rate of the Middle Ages. Here again, in the 18th century knowledge began

employment and marriage opportunities did not keep up with this increase of population. Women, in particular, were often faced with a future blessed with life and health but vitiated by lack of opportunities in a world that was still run for and by men.[11] Human society was suddenly faced with a broad swathe of population who had life and leisure. In a Catholic culture this was a boon to religious vocations. That two or three of a family of twelve or fourteen children joined religious life or went off as missionaries was no loss to the family. Founders of religious congregations had a ready pool of applicants. Needs were great in the new big cities: a school here, orphans there, a hospital relying on new medical knowledge in another place. The Josephites in Australia, the 'Holy Washtubs' in Ireland and England, the 'Madams of the Sacred Heart' and the 'Gray Sisters' in France could all find recruits for their own particular charism.[12]

The development of railroads and steamships suddenly made international travel much less of a risk than it had been in the past. Nationalist pride fostered congregations of religious priests working as missionaries: the German Divine Word Fathers, the Belgian Scheut Fathers, the Irish Maynooth missionaries. The Protestant congregations also took to the sea with a similar combination of nationalism and evangelism, evident for instance in George Leslie Mackay. Whilst former missionaries such as St Francis Xavier arrived in the East with little more than a crucifix, the new

---

to replace ignorance." (Ch. 1) available at http://www.amazon.com/Population-Industrial-Revolution-Economic-History-ebook/dp/B00GHJLAKC/ref=sr_1_4?s=books&ie=UTF8&qid=1411521077&sr=1-4&keywords=health+wealth+population.

11 Melanie Phillips refers to "chronic female unemployment": Melanie Phillips, *The Ascent of Woman: A history of the suffragette movement and the ideas behind it* (London: Abacus, 2004), p. 21.

12 Bl. Mary McKillop founded the Josephites in Australia. Frances Taylor founded the Poor Servants of the Mother of God in London in 1869. They were known as the "holy washtubs" because they ran a laundry service for poor people. St Madeleine Sophie Barat and her companions founded the Religious of the Sacred Heart of Jesus in France in 1800 (affectionately called the 'Madams' in England). The Daughters of Charity of St Vincent de Paul (known in France as the 'Grey Sisters') were founded in Paris in the 1630s and ran hospitals and schools, catering especially for the poor.

missionaries brought the new international languages, and the new science and learning that would 'improve' the lives of the natives. Where Matteo Ricci had sought to adapt to the clothing and culture of Ming China, the new missionaries clad their neophytes in the proper garb of imperial culture and took the 'poor' children into schools of Western learning. Foot-binding, semi-nakedness and head-hunting were consigned to the pages of superstition and the light shone on toothpaste and copperplate script.

By the mid-twentieth century, though, the light began to go out. Colonised peoples wondered why they needed to be colonised; Gandhi reverted to Indian cotton and the state took over the tasks of education, medical work, social concern and even burials (regulating cemeteries for instance) that had once been in Church hands. Meanwhile, the numbers entering religious life or volunteering as missionaries began to fall to their pre-nineteenth century levels. Europe and America no longer had the vast surplus population that had triggered such an extraordinary phase in ecclesiastical history. To lament this change, to hope that somehow it will be reversed, is to misunderstand the fact that it was a historical aberration in the first place.

With its decline has gone the decline of Church-based institutions. Schools, universities, care-homes and hospitals are no longer served by dedicated staff belonging to a founding religious body. In many cases the original religious inspiration has been diluted to the point of zero, as with Harvard University, or has petered away into historical nostalgia. And yet the state still fails to reach out to all in need. State-take overs of previously Church-run institutions cannot cope with new levels of poverty and need that have arisen.

2.5 Networks of Christian inspiration

The growth points of social commitment in the digital age rely precisely on the instruments developed by that technology along with a response to the gap that technology creates. Take, for example, the community of Sant'Egidio in Rome: a group of pious Catholics gather together to help the homeless in Rome. Founded after the Second World War, the Community identifies with outcasts in society, helps refugees, speaks against the death penalty and undertakes peace building and mediation in the world's conflict zones. It is green, on Facebook and very active on the internet. Members are generally lay people and volunteers are welcome. In the same breath one could mention the volunteers associated with Mother Teresa of Calcutta or those who work with the Jesuit Refugee Service. Here we have global networks that both deal with individuals and, at least in the case of Sant'Egidio and the Jesuit Refugee Service, are involved in advocacy to change the structural causes of the evils encountered. At the same time these groups provide a family setting and companionship that is often lacking in the modern family and in the world where virtual communication has replaced the family dinner as the significant moment for exchange and sharing.[13]

While the above are Catholic examples, it should be pointed out that all are open to ecumenical approaches. One does not have to be a Catholic to serve in Mother Teresa's home for the dying in Calcutta. The issues addressed are also frequently on the agenda of committed NGOs and international bodies such as Amnesty International, Greenpeace and the Campaign against Landmines. The Ecumenical Patriarch, Bartholomew I, inherits the See of Constantinople, but is better known today for his Green credentials.

---

13 While not engaged in social action to the same extent, the monastery of Bose in Italy is also an example of a new type of religious life. The prior is a layman, not a priest. Monks are Catholic, Protestant and Orthodox; guests are welcomed in their hundreds. Likewise, in the Protestant tradition there is the community at Taizé in France, founded by a Protestant but with both Catholic and Protestant monks and huge numbers of young people who come for summer camps. Both Taizé and Bose overcome barriers between groups by creating a common style of life together. In caring for the physically and mentally challenged, Jean Vanier has set up L'Arche, homes in which carers and cared live together as a community. Again religious boundaries are overcome.

Affectionately named "fish and chips", the late Archbishop Derek Worlock (Catholic) and Bishop David Sheppard (Anglican) of Liverpool always spoke with one voice in their social utterances.[14] Whilst the nineteenth century institutions blazoned their religious identity in every act of their social work, the current networks and campaigners bring a critical voice to the whole of society, inspired by Christian teaching, but deliberately reaching out beyond their own sect and beyond the bounds of Christian confession to embrace issues of universal social concern.

Thus, in this short, and necessarily insufficient, account we have seen five different ways of responding to social needs. The monastery provided resources for intensive coverage of local needs. The university and hospital/hostel catered to a mobile clientele and spread universal values to society, raising standards of education and hygiene. The utopia on earth model showed that it was possible to create pockets of idealism and social concern but only by opting out of the surrounding society. The industrial revolution and the expanding demography of Europe enabled the Churches to set up their own worldwide network of social institutions that sought to provide the benefits of civilisation to all. Whilst different from the previous idealistic model, the new institutions nonetheless shared in the exclusivity of the previous model, encouraging conversion into the faith as well as the fruits of medical science or Western learning. The new networks, whilst rooted in a Christian background, do not depend on institutional buildings and staff, but on the internet and on voluntary staff who help for limited periods of time. Moreover, they meet the concerns of secular groups and work with them. The exclusivity of the past is gone.

Just as Christianity does not espouse any particular political model as the perfect polity for the world, so too it does not need to be limited by any

---

14 For a statue commemorating the two, see http://en.wikipedia.org/wiki/Sheppard-Worlock_Statue.

one model of social commitment. Of course, previous models may continue to exist and may overlap with one another. The invention of M. Google need not imply that the Institut Catholique in Paris must close. Rather, what matters more is not to become so wedded to any one particular mode of social engagement that our only response to its inevitable shrinkage is to lament the good old days of the past. The Holy Spirit is more inventive than the plans of mice and men.

3 The Theory of Social Concern

In the next part of the paper I wish to address changes in the theory of social commitment. This is valuable too since the practical changes outlined above do not happen in a purely theoretical vacuum. The initial period, at the end of the Roman empire, is the so-called Patristic period of Sts Ambrose and John Chrysostom. Their comments on poverty and equal distribution of goods were to have a long-lasting impact in the Church. In the middle ages the key concepts were those of liberty and dominion. Formulated in canon law and expounded in the universities these concepts provide a backdrop to the medieval era. They also serve to help theologians deal with the issue of the New World. The question then was whether the Amerindians had dominion over their own land. If, as some argued, they did, then the colonial enterprise had to be put in question. In short, colonialism could be interpreted as manifestly unjust. This forms the theoretical background to the Jesuit Reductions. The contribution of the nineteenth century can be traced firstly among Protestants, especially in the anti-slavery movement, and then among Catholics, where the Popes began to write lengthy letters addressing issues of labour and capital that were to give rise to the social doctrine of the Church. In the present time this has expanded as it seeks to find a middle way through the classic capitalist-socialist divide.

3.1 The Patristic defence of the poor

At the time when the Roman empire became Christian, Christianity also began to flourish in the world of wealth and prestige. This was both a boon and a burden. It is thus no coincidence that we find classic statements on the duty of the rich to help the poor in the writings of the fourth century church Fathers: Ambrose (c. 340-397), Basil the Great (c. 329-379), John Chrysostom (344-407) and later Gregory the Great (c. 540-604). The emphasis is on the common ownership of all goods, as St Ambrose says:

> Not from what you own do you bestow upon the poor, but you make return from what is theirs. For what has been given as common for the use of all, you appropriate to yourself alone. The earth belongs to all, not to the rich... Therefore you are paying a debt, you are not bestowing what is not due.[15]

St Gregory repeats this in similar words.[16] In #329, the *Compendium of the Social Doctrine of the Church* gathers together some of the sayings of the church Fathers under the heading "Riches fulfil their function of service to man [*sic*] when they are destined to produce benefits for others and for society".[17] The following quotations outline how wealth must be used to help

---

15 Ambrose, *On Naboth*, 11 (Migne, *Patrologia Latina* 14, 747); English translation from Charles Avila, *Ownership: Early Christian Teaching* (New York: Orbis, 1983), p. 66. Quoted in Ruston, Roger, *Human Rights and the Image of God* (London: SCM Press, 2004), p. 42. 你不是從你所有的賜給窮人，反而是你歸還原來是他們的東西，因為，本來你們把大家可以使用的，當作自己的財產。土地屬於大家，不屬於富有的人⋯⋯因此你只是還債，並非贈送可以不給的東西。

16 *Catechism of the Catholic Church* # 2446 quoting St Gregory the Great, *Pastoral Rule* 3: 21 (Migne, *Patrologia Latina* 77, 87): "When we attend to the needs of those in want, we give them what is theirs, not ours. More than performing works of mercy, we are paying a debt of justice." 天主教教理第2446號引聖大額我略《牧民守則》：「當我們給與貧窮者必須的物品，我們不是施予他們我個人的慷慨，我們是還給他們原來是他們的東西。與其說我們完成一項愛德的行為，不如說實行正義的行為。」

17 *Compendium of the Social Doctrine of the Church* #329 quoting *The Shepherd of Hermas* Bk III, Allegory I in Mignes, *Patrologia Graeca* 2, 954. *Compendium of the Social Doctrine of the Church* available at http://www.iustitiaetpax.va/

others and only then is it a blessing. If it is stored up it becomes foul like water that becomes stagnant if not allowed to flow. Just as Adam is given responsibility to look after the earth in the *Book of Genesis*, so too the rich man has responsibility for the riches in his possession, to spend them wisely for others.

Similar sayings are listed in Gratian's *Decretal*. Composed in the twelfth century, this work was the standard text of canon law for the middle ages. The original text is annotated top and bottom, left and right as canonists used its essential sayings to reflect on questions such as whether a poor person who, in time of need, 'stole' from a rich person was really a 'thief' or not.[18] Medieval lawyers were not content merely to repeat the past. Rather they developed the fundamental concepts that would enable them to tackle social issues. Particular attention must be drawn to three terms: dominion, liberty and law/right.

'Dominion' derives from the Latin word 'dominus' (master) and refers to anything over which a person has some degree of control. The primary area in which one has such dominion is that of one's life decisions, marriage for

---

content/giustiziaepace/it/archivio/documenti/compendio-della-dottrina-sociale-della-chiesa--aggiornamento-lin.html (in Chinese and in English) (consulted 24 Sept 2014).

 # 329: Riches fulfil their function of service to man when they are destined to produce benefits for others and for society. "How could we ever do good to our neighbour," asks St. Clement of Alexandria, "if none of us possessed anything?" In the perspective of St. John Chrysostom, riches belong to some people so that they can gain merit by sharing them with others. Wealth is a good that comes from God and is to be used by its owner and made to circulate so that even the needy may enjoy it. Evil is seen in the immoderate attachment to riches and the desire to hoard. St. Basil the Great invites the wealthy to open the doors of their storehouses and he exhorts them: "A great torrent rushes, in thousands of channels, through the fertile land: thus, by a thousand different paths, make your riches reach the homes of the poor". Wealth, explains Saint Basil, is like water that issues forth from the fountain: the greater the frequency with which it is drawn, the purer it is, while it becomes foul if the fountain remains unused. The rich man – Saint Gregory the Great will later say – is only an administrator of what he possesses; giving what is required to the needy is a task that is to be performed with humility because the goods do not belong to the one who distributes them. He who retains riches only for himself is not innocent; giving to those in need means paying a debt.

18 Ruston notes that, in this case of an emergency, Thomas Aquinas concluded that what was taken in fact 'belonged' to the poor person and hence there was no theft; others argued that the act of stealing was a lesser evil than the rich man's prior claim to property. (Ruston, *Human Rights and the Image of God*, p. 43.)

example. Land and other physical property is secondary, and in feudal law, was often dependent on the former. Marriage or becoming a priest or a religious required a public statement before God.[19] This demands freedom on the part of the person taking the oath. Coerced statements might be legally binding but if coercion could be proved and the coerced party no longer wished to remain in the relationship then it could be annulled on the ground of coercion. Hence the church insisted on people marrying freely and on the appointment of bishops and abbots without political interference. In these basic choices of life people had to be able to exercise their rightful dominion or power of control.

This brings us to the more complex idea of 'right'.[20] Two things are operative here. Firstly the law laid down the objective norms for marriage, ordination, appointment of bishops, testimony in a law court and so on. There is nothing very controversial about this. But when the mendicant Orders were formed, especially the Franciscans, a dilemma arose. Wishing to imitate the poverty of Jesus, Franciscans friars took a vow to renounce all temporal goods, ie. to own nothing, to have dominion over nothing. This freed them to travel anywhere and rely on begging for their material needs. Following the precept that wealth should be used for the poor, rich admirers of the friars donated lands and houses for their use. So the friars were 'using' houses that belonged in law to their benefactors. Now some Franciscans wanted to go further and argue that even the use of these goods should be given up. The logical, if not actual, result would be that they would be turned out to wander in the forests without anything to eat or drink, since they

---

19 A private exchange of vows between two persons was also considered valid. Note that marriages were usually carried out in the church porch not inside the church itself. The priest, if present, was only a witness; the ministers of the marriage are the couple themselves.

20 My discussion is informed by Annabel S. Brett, *Liberty, Right and Nature: Individual rights in later scholastic thought* (Cambridge: Cambridge University Press, 1997).

could not 'use' food! But that would lead to their imminent death, and since suicide was forbidden by the Fifth Commandment, they had better eat something. Well, they argued, all their food and drink and housing and clothing belonged to the Pope, as head of the church on earth.

Hence the question arose: is it possible to give up dominion over everything, even over the use of basic necessities? Surely the law should prevent people systematically reducing themselves to such poverty that they would die the next day? Moreover, the Pope pointed out that he could hardly reclaim the apple the friar ate for breakfast. Thus while it might be noble to renounce dominion in the sense of ownership, this could not possibly include the renunciation of the *use* of everything. Human society requires that we use many things which we cannot claim as our own: the seats in the bus or train, the road I walk along, the communications satellite by which I send my E-mail. Of course the holy friar might say that his vow of poverty should include the renunciation of the use of ice-cream and chocolate cake, but he cannot say that it is a blanket condemnation of all usage. There must be a difference between what ought to be used and what can be used or not used.

This leads to the solution in terms of 'right'. Canon lawyers argued that the law must set down the use of some things – food, drink, housing – as basic necessities to which people could all lay a claim. Ownership of other things, such as castles, mills and a horse, could be protected by law but people who did not have them could not claim them as necessities. Thus the objective law gave rise to a claim-in-law or 'right'. Latin used the same word '*ius*' to talk about both law and right.[21] Furthermore, just as dominion was characterised not primarily as 'objects' but as a power of control, so too 'right' is seen as a power to make demands for what can be used. Using the

---

21 This practice is followed in French (droit), Spanish (derechos), German (Recht) and many other European languages. English is peculiar in that it uses the Danish word *lagu* (law) for the objective norm and the Germanic 'right' for the claim-in-law.

Aristotelian distinction between 'act' and 'potency', a right is understood as a potency or potential claim, that may be transmuted into an actual claim when circumstances require. In other words, the friar can happily eat the apples donated by the nobleman without needing to have recourse to the court, but should he be starving in the street because the noble refuses to give him an apple then he may go to court and make his potential claim active and the court must grant him the apple. In modern terms, the old lady does not need to take the bus company to court for failing to provide seats in its buses, but if one day the government abolishes all bus routes, she surely does have a right to reclaim her seat in a bus.

The natural law tradition grew out of these roots. There is a lot of misunderstanding about natural law. Many critics, indeed I would say most, spend all their fury shooting down a pure chimera. They imagine that natural law is a deductive set of unchanging norms, a doctrinaire straitjacket imposed on human society. Writing about the precepts of the natural law in 2009, the International Theological Commission states:

> These do not constitute a ready-made code of abstract demands, but a permanent and normative principle of inspiration. (#11)
> It is not a closed and complete set of moral norms, but a constant source of inspiration. (#27)
> This natural law has nothing stationary about it. It does not consist in a list of definitive and unchanging precepts. (#113) [22]

Indeed the document rules that the desire to deduce the precepts of the natural law *a priori* from a definition of the essence of the human being is a

---

22 International Theological Commission, *The Search for Universal Ethics: A new look at natural law.* (my translation from the French). For more on this see my book *Finding Truth in Life: A philosophy of human rights* (New Taipei City: Fu Jen University, 2012), pp. 100-101.

modern rationalist error (#33). Properly understood, natural law is a dynamic use of principles. It is what lies at the heart of Catholic social teaching today. New problems arise and so new solutions are required. Moral sensitivity grows and so what was acceptable in the past (slavery or capital punishment are two glaring examples) is forbidden today. Just as a live oak tree grows without becoming a pine tree so too natural law follows the same principles now as in the past but in new contexts. Moreover, awareness of what those principles are is also subject to growth and development.[23]

3.2 Defence of the Indians

The natural law tradition was honed in the context of the discovery of indigenous communities in the Americas. Theologians were interested in the question as to whether or not these peoples should be allowed to exercise dominion over their lands. The answer from Bartholomew de Las Casas and Francesco de Vitoria was a resounding 'yes'.[24] That the Amerindians were not Christian, that they did not have a literate culture, that they rejected the missionaries were not obstacles to this assertion of their right to dominion. On the other hand, the theologians still believed that the Gospel was good for them and that the Spanish had a right to preach the same Gospel. But the Amerindians had to be able to make a free choice of belief and should be free of the iniquities of Spanish colonialism. The compromise is to be found in the Reductions, where Amerindian cultural islands adopted Christianity but outside the control of European colonial masters.[25]

---

23 In a Chinese context this idea should not be too difficult to understand. The concept *cheng* 誠 (sincerity/integrity) in the *Mean and Harmony* 中庸 is what binds together the beginning of things as the 'mean' *zhong* 中 and their ending in harmony *he* 和﹕誠者物之終始 *chengzhe, wu zhi zhongshi*. (*Mean and Harmony* 中庸 #25)

24 Las Casas' argument is set out in his *Devastation of the Indies* (Baltimore: Johns Hopkins University, 1922); Vitoria's arguments are in James Brown Scott (ed.), *The Spanish Origins of International Law: Francisco de Vitoria and his law of nations* (New Jersey: Lawbook Exchange, 2000 [1934]).

25 One negative consequence of this was that the colonists turned to African slaves for labour on their estates. Partial

The same principle of dominion is operative even in the philosophy of John Locke, although Locke was to argue that the effort of labour exerted in farming gave the farmer greater rights to ownership. Locke's thesis lies behind the modern idea of private property. However, it should be noted that Locke believed, wrongly, that there was always sufficient land available for everyone and hence non-agricultural peoples could still enjoy their claims to fish and hunt. Locke imagined that the colonisers – including himself as the owner of American property – could enjoy dominion of their agricultural lands whilst the rest of the American mainland was *terra nullius* over which the Amerindians could roam at will. He failed to realise that indigenous people needed precisely the type of protection of their native dominion afforded by the theories of Las Casas, Vitoria and the Jesuits.

3.3 Opposition to the Slave Trade

Turning from the Catholic tradition we look at the formation of a new form of social engagement that is outstanding in late eighteenth century England. This is exemplified by the Clapham Sect, a group of evangelical Anglicans deeply concerned with social issues. Its best-known member was William Wilberforce (1759-1833), who as Member of Parliament campaigned for the abolition of the slave trade and later of slavery as such.[26] The slave trade was abolished in 1807 and slavery in 1834 after the passage of the Slavery Abolition Bill which passed the lower house of parliament in 1833 as Wilberforce lay dying at home. Wilberforce and his friends took practical steps to abolish slavery by founding a colony of freed slaves in Sierra Leone on the model of, and with similar problems to, the Jesuit Reductions. But the Clapham Sect also undertook defence of many other causes. They formed a

---

liberation for the Amerindian was thus bought at the price of slavery for the African.

26 http://www.anti-slaverysociety.addr.com/huk-wilberforce.htm

Society for the Suppression of Vice which aimed at improving the lives of the poor. Wilberforce's concerns reached far and wide, including the promotion of Christian knowledge.[27]

There is a very clear link between the piety and social engagement of the Clapham Sect and the growth of Protestant mission societies. The Church was impelled to take the Gospel to the poor in their own country and to the pagans in the newly opened colonies. The Church Missionary Society and British and Foreign Bible Society were all active in the China missions. Moreover the basic method of working was similar. A group of ardent persons gathered together as individuals to face the vast mass of the uninitiated and to campaign. While they might work together with other groups on some issues they could also see others as potential rivals. They had a strong, fighting belief, in the rightness of their own version of the truth and were prepared to make this prevail in spite of opposition. We only have to think of the way different mission bodies competed for converts to their own brand of Christianity. To be within 'my' fold meant salvation but to be in the fold of another group could be explicitly identified as belonging to Satan, whilst all the groups were competing for converts among the uninformed masses. Thus the missionary bodies played out the same social dynamics that were found in the great moral crusades with the crusaders (eg. Clapham sect), the Satanic 'lodges' (eg. the slave-owners) and the general mass of the people who had to be won over.

---

27 In fact, Wilberforce – dubbed 'the prime minister of a cabinet of philanthropists' – was at one time active in support of 69 philanthropic causes. He gave away one-quarter of his annual income to the poor. He fought on behalf of chimney sweeps, single mothers, Sunday schools, orphans, and juvenile delinquents. He helped found parachurch groups like the Society for Bettering the Cause of the Poor, the Church Missionary Society, the British and Foreign Bible Society, and the Antislavery Society. (http://www.christianitytoday.com/ch/131christians/activists/wilberforce. html?start=2) (consulted 24 Sept 2014).

He also campaigned for legislation to prohibit the worst forms of child labor, cruelty to animals and the removal of political disabilities on Roman Catholics (anti-slavery website).

The winning over of the masses is, indeed, one of the distinctive features of this type of social movement. Bruce Hindmarsh describes the role the Clapham Sect played in this new tactic:

The Clapham Sect pioneered techniques of mobilizing public opinion that have become commonplace in democracies. They exploited the media outlets of the day: lectures, billboards, newspapers, and pamphlets. They made effective use of voluntary societies and unprecedented use of petitions to exert public pressure on Parliament.[28]

In her book on the women's suffrage movement, *The Ascent of Woman*, Melanie Phillips makes a similar point:

The anti-slavery movement had been of the greatest significance because it was at the root of so much else. It pioneered campaigning / techniques based on voluntary work and private subscription and the concept of the active citizen; it displayed anti-political tendencies; it championed the provincial masses against metropolitan sophistication and expertise. It had connections with female suffrage, women's rights, temperance and prison reforms.[29]

Phillips draws attention to another motivating factor in nineteenth century campaigning: an assertion of the human being as something more than just an animal. If medieval thinkers could think of 'man' as being the image of God, the scientific discoveries of the nineteenth century, culminating

---

28 Bruce Hindmarsh, "William Wilberforce and the Abolition of the Slave Trade: A Gallery of Aristocratic Activists," *Christian History* 53 (1 Jan 1997) available at http://www.ctlibrary.com/ch/1997/issue53/53h023.html (consulted 20 Sept 2014)

29 Melanie Phillips, *The Ascent of Woman*, pp. 112-113.

in Darwin seemed to portray 'him' as a mere monkey or ape:

> [The] deep and abiding trauma of the Victorian period [was] the appalling vista Darwin had opened up that man was not created in the image of God but was instead no more than a sage brute. The overwhelming need to defeat this terrible prospect lay behind the preoccupation of the age to transcend animal appetites through spiritual purity.[30]

Campaigns against vivisection, slavery and in favour of female suffrage all shared this common thread, as too did the effort of missionaries in Hawai'i to clothe the semi-naked islanders, or to provide the 'proper' education for the 'savages' of the colonies. Opposition to suppression of prostitution, for instance, involved concern for the prostitutes themselves, but also fierce opposition to the way (male) doctors could treat the female body to check for sexual diseases. This smacked of the way animals were dissected. Moreover the same ethos of the brutish nature of the male and the 'spiritual' nature of the female played a part in the suffrage movement itself, with some calling for women to be involved in parliament so as to lift the moral tone, whilst others (including women) opposed it because the world of politics was a male world of brutish animals, beyond redemption. Women should be involved in purer pursuits outside the halls of Westminster.

One outstanding movement of this period is the Salvation Army, founded by William Booth in London in 1865 and currently preparing to celebrate its 150th anniversary.[31] The Army imposes strict standards on its members (no alcohol or tobacco) and combines a life of prayer with social

---

30 Melanie Phillips, *The Ascent of Woman*, p. 116.
31 See the Army's website at http://www.salvationarmy.org/ihq/home.

commitment in a disciplined organization. Booth's initial concern for poor, unwashed persons excluded from the churches of his day has led to the development of hostels for the homeless and a real concern for the poor. In today's world that concern has expanded. At the same time the Army is explicitly a missionary body and seeks to win converts. However, unlike some groups, it does not (at least in my experience) try to encroach on other Christian bodies. Rather it seeks to work with them. In this it can be seen as a prototype of the final model of social engagement I wish to present. Before doing that, we must, though, return to Catholic social engagement in the nineteenth century.

3.4 From Wilberforce to Leo XIII via Cardinal Manning

As a young boy Cardinal Henry Manning (1808-1991) knew of Wilberforce's campaign against slavery and later as an Anglican priest he got to know the people of his rural parish very well and so become acquainted with their condition of life. However, it was not until around the time of the First Vatican Council that he started to look more at solving problems of poverty. As Archbishop of Westminster he founded the League of the Cross, which campaigned against alcoholism. Every week the leaders of the League reported to him and so he gained greater knowledge of the conditions of the working men. He spoke on behalf of the League at mass popular meetings and in 1890 he noted, "The League has taken hold of the people, especially the working men. It was this that gave me a hold in the Strike of last year [1889]..."[32] His involvement in working men's issues led him to support Trade Unions. Already in 1874 he wrote that he had read a book on Guilds and decided that unions of working men involved in the same trade would be

---

32 Fitzsimons, John, "Manning and the Workers," in Fitzsimons, John (ed.), *Manning: Anglican and Catholic* (London: Burns Oates, 1951), p. 137.

beneficial, provided that they worked within the law.

Manning's ideas would carry to Rome. The occasion was an industrial dispute in North America/Canada in which a Canadian cardinal excommunicated workers who went on strike. The workers appealed to the American Cardinal Gibbons, who immediately consulted Manning. Manning's letter reads, in part:

> Up to the present the world has been governed by dynasties: henceforward the Holy See must treat with the people, and with bishops who are in close daily and personal relations with the people... The Church is the Mother, Friend, and Protectress of the People. As our Divine Saviour lived among persons of the people, so lives His Church...[33]

Cardinal Gibbons' statement to the Congregation of Propaganda reflects these ideas:

> And since it is acknowledged by all that the great questions of the future are not those of war, of commerce or finance, but the social questions, the questions which concern the improvement of the condition of the great masses of the people, and especially the working people, it is evidently of supreme importance that the Church should always be found on the side of humanity, of justice toward the multitudes who compose the body of the human family. As the same Cardinal Manning very wisely wrote, "We must admit and accept calmly and with good will that industries and profits must be considered in second place; the moral state and domestic condition

---

33 Manning, "Letter to Cardinal Gibbons," quoted in Fitzsimons, "Manning and the Workers," p. 142.

of the whole working population must be considered first... The conditions of the lower classes as are found at present among our people, can not and must not continue...[34]

Propaganda annulled the excommunication whilst Manning's status among workers was raised.

Manning's direct influence on Pope Leo XIII is attested as early as 1880. Two years after his election, the Pope is reported to have said that an encyclical he wrote condemning the slave trade was written because "he [Manning] put the idea into my head to do something for the slaves."[35] Two years after the London Dock strike of 1889 – the solution to which was brokered by Manning – Pope Leo XIII wrote *Rerum Novarum*, the first of the great social encyclicals. The Pope's thoughts on these issues were clearly influenced by Manning.[36] In a letter to the Cardinal dated 17 January 1891, the Pope wrote with a mention first of Ireland and then of the social question, "No less is the care which touches you as to the condition of working-men. We are engaged in the consideration of each matter, and as soon as we are able we will take pains that neither our duty nor charity are lacking to either cause."[37] In this rather formal way the Pope is saying that he is concerned about Ireland and working-men and will try to do something about both issues. In March, Archbishop Walsh of Dublin wrote to Manning to say that Pope Leo had spoken to him about the Encyclical and when it was completed in May the Pope gave a copy to Archbishop Walsh with a letter to Manning asking him to arrange the translation into English for England, Ireland and

---

34 Cardinal Gibbons, "Statement to Propaganda," in Fitzsimons, "Manning and the Workers," pp. 142-143.

35 Quoted in Shane Leslie, *Cardinal Manning: His life and labours* (Dublin: Clonmore & Reynolds, 1953), p. 157.

36 A recent article in *The Tablet* also emphasizes this point. It is illustrated by a union banner with a picture of the cardinal. See John Armitage, "Values lived through action," *The Tablet* No. 9065 (6 Sept 2014), pp. 7-8.

37 Quoted in Leslie, *Cardinal Manning*, p. 164.

the United States.

Leslie notes that in places the Encyclical is very close to a letter Manning had sent to a Congress at Liege which met in 1890. The wording is in fact rather different but the ideas are quite close. Thus Manning had insisted that "political economy is... a matter of human life," that human and domestic life comes before labour and wages. He also called for an eight hour day in mines and asserted that the right to unite for mutual protection was a "natural and legitimate right".[38] *Rerum Novarum* described treating men "like chattels to make money by" as inhuman. It called for "shorter hours" for those who work in mines and asserted that the State could not forbid "citizens to form associations".[39]

Hence Manning is the link between the activism of the Clapham Sect and Catholic social teaching that usually traces its origin to Leo XIII's encyclical.[40] The key texts of that teaching are set out in the following encyclicals: *Rerum Novarum* (1891) by Leo XIII, *Quadragesimo Anno* (1931) of Pius XI, *Mater et Magistra* (1961) and *Pacem in Terris* (1963) by St John XXIII, *Populorum Progressio* (1967) and *Octogesima Adveniens* (1971) by Bl. Paul VI and *Laborem Exercens* (1981), *Sollicitudo Rei Socialis* (1987) and *Centisimus Annus* (1991) of St John Paul II. Then in 2004 there appeared the *Compendium of the Social Teaching of the Church*, which depends for much of its content on quotations from the above encyclicals along with other Church documents. As can be seen from the dates (1891-1931-1961-1971-1981 and 1991) most of these encyclicals are deliberate updates of the first. Indeed, it is the world of work that formed the basis of *Rerum Novarum* which is

---

38 Quoted in Leslie, *Cardinal Manning*, p. 165.

39 Quoted in Leslie, *Cardinal Manning*, p. 165.

40 At Oxford Manning was a friend of the later Prime Minister, William Gladstone, and of Samuel Wilberforce, the third son of William. Manning's wife was the sister-in-law of Samuel Wilberforce, who presided at their wedding in 1833. She died of tuberculosis in 1837.

conspicuously the best part of the 2004 *Compendium*.

Another significant source of material for the *Compendium* is the Pastoral Constitution of the Church *Gaudium et Spes* promulgated at the Second Vatican Council. Virtually every paragraph of this document is quoted in the Compendium.[41] In the historical notes on the Church's social doctrine, the *Compendium* specifically draws attention to the fact that "[f]or the first time, the Magisterium of the Church, at its highest level, speaks at great length about the the different temporal aspects of Christian life".[42] In the same paragraph, *Gaudium et Spes* is noted as presenting "in a systematic manner the themes of culture, of economic and social life, of marriage and the family, of the political community, of peace and the community of peoples". Previous to Vatican II, the Church in her official documents tended to address only her own faithful. At Vatican II the Church realized that much of value was to be found outside her own confines and that this was to be welcomed in a positive spirit. This openness to the world is the chief feature which has enabled the Church to leave her own self-imposed ghetto.

Other parts of the *Compendium* also depend on a rich tradition in the Church. The section on politics (chapter 8) derives from reflections on the state that go back through Aquinas and Augustine to the Biblical dilemma over kingship in the *Book of Samuel*. Chapter 11 on peace draws on St John XXIII's *Pacem in Terris* and on the subsequent annual *Messages for the World Day of Peace* (1968-). The section on the family and marriage (chapter 5) also draws on a long ethical tradition. The section on the international community which deals, among other things, with development, poverty and debt, is clearly indebted to St John Paul II's encyclicals of 1987 and 1991. However,

---

41 The index to the *Compendium* lists all references to the Ecumenical Councils. In fact only three Councils are mentioned, and the first two (Lateran IV and Vatican I) only very briefly. The bulk of quotations from Vatican II come from *Gaudium et Spes*. See *Compendium of the Social Doctrine of the Church*, pp. 340-341.

42 *Compendium of the Social Doctrine of the Church* #96.

it must be supplemented by Benedict XVI's *Caritas in Veritate*. The chapter on the environment (chapter 10) quotes John Paul II's encyclicals and also relies on his many other speeches and writings. Thus as a whole the *Compendium* itself is uneven and the value of its parts unequal.

3.5 The principles of Catholic social teaching

Nonetheless, there are certain distinctive features of the Catholic approach that do deserve comment. Catholic social thought grew out of Leo XIII's encyclical as a middle path between socialism and capitalism. It is critical of the capitalist's accumulation of wealth and also of socialist collectivism. In this it remains true to its patristic origins. At the same time it seeks to find its own foundational philosophy and it does this by stressing the value of the human person. Quoting *Gaudium et Spes*, the *Compendium* notes:

> Everything is considered from the starting point of the person and with a view to the person, "the only creature that God willed for its own sake" (Gaudium et Spes #24). Society, its structures and development must be oriented towards "the progress of the human person" (Gaudium et Spes #25).[43]

The personalist current came to the fore with the work of the prolific St John Paul II. Personalism had developed in France with Emmanuel Mounier and spread to Poland, where John Paul II absorbed it. He was to stress the value of the worker rather than the value of the product (capitalism) or the claims of labour itself (Marxism).

At the close of the Second Vatican Council, in 1971, Pope Paul VI wrote

---

43 *Compendium of the Social Doctrine of the Church #96.*

an encyclical on development *Populorum Progressio* which applied the teaching of previous social encyclicals to that of development. Pope Benedict XVI explicitly refers back to Paul's encyclical when he wrote on economic issues with the assistance of a group of Italian economists. One of his consultants, Stefano Zamagni presented the encyclical *Caritas in Veritate* at the Vatican press office, saying:

> This encyclical aims to overcome a dichotomy that characterized the 20th century between the economic and social spheres. If we can instead incorporate the idea of the social element into the economy, the market itself becomes a force for civility.[44]

In short, it seeks to put the human person and ethical values at the centre of the financial world and thereby overcome the financial crises that have arisen.

One striking feature of this middle road to social theory is that it does not catch on to the current United Nations espousal of human rights. Of course, the Catholic Church today is not opposed to human rights. Indeed, it is especially concerned about the right to life and the right to freedom of religion. But the basic formulation of its position is not in terms of human rights. There is no true theology or philosophy of human rights behind its stance. Its fundamental principles, built on that of the dignity of the human person, are community-oriented: the common good, subsidiarity and solidarity (chapter 4 of the *Compendium*). Rights are discussed (in chapter 3) but as an exposition of the dignity and liberty of the human person. In other words, rights are a privileged form of language to express the nature of the

---

44 Quoted by Jeff Israely, "The Pope on the World Economy: Prophets, not Profits," *Time* (7 July 2009) at http://content.time.com/time/world/article/0,8599,1909020,00.html (consulted 19 Sept 2014).

human person, but not the only way in which this can be done. The reason for this lies in the chequered history of rights and the Church.

In the context of the French Revolution, rights were espoused by anti-clericals and led to massive persecution of the church. The Church tended to use the language of humanitarian concern, seeing the other as a recipient of charity, rather than as someone having a right to certain goods. St John XXIII was the first to make a positive step and accept the United Nations and its language of rights. Yet these still serve as a reinforcement for the long-standing charitable approach to human suffering. The *Compendium* describes them as "one of the most significant attempts to respond effectively to the inescapable demands of human dignity" (#152). While couched in the language of praise, this is also a reminder that the language of rights is only "one attempt" to express something deeper: ie. human dignity.

The three principles that then form the basis for Catholic teaching in social areas take human dignity as their foundation (#160). The principle of the common good and the universal destination of goods is simply a reformulation of the early Patristic position referred to above. Subsidiarity was present in *Rerum Novarum* (#101-3) and finds its formal definition in *Quadragesimo Anno* (#203), which definition is repeated in the *Compendium* (#186). According to this principle each level of an organisation has its own sphere of competence which should be free from interference. In concrete terms this can be translated into issues such as the state not interfering in church-run schools or hospitals. The principle of solidarity comes to prominence in the writings of the Polish John Paul II.[45] It is a willingness to give to others over and beyond what they can claim as their right. In short, it is a way of insisting on the principle of the common ownership of all things.

---

45 Footnote 421 of the *Compendium* traces the idea of solidarity back to *Rerum Novarum* and notes the different terms (eg. 'friendship', 'social charity', 'civilisation of love') used in the encyclicals.

Networks such as Sant'Egidio try to implement the above social Gospel. Indeed, awareness of this background can help to clarify their specificity as Catholic/Christian bodies. Along with other human rights' groups, Sant'Egidio is opposed to the death penalty. But its espousal of the cause of refugees and its peace-making activities are broader than the typical human rights NGO. It uses lobbying like they do but also practices personal charity and human contact. Solidarity is very much part of its way of acting.

Conclusion

In the first section of this address I distinguished certain models of social engagement that the Church has adopted. The models look quite different from one another. There is the international banking, hospitals and shipping of the military Orders compared to the idealism of the Pilgrim Fathers seeking to found a new arcadia in America. In the second part I have looked at the ideas which have inspired or been generated by the differing contexts in which the Church has found itself. In this latter part I have laid more emphasis on the continuity of thought, even noting how a predominantly Anglican body, the Clapham Sect, had an indirect influence on Catholic social teaching through the writings and example of Cardinal Henry Manning. Within any living tradition such as the Christian tradition there is bound to be a dialectic of continuity and innovation. This is a sign of life. The danger any body has to face comes when change no longer happens, when certain institutional formats become so rigid as to allow no new growth. The other danger is when changes are made that are not true to the central tradition of that body.

In today's context we probably still remain in awe at the vast institutions and networks built up in the nineteenth century. We perhaps long for the personnel and exclusive spirit of that era. I have tried to show that the nineteenth century institutions were not only merely one form of social engagement they were also, to some extent, an aberration that depended on a sudden increase in population. When we turned from the external buildings to the internal spirit of campaigning that marked the work of Wilberforce, we can see how this is better able to give us a model for the future, the model of networking and campaigning we see in Sant'Egidio. I would like to end with two quotations from Cardinal Newman's *Essay on the Development of Christian Doctrine*. In the first he talks about the danger of clinging to the past:

> one cause of corruption in religion is the refusal to follow the course of doctrine as it moves on, and an obstinacy in the notions of the past. (Ch. 5 #8)[46]

In the second he notes that discontinuity of external form does not necessarily deny identity of substantial ideas:

> An idea then does not always bear about it the same external image; this circumstance, however, has no force to weaken the argument for its substantial identity (Ch. 5 #9)

I pray that, with these ideas, we may look forward to a new era of social engagement between Christianity and China.

---

46 John Henry Newman, "An Essay on the Development of Christian Doctrine," available at http://www.newmanreader. org/works/development/chapter5.html

In the Beginning, There Were Hermeneutical Mistakes of Church-State Relations in Modern China *

Cheng-tian Kuo

Abstract

The hectic and slow progress of religious freedom in China is a direct result of restrictive religious policies, which have been guided by hermeneutical mistakes about religion-state relations made in the early 1900s. The phrase "separation of state and church was incorrectly translated and understood as total separation of state and church, instead of its American authentic meaning of "checks and balances between state and church. Even worse, the phrase has been employed to justify the state's domination over religion, while forbidding religion from criticizing the state. Chinese nationalism in the early 1900s further permeated the Chinese versions of the Bible by mistranslating different human groups into the state, thus, transforming the Bible into a nationalist textbook for the Chinese. The continued impacts of these hermeneutical mistakes on church-state relations in modern China are evidenced by the Christian Textbook of Patriotism and six major misconceptions of church-state relations commonly held by Chinese officials and intellectuals.

Keywords: Modern China, Church-State Relations, Separation of Church and State, Religious Freedom, Hermeneutics

---

* Paper presented at the International Symposium on Christianity and Social Responsibility in the Chinese Context, National Central University, TAIWAN, October 17-18, 2014. I thank Philip L. Wickeri for his helpful comments and Michael Hsieh for his very efficient research assistantship. National Science Council in Taiwan provides generous funding to this project (NSC 101-2410-H-004-118).

現代中國政教關係詮釋錯誤的起源

郭承天

摘 要

　　現代中國宗教政策導致宗教自由的緩慢與崎嶇發展，而這些政策的理念源自二十世紀初期政教關係概念傳入中國時，所發生的翻譯與詮釋錯誤。「政教分立」一詞被誤解為「政教分離」，而非美國原意、具有「政教相互制衡」意涵的「政教分立」。更糟的是，「政教分離」被國家用來合理化它對於宗教的控制，同時禁止宗教批判國家。二十世紀初期的中國國族主義更進一步滲入《聖經》的各種中文譯本，把各種人群團體都翻譯成國家或邦國，而使得《聖經》成為當代中國的愛國主義教材。這些詮釋的錯誤對於現代中國政教關係的持續影響，仍可見於《基督教愛國主義教材》以及中國官員與知識份子常抱持的六個錯誤的政教關係觀點。

關鍵詞：現代中國、政教關係、政教分立、宗教自由、詮釋學

I. Introduction

Thanks to the enlightened leaderships of Jiang Zemin and Hu Jintao, religious freedom of Chinese Christians made incremental progress from 1982 to 2012. In the past few years, however, the expansion of religious freedom for Chinese Christians reached a plateau, if not a limbo. In April 2014, a new provincial party secretary ordered tearing down those churches or church crosses which violated the building codes of Wenzhou city (Cao Nanlai called it "China's Jerusalem"). One year later, the city's party committee conducted an extensive campaign to purge party members who were Christian believers. The short-term factor of leadership transition at both the national and local levels is certainly the dominant cause. But the limited and hectic progress of religious freedom for Chinese Christians is partially rooted in long-term misconceptions of proper relations between the state and religion, starting with two kinds of hermeneutical mistakes in the early 1900s in China:[1] hermeneutical mistakes of the phrase "the separation of state and religion" and hermeneutical mistakes of those words related to the "state" in the Chinese versions of the Bible.[2] By revamping these misconceptions and revising current religious policies accordingly, Chinese

---

1 Theologians disagree on the definitions of Biblical interpretation, exegesis and hermeneutics (Bartholomew, Greene, Moller 2000; Corley, Lemke, Lovejoy 2002; Osborne 1991). In this paper, I use the term "hermeneutics" to include both exegesis (analysis of the meaning and morphology of scripture languages) and hermeneutics (application of Biblical verses to contemporary events). Although both exegesis and hermeneutics are subject to theological and ideological influence, hermeneutics is more so than exegesis. Thanks to Reviewers One and Two of this paper for this reminder.

2 In the past two decades, the literature on religious politics has expanded from research of church-state relations in Christian/Catholic countries to non-Christian/Catholic countries (Jelen and Wilcox 2002; Cheng and Brown 2006). Therefore, this paper uses "church-state relation" to refer to the relation between Christian church and the state, while "religion-state relation" refers to the relation between various religions and the state. Furthermore, the word "state" is used very flexibly in the literature on religious politics. It may refer to administration, government, state apparatus, party state, and politics, or their combinations. So is the word "religion" which may refer to theology, clergy, religious rituals, and faith community, or their combinations. In general, both state and religion are institutions that contain their respective elements. The literature on religious politics studies the relations between these two institutions.

Christians might start to enjoy more religious freedom.

The next section will discuss different hermeneutics of the "separation of state and religion" when the phrase was first introduced to Chinese politicians and intellectuals in the early 1900s. The third section analyzes the hermeneutical mistakes in the Chinese Union Version of the Bible. The fourth section studies the Christian Textbook of Patriotism to illustrate what long-lasting impacts these hermeneutical mistakes on conceptions of church-state relations in contemporary China. The fifth section briefly discusses other major misconceptions of religion-state relations in China as results of these hermeneutical mistakes. The last section concludes this paper.

II. In the Beginning, There Was a Hermeneutical Mistake

Although the phrase "the separation of church and state" was coined by Thomas Jefferson in this letter to the Danbury Baptist Association in Connecticut in 1802, the principle of church-state separation had been endorsed by the drafters of the U.S. Constitution.[3] Its content was made concrete in Article VI and the First Amendment of the U.S. Constitution. Article VI of the U.S. Constitution prescribes "no religious test shall ever be required as a qualification to any office or public trust under the United States." But it was the First Amendment of the U.S. Constitution that has been the most frequently cited exemplar for maintaining proper relations between the state and religion in modern democracies. It stipulates that "Congress shall make no law respecting an establishment of religion or prohibiting the free exercise thereof." Derived from this Amendment are the so-called "non-establishment clause" and the "free exercise" clause.[4] The first

---

3 Since most of Chinese religious groups are not Catholic or Christian, this paper will use interchangeably the phrases of "church-state relations" and "religion-state relations," pending on the context.

4 On the debate about church-state relations in the U.S., see Edwin S. Gaustad, *Proclaim Liberty Throughout All the*

component forbids the state from establishing any state religion, while the second forbids the state from interfering with religion. Through numerous rulings by the Supreme Court, particularly the Lemon v. Kurtzman of 1971, the state's promotion of or interference with religion is allowed only when it meticulously conforms to the criteria of "non-discrimination" and "non-excessive entanglement."

For the purpose of subsequent discussion, it is important to note that the word "separation" in this phrase and its authentic meaning were probably derived from the phrase "separation of powers" which the American founding fathers had in mind when they drafted the Constitution and the First Amendment. They embraced John Locke's political philosophy of separation of powers to construct the first modern democracy in the world.[5] In a nutshell, the separation of powers means two things: one, the three major branches of a government (administration, legislature and judiciary) are separate entities not subordinate to one another; two, these three branches of the government maintain checks and balances with one another. Therefore, when the founding fathers were drafting the First Amendment, they probably had in mind that the separation of church and state was to mean: one, the state and church were separate entities and were not subordinate to each other; two, the state and church would maintain checks and balances between them. All the U.S. Supreme Court decisions on church-state relations so far have reconfirmed these original interpretations. But so far, very few Chinese officials and intellectuals understand and embrace this authentic meaning of the separation of church and state. It all started with a hermeneutical mistake made in the early 1900s in China.

The hermeneutical mistakes is that the phrase was translated into

---

Land: A History of Church and State in America (New York: Oxford University Press, 2003); Philip Hamburger, Separation of Church and State (Cambridge, MA: Harvard University Press, 2004).

5 John Locke, Two Treatises of Government (Rutland, VT: Charles E. Tuttle, [1683]1993).

"zhengjiao fenlí" (政教分離) rather than "zhengjiao fenlì" (政教分立) by most Chinese intellectuals and politicians at the time and has been the most popular translation since. The former translation (called "SCX" hereafter for its wrong "X" translation) connotes that the state and religion are separate entities and have no interaction between them, like a divorced couple; while the latter (called "SCO" hereafter for its correct "O" translation) accurately captures the authentic meaning of the American separation of church and state. Even worse, the former was later used to justify the state's arbitrary intervention in the internal affairs of religion while forbidding religion from intervening in the state; SCX becomes a one-way separation. The former rejects the latter's implication for a mutual check-and-balance relationship between the state and religion. The following sections elaborate on these points.

In the archive of the Renmin University Library in Beijing, I found 28 newspaper reports and popular journal articles, published from 1904 to 1937, that dealt with the subject of religion-state relations. Among them, only 7 adopted the correct SCO translation, while 21 used the wrong SCX translation. But even among the seven that adopted the SCO translation, most opted for the SCX meaning to prescribe proper religion-state relations.

In the mind of most Chinese intellectuals at the time, the French case of church-state separation seemed to be the exemplar of SCX. Two articles, published in 1906 and 1907, adopted SCO in their titles to report news about France's new law (1905), which terminated all state subsidies to the Catholic Church (Article 2).[6] Articles 3 to 15 forced the Church to transfer its management authority to the state. Article 16 even forbid clergy from commenting on politics in places where they conducted prayer or read the

---

6 *The Eastern Miscellany* (Shanghai), 1906, vol. 3 (4): 26 (Rome: Rome bishop strongly protests against the separation [fenlì] of church and state in French); *The Eastern Miscellany*, 1907, vol. 4 (2): 4-12 (The new separation [fenlì] Law of church and state in French).

Bible. The French government literally treated the Catholic Church as a public educational institution that needed to be closely supervised by the state. Among the 21 Chinese articles that adopted the SCX translation, five dealt mainly with the French new law.[7]

In theories of religion-state relations, the French case has been regarded as an extreme and inappropriate model of religion-state separation, forbidding any interaction between these two institutions, such as wearing religious symbols in public schools.[8] In reality, it provides justification for the state's arbitrary intervention in religion, while forbidding religion from intervening in the state. In this sense, the SCX translation accurately described the idiosyncrasy of the French case. According to the annual Religious Freedom Report by the U.S. State Department, France is constantly criticized for minor violations of religious freedom.[9] Unfortunately, many important political leaders and intellectuals during the early Republican era, including Zou Enlai and Deng Xiaoping, had studied in France and enthusiastically embraced the SCX model.[10]

Among the 28 Chinese articles, several of them discussed religion-state relations in Tibet. Some used the SCO translation,[11] while others used the

---

7 *Law and Politics Magazine* (Tokyo), 1906, vol. 1 (1): 2 (Summaries of current events: The problems of separation [fenlí] of church and state); *The Diplomacy Review* (Shanghai), 1910, vol. 10 (10): 27 (Chronicle of events: French government carried out the separation [fenlí] of church and state); *The Universal Progressive Journal* (Chongqing), 1907, vol. 128: 10 (Issues: The problems of separation [fenlí] of church and state in French); *Sein Min Choong Bou* (Yokohama), 1906, vol. 4 (2): 90-91 (The separation [fenlí] of church and state case in French); *The Diplomacy Review*, 1906, vol. 6 (24): 15-16 (On the bargaining of separation[fenlí] of church and state in Europe).

8 Lorenzo Zucca, *A Secular Europe: Law and Religion in the European Constitutional Landscape* (New York: Oxford University Press, 2012), pp. xix-xx.

9 U.S. Department of the State, "France," International Religious Freedom Report, various years.

10 This sentence is inspired by Reviewer One.

11 *Kang Zang Qian Feng* (Nanjing), 1938, vol. 5 (4): 10-13 (A proposal to reform minority policies according to the separation [fenlí] of church and state in Xi-kang, Part I); *Kang Zang Qian Feng*, 1938, vol. 5 (5): 8-9 (A proposal to reform minority policies according to the separation [fenlí] of church and state in Xi-kang, Part II). *Kai Fa Xi Bei*, 1934, vol. 2 (1): 71-72 (Selected Public Opinions: The separation [fenlí] of church and state in Tibet from the historical perspective).

SCX translation, but all adopted the meaning of SCX. In 1910, the year before the Republican revolution, an editorial suggested the Qing dynasty to adopt the SCX principle in dealing with a new political crisis in Tibet: a senior Dalai just returned home from abroad, with the help of the Great Britain, in an effort to restore traditional theocracy and to abolish the rule of a junior Dalai who was appointed by the Qing dynasty. The editorial recommended SCX to thwart the conspiracy of the senior Dalai, which apparently is interference in Tibet's religious affairs.[12] Another two news reports said that there was already a consensus among the cabinet members of the Qing dynasty to adopt the SCX principle in dealing with the Tibetan question. The Qing government notified all embassies to China that it would not accept any diplomatic agreement made unilaterally by Dalai without the explicit approval from the Qing government.[13]

There was one news report on a British bill introduced to the parliament to remove the Church of England its status as the state religion. This news report used the SCX translation and declared that, following similar SCX policies adopted in France and Spain, religion would no longer be able to resist state domination.[14]

Dr. Sun Yatsen, the founding father of the Republic of China, was probably the only intellectual/politician in the early 1900s that adopted the SCO translation with its authentic American meaning in mind. After all, few Chinese politicians had lived in the U.S. as long as he did, or acquired dual citizenship in the U.S.[15] He inserted the principle of SCO in various drafts of

---

12 *Yu Ze Sui Bi*, 1910, vol. 1 (10): 6 (The proposal for separating [fenlí] church and state).

13 *Da Tong Daily* (Shanghai), 1910, vol. 13 (19): 29 (Hard News: The foundations of separation [fenlí] of church and state in Tibet). *Guo Feng Daily* (Shanghai), 1910, vol. 1 (14): 101-102 (Major Events in China: An opportune moment to separating [fenlí] church and state in Tibet).

14 *The Diplomatic Review*, 1907, vol. 13 (19): 23-24 (On separation of church and state in the United Kingdoms).

15 *Apple Daily* (Taipei), June 6, 2011, Sun Yat-sen, the founder of nation, is an American, http://www.appledaily.com.tw/appledaily/article/headline/20110606/33439605/, accessed September 2, 2014.

the Constitution. Article 5 of the Temporary Constitution (linshi yuefa) says that "all people of the Republic of China are equal regardless of race, class and religion." Article 6 stipulates that "the people have freedom of religion."

One can argue that these constitutional articles serve only passive protection of religious freedom and do not reflect the component of "checks and balances" of the SCO principle. Indeed, in his reply letter to a Chinese Buddhist organization, which was concerned about the possible abuses of the Temporary Constitution by Chinese warlords in granting religious autonomy, Dr. Sun seemed to adopt the SCX principle by saying that "In modern states, the separation of state and religion is strictly followed. Believers are devoted to the practice of religious life and never interfere with politics, while the state would do its best to protect religion."[16] In his reply letter to two Methodist leaders, Dr. Sun also used the term of SCO to discourage foreign missionaries from interfering with Chinese politics. He complained about the misbehaviors of some foreign evangelists who occasionally interfered with Chinese local politics. He also warned against those evangelists who intended to use state power for proselytism.[17]

But Dr. Sun moved from the SCX principle to the SCO principle in other letters or speeches in 1912. Addressing to a French Catholic church in China, he wished that all religions in China would worship the all-mighty God in order to complement the insufficiency of secular laws. He also wished that national politics make progress so that religions can also make improvement. Politics and religion complement each other.[18] In his speech at a church in Beijing, he proudly mentioned that many Chinese revolutionaries

16 Sun Yat-sen, "On freedom of religion: reply to the Buddhist Association," *Complete Works of Sun Yat-sen*, vol. 4 (Taipei: Modern China Press, 1989), pp. 250-251.

17 Sun Yat-sen, "On Chinese Autonomous Christian Church: reply to the Methodist Episcopal Church's Gao Yi Sheng and Wei Ya Jie," *Complete Works of Sun Yat-sen*, vol. 4 (Taipei: Modern China Press, 1989), p. 206.

18 Sun Yat-sen, "Religion and Politics," *Complete Works of Sun Yat-sen*, vol. 3 (Taipei: Modern China Press, 1989), pp. 50-51.

were Christian. Religion and politics are closely connected. The operation of national politics relies on religion to amend its insufficiency. So, he urged Christians to participate in politics.[19] In a speech delivered to a Christian association in the southern city of Guangzhou, he re-iterated his SCO principle: "Brothers and sisters, you are believers in a church, but you are also citizen of a nation... Christians should uphold both Christian ethics and national responsibilities in order to bring both politics and religion to perfection."[20]

A decade later, deeply frustrated by warlord politics during the early Republican era, Dr. urged Christian youths to get actively involved in politics to save the newborn nation. Addressing to the Chinese YMCA in 1924, he urged the Chinese YMCA to follow the exemplar of Joshua to rescue the Chinese people from the encroachment of warlords and to lead the Chinese people to the land of milk and honey.[21] In a long speech delivered at a YMCA conference in Guangzhou in 1924, he mentioned that American YMCA was active in American politics but Chinese YMCA was, strangely enough, not active in Chinese politics. He exhorted Chinese YMCA members to apply their Christian virtues to national politics, to "save the nation with virtues" (renge jiuguo). He cited the revolutionary martyrs of Lu Haodong and Shi Jianru who were both YMCA members and KMT members. He even promised the YMCA branches in Guangzhou that he would authorize them to govern a couple counties in Guangdong Province as experiments of "save the nation with virtues."[22]

19 Sun Yat-sen, "To amend deficiencies of politics with morality of religions," *Complete Works of Sun Yat-sen*, vol. 3 (Taipei: Modern China Press, 1989), p. 75.

20 Sun Yat-sen, "Christians in China should also apply Christian teachings to undertaking national duty," *Complete Works of Sun Yat-sen*, vol. 3 (Taipei: Modern China Press, 1989), pp. 132-133.

21 Sun Yat-sen, "Encouraging young Christians in China," *Complete Works of Sun Yat-sen*, vol. 9 (Taipei: Modern China Press, 1989), pp. 626-627.

22 Sun Yat-sen, "Citizens save their country with their moral quality," Complete Works of Sun Yat-sen, vol. 3 (Taipei:

However, the SCX translation, both in name and in substance, prevailed over the SCO translation in the mind of Chinese politicians and intellectuals in the early 1900s. After all, it was an era when Chinese nationalism just came out the political delivery room.[23] Most politicians and intellectuals fanatically embraced this "new religion" of nationalism with an aim to cleanse the national humiliation caused by Western imperialism and Chinese warlordism. While Catholicism and Christianity were treated as instruments of Western imperialism and needed to be "separated" from the state, traditional Chinese religions were regarded as instruments of feudal forces (warlords and Qing loyal family) that needed to be brought to the knees of a Leviathan state. In terms of religion-state relations, they preferred the French model of étatisme (strong state) rather than the more balanced American model of checks and balances.

In the mind of Chinese Christians in the Republican era, the misconceptions of religion-state relations were molded by the above nationalist program that could still be adjusted should zealous nationalism fade away. Unfortunately, Chinese nationalism did not stop at the gate of religion, but bodaciously permeated the very foundation of the Christian belief, the Bible, through hermeneutical mistakes in the Chinese versions of the Bible.

III. In the Beginning, There Was Another Hermeneutical Mistake

The most popular Chinese version of the Bible, which is also the most

---

Modern China Press, 1989), pp. 352-360.

23 Shi-jie Cha, *Minguo Jidujiao Shi Lunwenji* [Essays on the History of Christianity in the Republican Era] (Taipei: Yuzhouguang Press, 1994); Ren-chang Ye, *Wusi Yihou De Fandui Jidujiao Yundong: Zhongguo Zhengjiao Guanxi De Jiexi* [Anti-Christian movement after the May 4th Movement: Analyzing the relationship between politics and religion in China] (Taipei: Jiou Da Press, 1992).

common reference for Chinese Christian scholarship, is the Union Version
（和合本）. The translation of the Union Version, which lasted from 1906
to 1919, was led by foreign theologians and missionaries with auxiliary
assistance from Chinese Christians.[24] It was a time when nationalism reached
its zenith in the Western world and blossomed in China. Both the Western
translators and Chinese assistants were probably baptized everyday by the
nationalist holy water. The critical impact of nationalism on the Union
Version is mistranslation of words that are not entities of a state into states.
The author of a previous Chinese version of the Old Testament, Jewish
Bishop Samuel Isaac Joseph Schereschewsky, had warned his successors, who
were not of Jewish background, about possible mistranslations of those
Hebrew words that are not entities of a state into states. Somehow, the
translation committee of the Union Version failed to heed his critical warning
when they started their new translation based on his draft.[25] Without
exception, all other less-popular Chinese versions of the Bible, such as the Lu
Zhenzhong Version（呂振中譯本）, the New Translation Version（新譯本）,
the Contemporary Version（當代聖經譯本）, and the Contemporary
Chinese Translation Version（現代中文譯本）made similar hermeneutical
mistakes. Even if these translators had in mind the difference between nation
and state, they and their readers did not make such a clear distinction under
the influence of imported modern nationalism.[26]

---

24 *Holy Study Bible* (Hong Kong: The Rock House Publishers, Ltd., 2005), p. 1967; Wei-ben Zhao, *Yijing Suyuan*
[Origins of Biblical translation: The history of Translation of Five Modern Chinese Bibles] (Hong Kong: China
Theology Graduate School, 1993).

25 Ai-lian Yi [Irene Eber], *Shi Yuese Chuan: Youtai Yi Zhujiao Yu Zhongwen Shengjing* [Biography of Samuel I. J.
Schereschewsky: The Jewish Bishop and The Chinese Bible] (New Taipei City: Chinese Christian Literary Mission
Publishing Group Ltd., 2013), pp. 245-252. So far, I have not found other documents describing the worldview and
background of these translators.

26 Reviewer One suggests that in ancient Chinese classics, the concept of bangguo（邦國）might include both state and
people/ethnic group; such as "ming wei bang ben"（民為邦本）。 However, as this paper argues, the Chinese terms
"bangguo" probably denote the government/dynasty, rather than the people, and even more unlikely the modern
state.

Using both Chinese and English Bible study software programs,[27] Kuo conducts an intensive hermeneutical study of these translational errors.[28] It suffices to summarize his major conclusions here. Due to their lack of hermeneutical materials, both the Western translators and Chinese assistants of the Union Version extensively mistranslated various kinds of human groups that are not states into states. Even if occasionally they made the correct mistranslation, they did not apply the correct translation consistently throughout the Bible. The number of mistranslations in the Union Version is more than 3,000. These include eleven Hebrew words and four Greek words that are mistakenly translated into Chinese state: guo, bang, bangguo, and other similar terms.

In the Old Testament, the only Hebrew word whose meaning comes close to a modern state is kingdom or dynasty（王國，王朝）. The other eleven Hebrew words that are mistranslated into a state actually refer to other people, tribes, people living in certain areas, other ethnic groups, visitors, outsiders, ethnic groups, language, clans, strangers, and God's people. It is likely that the Israelis had a precarious history of thousands of years during which they encountered different "groups" of people with different degrees of friendship or hostility. Therefore, they probably developed different words to describe these groups of people for easy identification of threat. To lump these groups of people into a "state" is a reflection of the lack of hermeneutical knowledge on the part of both the Western translators and Chinese assistants of the Union Version.

In the New Testament, the only Greek word whose meaning is similar to a modern state is kingdom or dynasty（王國，王朝）. In fact, in the

---

27 For Chinese versions, Almega Bible Tools 4 contains Lu Zhenzhong Version, the New Translation Version, the Contemporary Version, and the Contemporary Chinese Translation Version. For English versions, BibleWorks 9.

28 Cheng-tian Kuo, Guozu Shenxue De Minzhuhua: Taiwan Yu Zhongguo Dalu [Democratization of Nationalist Theologies: Taiwan and Mainland China] (Taipei: Chengchi University Press, 2014), Chapter 3.

Septuagint, all Hebrew words for kingdom were correctly translated as *basileia* .[29] There are only four other Greek words in the New Testament that come close to a state, probably because the Jews, as a community, under the Roman Empire had stopped traveling extensively outside the Empire like their ancestors. The Roman Empire also annexed nearby kingdoms to make the world system simpler in the eyes of the Jews. Furthermore, the Greek language, is also a more precise language than Hebrew. All these factors probably contributed to the fact that the Union Version did a better job in translating these Greek words than Hebrew words. The other three Greek words that refer to tribes, other places and clans are mostly translated into words other than a state in the Union Version. But still, the most used word in the New Testament referring to a large community of people, is frequently mistranslated into "other states" (waibang) or "people from other states" (waibangren) in the Union Version.

These translational mistakes immediately generate new theological interpretations different from the original intent of Biblical verses. Kuo composes a list of 151 verses where the Union Version makes important translational mistakes.[30] For instance, one of the most often cited verses in Chinese political theology is "Righteousness exalts a nation, but sin is a reproach to any people" (Proverbs 14: 34). The Septuagint correctly translates nation as ethnos (nation or ethnic group), not a state. But the Union Version translates it as a state (bangguo). So the origin intent of the whole verse is to promote righteousness among the common people. But because of this mistranslation, the Union Version breaks the verse into two parts: to encourage public officials to uphold justice, and to discourage the common people from doing evil. Most Chinese Christians (in China, Taiwan and

---

29 BibleWorks 9.
30 *Supra* note 24, at pp. 285-297.

Hong Kong) today continue to cite this translation of the verse when they pray for or comment on national politics.

Another example of the translational mistake that generates new theological interpretations is related to the controversy whether secular states continue to exist in the new heaven and new earth. Revelation 21: 24 says that "By its light shall the nations (*ta ethnei*) walk." The original meaning of the verse is that believers of different "ethnic groups" will walk by its light. However, the Union Version translates "the nations" as "the states" (lieguo) and the verse becomes: "By its light shall the states walk in the city." But how can the states, which are governmental institutions, walk in the city? People can walk, but not governmental institutions.

The impacts of these hermeneutical mistakes on Chinese Christian theology are significant. First, most Chinese Christians would think that the history of Israel is a history of modern states fighting with one another, which is similar to the modern history of China defending itself against imperialist states. The primary responsibility of Chinese Christians would be patriotic to the Chinese state against imperialist states. Secondly, the misery of the Israelis was caused by a lack of centralized state, while the belief in God played only a secondary role. Again, the primary responsibility of Christians would be patriotic to the state; loyalty to the religion, second. Love your state first, then, love your religion (aiguo, aijiao). Thirdly, the new heaven and new earth will be composed of modern states, probably including the Chinese state, although probably not under the atheist leadership of the Chinese Communist Party. Therefore, Chinese Christians should embrace Chinese nationalism in this world in preparation for the coming of new Jerusalem, which would preferably descend upon somewhere in China.

IV. An Exemplar of Hermeneutical Mistakes: the Christian Textbook of Patriotism

The omnipotent and omipresent combined influence of these hermeneutical mistakes in the translation of religion-state relations and in the Chinese versions of the Bible is best exemplified by the Christian Textbook of Patriotism (jidujiao aiguo zhuyi jiaocheng; hereafter, CTP), which is the textbook of a required course for all freshmen in Chinese theological seminaries and is used in compulsory political study courses of large Three-Self churches in most major cities.[31] It was one of the religious textbooks of patriotism sponsored by the State Administration for Religious Affairs in the early 2000s with the aim to solidify the religious legitimacy of the CCP leadership after the 1989 Tiananmen massacre of students. The Catholic Textbook of Patriotism contains similar hermeneutical and hermeneutic mistakes as the Christian Textbook, but due to the limit of this paper, it will not be dealt with here.[32]

In addition to its introduction and conclusion, the Christian Textbook of Patriotism contains nine chapters. Chapter One proposes that patriotism is consistent with the Bible and Christian traditions. It extensively cites verses from the Old Testament and the New Testament, as well as works of church fathers, St. Augustine, Thomas Aquinas, Martin Luther, and John Calvin, to substantiate this proposition. Chapter Two traces the advent of Christianity in China, exposing the evil behaviors of missionaries in the late Qing dynasty and the early Republican era, but says that not all Chinese Christians were

---

31 The following is adapted from Cheng-tian Kuo, "Chinese Religious Reform: The Christian Patriotic Education Campaign," *Asian Survey*, 51 (6) (2011): 1048-1053.

32 Chinese Patriotic Catholic Association and Bishops Conference of Catholic Church in China, *Zhongguo Tianzhujiao Duli Zizhu Ziban Jiaohui Jiaoyu Jiaocai* [Catholic Textbook of Patriotism] (Beijing: China religious culture Publisher, 2002).

bad. Chapter Three recognizes contributions of Chinese Christians (including Sun Yatsen) to the 1911 Revolution, the patriotic movement of the early Republican era, the anti-Japanese war, and establishment of the People's Republic of China. Chapters Four and Five elaborate the development of the Three-Self Patriotic Movement in the past fifty years, presenting new religious/political dogmas and doctrines adapted to the emerging new political environment. Chapter Six provides justifications of the existence of the all-encompassing hierarchy of the National Committee of Three-Self Patriotic Movement of Protestant Churches and the China Christian Council. Chapters Seven and Eight pay tributes to eighteen founders and exemplars of the Three-Self Patriotic Movement. Chapter Nine discusses the more recent developments in church reforms led by Bishop Ding Guangshun. The ultimate goal of these reforms is to realize the "Construction of the Socialist Harmonious Society," which Party Chairman Hu Jintao championed at his inauguration in 2002.

The CTP is significantly different from the older propaganda works in terms of theological sophistication.[33] In one pioneering book, the CTP constructs an indigenous nationalist theology that is both comprehensive and consistent. It starts with the sacred religious scriptures and traditions. Then, it reconstructs the origin and development of Christianity in China in order to transform the hitherto imperialist, exploitative Christianity into a native, patriotic Christianity. It justifies the existing Christian hierarchy and provides eighteen recent exemplars of Chinese patriotic Christians for common Christians to emulate. Older propaganda works might have dealt with these

---

33 These propaganda books include *Weile Zhengyi Yu Heping* [For Justice and Peace]; *Qianshi Buwang Houshi Zhishi* [Lessons learned from the past can guide one in the future]; *Zhongguo Jidujiao Sanzi Aiguo Yundong Wenxuan, 1950-1992* [Selections of three-self patriotic movement of protestant churches in China, 1950-1992]; *Wu Yaozong Xiaochuan* [Biography of Wu Yao-zong], *Huiyi Wu Yaozong Xiansheng* [Wu Yao-zong in retrospect]; *Zhao Zichen Wenji* [Selected Works of Zhao Zi-chen]; *Ding Guangxun Wenji* [Selected Works of Ding Guang-xun].

subjects separately but have not matched the breadth and consistency of the CTP.

Furthermore, old propaganda works did not extensively cite from the Bible to substantiate their arguments, thus, lacking religious legitimacy in the eyes of lay believers. Neither did they refer to important Western theological works based on liberal or conservative theology. Most of them consisted of proclamations and reiterations of state religious policies, official stories of modern Chinese Christian history, news of international religious exchanges, and personal witnesses related to the "insightful" and "correct" state religious policies. To avoid the political risk of innovative ideas, many propaganda works simply plagiarized sentences from existing publications and state proclamations.

Different from these propaganda works, the CTP cites extensively from the Bible and Western theological works to justify patriotism. For instance, Chapter One proposes that patriotism is consistent with the Bible and Christian traditions. It argues that the concept of a sacred nation originated in Genesis 12: 1-2 in which Jehovah promised Abraham establishment of a great nation (not a "state"). Since then, "national sovereignty and territorial integrity became sacred." Moses, "taking the burden of national independence and freedom, 'liberated' Israelis and consolidated state-building through the Law of Moses." David established a strong state to protect religious freedom. Later, political fragmentation and decline of the state led to religious fragmentation and decline. The Books of Daniel and Esther re-iterate the truth that "without state protection, there is no religious independence and freedom." Psalmists (e.g., Psalm 126) reveal a strong sense of patriotism. "Having a burning heart for patriotism is a requirement of all Jehovah prophets," as witnessed by Elijah, Elisha, Amos, Isaiah, Micah, and Jeremiah. Does patriotism lose its importance in the New Testament? No, the authors of the CTP say. Jesus himself was a great patriot, presumably to the lost

Jewish state. The Great Commission is interpreted as Jesus' love for his nation-state. And the New Heaven and Earth is a reconstruction of his "mother nation." Jesus' disciples were also patriots. They wanted to establish the Messiah kingdom based on Jewish idealism and patriotism.

Authors of the CTP further cite from works of church fathers, St. Augustine, Thomas Aquinas, Martin Luther, and John Calvin to substantiate the patriotic proposition. Quintus Septimius Florens Tertullian, St Justin Martyr, and St Polycarp of Smryna of the first to third centuries exhorted Christians to pray for the Roman emperor and the polytheist state even when they were mistreated. These church fathers "sacrificed their lives in order to demonstrate to the world that Christianity was the most patriotic force in the state." St Augustine promoted citizen virtues and encouraged Christians to become the foundation of national harmony and stability and to defend the state. Thomas Aquinas urged Christians to obey the law and the officials. Martin Luther's religious reform expelled the exploitative Holy Sea from his fatherland and contributed to Prussian national self-determination. John Calvin established national churches in Geneva free of Papal control. In order to strengthen the credibility of these patriotic interpretations, CPT authors cite works written by liberal and neo-conservative Western theologians/ philosophers such as Jürgen Moltmann, Dietrich Bonhoeffer and Leonard Trelawney Hobhouse. Most of these cited (translated) works were published after 1991, reflecting the increasing exposure of Chinese theologians of younger generation to sophisticated theological thoughts that provide an alternative perspective to government propaganda works.

There is little doubt that CTP authors have deliberately interpreted or misinterpreted these Biblical verses and Christian traditions in order to justify Chinese patriotism. Borrowing from Luke 5: 37, one senior Christian theologian I interviewed commented: "it is new wine in the old propaganda bottle." However, an in-depth discussion of Biblical verses and Western

Christian traditions to justify Chinese patriotism had been rare before the CTP was published. Most of older Chinese theologians did not have access to these translated works or did not have foreign language skills to read the original texts. Younger seminary students and Christians, particularly in urban family churches, think "foreign priests deliver better sermons." The CTP authors must have felt it necessary to place this discussion right in Chapter One in order to strengthen their appeal to younger Christians. The side-effect of this discussion is that it may open up a Pandora's box of other "pernicious, politically incorrect" discussions of religion-state relations. And it does.

The most interesting part of the CTP is its impressive emphasis on political prophetic roles of Chinese Christians, hitherto a taboo in Chinese theological seminaries and in Three-Self churches. Instead of patriotism alone, "patriotic but politically critical" seems to be the quintessential theme of the textbook. The CTP authors do this in a very subtle way and place these critical messages in between patriotic statements. For instance, Moses Law was patriotic but "its core was liturgy... A nation cannot be strong without a worship center." Do the CTP authors want to convey a message of religious freedom to the readers? The Books of Psalms, Daniel and Esther, as well as the prophets praised patriotism. But the CTP authors spent almost ten pages to explain that the decline of Israel was due to government corruption and distributional injustice. Isaiah urged people not only to relinquish evil behaviors but also to uphold social and political justice, i.e. to vindicate the disadvantaged people. Micah was a patriot but shared with Isaiah the abhorrence for official corruption. Jeremiah was a patriot but risked his life to criticize the Jewish rulers. Jesus was a patriot but he "showed true love by respecting human dignity." By these comments, are the CTP authors talking about basic human rights? St Augustine promoted patriotism as well as the "interdependent and re-enforcing relationships between state and church."

He urged Christians to "reform the state in order to reinvigorate national unification and strength." Thomas Aquinas asked Christians to obey the government but also to promote justice and social equality. Martin Luther pursued both national self-determination as well as freedom and equality.

These prophetic messages are not limited to Chapter One alone, which focuses on the Bible and Western Christian traditions; they are spread sporadically in other chapters of the textbook. For instance, Chapter Three eulogizes those patriotic Christians who participated in liberation of the Chinese people from feudal forces and imperialist powers. This serves to justify Christian participation in political reforms. Chapter Four criticizes some anti-revolutionary Christians during the anti-Japanese war because they "promoted unconditional obedience to the (Japanese) government in the name of Christ." Chapter Five provides justifications for the TSPM, but CTP authors periodically remind the readers of the importance of religious freedom and democratic legal institutions. Chapter Seven is devoted to introducing Wu Yaozong, the champion of the TSPM and a sincere follower of liberal Social Gospel. Among his patriotic behaviors, Wu touted Christians to promote a more "equal and reasonable" socialism. At the end of each chapter, the authors encourage the readers to apply the gist of the chapter to current social and political issues in China.

In addition to what is theologically and politically innovative in the CTP, what is missing also deserves discussion. The minimal role of the Chinese Communist Party in modern Chinese Christianity is one such missing point. A typical patriotic theology usually would have some theological justification of the contemporary ruler and some elaboration of the contribution of the political guardian to the religion. The CTP does not contain much information on these topics. When I pointed out this puzzle at a meeting with about thirty SARA researchers, they seemed stunned and could not explain it. They promised to add materials related to the CCP in the next edition of CTP. Later, a senior SARA researcher, in private, offered an explanation for the CCP's minimal role. The textbook was written by a believer/theologian who knew that he should not theologically over-eulogize the CCP in the text because of political considerations. Otherwise, the book would lose its legitimacy in the eyes of ordinary believers. The author intended to write a textbook that was acceptable to believers in both Three-Self churches and family churches.

V. More Hermeneutical Mistakes of Religion-State Relations in China

The hermeneutical mistake of the phrase "the separation of religion and state" along with the hermeneutical mistake in the Chinese versions of the Bible in the early1900s were responsible for the development of additional six major misconceptions of proper relations between the state and religion in China for the whole century and till now. These are: (1) In traditional China, the state tightly controlled religions, while religions were submissive to the state. (2) Religious freedom would cause political instability. (3) Traditional Chinese religions are obstacles to China's modernization. (4) Catholicism and Christianity are instruments of Western (neo-) imperialism. (5) Religious sovereignty infringes upon national sovereignty. And, (6) Western religious freedom is not applicable to the Chinese context. Based on the previous discussion, these misconceptions are rebutted in the following.

1. In traditional China, the state tightly controlled religions, while religions were submissive to the state. This is an "imagined" utopia, using Benedict Anderson's reference to nationalism as "imagined community," with which Chinese nationalists imposed their political program on historical facts. The majority view of recent scholarly findings is that the Chinese state was a

religious state, while the Chinese society was a religious society.[34] Neither one dominated the other, but rather, they lived in harmony with each other. Religious tolerance and freedom was the norm rather than the exception, due to the long tradition of religious pluralism and religious syncretism. By comparison, Chinese people in traditional China probably enjoyed more religious freedom than their counterparts in the West before World War II.

2. Religious freedom would cause political instability. Historically, most of religious rebellions were instigated by corrupt officials who caused local political instability, not the other way around; for examples, the Yellow Turban Rebellion (184 AD), the Taiping Rebellion (1850-1851), and the White Lotus Rebellion (1900). Most Chinese religions are, by nature, conservative and pro-government.

3. Traditional Chinese religions are obstacles to China's modernization. Chinese religions underwent modernization in the Republican era and continue to do so in the Communist China.[35] In fact, major religions successfully adapt to new environments all the time.[36] Christianity was a modernized religion derived from Catholicism. Catholicism underwent modernization in the early 1960s. Even "fundamentalist Islam" is a selective adaptation to the pressure of modernization. Currently, all the five major religions in China have been modernized and significantly contributed to the socialist construction programs.[37] In Taiwan, Chinese religions, such as Ziji,

---

34 Vincent Goossaert and David A. Palmer, *The Religious Question in Modern China* (Chicago, IL: University of Chicago Press, 2011); John Lagerwey, *China: A Religious State* (Hong Kong: Hong Kong University Press, 2010); Kenneth Dean, "Further Partings of the Way: The Chinese State and Daoist Ritual Traditions in Contemporary China," in Yoshiko Ashiwa and David L. Wank, eds. *Making Religion Making the State* (Stanford, CA: Stanford University Press, 2009).

35 C.K. Yang, *Religion in Chinese Society: A Study of Contemporary Social Functions of Religion and Some of Their Historical Factors* (Berkeley, CA: University of California Press, 1961); Fenggang Yang, *Religion in China: Survival and Revival under Communist Rule* (New York: Oxford University Press, 2012).

36 John L. Esposito, Darrell J. Fasching, and Todd Lewis, *World Religions Today*, 2nd ed. (New York: Oxford University Press, 2006).

37 P. R. C. Center for Religious Research of China, State Administration for Religious Affairs, ed., *Zhongguo Wuda*

Foguangshan and Yiguandao, have adopted modern management and established branches in more than 100 countries.

4. Catholicism and Christianity are instruments of Western (neo-) imperialism. Some of them were, but most of them were devoted to evangelism and modern education.[38] We need to differentiate pure religious organizations from politically motivated religious organizations. The majority of Chinese Christians and Catholics, both the Three-Self and family churches, are loyal supporters of the CCP regime, although they disagree with the extent of religious autonomy.[39] Besides, Chinese Christians are so divided to have a coherent political influence. Western Christianity also learns from past experience to respect local autonomy and politics in China.

5. Religious sovereignty (宗教主權) infringes upon national sovereignty (國家主權). Religious freedom aims to promote religious autonomy (宗教自主權), not religious sovereignty. There is no such concept of religious sovereignty as religious freedom is concerned. Nor the concept of religious sovereignty can be found in theories of religion-state relations. The Holy See (the Vatican State) is an exception that proves the rule. It functions mainly as the religious coordination center of Catholic religious organizations worldwide. By religious freedom, it means only the freedom to choose religion, to practice religion in private and in public, to make own decision on religious management and doctrine, and to disseminate their religious doctrine without discrimination and harassment from the government. On the one hand, religious freedom is practiced under the constraints of social norms and the rule of law. On the other hand, state sovereignty, as defined in

---

Zongjiao Lun Hexie [Chinese Five Great Religions Commenting on Harmony] (Beijing: Beijing: China religious culture Publisher, 2010).

38 *Supra* note 28; National Committee of Three-Self Patriotic Movement of the Protestant Churches in China and China Christian Council, *Jidujiao Aiguo Zhuyi Jiaocheng* [Christian Textbook on Patriotism] (Beijing: China religious culture Publisher, 2006).

39 Declaration of Family Churches in China, 1998 (unpublished).

its first appearance in the Westphalia treaty of 1648, explicitly excluded religious autonomy from its jurisdiction. The practice of religious autonomy can hardly infringe upon national sovereignty, unless the controversial religious organization promotes non-religious goal of national independence. In return, the state should refrain from interfering with religious autonomy.

6. Western religious freedom is not applicable to the Chinese context. Taiwanese compatriots experimented with a similar Leviathan rule by the Leninist party-state from 1949 to 1987.[40] Most religions practiced medium level of religious freedom and supported the KMT government. The Presbyterian Church in Taiwan supported the KMT government from 1949 to 1972. It was the incompetent secret police, who constantly violated the PCT's religious freedom, drove the PCT to the opposition movement. It also thanked to the major religious organizations, which developed democratic culture within their organizations, to promote peaceful transition to democracy. According to the US Religious Freedom Reports, Taiwan is a model of religious freedom among all democratic countries.[41] Western religious freedom is proven applicable to the Chinese context.

VI. Conclusion

The hectic and slow progress of religious freedom in China is a direct result of restrictive religious policies, which have been guided by hermeneutical mistakes about religion-state relations made in the early 1900s. The phrase "separation of state and church" was incorrectly translated and understood as total separation of state and church, instead of its American authentic meaning of "checks and balances between state and church." Even

---

40 Cheng-tian Kuo, *Religion and Democracy in Taiwan* (Albany, NY: State University of New York Press, 2008).
41 U.S. Department of the State, "Taiwan," International Religious Freedom Report, various years.

worse, the phrase has been employed to justify the state's domination over religion, while forbidding religion from criticizing the state. Chinese nationalism in the early 1900s further permeated the Chinese versions of the Bible by mistranslating different human groups into the state, thus, transforming the Bible into a nationalist textbook for the Chinese.

The combined and long-lasting influence of these hermeneutical mistakes can be found in the Christian Textbook of Patriotism (CTP), which serves as a standard textbook in a required course for all freshmen in theological seminaries. Clergy and leaders of lay believers of churches in major urban areas are also required to study this textbook. The CTP extensively mistranslated and misinterpreted Biblical verses in order to provide religious justification for Chinese patriotism. However, the CTP also contains hidden messages of religious freedom that reflect the growing dissatisfaction of Chinese theologians toward the lack of religious freedom.

Additional six hermeneutical mistakes of religion-state relations in China are briefly rebutted. Based on recent scholarly findings and contemporary theories of religion-state relations, these hermeneutical mistakes are amended as the following: (1) In traditional China, the state did not tightly control religion. They largely lived in symbiosis with high levels of religious freedom and tolerance. (2) Religious freedom did not cause political instability. It was political corruption and incompetence that instigated religious rebellions. (3) Traditional Chinese religions have been modernized and contributed to China's modernization. (4) Catholicism and Christianity are no longer instruments of Western (neo-) imperialism. (5) Religious sovereignty, which is an hermeneutical mistake of "religious autonomy," does not infringe upon national sovereignty. And, (6) Western religious freedom is applicable to the Chinese context, as evidenced by the high degree of religious freedom and democracy in Taiwan.

（本文曾刊登於《史匯》第19期 [2016年6月]，頁175-200）

私人信仰方式與基督教的社會關懷：
以改革開放後的江浙城市為例

李向平

摘要

　　基於社會結構及其近十年來的變遷，中國當代基督教的基本信仰已經呈現了一種私人化的信仰方式。

　　這種信仰方式促使基督教的社會關懷方式也發生了極大的改變，因此，在基督教慈善層面，個體的或者是面對面的慈善互助，已經成為當代基督教關懷社會、他人的主要方式，同時也超越了登記教會與不登記教會之間的體制差異。一方面，這是強調「信主」與「不信主」之不同所形成的關懷方式，更願意說明信主的人，而不太願意幫助教會外的人；一方面，這也是基督教教會局限於體制差異所只能踐行的一種關懷方式。儘管教會組織的慈善活動也在進行，但是，個體的慈善方式無疑成為了當代中國基督教關懷社會現實的一個重要特徵。

　　本文將從當代中國基督教的運行機制、慈善資源的動員、基督徒的私人信仰方式等不同層面，對此問題進行討論。

關鍵詞：私人信仰方式、制度性私人化、社會進入機制、基督教關懷、個體慈善方式

一、問題的提出

著名的宗教社會學家侯賽・卡薩諾瓦，曾經就當代世界宗教的世俗化、私人化及其公共化之間的關係進行了深入而獨到的研究。[1]卡薩諾瓦用大量的經驗事實論述了，在現代社會普遍存在的社會分化趨勢之中，宗教本身不得不隨之發生相應的結構分化。但這種分化，並非如宗教世俗化理論所預測的那樣，呈現為一種宗教的「私人化」，反而呈現了一種所謂的「去私人化」（de-privatization）傾向。這已經成為當代社會中的普遍宗教現象，由此形成的「公共宗教」卻不會威脅現代社會的個人自由及社會結構分化原則。卡薩諾瓦基於西班牙、波蘭、巴西以及美國的案例，論證了宗教的公共參與在保護現代自由與權利、保護生活世界免遭行政國家的「殖民」，進而推動集體倫理反思。

傳統中國宗教的那種公共形式，在現代社會原則的制約之下已難以為繼，它已經遭到分解，必欲在無限的秩序概念之中還原它的有限性，即將對天人合一或天下國家的權力秩序的合法證明，轉變為對於社會秩序或其他部分社會秩序的具體適應。「天下」本來就是被社會分割的結構，「天下」的意識本身亦必須還原為社會、社區、甚至是私人的宗教信仰方式。於是，這種公共崇拜的表達形式，就分解在現代社會諸種有效性的制度分離中，進而導致現代國家也放棄了它對公民靈魂進行拯救的工作，放棄了它千百年來對於個人精神權的掌控，而把拯救靈魂的事情交由私人、社會自己去料理。這樣做的目的不是為了其他，而是為了「……國家成功地做到不用宗教而進行自我組織」[2]。各個社會領域均有自己的組成法則及其界限，彼此難以共用、甚至逾越。

在這樣一個制度分割和社會治理的狀態中，宗教的功能明顯縮

---

1 José Casanova, *Public Religions in the Modern World*. The University of Chicago Press, 1994.
2 京特・雅科布斯，《規範・人格體・社會——法哲學前思》（北京：法律出版社，2001），頁52。

小、減弱了，然而，重要的是，宗教的社會功能及其表達形式也將隨之而相應縮小，從天人合一的路徑進入了另一個領域——即社會治理的領域。因此，宗教與權力進行了原則上的分割、功能上的分割，促使宗教還原為它本來的自身發展形式，私人的信仰也開始成為私人的東西。為此，與傳統社會秩序相比較，現代社會的基本公共制度不再深入地影響個人意識與個性的形成，儘管這些制度的功能上合理的機制對人們施加了大量的行為控制，然而，個人的精神認同、信仰方式基本上成為一種私人現象。

在此背景之中，當代中國宗教及其信仰的世俗化問題，同樣也涉及到中國宗教的私人化或公共化、社會化的相關問題，涉及到宗教及其信仰方式的祛魅或復魅、個體化的宗教信仰方式如何建構、私人化的信仰方式與其信仰公共化要求，是否具有內在的關聯，等等。

由於社會結構及其近十年來的變遷，中國當代基督教的基本信仰也已經呈現了一種私人化的信仰方式。這種信仰方式促使基督教的社會關懷方式也發生了極大的改變，因此，在基督教慈善層面，個體的或者是面對面的慈善互助，已經成為當代基督教關懷社會、他人的主要方式，同時也超越了登記教會與不登記教會之間的體制差異。一方面，這是強調「信主」與「不信主」之不同所形成的關懷方式，更願意說明信主的人，而不太願意幫助教會外的人；一方面，這也是基督教教會局限於體制差異所只能踐行的一種關懷方式。儘管教會組織的慈善活動也在進行，但是，個體的慈善方式無疑成為了當代中國基督教關懷社會現實的一個重要特徵。

誠然，本文討論的私人信仰方式，主要是著重於梳理或討論當代不被制度所認可的「個體」信仰方式，導致了信仰者在服務社會之際無法使其信仰呈現一種公共信仰方式。為此，當代中國基督教的私人信仰方式，如何能夠從個體的被局限於私人的信仰方式，轉型為公民的信仰方式，或者是在基督教慈善資源的動員方式等不同層面，建構為個體的與公共的信仰方式。對此類相關問題進行的討論，也正是討論當代中國宗教的信仰方式等重要問題。

二、 私人化的信仰方式

改革開放三十年以來，中國社會中的宗教信仰自由問題，已經從有沒有宗教信仰自由的問題，變成了宗教信仰如何自由的問題，或者說從有無自由轉變成多少自由、如何自由的問題，以及宗教自由如何在法制社會之中得以實踐的問題了。

個人層面的信仰自由，解決了個人的信仰問題，但並非等同於宗教的自由。私人性的信仰自由，指的是個人的精神與信仰層面，但不能完全包括個人信仰的生活實踐與表達層面。個人信仰的實踐與表達，實際上也不會局限於私人的範圍了。因為公民個人的信仰不會總是局限於個人的腦袋之中，不能說出來，不能活出來。因此，宗教信仰自由原則的三十年社會實踐，能夠告訴我們的是個人的信仰自由與社會的宗教自由，其實是兩個不同卻又緊密聯繫的兩大層次，它們難以分隔，更不可能人為割裂。而宗教事務的依法管理，其本質就是在宗教信仰自由原則基礎上對社會性宗教自由的一種最基本的定義方式。既強調了宗教信仰的社會性，同時也肯定了信仰宗教的個體性，從而能夠將私人層面的信仰自由與公共社會層面的宗教自由，在現代法制建設之中整合起來。

回顧三十年前的1982年中共中央19號檔，這就需要我們重新理解檔與憲法規定的「宗教信仰自由」這一概念及其原則。如果僅僅是把宗教信仰之自由理解為或局限於公民之間私人的事情，那麼，不同信仰之間如何能夠體現信仰上的相互尊重呢？要不就把宗教信仰局限於為私人交往關係與信仰者的個體神祕認同之中。所以，不同信仰與宗教信仰之間如何尊重的問題，似乎還有一個信仰與宗教信仰社會實踐的公共領域建構的問題。只有在宗教信仰被社會某一層次共用認同的基礎上，宗教信仰才能成為社會、文化建構的重要資源之一。至於那種局限於私人認同、私下交往的宗教信仰方式，則很容易被祕密化、神祕化、巫術化，處於現代社會之邊緣。這就是中國有了信仰、卻又呈現信仰無用、信仰缺失的基本原因。

相對於個人崇拜、中國人處於被信仰的權力共同體而言，私人信仰的形成，實屬社會進步的結果。它與1980年代以來個人主體性確立與自我的發現相互配合，具有人心解放、權力解構的一定作用。它拆解了那種一元、單極、帶有象徵權力獨斷特徵的信仰結構。人們僅僅信奉自己。為此，私人的信仰可說是開啟了一個個體主義新時代，一種更為私人化、情感化和更民間化的信仰方式。

　　然而，問題也出在這裡。僅僅是私人或私人的信仰，或許會導致信仰本身所包含的公共性喪失，而信仰之公共性所賴以依託的社群或共同體缺失，會使一個社會信仰的公共性始終無法建構，導致一個社會公共信仰的缺失。在公私領域尚且無法界定的時代，私人信仰也無法再度提升為聖人信仰的前提下，私人信仰有可能演變出一套私人主義的意義模式。他們不期待自己的身分改變，甚至不期於與他人交往、互動，而是漸漸地把他們的私人信仰構成一種亞社會、亞文化生活方式，變異為一種僅僅關心自己利益、自我滿足的精神關懷。

　　在打天下、先得人心的傳統社會，人心幾乎等同於信仰以及對權力更替的信仰，私人信仰幾乎不可能；而國民時代，民族國家如同世俗之神，私人信仰同樣難構成。而整個二十世紀以來，宗教被道德、美育、科學、哲學等「主義信仰」所替代，私人信仰依舊給人焦慮。而真正的私人信仰，只有在1980年代後的改革開放中，才得以漸漸呈現。特別是當信仰之公共性不能依託於自由社群之時，私人信仰便可能被推向了個人內在、單一的道德修養，最後未能為信仰之公共性提供孕育、滋生的土壤，變質為單純的私人之事。

　　實際上，私人信仰是自然狀態下的信仰方式，而公民信仰則是社會交往中的信仰方式，同時也是承載了私人信仰公共性與社會性的實踐方式。私人信仰只有演進為公民信仰，才有可能構成良性互動的社會秩序。因個體的私人修持，只能淨化自我，甚至連自我也無法淨化。個體私我的關懷，缺乏終極。而終極的關懷形式，就在於神人、神聖信仰的公共互動之中。與此相反，當代中國為什麼會頻頻出現「貪官信教」的權力困惑？即是因為這些官員們「信仰走私」，這與

他們的「權力走私」，往往一脈相承、彼此推動。各人只信自己的，無法交往、難以認同，也不會彼此制約。

因此，現代社會的「制度分割給個人生活留下了未加組織的廣大領域，也給個人經歷的中心意義脈絡留下了尚未決定的廣大區域，從來自制度分割的社會結構間隙中出現了所謂『私人領域』。」在此前提之下，「宗教被定義為『私人事務』，個人就有可能從『終極』意義的聚集中挑選他認為合適的東西——只聽從有他的社會經歷所決定的偏好的引導。」[3]

在這裡，既有宗教的問題，亦有信仰層面的私人關係的限制。信仰的神聖性，必定出自於信仰的公共性與社群性。實際上，「沒有法律的宗教，將失去其社會性和歷史性，變成為純屬於個人的神祕體驗。法律（解決紛爭和通過權利、義務的分配創造合作紐帶的程式）和宗教（對於生活的終極意義和目的的集體關切和獻身）乃是人類經驗兩個不同的方面；但它們各自又都是對方的一個方面。它們一榮俱榮，一損俱損。」[4] 宗教如此，宗教的信仰方式同樣如此。缺乏法律共識的信仰，將失去其公共性與普遍性，變為特殊群體的象徵權力構成；而以憲政建設為基礎的信仰，才會建構一個公共的信仰平台，構成社會層面的公共信仰。當人們只信任自己的信仰，不信任私我之外的任何存在之時，最終將導致更為深層的另一種信仰危機、權力危機——我們的信仰如何被信任!?什麼才是值得信任的權力？什麼才是被認同的信仰方式？

三、從信仰方式到社會關懷方式

曾經有一種觀點認為：美國的基督教具有一種過度諾斯替化（即私有化）的傾向，意思是「他們的信念與行為，都傾向認為信仰與救

---

3 湯瑪斯‧盧克曼，《無形的宗教——現代社會中的宗教問題》（香港：道風山漢語基督教文化研究所，1995），頁108、109-110。

4 哈樂德‧J‧伯爾曼，《法律與宗教》，梁治平譯（北京：三聯書店，1991），頁95。

恩本質上是個人的事，與文化和歷史無關。」[5] 這種把福音私人化的過程，同時就會表現出很強的實用主義的味道。一方面，教會是屬靈的家，信徒躲在教會圍牆之內，只會尋求和經歷內在生命的屬靈經驗，追求個人道德生命的改善和突破，在屬靈的家裡要過的是一種「分別為聖」的屬靈生活。另一方面，教會的牧養事工，也是過度重視個人心理輔導的服務有關。[6]

特別是在當代社會高舉個人主義的文化思潮之中，基督徒由此而高舉的個體主義和立己心態，可能也強化了信仰私有化、福音私人化的傾向。中產人士一旦成為社會上的既得利益者，自然就會想維持穩定的社會局面，除非威脅到自己的利益，否則不會隨便直接介入社會政治活動。正如克拉普說的：「發現或許只有最富裕、在社會上最穩定的人才可以不理會社會、經濟和政治的問題，可以一味專注於抽象的內在健康。」[7] 與此傾向相互整合，那種被固有制度定義為「私人事務」的信仰方式，就很有可能從「終極」意義的聚集中，只去選擇信仰者自己認為合適的東西，或者是只聽從信仰者個人偏好的引導。

在此問題層面，如果就基督教教會的社會服務特徵而言，人們也不難看出這種信仰方式對其社會關懷或社會服務方式的深層聯繫。儘管各種資料顯示中國基督教信徒超過3,000萬，或者說是在2,300～4,000萬之間，但在當代中國社會龐大的人口基數中，基督教群體的比例還是偏低的，[8] 而基督教作為普通中國人眼中的外來宗教，始終還是受到中國社會不少人的排斥或誤解，由此嚴重制約了基督教教會對社會服務的深度與廣度。

---

5 克拉普（Rodney Clapp），《非凡的凡民——教會在後基督教世界中的文化身分》，陳永財譯（香港：香港基督徒學生福音團契，2010），頁24。

6 趙崇明，《佔領中環與教會政治》（增訂版）（香港：基道出版社，2014），頁61。

7 克拉普，《非凡的凡民——教會在後基督教世界中的文化身分》，頁80。

8 江蘇教會現有基督徒超過180萬人，約佔總人口2.3%（江蘇省2010年第六次全國人口普查主要資料公報江蘇人口7,866萬）；浙江省現有基督徒約180萬，佔3.3%（浙江省2010年第六次全國人口普查資料浙江省人口約5,442.69萬人）；上海現有基督教信徒21.8萬人（上海市第六次全國人口普查全市常住人口為23,019,148人，以這個資料計算，基督教徒在上海市人口中所佔比例不到1%）。

在長江三角洲（以下簡稱長三角）的基督教公益慈善事業中，教會作為一個基礎力量貢獻了絕大部分的資金、人力資源支援。[9] 長三角基督教開放堂點共計約 8,192 處，[10] 他們的公益慈善參與限於其宗教團體身分，通常以直接的資金、人力輸出為主。公益慈善參與的範圍主要包括敬老養老服務、社區服務、社會救濟、社會援助及教會內部的肢體互助。這些以基督教堂點為主體開展的公益慈善事業中，堂點負責公益慈善運作及財物支持，多數教堂的教牧職員不足十人，因此，主任牧師、長老成為公益慈善事業的主持者，並不特設專門的事工部門。在敬老養老服務、社區服務、教會內部肢體互助中，堂點直接參與，能跟蹤服務、自行監督，而在社會救濟、社會援助等與其他社會機構合作開展的公益慈善活動中，跟蹤服務及監督需要合作機構或團體回饋，教會較少有直接參與的機會。

然而，長三角地區基督教堂點各自行動，聯合性弱，社會參與程度低，同時又因信徒每週有限的事奉，長三角基督教以堂點開展的公益慈善呈現出小規模、有限範圍、不完整、大多局限於教會內部服務等特徵。

（一）肢體互助

《新約聖經》中耶穌教導信徒：「你們要彼此相愛，像我愛你們一樣，這就是我的命令。人為朋友捨命，人的愛心沒有比這個更大的。」[11]

因著耶穌的教導，教會內部的肢體互助一直是基督教優良的慈善傳統。這種宗教團體的互助形式互動方式直接、說明及時，也是基督

---

9 文中所用資料主要來源於華東師範大學宗教與社會學研究中心 2012 年上半年開展的長三角基督教公益慈善調查；參李向平主編《中國信仰研究》第三輯（上海人民出版社，2013）。

10 2009 年江蘇省民宗局資料，江蘇登記的活動場所共 4,323 處（教堂 476 處和固定處所 3,847 處）；2012 年浙江省基督教兩會統計，浙江省基督教教堂 1,200 餘所，聚會點 2,500 多處；上海民族與宗教網公布 2011 年底統計資料，上海市開放的基督教堂點 169 處。

11 《新約·約翰福音》第 15 章 12-13 節。"This is my commandment, That ye love one another, as I have loved you. Greater love hath no man than this, that a man lay down his life for his friends."

教教會保持其凝聚力的重要途徑之一。長三角地區教會內部的肢體互助主要有兄弟教堂的修建、教會內部兄弟姊妹的救助[12]和地區各教堂對神學院的辦學資助等。在各地區教會堂點所從事的社會公益慈善中，肢體互助佔了絕大部分的支出金額。而單從捐贈金額來說，對地區或中西部貧困地區教堂、教會的慈善捐助又比教會內部的貧困救濟要多得多。以無錫市基督教兩會「社會服務愛心公益基金」的活動為例，其26項資助活動中，有19項是明確指向信徒，而上海地區的基督教堂用於社會性公益慈善的除自然性災害外的支出一般在20%以內，浙江地區教會堂點的公益慈善也主要是針對教會內部困難的兄弟姊妹的救助和對貧困地區教堂修建的支援。

長三角地區教會對貧困地區的教堂修建包括省市內貧困地區和中西部貧困地區，這種援助資訊一方面通過地區兩會和全國兩會獲得，也有貧困地區教堂主動尋求援助的情況。援助內容主要是現金資助，一般幾千至幾萬不等。

浙江省基督教兩會於1984年秋開辦浙江神學院，2011年已被國家宗教局批准為宗教高等院校，辦學資金主要由地區兩會、教會堂點及基金會支持。上海市內有華東神學院一所，成立於1985年，由上海、浙江、福建、山東、江西四省一市的基督教兩會聯合創辦。華東神學院的辦學資金多由各地教會資助。上海地區每年3月的第三個禮拜，稱為「神學奉獻日」，上海地區各教堂所得奉獻都會捐給華東神學院，不過因為華東神學院資金相對充裕，因此也有教堂會將一部分資金捐助給其他貧困地區的神學院。所捐金額根據各地區教堂奉獻所得從幾萬到幾十萬不等。[13]江蘇境內還有金陵協和神學院和省基督教聖經專科學校兩所院校，其中金陵協和神學院由基督教全國兩會所辦，各地教會堂點會援助辦學資金和書物。

---

12 教會內部的救助內容主要包括傷殘、養老、貧困家庭、貧困學生的補助等。

13 據本次調查所得資料，上海市國際禮拜堂、景靈堂、普安堂、莘莊耶穌堂、閘北堂等堂每年對神學院援助在20～60萬之間。

（二）信徒個體之間的互助

　　基督教各堂點僅是一個宗教活動場所，由此形成的長三角地區的各地區教會並不能開展營利性活動。因此，基督教信徒實際上成為基督教開展社會公益慈善的財物來源和人力資源的根本。在教會堂點從事的（主要在養老敬老服務、社區服務方面）、教會組織的（包括公益慈善項目和機構）公益慈善中，基督教信徒都是免費的、帶著基督教人文關懷的義工團體。然而，還有不少基督教信徒對社會公益慈善的貢獻則要大得多。他們出於對目前體制內慈善機構的不信任，走出了一條面對面的個體慈善模式，同時也在一定程度上超越了宗教體制的內外局限。

（1）「老闆基督徒」

　　老闆基督徒由浙江大學教授陳村富赴浙江溫州調研後提出，老闆教徒是基督徒，但他們的職業，他們的經濟，他們的生活方式，都是現代經濟的產物，跟現代經濟緊密相關。[14] 浙江地區的老闆基督徒因地方經濟發展特點，因而他們多從事小商品加工、開個體經銷店等。同時，因為這些老闆基督徒財力雄厚、社會資源多，他們擁有更多的社會公益慈善資金資源。浙江地區的基督徒企業家從事慈善事業的形式多種多樣，包括向教會奉獻錢物、結成團契進行服務、參與支援慈善基金會等等。僅在2012年中國基督教公益慈善事業經驗交流會表彰的浙江籍企業家基督徒就有三位，即上海人民企業集團董事長金福音、浙江慈溪市振成機械有限公司董事長應成釗、杭州中慶建設有限公司董事長孔慶生。

　　老闆基督徒所參與的社會公益慈善涵蓋範圍廣泛，包括社會救助、養老服務、社區服務等，慈善參與形式也包含直接的經濟補助、提供便民服務、創立慈善基金、公益慈善機構等。老闆基督徒的公益慈善參與多以企業的名義展開，有的基金會及項目都以企業命名，如「上海人民企業集團愛心互助基金會」、「中慶扶貧幫困基金」、寧

---

14 張邦松，〈溫州老闆基督徒調查[J]〉，《經濟觀察報》（2010年3月26日）。

波伊司達潔具有限公司的「伊司達慈善扶貧／助學基金」、及其出資修建的八所「伊司達愛心學校」等。

（2）孫金耀夫婦與廣慈殘疾兒童福利院

廣慈殘疾兒童福利院是上海一個民間私人慈善機構，法人代表就是孫金耀先生。1998年，在劉勇志女士（孫金耀先生的母親，上海人，年輕時在教會學校上學，是基督徒）的願望下，由現任院長孫金耀先生及夫人開辦。孫院長及夫人全權負責管理，包括行政、財務。福利院有八個員工，其中一名老師，都是社會上招聘的。福利院的管理模式可以說是一種家庭式的管理。其運行資金來源主要是由孫院長的家族企業提供資金，當地民政部門對於院內兒童有部分資助。

廣慈福利院辦院十四年，已培育60多名殘疾兒童出院回歸社會，現在院41名殘疾兒童（這些兒童都是孤兒）。但是福利院在運行的過程中依然遇到不少的困難。資金方面，福利院的資金能保持其日常開銷，但用於殘疾兒童看病的花費很大，因而造成一定的資金緊張，福利院因此會開展一些義賣活動以補貼運作費用。福利院兒童教育方面，適齡兒童就讀特殊學校，同樣因為戶籍及上海市內特殊學校名額有限等原因，一直是福利院的難題，院內一些兒童八歲了還無法上學。職工方面，由於福利院地處偏遠郊區，招收不到長期穩定的護工團隊，同時院內教學也缺少專業化的師資力量，院內兒童的生活和學習仍存在一定程度上的不便。

因此，廣慈殘疾兒童福利院屬於一個獨立運作的、由基督教信徒創辦的慈善機構。這種慈善模式面臨的困難是多面的，儘管孫先生家的家族企業能為福利院提供大部分的運作資金，但是當福利院面臨大額的醫療費用時便出現困難；另一方面，非營利性的運行方式使得福利院負擔不起相對高額的雇工費用，也使得福利院護理及教師人員出現短缺。

以上兩種基督徒個人的社會公益慈善參與類型，前者在浙江地區相對較多，而像廣慈殘疾兒童福利院這樣的慈善參與形式在基督徒中很少。老闆基督徒的社會公益慈善參與多以企業名義展開，因此與社

會、政府關係融洽，而有營利性的公司作為基礎的公益基金、慈善專案都能保持其持續性，同時溫州多數企業家基督徒有家庭教會的背景，但是這種體制的限制在公益慈善參與中得到超越，他們的慈善參與使教會堂點、團契和家庭教會信徒成為一種立體的慈善動力。而基督徒個人名義創辦的廣慈殘疾兒童福利院，作為私人辦理的福利院不屬於政府購買服務、不享受政府福利院待遇、培育的殘疾兒童因其戶口限制不享受上海市醫療保險保障，與企業家基督徒的慈善開展形式來說沒有教會、團契背景，因而其開辦面對諸多困難。

（三）社會服務的總體特徵

本次調查所觀察到的長三角地區基督教公益慈善參與主體、公益慈善參與形式、參與涉及領域多樣，地區基督教社會公益慈善也有所差別。

其主要特徵是：在公益慈善參與主體方面，上海地區以教會堂點、教會組織為主體的社會公益慈善較多，而江浙地區除此之外基督教基金會的發展要更突出；參與形式方面，上海地區各教會堂點和基督教兩會組織的參與形式相對普通，教會堂點多以財物捐助為主，其中肢體互助佔多數；而青年會、女青年會通過購買政府服務創辦社區服務中心的形式點多、影響廣泛，浙江地區市兩會開展的社會公益慈善規模較大，地區兩會、團契、及信徒通過創辦慈善基金會、公益慈善機構開展的公益慈善形式普遍，江蘇省基督教公益慈善活動以愛德基金會為首鋪開的社會公益慈善形式多樣，基本涵蓋本文中提到的幾類慈善形式；慈善參與領域方面，江浙滬三地基督教各慈善參與主體的參與領域多樣，其中愛德基金會的社會組織培育中心、杭州教會醫院（將敬老院和醫院整合，納入醫保範圍）所涉及領域獨特。

在長三角各地區基督教參與社會公益慈善的特徵上，還有一些共同的特徵需要說明，即基督教社會公益慈善的信仰背景的特殊性、超越宗教的社會性、整合各教會和信徒的超體制性。基督教教會堂點、教會組織、信徒等參與社會公益慈善遵循基督教「愛鄰人」的慈善思

想，在慈善行為中遵循《聖經》中基督的訓導（「你施捨的時候，不要叫左手知道右手所做的，要叫你施捨的事行在暗中。」[15]）默默地奉獻。他們在教內肢體互助、社區服務、養老服務、特殊群體服務等慈善活動中，儘管其專業性還有待提高，但其細緻、無私的奉獻卻無異是值得稱道的。

同時，長三角地區基督教背景的慈善逐漸走向社會公益慈善，各地區青年會、女青年會、各種基督教背景的基金會、各種社會公益慈善機構通過形成獨立於教會的社會性團體，突破了宗教身分的活動限制，促進基督教更全面參與社會發展。在基督教各慈善參與主體開展的主要以基督教基金會的形式、財物募捐的活動中，各基督教堂點、教派能打破體制限制通力合作，也為基督教進入社會提供了新的途徑。

四、社會化與私人化的矛盾

中國人人際關係的社會取向，促使中國人必須時常地改變自己，同時又不宜使自己的改變過於頻繁，從而在道德心性深處構成了一個潛在的衝突。為了解決這個衝突，中國人只好將自己分為兩個層次，一個是「公己」（public self）的層次，另一個是「私己」（private self）的層次。其公己關係，可以隨人際作用而調節，私己則不必因為他人影響而輕易改變。對中國人而言，公己主要是對他人「演戲」的自己，是角色，私己是對他人保密的自己。公己重應變，私己重穩定。[16] 換言之，公己是一種角色要求，無法穩定也不需要穩定；私己欲求穩定而無法做到穩定，常常聽從公己的諸種要求而不能自己。所以，這種矛盾表現於傳統中國宗教、信仰之間的時候，就是一種公共

---

15 《聖經·馬太福音》第6章3-4節。"But when you give your alms, do not let your left hand know what your right hand is doing, so that your alms may be done in secret; and your Father who sees in secret will reward you ."

16 楊中芳，〈試論中國人的「自己」：理論與研究方向〉，見楊中芳等主編《中國人·中國心——人格與社會篇》（臺北：遠流出版公司，1991）。

宗教與私人信仰之間的衝突了。

這個公私矛盾，有其表達形式卻還沒有明確的界限，實際上就源自於中國宗教神人關係及其內在的兩向性矛盾。這種兩向性，在其最廣泛的意義上是指對於指定給社會中的一個身分或一組身分的態度、信念和行為之相互衝突的規範期望，它在最狹窄的意義上則是指某一單一身分之單一角色所必須同時滿足的相互衝突的規範期望。從社會學的兩向性出發，我們可以將社會角色視為一個由規範和反規範構成的動態組織，而不是將它視為一個由各種居於主導地位的特徵構成的複合體。主要的規範和次要的反規範輪流制約著角色行為，從而造成了兩向性格。[17] 合法與非法、公己與私己……，神人互惠關係、人際倫理關係、和諧與衝突等等，均在不同程度上源自於這種規範與反規範的矛盾、衝突，具有了雙重性質，「在於否定和肯定的抉擇組合的複製：這構成權力。」[18]

基督教的私人信仰方式及其社會服務方式，就是在這樣一種社會結構之中，真正擔心的倒不是私人信仰的非正當性或非公共性。它總是在期待著自己的信仰方式和內容層面能夠合法化或公共化。這些私人信仰或私人型象徵資本的擁有者總是在希望以自己的「越位」形式能夠促使自己的身分改變，導致信仰的方式能夠合法公共化。

毫無疑問的是，通過長三角地區基督教服務社會的調研及其總體情況來看，基督教及其社會影響具有很大的改善與深入，僅只是因為宗教行政管理制度的約束，其服務社會的深度與廣度還是很有局限性。比如，教會內部的服務強度與廣度，遠遠大於對教會之外社會群體的服務，肢體互助成為慈善公益事業的主體，佔據了教會用於公益慈善事業的主要經費。同時，幾乎所有的基督徒在被問及，在教會內部的弟兄姊妹與教會外部的陌生人同時都有困難之際，你首先會幫助誰的問題時，一般都會回答說：先幫助教會內部的弟兄姊妹。幾位教

---

17 金耀基，《中國社會與文化》（香港：牛津大學出版社，1991），頁15，注35、36。
18 尼克拉斯·盧曼，《權力》（上海：人民出版社，2005），頁70。

會的主要牧師也曾表示過這樣的顧慮：如果把教會的社會服務指向教會之外的一般人群，那麼，教會可能就無法募集應有的錢款了……。

當然，之所以會出現這樣的傾向，一方面是對於宗教施行行政管理的制度局限性所致。法規是公共事務，宗教及其信仰方式卻被視為個人的私事，無法直接進入社會領域。另一方面，則是基督教的社會化與教會福音、基督教信仰方式的私人化，在目前基督教與社會的關係之間，已經構成了難以化解的矛盾。

基督教信仰的概念，可以是一個生活方式的概念，同時也可以是一個社會性的概念；如同宗教不僅僅是一個組織或場所的概念，同時更是一個社會性、社區活動形式的概念。因此，信仰與宗教概念，完全可以從個人和社會、社區、信仰團體等不同層面來加以理解。正是這一不同層面的差異，能夠構成基督教社會服務及其慈善公益事業的成就，同時也能夠建構基督徒信仰方式的私人化特徵。關鍵是要在兩者之間，能夠具有一種制度作為仲介，具有一種法律加以整合，以完成從信仰者個體到宗教群體之間的互動。一旦其間發生斷裂，基督教的個人主義就會變遷為一種私人化的信仰方式，就會不斷地隔離了宗教與社會之間的有機互動與彼此影響。

比較而言，當代中國社會變遷及其與宗教信仰方式之間的分化問題，惟「社會」一詞最適宜於表達的方式，就是在社會建設之中信仰方式的總體構成。這是因為，在一個大社會之中往往存在著不盡相同的「部分性社會」（partial society）重合的現象，而且每個個人都有如宗教信仰者那樣，他們除了作為大社會的一個成員之外，還可能是其他許多局部社會的次級秩序或這些「部分性社會」中的成員。這些部分社會及其秩序、成員身分的相互重疊，正好是對於一個社會整體秩序的自覺認同，進而決定了當代中國社會建設之中宗教功能與信仰方式的社會認同形式，決定了宗教與社會相互適應的社會存在形式。

值得指出的是，私人生活或更廣義的整個文化領域，在今天正一步步進入政治的領域，正如經濟在工業革命和工業時期進入政治領域一樣。一整套新思潮已經表明了——各種政治組織的成敗在此並非決

定性標準——私生活（private life）比任何時候都更是一種公共事務，更是一種社會運動的場域和各種新興的社會衝突的主要議題。[19]在此基礎上，那種基於現代憲政的個人認信的自由，宗教認同及其民族認同的個人化現象，反倒不失為宗教、民族資源社會化整合的重要路徑之一。對於一個總體社會的變遷而言，私人化的東西就是很政治的。

在這裡，這種個體化即意味著人們能夠獲得一種制度性的推動力，它的目標是個人而不是集體。「如果還以為個體化只是影響某個群體，而不去全面思考它對社會結構造成的深刻變化，並通過社會學分析把這種作用揭示出來，那就完全錯了。」它對於現代社會公民之間的共識和認同方式來說，只是一個極好的結論——「私人的便是政治的。」[20] 從個人的社會化與政治社會化的關係，再度展開了另一種社會化的時代主題。

這是因為，現代社會之中公民的個體活動被一個「當為的秩序」解釋的時候，社會才能夠存在，個體的社會化過程就由此開始了。[21]可以說，這個「當為的秩序」，就是個人社會化乃至政治社會化的核心問題。它在共同理解中所生產出來的規範的有效性，涉及到社會。這也就是說，只有在規範提供了指導交往的標準時，只有當規範決定著必須如何與某種行動相聯結時，社會才能夠產生。

而宗教群體的社會組織形式或者是社團形式的宗教組織，它們能夠將此「私人事務」整合成為社會公共事務，納入當代社會法律規範之中。儘管在當代中國社會之中，這個規範還在建設，國家、政治等公共權力秩序對於個人意識與個性的形成尚有重大的影響，並通過這些制度功能上的合理「機制」對個人予以大量的行為控制，然作為公民個人的宗教信仰在一定程度上已基本成為一種私人的現象了，成為

---

19 阿蘭‧圖海納，《行動者的歸來》，舒詩偉等譯（商務印書館，2008），頁26。
20 烏爾里希‧貝克、[英] 安東尼‧吉登斯、斯科特‧拉什著，《自反性現代化——現代社會秩序中的政治、傳統與美學》（商務印書館，2014），第71、83、60頁。
21 京特‧雅科布斯，《規範‧人格體‧社會——法哲學前思》（北京：法律出版社，2001），頁42、45。

憲法保護的私人權利了。其中的問題是，如何實現從私人化到個體化的轉變？！

在此基礎上，個人信仰的社會意義才得以突顯出來，其意義幾乎等同於當代中國第一次把合理的個人財產列入憲法保護範圍一樣，把私人信仰真正的變成個人的精神權利。這就是說，在當代中國憲政的建設之中，其中有一個非常重要的問題，就是國家世俗權力與私人－公民精神權利的制度分離。這是一個相當重要的兩權分離。只有此二者的制度分割，公民的最基本的精神權利才能得到根本的尊重和保護，而不會再次成為制度外的純私人事務，最後在信仰方式層面上，構成了私人化而公共化的發展可能。

然而，信仰方式的私人化現象，是否意味著即是一種私人性的退出，是否象徵著公共性的退出，進而引發廣泛的公共呼籲運動？不過，當這種退出的規模達到一定程度之際，這也許會成為一種公開的集體行動，促使政府的無能與合法性的危機，徹底的展現在公眾的面前。[22]

為此，私人性的退出，對於民主轉型而言，是一把雙刃劍：它將是弱者的武器，還是強者的工具？這最終取決於每個信仰者個體的選擇、國家的應對以及社會整合的能力。

---

22 參阿爾伯特·O·赫希曼，《退出、呼籲與忠誠》，盧昌崇譯（北京：經濟科學出版社，2001）。

【關懷機構】

中華基督教青年會的「全人關懷」：
以《青年進步》（1917-1920）為中心的探討

李宜涯

摘要

「中華全國基督教青年會」（YMCA）是民國初期在社會與學校界最為特出的教會團體。青年會與其他教會機構不同之處，就在於其提出了一套有益國家、社會、個人的「德智體群」的論說與活動，廣受各界歡迎，成為當時發展最快的基督教團體。青年會所提出之論說與活動，以今日的觀點來看，相當符合「全人教育」的理念，也就是在塑造出一個有人格、有學識、健全體魄又具有公民意識的現代青年。本文即是以 1917-1920 年該會機關報《青年進步》為中心，爬梳其中所倡導「德、智、體、群」的內涵與活動特色，並探究其所呈現「全人關懷」的思考與模式，是否可作為當代教育所提倡「全人」之嚆矢。

關鍵詞：基督教、中華基督教青年會、《青年進步》、全人教育

一、前言

　　自教育部在1999年揭櫫，以「全人教育」[1] 作為二十一世紀的臺灣教育願景後，「全人」一詞隨即成為眾多學校與社會機構最愛用的名稱。許多社福機構甚至以「全人關懷」表達其組織工作的理念與目標。事實上，早於二十世紀初期，在中國發展最快，最受社會大眾注意的教會組織——中華基督教青年會，即已推展類似的概念。

　　過去學術界對於青年會在華的發展多有注意，無論中、英文的著述都相當不少。[2] 然而在學界研究中，卻很少有人關注到這組織社會教育的層面。目前對於中華基督教青年會的研究多係歷史鋪陳，雖然或多或少的利用到其機關報《青年進步》[3]，但多聚焦在青年會在華

---

1 http://content.edu.tw/wiki/index.php/%E5%85%A8%E4%BA%BA%E6%95%99%E8%82%B2

2 學界與教會界已經注意到青年會在中國近代歷史的重要，有不少的論著。通論性的有：陳秀萍，《沉浮錄：中國青運與基督教男女青年會》（上海：同濟大學出版社，1989）；王成勉，〈中華基督教青年會初期發展之研究〉，《全人教育國際學術研討會論文集》（臺北：宇宙光出版社，1996），頁239-260；趙曉陽，《基督青年會在中國：本土和現代的探索》（北京：社會科學文獻出版社，2008）。而由於青年會的宗旨就是在「德智體群」的提倡，故在這方面的專著比較多。在智育方面過去的作品有：王成勉，〈余日章與公民教育運動〉，收錄於林治平主編，《全人教育國際學術研討會論文集》（臺北：財團法人基督教宇宙光傳播中心出版社，1996），頁239-260；Charles Andrew Keller, "Making Model Citizens: The Chinese YMCA, Social Activism, and Internationalism in Republican China, 1919-1937" (Unpublished Ph. D. Dissertation. University of Kansas, 1996)。在體育方面的著作，有蔡政杰，《基督教青年會與中國近代體育之發展（1895-1928）》（臺北：國立臺灣師範大學體育研究所碩士論文，1992）；李鎮華，《基督教青年會在華傳播競技運動（Sport）的本土化歷程（1885-1928）》（臺北：國立臺灣師範大學體育學系碩士論文，2004）；Kimberly Ann Risedorph, "Reformers, Athletes and Students: The YMCA in China, 1895-1935" (Unpublished Ph. D. Dissertation. Washington University, 1994); Andrew D. Morris, *Marrow of the Nation: A History of Sport and Physical Culture in Republican China* (Berkeley: University of California Press, 2004)。在文化交流與社會改革方面，直接相關的著作有：劉遠城，《中美文化交流的激盪：基督教青年會對晚清社會的適應與交融，1985-1911》（臺北：淡江大學美國研究所博士論文，1999）；左芙蓉，《社會福音‧社會服務與社會改造：北京基督教青年會歷史研究1906-1949》（北京：宗教文化，2005）；Wenjun Xing, "Social Gospel, Social Economics and the YMCA: Sidney Gamble and Princeton-in-Peking" (Unpublished Ph. D. Dissertation. University of Massachusetts, 1992); Jun Xing, *Baptized in the Fire of Revolution: The American Social Gospel and the YMCA in China, 1919-1937* (Bethlehem, Pa.: Lehigh University Press, 1996). 以上文獻請參見李宜涯〈激流中的砥石——五四時期《青年進步》小說分析〉一文的註一，《淡江中文學報》，2014年。

3 中華基督教青年會非常重視文字出版工作。1895年青年會在華成立，1896年6月即出版《基督會報》，1897年2月發行《學塾月報》。在1902年成立青年會書報部，3月，《學塾月報》改名《青年會報》，並於1906年2月再改名為《青年》。1911年另外創辦《進步》，以接觸中國的知識界。《進步》面向社會上層及學生，不沾宗教，而在發展其新知識與新道德，《青年》則是以青年會四育為宗旨，寓宗教於

的活動與發展，卻忽略了青年會本有一套全人關懷的理念，也極少涉獵他們如何在華人情境下來落實。

　　《青年進步》編者係有系統的藉由現代化的教育觀點，提出一套有益於國家、社會與個人的「德、智、體、群」論說及活動，以今日觀點來看，頗符合「全人關懷」的理念，也就是在塑造一個有人格、有學識、健全體魄又具有公民意識的現代青年。而本文企圖以1917-1920《青年進步》為中心，爬梳其中所倡導「德、智、體、群」的內涵與活動特色，並探究其所呈現「全人關懷」的思考與模式，可作為當代教育所提倡「全人」之嚆矢。

二、從廢除科舉到《青年進步》的全人關懷

　　中國傳統教育向來以科舉功利為導向，但隨著晚清時局大變，西方勢力挾著船堅砲利而來，不合時宜的取才制度已無法應付時勢。知識份子遂呼籲廢除行之有年的八股取士制度，留心於經世之學，並從教育改革開始著手。他們主張學生能發揮其才學、心性及思想。例如二十世紀初期著名學者王國維，即在這股潮流中，提出講究新式教育所追求的真、善、美，以符合時代所需。[4]

　　而廢除科舉後所展現的新式教育，正顯現改革後的人文通才教育，尤其在五四時期，知識份子更對教育提出自己的理念，大半知識份子都認為教育就是要從德、智、體、群的角度著手，旨在培育「通

教育中，為當時「銷路最廣」的基督教刊物，遍佈全國17省，甚至遠至香港、日本、美國。1908年銷售3,700冊，至1911年時已達69,977冊。1917年3月，《青年》與《進步》合併為《青年進步》，作為青年會全國協會機構刊物。它保持著兩個刊物的傳統，介紹歐美最新社會宗教思潮和發展，用淺顯文字研究現代社會政治，關注中國社會現實問題，同時有各式各樣的文學與文藝作品，廣受教會內外人士的好評。該刊物一直發行到1932年「一二八事變」，日軍侵華，毀損《青年進步》的印刷所為止，《青年進步》共出版150期。從1896年的《基督會報》到1932年《青年進步》停刊，青年會之機關報共發行了三十七年，是二十世紀在華基督教刊物中，面向社會且又發行廣大、極富特色的刊物。

4　王國維〈論教育之宗旨〉：「完全之人物，精神與身體必不可不為調和之發達。而精神之中又分為三部：知力、感情與意志是也。」轉引自黃俊傑，《大學通識教育的理念與實踐》（臺北：中華民國通識教育學會，1999），頁48。

才」。[5] 而放在時代脈絡來看，這也與1917年的《青年進步》撰稿者所提倡的「教育」理念，有異曲同工之妙。

（一）廢除科舉後的人文通才教育

中國近代以前，視科舉制度為培養國家官吏的體制，也是傳統士大夫晉身的主要途徑。換句話說，科舉制度維繫了帝國與社會之間的關係，並在一定的程度上攏絡或安撫大部分的知識份子。然而，在光緒31年（1905年）廢除科舉後，改採西方的新式教育，此舉使社會進入新的面貌，而中國傳統知識份子也面臨新的挑戰，需要適應與傳統迥異的教育型態。王國維（1877-1929）在1906年〈論教育之宗旨〉一文，就新式教育所講求的真（智育）、善（德育）、美（情育）三德多作著墨，強調教育必須精神與身體並重，缺一不可：

> 教育之宗旨何在，在使人為完全之人物而已。何謂完全之人物？謂人之能力無不發達且調和是也。人之能力分為內外二者：一曰身體之能力，一曰精神之能力。發達其身體而萎縮其精神，或發達其精神而罷敝其身體，皆非所謂完全者也。完全之人物，精神與身體必不可不為調和之發達。而精神之中又分為三部：知力、感情與意志是也。對此三者而有真善美之理想：真者知力之理想，美者感情之理想，善者意志之理想也。完全之人物不可不備真善美之三德，欲達此理想，於教育之事起。教育之事亦分為三部：智育、德育（即意志）、美育（即情育）是也。……然人心之知情意三者，非各自獨立，而互相交錯者。如人為一事時，知其當為者知也，欲為之者意也。而當其為之前又有苦樂之情伴之：此三者不可分離而論之也，故教育之時，亦不能加以區別。有一科而兼德育智育者，有一科

---

5 如蔡元培〈中國現代大學觀念及教育趨向〉一文，以制定體育教育計畫、培養學生美術與自然的鑑賞能力以及進行社會服務，作為培養北大學生的性格與品性。詳見楊東平編，《大學精神》（臺北：立緒文化，2001），頁3-11。

兼美育德育者，又有一科而兼此三者。三者並行而得漸達真善
美之理想，又加以身體訓練，斯得完全之人物，而教育之能事
必矣。[6]

王國維強調，教育必須精神與身體並重，缺一不可。其中精神又可細
分為知力、感情與意志，分別代表著真（智育）、善（德育）、美
（情育）三德。以現在的眼光來看，王國維的教育觀展現出明顯的現
代教育的意涵。

　　然而王國維的觀念仍有所缺漏。如黃俊傑所指出的，王國維的教
育觀以「人」為主體，卻只注意到人的內在統一性，缺乏了人對社
會、世界的關懷，而這樣的教育觀，亦無法處理人之存在以外的所有
事物。簡單來說，黃俊傑認為王國維的教育觀所呈現的是一種「內部
的」（intra），而非「內外交輝的」（inter）。[7] 但即使是如此，王
國維能夠提出超越近代以前中國的教育制度，已經是一大突破，值得
讚許與思考。

　　近代以前中國的教育制度，就是科舉制度。科舉制度主要是國家
培養官吏的手段，也是傳統士大夫晉身的唯一途徑。科舉制度不僅使
傳統農業社會中菁英份子成為帝王專制下的臣民，更在某種程度上造
成傳統士大夫與他們所處的社會脫節。另外，傳統的科舉教育內容，
是講求統御與治理帝國之道，強調的是人與人之間的關係網絡，而非
人與自然社會的關係。[8]

　　換句話說，科舉制度維繫了帝國與社會之間的關係，並在一定的
程度上籠絡，或者是安撫大部分的知識份子。然而，中國在1905年
廢除科舉後，改採西方的新式教育，此舉勢必使社會進入新的面貌，
傳統的知識份子也將面臨新的挑戰，即如何適應沒有科舉的生活。這
時期很多知識份子都在思考一個問題，即中國的教育制度該怎樣發

---

6 轉引自黃俊傑，《大學通識教育的理念與實踐》（臺北：中華民國通識教育學會，1999），頁48。
7 黃俊傑，《大學通識教育的理念與實踐》，頁49。
8 黃俊傑，《大學通識教育的理念與實踐》，頁52。

展？

　　到了1919年，因山東問題無法在巴黎和會獲得滿意的解決，引起「五四運動」，在求新求富強的浪潮下多以西方為師，各式各樣的思想都在這個時期被介紹到中國，也影響中國近代知識份子重新看待教育。以蔡元培為例，其於1925年在歐洲應世界學生基督教聯合會撰寫〈中國現代大學觀念及教育趨向〉[9]一文，內容除了闡述當時北京大學的發展趨向及教學目標外，更值得注意的是，蔡元培在其演講稿中談到北大培養學生的性格及品德所採取的三個措施：

> （甲）制定體育教育計畫：（1）每年進行各種運動技能比賽。與外界舉行比賽和其他的室外比賽，吸引了所有北大師生，其水準可與西方相比。足球、網球、賽馬、游泳、划船等活動同樣令人喜愛。（2）可志願參加某些軍訓項目，特別是童子軍運動正在興起。
>
> （乙）為培養學生對美術與自然的鑑賞能力，成立了雕塑研究會與音樂研究會。
>
> （丙）學生們利用課餘時間在為學校附近的文盲及勞工社會服務，深受公眾的讚賞。其中最突出的是在鄉村地區開展平民講習運動和對普通市民開辦平民夜校。學生們透過這些活動，極大地促進了自己的身心發展。[10]

從這段講稿中可以看出，蔡元培重視學生體能及美學鑑賞能力，並且要抱持服務精神，以人為本，關懷鄉村地區的平民教育。德智體群美是他的教育理念。

　　著名歷史學家雷海宗（1902-1962）在1940年則指出，中國的教育有個嚴重的缺陷，那就是只知道培養「專家」，而不知道培養「全

---

9 蔡元培，〈中國現代大學觀念及教育趨向〉，收入楊東平編，《大學精神》（臺北：立緒文化，2001），頁3-11。
10 蔡元培，〈中國現代大學觀念及教育趨向〉，收入楊東平編，《大學精神》，頁9。

人」。因此,他在〈專家與通人〉[11]中講一段饒有興味的話,如下:

> 今日學術界所忘記的,就是一個人除作專家外,也要作
> 「人」,並且必須作「人」。一個十足的人,在一般生活上
> 講,是「全人」,由學術的立場講,是「通人」。我們時常見
> 到喜歡說話的專家,會發出非常幼稚的議論。這就是因為他們
> 只是專家,而不是通人,一離本門,立刻就要迷路。他們對於
> 所專的科目在全部學術中所佔的地位完全不知,所以除所專的
> 範圍外,若一發言,不是幼稚,就是隔膜。[12]

換句話說,雷氏的「全人」觀,就是建議人應該多觀察社會各種面
向,多與社會接觸,並要對其他學科有基本的了解,認為教育並非要
培養「專家」,而是培養「通人」。這個「全人」的提出,可說是現
代「全人教育」的先聲。

社會學家潘光旦(1899-1967)則認為,普通教育的重點在於把
人視為一個本體,且他認為人是囫圇的,因此教育就必須注重人的整
體性格,才不會培養出畸形的人。但是,潘光旦的教育理論與他人不
同的地方是,他並不強調合作(群)的重要性,反而認為應該培養學
生獨立的精神,並訓練學生單獨完成工作的能力,這點是潘光旦與其
他教育家不同的地方。[13]

五四時期的知識份子都曾對教育提出自己的理念,這對創建現代
教育發揮很重要的作用。其中,較值得我們注意的是,這些知識份子
大半都認為教育就是要從德、智、體、群的角度著手,旨在培養「通
才」,而非「專家」。這與1917年創刊的《青年進步》之撰稿者所
倡導的「德智體群」教育理念,有異曲同工之妙。也就是基本上都是
希望透過教育,培養「通才」,而非培養「專家」。兩者是否相互影

---

11 雷海宗,〈專家與通人〉,收入楊東平編,《大學精神》,頁175-178。
12 雷海宗,〈專家與通人〉,收入楊東平編,《大學精神》,頁176-177。
13 潘光旦,〈論教育的更張〉,收入楊東平編,《大學精神》,頁195-206。

響，值得探究。

（二）《青年進步》的全人關懷

　　現代學者多根據教育部出版的《德智體群美五育理念與實踐》中所提出的五育詞條[14]，作為全人教育定義。然而，若是將時間軸往前挪，可以看到早在1917年創刊的《青年進步》，就具有全人關懷模型。依據《青年進步》目錄，其自發刊起，有系統的將內容分為十大類：一德育，二智育，三體育，四社會服務，五會務，六經課，七通訊，八記載，九雜組，十附錄。從中，可以清楚看到編者有意識的區分「德、智、體、群」，以求新求變的方向來建造青年的新品格與新視野，試圖讓現代青年具有新知識、新科技與新教育的素養。

　　誠如范萓誨[15]〈現代青年之人格〉中所提，討論現代青年應該具備何種人格，而人格又應該由德育、智育、體育來養成：

> 基督教青年會，何為而有乎？為現代青年而有也。基督教青年
> 會，於現代青年，何所裨益乎？為欲養成其人格也。蓋基督教
> 青年會，本基督為人類犧牲之精神，願以德育、智育、體育養
> 成青年之人格。於世界，於國家，於社會，於家庭之間，而亦
> 使之清夜捫心，無屋漏衾影之慚。故現代青年在基督教青年會

---

14 教育部編印，《德智體群美五育理念與實踐》（臺北：教育部，2007）。德育：當代德育就廣義外延而言，實可謂一種價值教育、生命教育、人權教育、法治教育、民主教育，以及公民資質教育。德育不應是意識型態灌輸，不宜簡化為生活常規要求，亦不可能是外來或傳統文化之複製與再現；而是針對道德核心價值，在民主開放社會中之轉化、重建、溝通與共識形塑，其兼具認知、情感與行動等多元層面及深度意涵，以期達到私人領域、公共領域以及專（職）業領域等共榮共善之理想。（頁15）智育：智育有三個重要的元素，即培養人有「論證」、「批判思考」、「探究」的能力。這三個元素又稱為「智育三元素」。（頁59）體育：體育是以身體學習運動技能以提升運動興趣，逐而實現人類身體卓越的自我理想；又如，透過運動概念的建立與養成以促進身體的適能，在此過程中得以體驗及體悟運動的精神並落實道德行為，最後促進人際之互動關係。（頁107）群育：有組織、有紀律、有品德與愛心，能分工合作以及團結進取的一群人，才是真正的群。依據群育的目標，群的關係包括：他人、團體、社會（含國內外）與自然（含生命與非生命）。（頁145）美育：美育是有關於美感認知與情意養成的教育。換言之，它是一門有關於製作、感受與了解藝術及其有關事物的教與學，同時也是一門經由藝術發現世界與自我的學科。（頁195）

15 范子美，號范萓誨，為《青年進步》主編。

中，既得有基督教平等自由之釋放，至仁博愛之感動，知人類
之尊貴，識人格之重要。[16]

胡誨並闡述青年會的宗旨在於透過人格培養，能作用於世界、國家、
社會及家庭之間，推己及人，並藉此方式使人類得以追求平等、自由
與博愛，裨益於社會。

　　除此之外，《青年進步》作為青年會之機關報，內容亦闡明服務
青年之宗旨，在於培養三育（德、智、體），並且要有救濟人群的服
務精神（群）：

> 若夫全國協會之所以立，其與各地方城市學校基督教青年會，
> 實為一致，同以三育及社交，造福青年為宗旨，同本救主博愛
> 之精神，犧牲一切，以救濟人群為職志。[17]

姑且不論所有人格與三育的養成，應首本基督教的精神，僅由其論
述，可以看出《青年進步》在情境上已充分展現「全人關懷」，以人
為本，不只重視人的內在品質，更透過人群服務，達到自我完成與社
會的和諧互動。

三、青年會與《青年進步》的現代全人觀

　　《青年進步》雖為基督教刊物，文章帶有宣教意味。然而，除了
宣教之外，《青年進步》亦積極與社會時代互動，期盼為當代中國塑
造一個符合新時代的青年形象，其中「教育」是很重要的方法。

---

16 胡誨，〈現代青年之人格〉，《青年進步》，第一冊（1917年3月），頁5-6。
17 余日章，〈說明中華基督教青年會全國協會之任務〉，《青年進步》，第六冊（1917年3月），頁14。

（一）《青年進步》眼中的現代青年形象

　　對於《青年進步》眼中的現代青年有何指標呢？以及現代青年應該具備怎樣的條件？《青年進步》的主編皕誨在〈現代青年之人格〉[18] 一文中就談到，世間有了基督教之後始有人類一詞，而有人類後，就會產生人格。其中，人格之養成，對於青年的影響甚鉅。因此皕誨根據倫理學之次序，把現代青年應養成的人格分成五類：即（1）對於世界之人格；（2）對於國家之人格；（3）對於社會之人格；（4）對於家庭之人格；（5）對於自己之人格。皕誨並認為應以德育、智育、體育養成青年之人格於世界、於國家、於社會、於家庭之間，藉此方式使人類得以追求平等、自由與博愛，並培養良好之人格，裨益於社會。

　　而在〈現代青年之責任〉一文中，皕誨更是明確點出現代青年應要具備七點責任，即從對家庭倫理的責任開始，逐步擴展至學識上的責任、然後是職業上的責任、道德上的責任、健康上的責任、服務上的責任，以及使命上的責任。簡單的說，皕誨眼中的現代青年，除了必須重視人際關係外，還要重視人與社會之間的關係，並努力服務社會、服務國家，進而服務世界。

　　那到底怎樣才算是皕誨眼中成功之青年呢？在〈青年之成功〉[19] 一文，皕誨就談到一個成功的青年必須必備三個條件：即思考、勤奮和健康。皕誨認為，青年有了思考後，才能鑑往知來，不至於發生「鹵莽滅裂之弊」。懂得思考後，皕誨認為青年還要勤奮，而勤奮不只是要做好本分的工作，還得在職務外有犧牲奉獻的精神。皕誨認為，青年具備以上兩點後，還必須要保持身體健康，並設法改善衛生環境，若沒有健康，「雖有思考之心，而腦力不足，雖有勤奮之志，而體力不勝，是亦無可奈何者也。」[20]

---

18 皕誨，〈現代青年之人格〉，《青年進步》，第一冊（1917年3月），頁1-6・1。
19 皕誨，〈青年之成功〉，《青年進步》，第六冊（1917年10月），頁1-3・1。
20 皕誨，〈青年之成功〉，《青年進步》，第六冊（1917年10月），頁2・1。

王衷海在〈告今日社會之青年〉[21] 一文中，則是特別強調國家與青年的責任。王氏說：「國家極大之問題，皆係青年職務之所在」，是故，他提了七點青年的職務，即：（1）改良社會也；（2）普及教育也；（3）振興實業也；（4）整頓財政也；（5）擴張軍備也；（6）整理內治也；（7）穩固外交也。並強調青年在求學期間，必須積極朝上項七點目標邁進，將來為社會出一份心力。

退心則認為，青年即等同於能力的代名詞。而在應付世界上的各種挑戰時，青年就會耗損這些能力，那如何恢復能力呢？退心談到：

> 然則青年當如何恢復其能力乎？曰：注意於修養之功而已矣。吾人欲體魄之強健者，必使居處衣服、飲食一一適宜，更為各種運動遊戲以佐之。欲學問之優異者，必費十餘年或數十年之力，從學識優美之名師，選古今名人之著述而研究之，則世人於身體智能無不知有修養之必要矣。……。[22]

在退心眼中的青年，應該具備良好的體魄，並時常鍛鍊，另一方面也須努力學習新知識，充實自己。

從以上三位撰稿者的言論，我們可以拼湊出《青年進步》眼中的標準青年形象，除了要努力學習新知識，時常充實自我外，還必須保持健康的身體，並時常鍛鍊自己的體魄，最重要的是，青年們應該養成服務的精神，以備將來服務於國家、服務於社會，最後服務於世界。

（二）《青年進步》的四育

下文試圖以「德育、智育、體育、群育」來分別討論《青年進步》的作者群如何看待這四育，四育的精神該如何的達成。

---

21 王衷海，〈告今日社會之青年〉，《青年進步》，第三冊（1917年5月），頁1-2・1。
22 退心，〈青年與能力〉，《青年進步》，第十一冊（1918年3月），頁3。

1. 德育

　　《青年進步》作為基督教青年會之機關報，其中文章多以宣教為主。而基督教所講求的犧牲奉獻精神，正是《青年進步》作者群欲以教化國民青年之處。所以在德育之部，諸如任夫〈基督教之精神〉[23]、知正〈基督教與中國社會之關係〉[24]、陳安仁〈釋宗教〉[25]、揚鐸〈我之證道譚〉[26]，皆是從基督教義出發，提出品德教育，摒除中國青年的貧弱心理，以振興拯救中國。

　　誠如揚鐸〈我之證道譚〉一文，從談論國人通病「做官心」及「利己心」，來指出過去受孔孟教育，只求「或勞心，或勞力。勞心者，治人；勞力者，治於人。治於人者食人，治人者食於人，天下之通義也。」[27] 所以國人普遍以讀書為尚，視做官為目標，但基督教立教則是以「非以役人，乃役於人」[28]，並非以治理群眾為核心，而是能為公眾犧牲，為公眾之奴隸。並且闡明基督教「克己利人」，不似國人只知克己而養成鄉愿，只知利己而淪為盜賊，這些流弊使國人如一盤散沙，揚鐸遂以基督教義為救中國的良方。

　　正如同任夫〈基督教之精神〉一文所論，期望以基督教的利濟之心，創造一個和平世界：

> 自基督出，苟人視一切艱難痛苦而甘之，吾人以義務之所在，與希望之無窮，激發人類利濟之心，使造成一種公理和平友愛之新世界，即人間天國者。[29]

---

23 任夫，〈基督教之精神〉，《青年進步》，第三冊（1917年5月），頁1-5。

24 知正，〈基督教與中國社會之關係〉（上海浸會大學社會學教授美國克爾布 Daniel H. Knlp II 著），第三冊（1917年5月），頁6-10。

25 陳安仁，〈釋宗教〉，《青年進步》，第六冊（1917年8月），頁1-8。

26 揚鐸，〈我之證道譚〉，《青年進步》，第四冊（1917年6月），頁15-21。

27 揚鐸，〈我之證道譚〉，頁19。

28 揚鐸，〈我之證道譚〉，頁20。

29 任夫，〈基督教之精神〉，頁5。

如此推己及人與犧牲奉獻的精神，正是《青年進步》所提倡的。這與教育部定義的當代德育：「就廣義外延而言，實可謂一種價值教育、生命教育、人權教育、法治教育、民主教育，以及公民資質教育。」看似相近，但就宗教的情操與精神而言，《青年進步》的德育顯然更強調宗教心靈（spirit）與社會文化生活相結合，不僅僅只是世俗道德（moral）的實踐。人格統整很重要，但唯有基督的靈在其中，才能創造出「人間天國」。《青年進步》作者都在文章中有著宗教靈命的呼喊，但也摻雜自己對於改革中國社會的期望，並期望讀者能與之進一步實現。這樣的德育，包含了宗教的「信念」與「實踐」的信仰體系。

2. 智育

《青年進步》中的智育部分，呈現幾個很重要的特色：其一，撰稿者大多藉由翻譯外國的雜誌、著作，向讀者介紹歐美的新知識、新器物以及新觀念，其中包羅了歷史、科學、制度、身體衛生等議題。如葆穌〈人類體格長短之生理上研究〉[30]、周承恩〈陽曆正議〉[31] 以及鄭兆榮〈森林補助社會其利益若何〉[32] 等。而秋水在第一冊跟第三冊亦各發表一篇〈科學譚屑〉[33]，主要就是透過翻譯美國科學雜誌，向讀者介紹西方的科學動態與避火梯、天文攝影機等新器物。另外，錢泰基亦透過選譯《圖畫世界》（*The Illustrated World*）雜誌的文章，向讀者介紹歐美正在研發的水陸空中行駛機計畫，而這種飛機完成後可以「馳騁於陸地，駛行於洋海，翱翔於空中，駕機之人自機房駕之而出，遊行地面縱意所至，江河當其前，則越空而行，此非夢想

---

30 葆穌，〈人類體格長短之生理上研究〉（譯美國哈佛大學生理學教授華爾德．加能 Walter B. Cannon 著），第八冊（1917年12月），頁23-27。

31 周承恩，〈陽曆正議〉，《青年進步》，第五冊（1917年7月），頁6-10．3。

32 鄭兆榮，〈森林補助社會其利益若何〉，《青年進步》，第五冊（1917年7月），頁1-6．3。

33 秋水，〈科學譚屑〉（選譯美國科學雜誌），《青年進步》，第一冊（1917年3月），頁14-18．2；秋水，〈科學譚屑 附圖二〉（選譯美國科學雜誌），《青年進步》，第三冊（1917年5月），頁16-20．3。

也。」[34]

　　除了介紹新知識與新器物外，由於受到第一次世界大戰的影響，《青年進步》的撰稿者也開始向讀者介紹歐洲的情況。如錢泰基在〈英倫海峽通車之計畫〉[35] 一文，就透過翻譯《圖畫世界》雜誌中的文章，向讀者介紹英、法曾於 1860 年代共同開築往返雙方的海底隧道的計畫，然在 1882 年，因英國懼怕隧道告成後，法國能藉此隧道將其軍隊直開往英國本土而作罷。

　　簡言之，這些內容都是當時國民尚未明白或尚未清楚知道的新知識以及新器物，或者是第一次世界大戰中歐美各國的情勢，故作者希望藉由選譯美國各種雜誌的方式，向讀者介紹歐美最近的新發明與動態，以期讀者能夠掌握世界的脈動。

　　其二，《青年進步》也檢討國內的教育現況，並提出改革之道。他們認為「教育為神聖事業，國家富強，社會文明，人群進化，皆繫於是。」[36] 教育與國家社會以及人群的關係密不可分，而智育正是提升整體素質的關鍵。欲提升，首先必須檢討傳統內部教育弊病，陳安仁〈吾國教育之受病原因〉即提出當時教育的四大弊端：（1）國家浮慕教育虛名而無其實際也；（2）人心以教育求虛榮而不重實例也；（3）國是以教育為敷衍而未嘗積極進行也；（4）教育家以教育為名譽鋪張而未嘗求適應於個人之生活能力也。正因為有這四個弊端，使得中國的教育無法與歐美的教育相提並論，更是無法適應世界潮流。[37] 可是在這篇文章中，陳安仁卻沒有提出一個解決的辦法。

　　但是，在其他各篇章中，我們可以看到《青年進步》的作者紛紛提出改革中國傳統教育的方法。如任夫在〈學校編制中學生自治之實

---

34 錢泰基，〈水陸空中行駛機之預測〉（譯《圖畫世界》*The Illustrated World*），《青年進步》，第五冊（1917 年 7 月），頁 11-13．3。

35 錢泰基，〈英倫海峽通車之計畫〉（譯《圖畫世界》*The Illustrated World*），《青年進步》，第五冊（1917 年 7 月），頁 13-15．3。

36 胡宗瑗，〈今後吾國教育之訓練方法〉，《青年進步》，第三十八冊（1920 年 12 月），頁 20。

37 陳安仁，〈吾國教育之受病原因〉，《青年進步》，第十三冊（1918 年 5 月），頁 23-25。

驗〉[38] 一文中，即以自己為例，向讀者介紹其在公立學校辦理學生自治的成效。任夫認為，學校辦理學生自治，不只是一種民權主義的表現，亦可培養學生高度自動自發的精神，也可培養學生服務的精神，且作者認為，若此制度運用得當，可減輕教職員的行政負擔，故他呼籲「凡學校之情形合宜者，必可採用其制度，造就有思想、有才能之國民。此種國民出而擔任國家社會之服務，較諸疇昔迂拘不化時之學士優勝多矣。」[39]

此外，由於西方勢力的影響，國人學習英文的情況蔚為風潮。然而因為過於強調英文的重要性，導致國人荒廢中文者，比比皆是。有感於此，來自長沙雅禮大學的彭慎行，發表〈中文英文並重策〉[40]，提出七點改良之策，告誡讀者在追求英文之際，亦不可忽略國學的重要性。

另外，受到西方教育的影響，使得白話文運動勃興。然而當時的中國，正處於新與舊的變動之下，許多事物都擺盪於傳統與革新之間，形成矛盾對立的現象。其中，以國文科所遭遇的衝擊最大。有鑑於此，皕誨在〈初等國文教科之改革論〉[41]，就談到現今的國文科教育，應當學以致用：

> 竊謂為今之計，國民學校國文讀本宜採取從前文士所鄙棄之村
> 塾教法而變通之。取幼學生目所能見，耳所能聽，腦力所能涉
> 想者，導以寫作技巧，使其回家能為母親計米一石，柴百斤，
> 更能作一便條，以家事告其出門之父親，則其國文已大成，稍
> 加以種類之推廣，如上文所舉契約之屬，則恢恢乎有畢業之程
> 度矣。[42]

---

38 任夫，〈學校編制中學生自治之實驗〉，《青年進步》，第三冊（1917年5月），頁1-4．3。
39 任夫，〈學校編制中學生自治之實驗〉，頁4。
40 彭慎行，〈中文英文並重策〉，《青年進步》，第七冊（1917年11月），頁26-28。
41 皕誨，〈初等國文教科之改革論〉，《青年進步》，第六冊（1917年10月），頁1-5．3。
42 皕誨，〈初等國文教科之改革論〉，頁2．3。

另外，皕誨也認為，現今國文科教育應拋棄傳統的之、乎、者、也，全面以白話文為主，並依循漸進教導學生用白話文學習知識，即「初等小學純用白話，自高等小學以至中學則用淺近文義，然仍務令與白話不甚相遠，至於高雅之古文，無論唐宋體，無論秦漢體，皆為大學堂文學專科之研究，非文學科固不必問津也。」[43]

而白話文的重要性，誠如皕誨在文末所說：「若夫真共和，則平民而已。平民相與交接，則白話而已。白話故平等，白話故自由。嗚呼，世徒以吾國有華美之文學為吾國光，而不知吾國正以此華美之文學陶鑄國民陷於不可振拔之奴隸根性中，至今為平民主義之阻力也。然則初等小學白話課文之普行，其亦鞏固共和之一大關鍵乎。」[44]

除了指出中國的教育弊病外，《青年進步》作者亦介紹歐美國家的教育情況，供讀者參考。如錢泰基在第六冊發表〈丹麥之教育狀況〉一文，作者透過翻譯的方式向讀者介紹丹麥的義務教育施行情況與教育環境：「丹麥行強迫教育制，兒童以七歲入學讀書，故丹麥全國幾無人不讀書者。學校生活，以遊戲為一重要部分，學校場中，每見有教員指揮學生，為足球戲，或棍球戲，年齡較幼之學生則教以歌唱。」[45]可見國家教育之重要性，並且使學生運動遊戲，強健體魄。

除此之外，錢泰基的〈美國之兒童博物館〉一文，也提倡重視兒童教育。他指出「兒童博物館之組織，在一切陳設品物，與兒童之知識相齊，性質相合，聘請講師，以指示一切。品物之上，各有標題，附以淺顯之解說，使兒童一目了然。院中陳設之法，亦宜深為注意，凡物必與兒童相稱，高度勿逾其首。」[46]這樣的見識，在中國是相當特別的。

其三，翻譯成功人物的故事，藉此激勵青年讀者積極向上之心。

---

43 皕誨，〈初等國文教科之改革論〉，頁3‧3。
44 皕誨，〈初等國文教科之改革論〉，頁5‧3。
45 錢泰基，〈丹麥之教育狀況〉，《青年進步》，第六冊（1917年6月），頁6。
46 錢泰基，〈美國之兒童博物館〉，《青年進步》，第四冊（1917年6月），頁29。

如錢泰基在〈東西文化論衡為印度詩聖臺莪爾而作〉[47] 一文中，就先開宗明義說明東西文化的差異：

> 東西文化各自不同，東方之不能同化於西方，猶之西方之不能同化於東方也。故東方文化以中國、印度為大宗；西方文化以歐美列強為極盛，天之生人各適其地之宜，豈必從同，然後為美哉。雖然東方之人、西方之人要非不可互通意見，互示尊敬，因之互有取法也。[48]

因此錢氏向讀者介紹臺莪爾（Sir Rabindranath Tagore，按：即泰戈爾）。希望藉臺氏之例，說明東西文化雖不能同化，但能夠互相取法也，而臺莪爾就是一個最好的例子。

然而作者也認為，西方人對於事物比較重視科學的觀察，凡事必求正確之界說，而東方人較傾向於「深求正確解說之意念，以為心靈之一切經歷超過於學說之上屬於一特異之世界」[49]，即使是臺莪爾也不能例外。故東西文化最大差異，「直言之，東方人士無神學而但有宗教，西方人士有時且無宗教而但有神學矣。」[50] 另外錢氏亦透過翻譯外國成功人物的故事，藉此鼓勵讀者積極向上。

教育的重要性與中外教育的良莠與改革方向，是《青年進步》不斷在雜誌中的叮嚀與呼籲，智育的提升，應是《青年進步》在宣教之外，很注重的一環。

---

47 錢泰基，〈東西文化論衡為印度詩聖臺莪爾而作〉（譯美國立孟·阿勃脫Lyman Abbott原著），《青年進步》，第一冊（1917年3月），頁1-6·2。
48 錢泰基，〈東西文化論衡為印度詩聖臺莪爾而作〉（譯美國立孟·阿勃脫Lyman Abbott原著），頁1·2。
49 錢泰基，〈東西文化論衡為印度詩聖臺莪爾而作〉（譯美國立孟·阿勃脫Lyman Abbott原著），頁5·2。
50 錢泰基，〈東西文化論衡為印度詩聖臺莪爾而作〉（譯美國立孟·阿勃脫Lyman Abbott原著），頁6·2。

3. 體育

　　對於《青年進步》的作者群而言，如何加強國人的體魄精神，是不容忽視的當務之急。正所謂有健全的身體，而後有健全的精神，而且「保衛學生之健康，間接始其於智育德育有所長進」[51]，可看出身強體壯影響智育、德育的發展，所以體育議題在《青年進步》所佔篇幅甚多，積極撰寫或翻譯相關文章，向國人介紹體育運動方面的知識與重要性。

　　惲代英於〈學校體育之研究〉一文中，即指出「學校之不可不重體育」[52]。而美國青年協會體育幹事麥克樂的〈新體育觀〉，更進一步指出：「教育系統裡邊，非加入體育，那教育底制度，就算是不完全。因為無論德育、智育、社會教育，沒有不和體育有密切關連的。」[53] 體育所涉及的層面廣泛，並且能透過遊戲運動，來達到德育目標：

> 用體育去教人，最容易使人感動。在美國各地底青年會，德育感動人底力量最強，但是，體育也是有同等底力量。即此，可以證明體育和德育是並行的。……運動員作禱告的力量，和運動身體的力量，都是為社會服務增加能率的。[54]

由此看來，教育制度下不能沒有體育，且體育與德育、智育與社會教育密切相關。能從體育養成服務精神，以備將來服務於社會、服務於國家乃至於服務於世界。

　　正所謂有健全之身體，而後有健全之精神。故提倡體育活動似乎是《青年進步》撰稿者最為熱心的事，其所佔篇幅亦多。如惲代英所

---

51 惲代英，〈學校體育之研究〉，《青年進步》，第四冊（1917年6月），頁2。
52 惲代英，〈學校體育之研究〉，頁2。
53 麥克樂，〈新體育觀〉，《青年進步》，第三十六冊（1920年10月），頁13。
54 麥克樂，〈新體育觀〉，頁37-38。

寫的〈學校體育之研究〉[55]、〈運動之訓育方法談〉[56]，皕誨所著的〈簡易運動法之六段錦〉[57]，任夫所撰的〈參觀第三次遠東運動會之心得〉[58]，潘知本所介紹的〈足球捷徑〉[59]、蜇庵所節譯的〈學力與體力關係之測驗〉[60]都是屬於這類範疇。

上述之文章都有一個特色，就是向國人介紹體育運動方面的知識與重要性。例如皕誨的〈簡易運動法之六段錦〉一文中，就把中國古運動法之八式簡化成六式來教導讀者。而這六式包含了「自頸而肩、而胸、而背、而臂、而腿，人身前後左右上下無不完全，而肺部與腹部亦包括其內，則此六式已統全身之各機件。」[61]皕誨認為，若每日「早起後操六段錦一偏，夜臥前操八段錦一偏，中間午後旁晚參以各種遊戲運動，則人身體上之健康與壯碩，自有不待言者。」[62]潘知本在第六冊跟第七冊亦分別發表〈足球捷徑〉兩文，向讀者介紹足球運動的練習方法，以及足球規則等。

而蜇庵所節譯的〈學力與體力關係之測驗〉，是藉由介紹歐美心理學學者所作的各種機械實驗（如握力測驗、電流與手的振動數、賽跑等等），說明學力與體力是相互而不相離的：

> 於是更有人以各種運動，如跳高、跳遠、賽跑等，證明其與學業之成績亦有極大之關係，即學力優勝者，此等運動之能力必優勝於人。惟其優勝之故，在於意志之努力，此努力表現率成一時的力量，而筋肉運動之以機械的持續著轉，不能與意志相

---

55 惲代英，〈學校體育之研究〉，《青年進步》，第四冊（1917年6月），頁1-6．2。

56 惲代英，〈運動之訓育方法談〉（譯美國《體育雜誌》，Carl Easton William原著），《青年進步》，第八冊（1917年12月），頁41-47。

57 皕誨，〈簡易運動法之六段錦〉，《青年進步》，第五冊（1917年7月），頁16-18．3。

58 任夫，〈參觀第三次遠東運動會之心得〉，《青年進步》，第五冊（1917年7月），頁24-27．3。

59 潘知本，〈足球捷徑〉，《青年進步》，第六冊（1917年10月），頁1-8．4。潘知本，〈足球捷徑〉，《青年進步》，第七冊（1917年11月），頁49-57。

60 蜇庵，〈學力與體力關係之測驗〉，《青年進步》，第十三冊（1918年5月），頁25-29。

61 皕誨，〈簡易運動法之六段錦〉，頁16．3。

62 皕誨，〈簡易運動法之六段錦〉，頁16．3。

連而為智能之發展，以是證學力體力關係，若何要亦未可作為正確焉。[63]

但是，最值得我們注意的還是《青年進步》的撰稿者對於體育的看法。他們都認為體育的宗旨並非為培養一運動家，而是要讓民眾普遍養成運動的習慣，並從運動習慣中發展出興趣，進而持之以恆的練習。如惲代英在其所寫的〈學校體育之研究〉就明白指出學校的體育宗旨應該是要讓全體學生都能具備運動的能力，而非是為了體育競賽而提倡運動。故他提出改良之法，目的就是為了「改片段的體育為有系統的體育；改偏枯的體育為圓滿的體育；改驟進的體育為漸進的體育；改枯燥的體育為有興趣的體育是也。」[64]而此文另一特色，就是惲氏指出了男女運動強度有別的觀念：

> 女學之體操不應與男子學校同一宗旨，同一手續是也。女子有分娩之義務為男子所無，故男子之體操可以強健為惟一目的，至女子則不但須強健，且須易於他日分娩之事業。此男女需要之不同，而其體操即應各異者也。合度之強健固於女子之分娩有益無損，然若一意從強健做去，則其筋骨必皆變為堅固，分娩之時盤骨不張。試觀歐美體育界之女子每遭難產之惑，野蠻人種或鄉居農婦亦每有因分娩而死者，此可知女子雖應強健，而過度之強健反為不祥之物，不可不慎也。[65]

而任夫所寫的〈參觀第三次遠東運動會之心得〉更是尖銳地指出中國在運動會失利的原因，就是因為太過於注重競賽成績，以及太過於注重培養專業的運動員，反而忽略了遊戲性運動的重要。故任夫認為改良之道，就在於「體育普及，使全國人人皆能領受其奮發活潑之

---

63 蜇庵，〈學力與體力關係之測驗〉，頁26。
64 惲代英，〈學校體育之研究〉，頁3.2。
65 惲代英，〈學校體育之研究〉，頁6.2。

趣味，凡男女老幼咸養成遊藝之習慣，自然能收健體明效，產生運動之能手。」[66]

至於運動的訓練方法，惲代英在其翻譯的〈運動之訓育方法談〉一文中有更詳細的論述。此文最大特色在於作者告訴讀者一個重要的觀念，那就是施以過多的訓練將會使得訓育適得其反，並且會扼殺「人類體育的最高可能性」。[67]故作者認為培養國民活潑的運動生活，並使國民不要汲汲於名次之爭，才是運動訓育的最高原則。

4. 群育

《青年進步》雖未標明群育項目，但在「社會事業」項目中，卻隱含著群育的概念，包括家庭、團體、社會與自然間的關係。

以劍衡〈今後家族主義之遞變〉一文為例，其從家族概念出發，首先提出中國頹靡的現象，在於「盤旋於身家榮辱得失之間，此外實無用其思想之餘地。於是一身既不能自拔，私德即不能完全，又遑能責以公共之問題乎？對於社會無公共之觀念，惟以種種惡業，荼毒社會，熏化傳染，輾轉煽播，致成痿痺不仁之中國。」[68]而種種情形推源禍始後，皆因「家族主義」所釀而起。且家族愈大，其內容愈有不堪告人之苦，由其貪婪官僚視錢如命，為子孫作牛作馬，使青年缺乏自助之力，對於家庭失去互助之誼，視骨肉如寇讎，使兄弟鬩牆。遂作者認為該學習歐美，應先發達個人之性能，爾後才能使家族團結：

> 然而人類之惡，固由感情而起，而善亦由感情而成。今而後果
> 能力鋤舊惡，展發類固有之情感，則新猷煥著，家無廢丁，施
> 家庭教育之法，對於子女，應毋歧視，使人人有自助之本能，
> 如此則無形間，即得家庭之互助，智識趨於平等，性情趨於雍
> 和，家族之興，可翹足而待，此理性與感情得適當之調

---

66 任夫，〈參觀第三次遠東運動會之心得〉，頁25．3。
67 惲代英，〈運動之訓育方法談〉，頁47。
68 劍衡，〈今後家族主義之遞變〉，《青年進步》，第四冊（1917年6月），頁17。

和。……歐美最優良之自治，固必以發達個人之性能為主，而
後始能集家族之團體，為社會之中堅，即政府行政能力，幼稚
而薄弱，或各省地方遼闊，自能消弭隱患於無形矣。[69]

由此可見，家庭關係影響群育深遠，甚至觸及社會、政治、國
家。而中國應該檢討過度的家庭主義，使人人有獨立思想，建立小家
庭而不依靠祖輩的餘蔭。

四、結論

中華基督教青年會是民國初期在社會與學校界最為特出的教會團
體。青年會與其他教會機構不同之處，就在於其提出了一套有益國
家、社會、個人的「德智體群」的論說與活動，廣受各界歡迎，成為
當時發展最快的基督教團體。青年會所提出之論說與活動，以今日的
觀點來看，相當符合「全人教育」的理念，也就是在塑造出一個有人
格、有學識、健全體魄又具有公民意識的現代青年。

但是，基督教青年會的「德智體群」超越了字面的意義。無論在
出發點，或是四育的協調性，以致發展的內涵，都具有基督教的情操
與使命，也是一種基督教的全人關懷。首先，基督教青年會的主張乃
是「本基督為人類犧牲之精神，以德育、智育、體育養成青年之人格
於世界、於國家、於社會、於家庭之間。」[70] 故青年會之運動源出於
基督救世、濟世之精神，更以這種精神來服務與改造現代青年。故青
年會的領導者以迄各級幹事，必須是基督徒，也要效法基督的精神來
奉獻自己和改善社會與國家。

第二，基督教青年會的「德智體群」的目的，除了達成「德智體
群」四育的發展與均衡外，更要將現代青年陶冶成「有基督教平等自

---

69 劍衡，〈今後家族主義之遞變〉，頁18。
70 皕誨，〈現代青年之人格〉，《青年進步》，第一冊（1917年3月），頁5‧1。

由之釋放，至仁博愛之感動，知人類之尊貴，識人格之重要。」[71] 這是體現基督教所教導的人格與品格。一般的學問、宗教、或是訓練方法，無從有「神創造人」、「人神有如同父子的關係」、「耶穌被釘死完成救贖」的觀念，所以對人的價值與人生命的意義，難以提升到這樣的境界。這也是基督教青年會全人關懷的特殊之處。

第三，基督教青年會雖然起源自英國，可是在許多國家都受到歡迎，其全人關懷乃是一個超越種族與國界的運動。而我們從上述的討論中，可以發現其在華快速發展的時期，並不是徒然的將「德智體群」照章引用，而是走向一種與本土文化相互論證的方式。例如在介紹青年會的德育時，側重其超越世俗道德（moral），或是孔學之「克己利人」，所以使人心不致流為鄉愿，國人不致成為散沙。而鄉愿與散沙正是當時中國之弊。而在論述智育時，青年會也沒有隨從全盤西化的風氣，在《青年進步》中固然介紹西方新知，也討論教育改進之道，但是卻在白話文運動下也提醒國學之重要。同樣的，也有文章利用泰戈爾的例子，來證明東西文化可以互相取法。這種一方面發揮基督教的全人關懷，另一方面則因應時代環境之需，應該是當時青年會「德智體群」四育的特色，也應是當時廣受社會歡迎的重要原因。

總的來說，中華基督教青年會在二十世紀第一個二十五年廣受歡迎的原因，除介紹新知外，最值得人們注意的乃是它開展了一系列德智體群的論說，藉以培養出符合現代的「全人青年」。《青年進步》可謂推動全人關懷之嚆矢，從以人為本的角度，培育身心健全的國民青年，傳達博愛、自由、平等的精神，使人和社會、國家與世界達到和平共處的狀態。此正如青年會的口號，他們不是在傳教，而是活出基督教。這種篤信力行的方式，在當時的確影響深遠。

（本文曾刊登於《淡江中文學報》，第 32 期 [2015 年 6 月]，頁 253-282）

---

71 菡誨，〈現代青年之人格〉，頁 5 · 1。

「尊重生命・改變生命」：基督教靈實協會的服侍理念及其實踐（1953-2013）

劉義章

摘要

　　基督教靈實協會（「靈實」）草創於上個世紀五十年代，迄今已有超過一個甲子的歷史。「靈實」誕生於香港當年的調景嶺難民營，始於一張卑微診桌、服侍流離失所者。今天，它的服務涵蓋五大範疇：「長者服務、健康服務、復康服務、福音事工、社會企業」；服務範圍從九龍調景嶺、將軍澳一隅擴展到香港多個地區，並延伸至中國大陸。「靈實」的服侍理念亦即其服務精神和核心價值是：「以愛心關懷及積極進取的態度、專業的精神，服務人群、傳揚福音。」本文嘗試探討：一、「靈實」六十年以來如何貫徹其服侍理念、特別是基督精神的實踐情況；二、從過去一個純教會慈惠組織發展成今天兼備公營機構和教會團體雙重性質的歷程；以及三、發展過程中所遭遇的挑戰及其克服。

關鍵詞：基督教靈實協會、「尊重生命・改變生命」、調景嶺、非政府機構

一、引言

香港在第二次世界大戰期間經歷了日本侵略軍佔領三年零八個月後，當1945年8月香港重光時，社會上百廢待興。今天，香港是中國最現代化城市之一；它能有這樣的成就乃基於多方面原因，其中包括政府與非政府機構等多方面的努力和貢獻。本文論述的基督教靈實協會（下文簡稱「靈實」）即是眾多優秀非政府機構之一。

「靈實」由幾位女宣教士在香港東九龍將軍澳的調景嶺開始。1950年香港政府在調景嶺設立一個難民營；宣教士為營中難民和學生施醫贈藥。

二、「尊重生命‧改變生命」——「靈實」的服務理念和核心價值

「尊重生命‧改變生命（Respecting Life‧Impacting Life）：以愛心服事關懷（With Love, We Serve and Care）」是「靈實」迎接六十週年時呈獻的服務理念、目標。回顧「靈實」半個多世紀的發展史，赫然發現「尊重生命‧改變生命」原來一直是這個機構、其同工在服侍時的寶貴精神所在。本文撰寫目的之一即在透過述說有關史實，以論證這種精神如何瀰漫、滲入「靈實」六十年來，其在社會關懷上為有需要人士所作出的醫治、教育以至「全人治療」等服侍。

六十年來「靈實」本著「以愛心關懷及積極進取的態度、專業的精神，服務人群、傳揚福音」為有需要人士提供包括健康、復康、靈性、長者、教育等方面的優質服務。儘管在不同時期，「靈實」因資源所限以致提供的服務環境和條件受到掣肘，然而，始終以被服侍者的最大幸福為核心目標。「靈實」草創時專為調景嶺難民提供醫療健康服務，迄今服務已是多元化。無論處於哪一個發展階段，「靈實」服侍者都為被服侍者貢獻所能提供的最好服務。「靈實」醫治病者，卻不止於醫治其肉體傷患，而同時看重其生命和靈魂，兼顧身、心、

靈、社、群等各方面的需要。從誕生那一天開始,「靈實」為被服侍者所提供的乃「全人醫治」——一種整全、配套的服侍。以下試以「靈實」在不同發展階段的故事為例,從而說明這種「全人醫治」的理念和實踐。

三、「全人醫治」服侍理念的實踐

(一)五大服務範疇:「長者服務、健康服務、復康服務、福音事工、社會企業」

「靈實」六十年來,服務範疇因應被服侍者的需要以及資源的增加而擴充,由起初的簡單治療逐漸發展至今天五大範疇——健康服務、長者服務、復康服務、福音事工和社會企業。以下按各個時期論述之。

(二)初期:1951-1969

「靈實」是中國大時代的產物。1949年中國大陸政權更替,包括前政府人員在內的許多難民逃至香港。他們起初棲身上環東華三院一帶,倚靠東華醫院每天供應兩餐度日。其後不久,香港政府把他們先遷至西環摩星嶺、再遷調景嶺荒原。這時許多基督宗教宣教士從中國大陸來到香港,當時難民遍布全香港,亟待救援。他們目睹難民的苦況,乃紛紛請准各自的差會留在香港開展救濟工作。原在湖南岳陽、沅陵從事二十四年醫藥傳教的美國復初會宣教士麥瑪莉(Miss Mary Edna Myers)是其中一位,她於1951年4月經廣州來到香港。旋即在調景嶺施醫贈藥,並教導學童有關衛生和醫學常識。她提著盛滿藥物的籃子、以一尊石塊為診桌,就這樣開始了調景嶺基督教醫務所,也是今天「靈實」的濫觴。同年7月蘇格蘭教會差會孫海倫教士(Helen D. Wilson)從湖北來到香港,10月挪威聖約教會差會葛瑞霖教士(Hanny Gronlund)亦從大陸而至,她們隨即加入麥教士行列。翌年,曾在雲南從事醫藥宣教的海富生醫生(E. Stuart Haverson)到醫務所診治肺病患者。挪威聖約教會差會司務道教士(Annie Skau)

於抗戰時期曾在陝西南部商洛地區從事醫藥宣教，1953年她從挪威來到香港加入醫務所事奉。在孫海倫教士建議下，為了醫護人員能專注於醫治和關顧病人，於1953年3月成立了調景嶺基督教醫務所委辦會（下稱「委辦會」），也就是今天「靈實」前身。「委辦會」由晏樹庭醫生（Frank Ashton）任主席、惠施霖牧師（Sterling H. Whitener）任秘書兼司庫，其他成員包括註冊護士諾蘭教士（Kristine Nodland）、袁結思牧師（Charles Reinbrecht）和葛瑞霖教士。晏樹庭醫生是倫敦傳道會醫藥宣教士（也是家族中的第五代宣教士），1929年前赴香港，任職於雅麗氏何妙齡那打素醫院前後三十七年（其中任院長二十八年，1935-1963年），在香港社會享有良好聲望，備受香港政府尊重。惠施霖牧師生於江西廬山，為第二代來華宣教士；1946年和師母惠寶琳（Barbara Whitener）受復初會差派到湖南岳陽、寧鄉一帶宣教和教授英文，1952年被差派前赴香港。諾蘭教士、袁結思牧師和葛瑞霖教士分別代表挪威信義會差會、美國協同路德會差會和挪威聖約教會差會。

1. 關顧肺病患者

肺結核病在1950年代香港一度十分猖獗，它的成因主要是身體過勞、營養不良。戰後香港百廢待興，經濟一時未能恢復過來、人們謀生不易，社會上許多人兩餐不繼；因此染病者眾。由於肺結核病具傳染性，病人要被隔離，有些甚至不為家人接納。調景嶺約有400名肺病患者，基督教醫務所從起初即照顧這些病人，之後更為他們專門設立療養病房。病人可以照料自己飲食起居，一些粗重工夫則由醫務所安排代勞。[1]

1954年8月28日由於颱風「艾黛」襲港，肺病房被烈風吹毀。「委辦會」為了更好地讓肺結核病人獲得治療和療養，決定在調景嶺

---

1 劉義章，《盼望之灣——靈實建基50年》（香港：商務印書館，2005），頁33。本文許多內容乃取材自此書。

附近的元洲興建一所肺病療養院。宣教士為此而努力籌募經費。例如：西門英才教士（Gertrude Simon）[2] 趁回美國休假述職，向家鄉一所學校學生講述調景嶺居民的苦況和需要後，「一個小男孩從座位站起來，滿臉嚴肅地說：『我要把我的心送給耶穌，買聖誕禮物的錢也要送給耶穌，讓可憐的小朋友可以買東西吃、買衣服穿。』愛的火焰很快從一班燃點到另一班，從一級到另一級，從一間學校到另一間學校。那小小愛心的奉獻，那小手所播的種子，終使世界改變成為天父的家。1955年春，一張二萬五千美元的匯票返過高山、越過大海來到調景嶺。」[3] 一位參觀過調景嶺基督教醫務所的信徒回到美國後，向教友描述醫務所、醫藥宣教士們住所如何簡陋，立時感動許多人捐輸。[4]

　　肺病療養院於1955年10月落成啟用，命名靈實，意謂「聖靈所結果實」（《聖經·加拉太書》第五章22-23節），由司務道教士擔任護士長，首任院長是姜彼得醫生。[5] 由於這時「委辦會」的服務範圍已經涵蓋調景嶺以外的將軍澳其他地區，於是名稱於1957年10月相應地易為將軍澳區醫援會（下稱「醫援會」）。儘管香港政府其時仍把調景嶺難民營視作權宜性安排，設立靈實肺病療養院標誌「委辦會」把香港醫藥救助視為長期事業。「醫援會」宗旨是：「本著基督精神，為本港社區貧苦大眾提供價廉的醫療和社會服務。」[6]「醫援會」提出「全人治療」概念，關心被服侍者的「整體健康」，兼顧他們身、心、智、社交和靈性多方面需要。

2　西門英才教士於1927年開始在湖北恩施從事醫藥宣教、主理孤兒院和開辦助產士學校；1949年秋從中國大陸來到香港後，參與救助難民工作。她在調景嶺開辦聖經學校，培養了香港戰後一代牧師、傳道人。西門教士關心調景嶺基督教醫務所，當她發覺在聖經學校協助教學的戴嚴華實女士曾接受過正規護士訓練後，即推薦予孫海倫教士。戴女士後來成為醫務所又能幹、又忠心的同工。

3　司務道口述、尚維瑞撰寫，《陝西羚蹤──司務道教士自傳之一》（香港：靈實醫院靈實福音佈道團，1983年出版、1999年第八版增訂版），頁29-30。

4　司務道口述、尚維瑞撰寫，《陝西羚蹤──司務道教士自傳之一》，頁29-30。

5　姜彼得醫生於1958年11月正式上任。姜醫生1929年蒙上帝呼召成為宣教士，二戰期間在英國皇家軍隊醫療隊服役。姜醫生於1947年前赴中國宣教，工場在山西太原；1953年任（香港）靈光醫務所院長。擔任靈實肺病療養院院長後，每週有三個下午仍到靈光醫務所服侍迄1961年12月。

6　劉義章，《盼望之灣──靈實建基50年》，頁41。

2. 關顧染有毒癖者

靈實肺病療養院1971年開始「福音戒毒」計畫。1970年代香港染有毒癮而同時患上肺結核病者人數以百計；他們也來到肺病療養院就醫。可是，如果這些病人不同時進行戒毒，他們獲得治癒的機會甚微。1961年1月由復初會差派而來的一對美國宣教士夫婦白和敦醫生和白嘉蓮（W. Benjamin & Carolyn Whitehill）加入「醫援會」行列。[7]白醫生有見及此，於是聯繫專門從事福音戒毒的基督教機構晨曦會，經過與之洽商，決定在肺病療養院試辦福音戒毒計畫以醫治染有毒癮的病人。院方把其中的和平病房闢作戒毒病房，由白醫生領導一個小組專責其事。曾在中國大陸學習有關福音戒毒的護士兼靈實護士學校教師史烈先生擔任戒毒病房護士；參與福音戒毒服侍的靈實同工還包括有林崇智醫生、姜彼得醫生、譚美娟姑娘和黃茵若姑娘等療養院同工。

靈實肺病療養院「福音戒毒」計畫內容包涵著「尊重生命・改變生命」元素。白醫生所領導的小組成員會為成功戒掉毒癮、並且信主的已經痊癒出院的前病友提供身、心、靈輔導。病人入住樓房頂層上鎖的和平病房；療程為三至六個月；除了服用藥物，還著重倚靠閱讀《聖經》和祈禱。他們痊癒出院後，繼續參加每週一次的福音聚會（在位於九龍城地區的靈光堂舉行）。「靈實」為病人提供出院後的支援，並協助他們不再染上毒癮。福音戒毒取得成功來之不易。「靈實」、療養院同工鍥而不捨，始終以愛心堅持此項服侍。其後由於社會進步，患上肺結核病而同時染有毒癖者的人數下降至每個月只得一兩宗。「靈實」乃結束福音戒毒服務，在院病人被轉介到離島石鼓洲戒毒所。時任療養院院長林崇智醫生按月前赴石鼓洲戒毒所跟進病人的情況。[8]福音戒毒服侍帶來一個意想不到而令人振奮的結果是：痊癒後的被服侍者當中不少信主以後，後來更成為全時間傳道人、專一

---

7 白醫生畢業於哈佛大學醫學院，乃「醫援會」首位美國專任、駐院醫生；他學習廣東話兩年以後即全情投入醫治工作。劉義章，《盼望之灣——靈實建基50年》，頁44。
8 劉義章，《盼望之灣——靈實建基50年》，頁138。

事奉。體驗了「靈實」「全人醫治」——「治身體、救靈魂」的服侍宗旨。[9]

從1953年「委辦會」成立到1957年易名「醫援會」，彰顯一眾宣教士長期服侍調景嶺和將軍澳地區有需要人士的決心；亦開啟「靈實」往下扎根、往上開展的十年。「醫援會」成員從1960年6名擴充至1969年23人，反映「靈實」為調景嶺、元洲以及將軍澳地區所提供的服務逐漸增加。隨著靈實肺病療養院的創辦，「醫援會」的社會關懷邁出新步履。在調景嶺、元洲荒原上，基督教醫生、護士與行政、技術人員（包括宣教士和華人同工）默默地、盡心盡力服侍貧困人士、病友；實踐「全人醫治」——兼顧其肉體和靈魂的需要，醫治其身體、向他們傳福音。「靈實」使陷於徬徨的難民得聞耶穌基督救恩，他們在人生感到絕望時獲得身體上的關懷、心靈上的慰藉，並且得著永生的盼望。[10]

（三）服務多元化時期：1970-1986

1. 華人接棒

「醫援會」踏入第三個十年，醫藥宣教士逐漸淡出領導層，由華裔或本土醫護人員接棒。1970年董事會主席一職由陳立僑醫生[11] 接替巴治安醫生[12]；兩年後靈實肺病療養院護士長司務道榮休，由黃茵

---

9 在「靈實」接受福音戒毒成功後進入神學院攻讀、畢業後成為全職牧者包括李賢義牧師（任香港基督教青少年牧養團契總幹事）、韋啟志牧師（曾在泰國北部山區宣教，後任香港威爾斯親王醫院）。

10 劉義章，《盼望之灣——靈實建基50年》，頁48。

11 陳立僑醫生生於新加坡，畢業於美國聖約翰普金斯大學醫學院；在沙撈越詩巫原住民中從事醫療宣教。1958年陳醫生來港出席「首屆亞洲基督徒醫生醫學研討會」時，曾參觀靈實肺病療養院。三年後他舉家從馬來西亞遷往香港。1968年陳醫生在巴治安醫生引薦下加入「醫援會」成為董事，三年後當選董事會主席迄1996年退休。陳醫生大半生服務社會基層和貧苦人士，自奉簡樸，踐行座右銘「簡樸生活、慷慨施予、敏銳思考」。Bernard Fong, *Out of the Shadow: Life and Times of Ding Lik Kiu.* Hong Kong: Haven of Hope Christian Service and Yang Memorial Methodist Social Service Centre, 1994. 筆者於2000年2月2日在陳醫生府上進行訪談時，他以其座右銘相贈；原文是：「To live simply, to give generously and to think vigorously.」

12 巴治安醫生（Edward H. Paterson）是家族第二代中國醫療宣教士，1920年生於江西，在上海、倫敦分別完成小、中學教育，1943年畢業於米德爾塞克斯醫院醫學院（Middlesex Hospital Medical School），五年後成為英國皇家外科學院院士。1949年由倫敦傳道會差派到天津從事醫藥宣教。1951年前赴香港，在那打素醫院任資深外科醫生。他自1953年秋到靈實肺病療養院診症，其後任「委辦會」（「醫援會」）董

若[13] 接任；再過兩年林崇智醫生[14] 接替姜彼得醫生為肺病療養院院長。醫務所主任護士由戴顏華實出任。數年間，「醫援會」經歷了管理層人事和部門主管交接，然而其服務工作依然穩步發展。1950至1970年代，「醫援會」為將軍澳附近鄉郊一帶村落人士提供醫療和教育等社會服務。儘管物質條件不充裕，「醫援會」同工本著「愛人如己」的精神關顧有需要的群體，備受政府和社會人士肯定。1973年開始，靈實肺病療養院（1976年改名為靈實醫院）獲得香港政府補助經費；與此同時，「醫援會」在調景嶺開展社區健康、護理、長者健康和「鄰舍層面社區發展」等服務。這些發展，一方面為靈實肺病療養院日後發展成公立醫院，以及為「靈實」為未來將軍澳新市鎮居民計畫多元社會服務奠下堅實基礎。

2. 社區健康

社區健康的定義是：「擁有共同組織或興趣，或居住於同一地區而在同樣法律管治下的人的整全健康——身體、精神和社群。」[15]「社區健康」通過專業人士包括醫生、負責社區發展者、教育工作者、經濟計畫者等彼此配合、協調，以及社區上居民或其代表共同參與建議、決策，一起謀求社區的整全健康——每個人的身體、精神、靈性和群體性。「醫援會」第二、三任巴治安醫生和陳立僑醫生都重視社區健康和基層保健。兩人從基督徒醫生的角度出發，深感社會有

事，1963年繼晏樹庭醫生出任「醫援會」主席。

13 黃茵若護士在廣華醫院護士學校接受培訓，畢業後曾服務於香港山頂明德醫院（Matilda Hospital），1957年9月加入靈實肺病療養院，乃首位本地訓練而任職療養院的護士。黃護士於1962年被派往英國深造，進修肺結核病護理學、護理行政學，在胸肺科實習。1965年她學成回港，任助理護士長；把英國先進胸肺科儀器和護理技巧引進療養院，為胸肺科進一步發展奠下良好基礎。

14 林崇智醫生畢業於香港大學醫學院，乃首位香港訓練的醫生加入「醫援會」行列。1968年7月，林醫生應白和敦醫生邀請到靈實肺病療養院服務，原先是暫代準備休假半年的姜彼得醫生；後來一做就是十六年。

15 原文是："'Community Health' is the total physical, mental, and social well-being of individuals who have common organization or interest in the same place under the same laws." Dr. L.K. Ding, "Community Health: A Problem of Definitions", paper presented at the Christian Conference of Asia Health Concerns Committee, Hong Kong, November 7, 1976.

限資源無法照顧每一位有需要人士的健康，因此必須引進「發展中國家」行之有效的方法，以社區人士作主導，讓各該社區成員參與本社區的健康服務。1970年代初「觀塘社區健康計畫」（Kwun Tong Community Health Project）和1972年3月啟用的秀茂坪健康中心，見證了他們為推動香港社區健康的先驅角色。今天，「靈實」社區醫療服務遍布將軍澳新市鎮，全面地實踐了「靈實」兩位前故主席有關「社區健康」的理念。[16]

3. 開展舒緩治療

1984年5月，「醫援會」醫務總幹事兼靈實醫院院長林崇智醫生離任赴美攻讀神學；董事會委任高級醫生高凌雲（Robert G. B. Graham）為署理醫務總幹事兼靈實醫院署理院長。[17] 在高醫生領導和推動下，靈實醫院確立轉型為多元專科復康醫院，讓來到醫院接受治療的病人得以重拾信心，使他們盡可能恢復原有的能力、其潛質得以發揮。[18] 1984年靈實醫院開始為末期癌症病人提供特別照顧，目的是：「使病人體會生命的價值，幫助他們重燃對生活的情趣。結果有些病人能重返家園，過著正常生活。」[19] 「解除病人痛苦，鼓勵他們善用餘下的生命、提高生命素質。病人在獲得多方面而又足夠的支持下：包括止痛藥、輔導服務和職業治療，這項服務目的已經達到，並且為很多病者的生活增添了一股生命力。」[20] 這項新服務在數年間取得良

---

16 劉義章，《盼望之灣──靈實建基50年》，頁59。

17 高醫生在英國完成中、小學後隨家人移民紐西蘭，考上奧塔克大學（Otago University）攻讀醫科；畢業後負笈倫敦深造熱帶醫學和公共衛生學，又曾攻讀一年婦產科文憑。他自小立志當一名傳福音的醫生，以醫學、醫術彰顯耶穌基督的慈愛和憐憫。1967-1968 年以紐西蘭政府人員身分在越南行醫，有時要在槍林彈雨下救治飽受戰火蹂躪的病人和傷者。高醫生在靈實服務了二十年（1968-1988），是一位忠心僕人和良醫。 Robert G. B. Graham, "My Years in Hong Kong and Those Before"(manuscript), July 2003.

18 "...Regaining what people had lost or achieving the maximum function, potential or ability that was possible under the circumstances and aiming for the best quality of life, and total personal care approach." Robert G. B. Graham, "My Years in Hong Kong and Those Before"(manuscript), July 2003.

19 將軍澳區醫援會，《將軍澳區醫援會年報，1984/85》（香港：將軍澳區醫援會，1985），頁40。

20 高凌雲，〈將軍澳區醫援會服務報告〉，《將軍澳區醫援會年報，1985/86》，頁38。

好開端，逐漸發展成日後全面性舒緩治療（善終）服務。[21]

（四）1987-2013 年服侍理念的實踐

　　1980 年代末香港政府落實將軍澳新市鎮規劃，新市鎮將會容納 50 萬人口。「醫援會」積極配合社區發展，因而當首個屋苑寶林邨落成時，迅即為市民提供所需醫療等社會服務。1987 年 1 月獲「醫援會」聘為醫務總幹事兼靈實醫院院長、原任教香港中文大學醫學院梁智達醫生上任。他隨即處理：1. 靈實醫院重建計畫；2. 靈實醫院加入醫院管理局[22]；3. 「醫援會」往後在將軍澳以及全香港醫療事業的角色；同時致力於提升靈實醫院醫療服務水平，包括為醫生和護士提供臨床講座和研討會，鼓勵他們進修。他聯同醫生巡視病房、觀察病者康復進度，定期舉行醫務會議。幾年下來，「醫援會」通過在將軍澳新市鎮開展醫療等社會服務，取得顯著成果，而靈實醫院在業界亦聲譽日隆。

　　為配合時代和社會變遷，「醫援會」董事會決定從 1990 年 8 月起，「醫援會」採用「基督教靈實協會」（Haven of Hope Christian Service）這一新名稱。[23] 當時，梁智達為了集中處理醫院重建計畫，徵得陳廣明醫生（1987 年 7 月加盟靈實）應允擔任院長。陳醫生在「靈實」發展史上關鍵時刻毅然受命，分擔醫院行政責任，讓梁醫生為醫院重建全力以赴，「靈實」發展大局從而得以穩住；今天靈實醫院以至整個協會的成績與陳醫生當年的付出和貢獻密不可分。1991 年 5 月，在獲得醫院管理局保證後：即保留和發揚靈實醫院「全人關懷」醫療哲學和基督教醫療文化傳統、確認醫院行政總監「由一位基督徒出任為佳」，靈實醫院正式加入醫管局。醫院過去數十年的表現

---

21 劉義章，《盼望之灣——靈實建基 50 年》，頁 142。

22 1980 年代初期香港政府改革醫療制度，成立一個醫院管理局，目標是把香港所有公立和受補助醫院納入全新的管理系統內。

23 這是由於香港政府已把將軍澳英文名稱從原來的 Junk Bay 改作 Tseung Kwan O，以及「醫援會」工作和取向已不再限於「救濟」（relief）。

和貢獻深獲政府和社會所肯定，自此員工薪酬福利等服務條件與公立醫院看齊。

陳廣明醫生不幸於1992年1月遽然去世；這對梁醫生、醫院和「靈實」都是莫大打擊。[24] 梁醫生與戴樂群醫生、陳健生醫生以及全體醫護同工合力共度時艱，1992年4月起梁兼任醫院院長。就在此刻，「靈實」聘得聶錦勳博士擔任執行總監，大大舒緩梁醫生等醫院和協會高層的行政擔子。自此，聶博士負責領導「靈實」中央行政事務，梁醫生專注於新醫院建造和醫院日常行政運作。[25] 1992年香港政府決定靈實將重建為一間復康專科醫院，提供老人科、胸肺科和善終（舒緩）治療科等專科治療。[26] 1997年4月、8月新醫院首、二期工程先後竣工，同年7月新醫院大樓開始投入服務；連接新醫院與將軍澳新市鎮的道路──靈實路亦相繼建成。重建後的靈實醫院為一間富有基督教特色、著重「全人關懷」的專科復康醫院，密切配合將軍澳新市鎮以及相關社會發展的需要。

我們從梁智達醫生就靈實醫院發展成復康專科醫院、而非地區性全科和急症醫院的看法，可見協會所堅持的「尊重生命・改變生命」服務哲學。他認為如果靈實醫院發展成地區醫院，它將因失去其特有的溫情文化而導致嚴重損失。[27] 另一方面，從長遠來說，香港也的確需要發展復康服務。從今天香港公立醫院情況、醫療制度發展來看，印證了梁醫生的顧慮和遠見。[28] 誠如「靈實」首任執行總監聶錦勳所

---

24 這是醫院領導層和「靈實」最艱難時刻，因為失去一位好弟兄、好夥伴，而梁醫生與陳醫生更是中學和大學同學。

25 聶錦勳博士1984年加入「醫援會」董事會，於1985-1992年擔任董事會副主席；1992年7月從其三十六年香港政府公僕生涯退休（時任拓展處處長）。聶博士人脈網絡和經驗豐富，在工程界地位崇高；梁醫生深感他擔任行政總監實在是上帝對「靈實」的祝福。

26 從1989年5月正式批准重建靈實醫院迄1992年，政府仍考慮把靈實發展成地區性全科、急症醫院；後來經多次派員實地勘察研究，發覺因醫院建於山坡上、對外交通不便，而決定不宜作為地區醫院。

27 梁智達認為按當時人力和物力而言，醫院未必能承受六百張病床的地區性全科、急症醫院規模的需要，醫護等員工也未必能適應相關工作環境；而「靈實」也未必能籌集所需資金進行重建工程。

28 以香港九龍區龍頭醫院伊莉莎伯醫院為例，醫護人員由於每天都極度忙於診治無數病人包括急症和遭遇意外事故者；他們往往捉襟見肘，能為病員做好基本需要的診治、療傷已經不錯了，幾乎完全談不上照顧到病人的人性尊嚴方面。

說：「我觀察到靈實有一班好的同工，這是主的恩典，又是前人如司務道教士以及那些全心事奉的弟兄姊妹留下的果子，使靈實協會建立了以基督為中心的優良服務精神。」[29]

這個時期主要工作包括：重建靈實醫院和恩光學校，在將軍澳新市鎮陸續開展各種社會服務：醫院透過社康護士把家居善終服務延伸到社區層面，先後在新市鎮多個屋苑包括寶林邨、景林邨、厚德邨、明德邨和翠林邨開設社區健康發展中心或/及長者服務中心、專科診所、智障人士日間活動中心暨宿舍、長者家居護理及支援中心、老人護養院及護理安老院。

主曆2000年，靈實董事會和管理層順服上帝的旨意，帶領整個機構團隊形成「異象二零一零」，成為靈實往後發展的導向指標。而在過去十多年，靈實的發展純然按著從上帝而來的異象，不斷完善原來的多種多元服務，同時開創切合新時代、新社會種種需要的新服務品種。在過去十多年（2000-2013年）我們看到一個接著一個這樣的新服務陸續出台，這是將來自上帝的異象轉化成事實的歷程，許多個美麗動人的故事。

2000年代初有1,300名員工；今天靈實擁有2,000名員工，每年接受靈實服務者數目超過30萬人次。在最近十多年，靈實真正做到與時俱進，在富有創意思維和擁有廣闊視野下，不斷開展回應新時期社會轉型中的需要。其間先後開拓了以下新服務：包括「靈實全護通」、「愛心傳餸計畫」、「護理見習生」課程，等等。其中，「靈實全護通」提供「一站式長者照顧服務」，服務理念為：「透過一站式的服務平台，為長者提供跨專業的照顧及護理。服務範圍包括：上門、日間及復康護理，安排院舍住宿，復康巴士接送及護老者培訓，更有針對認知障礙而提供評估、訓練及護理，加上體貼的心靈關顧，務求為長者及家人提供靈活妥善的服務。」[30]

---

29 劉義章，《盼望之灣——靈實建基50年》，頁79。

30 靈實十分重視被服侍者在屬下每一個單位接受服務的身、心、社、靈四方面的需要；其中對靈命的關顧可以創辦靈實寧養院作為說明的例子。筆者另撰文論述有關靈實寧養院的故事。基督教靈實協會網頁

四、「尊重生命・改變生命」——超越六十年的傳承

「靈實」堅持作為公共衛生醫療系統同時維持「自資營運」特色，這大有利於其提供貼近時代需要的服務、傳承「全人醫治關顧」的服侍精神。六十多年前，司務道教士與同工們以生命影響生命的服務精神救助調景嶺難民、服侍病人。

在靈實護士學校講堂，司教士教導她的學生要把病人視作家人。她自己以身作則，最為人津津樂道的是她擁抱即將離世的病人；不少病人就在她的懷抱中去世。當年她一位學生回憶少時立志要當護士和入讀靈實護校的歲月：[31]

> 小時候，我有個小小的願望，就是長大以後，要做一位白衣天使，協助醫生，希望能夠使病者得到安慰、醫治，為人群服務。十八歲那年，我和兩位好朋友結伴，決定去將軍澳靈實醫院做護士學生，為期二年。我們當年護士制服，很是漂亮，就像外國影片中的牛奶妹一般可愛。制服分為二件，裡面是一件灰白相間條子襯裙，左上方有一小口袋，可以放筆、剪刀，胸前扣上名字牌、掛錶；外面再穿一件背心大白裙、白絲襪、白護士鞋。頭上有一大四方巾，可摺成像修女頭巾大小的帽子，很大方、亮麗、莊重。記得當初入學，首先在課室密集上課四週；課程包括藥物學、倫理學、營養學、解剖學、內科、外科，等等。當年的護士長是司務道教士，她是一位頗為高大、和藹可親挪威籍的女傳道人。她除了教導我們藥物學、倫理學外，還教導我們接待病人，要像接待我們家人一樣；做事要謹慎、冷靜、細心，還教導我們如何面對黑暗、死亡。……往後走護理行業的工作上，使我體會到生命的無常——生命與死亡

---

www.hohcs.org.hk，「長者服務：長者家居照顧服務」。瀏覽日期：2015年3月18日。

31 盧志煌，〈我的青蔥歲月〉，撰於2015年4月，時居美國紐約。

都不是在人的掌握之中，乃是在造物者的主，在祂的手中，一切事物，都有定時。經過四週上課後，全班同學被分配到不同病房實習。在每個病房內都有自己同班同學，這樣心理上有點安全感，未感孤單。

司教士身體力行尊重生命、從而改變生命。一位靈實醫院早期病友這樣回憶：[32]

有一天，一位新來的護士由司教士帶領著來到我床前，那護士與我點頭後問道：「你是河南人？」我用河南鄉音回答說：「可不是。」我們兩人相視而笑，使用河南話交談起來了，說得很高興，教人有他鄉遇故知的感受。一個從外國而來的宣教士一定深深感受到異鄉人的孤寂，也明白異鄉人會想家。將心比心，司教士發現了一位同工和一位病人與我是同鄉，就特別介紹我們彼此相識。百忙中的司教士是一位在大事小事上都忠心的管家，也同時實踐了登山寶訓中的金句：「你們願意人怎樣待你們，你們也要怎樣待人。」（《馬太福音》七章12節）

1950年代加入靈實醫院行列的早期同工們這樣憶述：

司教士擁有捨己服務的精神，待病人如同待自己；不分晝夜、隨傳隨到，絕不耽延。她的好榜樣，影響同工至深，令我獲益良多。[33]
在司教士帶領下，大家同心協力工作，不斷把愛心獻給病人，並贏得病友的稱讚。司教士那種以身作則的精神，實在令人敬

---

32 唐文珍，〈懷念媽媽——司務道教士〉，基督教靈實協會五十週年紀念特刊編委會，《荒原上的雲彩》（香港：基督教靈實協會，2003），頁2-5。
33 史烈，〈靈實——神的傑作〉，基督教靈實協會五十週年紀念特刊編委會，《荒原上的雲彩》，頁6-8。

仰。她把全副身心投入到工作中，每天早上四時起床，晚上十二時過後才休息。如果夜間病房有急事，她必定隨時出來查看。她就是這樣忘我工作，毫無怨言，直到退休為止。因為她相信神能幫助她，並賜給她力量和信心。醫院同仁在她偉大榜樣的感召下，也都盡職盡責，勤奮努力，使醫院的服務素質不斷提高。她永遠活在我們的心中，永遠值得我們懷念。[34]

一九五七年九月，我成為靈實同工的一員。那時候的靈實因為經費有限（病人院費全免），所以設備十分簡陋，而病友也多來自困苦的環境。兩把長凳架著兩片木板就是睡床，穀殼放進麵粉袋就是枕頭。醫院雖然設備簡陋，卻最注意衛生和消毒，處處可見窗明几淨，一塵不染。雖然膳食簡單，但早餐卻必備雞蛋、牛奶，而護士就寢前再喝一杯牛奶，且早睡早起。因此，同工被肺病傳染的機會極少，記憶中在三十年來也只三數人而已。

半個世紀以來，同工們默默地在耕耘、結果子，為的是要叫神看見祂自己勞苦的功效，便心滿意足。記得曾有幾位原是目不識丁的女病友，在每天的早、晚禱中，學會了自己讀經、唱詩，還常常領著其他病友在涼臺外進行小組禱告呢！

記得曾有一位來自河南省的孤苦老人，臨終時流著淚，託我把僅餘的一點錢寄給在老家的兒子。又有一次，一位中年母親在大咯血中去世，我和三位同工合力抬著擔架，沿著仁愛房後面的崎嶇小徑，把她送往太平房料理。路上，她生前常常為丈夫、兒女流淚禱告的情景，油然浮現在我眼前。直至今日，仍歷歷在目。我深信，她有一天必會在天家與親人重聚。還記得有一位周媽媽，她很會編織美麗精緻的玫瑰塑膠花和小花籃，並常常禱告說：「神啊，我願在天堂上當你的一管掃帚。」無數的病友，在那簡陋的病房裡得著護理、治療，並獲得了神所賜

---

34 董德滋，〈數算神恩〉，基督教靈實協會五十週年紀念特刊編委會，《荒原上的雲彩》，頁9-11。

的全副軍裝，因而重新踏上征途；也有不少病友在同工們細心的照顧下，甚至在司教士的懷中通過了夕陽門，進入永生。[35]

誠然，司教士的好榜樣影響迄今（深信也會一直到永遠）。以下試以筆者所屬教會黎詩敏姊妹的胞弟黎有成弟兄在靈實司務道寧養院的經歷來闡明。有成先生去年（2014）7月患病，後來確診是癌症。詩敏姊妹和家人後來讓有成住進靈實司務道寧養院接受醫治和照顧。有成在入住寧養院的三個月期間，因著醫生、護士和院牧的愛心、細心和悉心看顧，前後判若兩人。在寧養院，他重拾人的尊嚴。他一面抗癌，一面過著充實、信心滿滿的生活；而最重要的是：經過自己慎密思量、教牧啟導，他接受主耶穌的救恩，決志信主，並且受洗。從家人口中，筆者聽到寧養院醫護同工如何讓弟兄昂首、喜樂和感恩地度過世上最後的歲月。在真道上啟導弟兄的教會馮牧師這樣懷念他：

> 「想到病痛雖在這些日子中折騰了你不少，但就是你那種甘於接受、無怨無悔地走下去，叫我看到、記得生命鬥士本來就有的本色。有成，天家見！」[36]

另一位牧養、看顧弟兄的教會傳道人姚姑娘憶述：

> 與有成初遇不是好的「日子」，那時腫塊令他說話不清，吞嚥不易。那時他臉上常帶一絲憂愁，卻不致唉唁苦澀度日！這已經很難得。在緊湊面見醫生的日子，抉擇不易，大家心情七上八落。但從頭一天起，他便願意一起禱告交託自己的將來給天父。當聽到有成決志的消息，我心是患得患失，寡言的他不知意思是否清晰。他是率直的人，直到從他口中道出：「我真的

---

35 馮黃茵若，〈美哉靈實〉，基督教靈實協會五十週年紀念特刊編委會，《荒原上的雲彩》，頁12-16。

36 黎有成先生安息禮拜儀節（於2015年4月27日星期一晚上七時三十分，假香港大圍寶福紀念館舉行）所附紀念冊子《懷念黎有成 1967-2015》。

信耶穌。」我心裡很開心，因為他真的信靠那信實的主！當見到他珍惜每天活著的機會，我為他感謝神，他把握活著的「好」不在於「多少日子」，乃在於「享受與人在一起」。如果痛楚令人「放棄自己」，那他正是對此提出「抗議的活見證」。他願意學習「神的話」，這很難得。當他真的體會「信耶穌的喜樂」時，他能與人分享：這是真實的──他願意作這「傳福音的人」。有成，我相信您今天已在樂園裡，您所撒的種子，神必會讓它生長。我很榮幸有您這位弟兄，您的仗打得漂亮，讓我們日後天家再會！[37]

一位弟兄這樣回憶有成弟兄從決志信主到接受洗禮後生命的改變：

有成弟兄從充滿決心去認識上主，接受水禮，從此一心依靠耶穌基督，到最後離世返回天家，都帶著堅定的信心，相信神愛他，與他同行每一步。聽見他在歸天家的前一天，在床上用僅餘的聲線向他家人說：「要信耶穌」；令我深深感受到他信主的堅決及他帶著患病的身體也把福音傳給身邊人的熱心。跟有成短暫的相處，就像跟相識了多年的朋友一樣，他帶給我一個很難忘的回憶及一個好好的見證，提醒了我縱使艱難，也有上主同在而得力量和平安，要把神的愛及訊息傳揚出去。願有成在天家與主同樂，也願他的家人及親友在地上得神的安慰。[38]

寧養院醫護、院牧對有成弟兄同樣留下深刻的印象。他的主診醫生這樣回憶：

---

37 同上註。
38 同上註。

猶記得有成入住寧養院的第一天，我被安排成為他的主診醫生。在收新症時，出乎意料地看見我教會的一位姊妹——詩敏，才知道我這位新病人是她的弟弟。世界真細小！感謝神奇妙的安排，也感謝神讓我能有服侍有成的機會。說實在，有成的癌病屬非常嚴重的一種，隨時會有併發症，處理特別困難。雖然醫護同事已做足準備去應付這些突發情況，但作為有成的醫生，我每天都感受到壓力，也感受到病人和家屬所面對的壓力。所以，我每天都為他禱告，希望他受的痛楚能減至最輕，相關的併發症不要發生，以及他仍能享受每天有素質的生活。感謝天父垂聽禱告，以上的三件事一一蒙應允。有成的病情穩定，艱難的日子不算太長。每天更可駕著他的電動座駕，時而到花園曬太陽，時而到復康部接受物理治療。偶爾亦與家人外出，到西貢、到寶琳等不同地方逛街、嘆（喝）茶，及回家，一家團聚。主的慈愛永不止息，祂的憐憫永不斷絕。現在有成已息去地上的勞苦，安居主懷，也願家人的心得著安慰！[39]

一位照顧有成弟兄的寧養院護士如此憶述：

Bobby [有成弟兄英文名字] 是我照顧眾多病人當中其中一位抗癌勇士！他為人友善，亦很體貼我們一班照顧同工。記得有一次為他護理背部傷口時，我另一隻手需要同時支撐他的身軀。他反過來慰問我們，擔心我們會累。又記得有一次，Bobby 往西貢回來送給同工的茶果及魷魚絲……他總是為人設想！縱使頑疾令他身體出現不同程度上的限制，但他從沒有怨天尤人。只心存感恩！Bobby 感恩與摯愛家人共處時光、同行及經歷天父一直給予的祝福！這是他在一次對話中所表達的。[40]

---

39 同上註。
40 同上註。

靈實司務道寧養院院牧這樣追憶他與有成弟兄相處的時刻：

> 他一向以為只要積極「想好D【往好處想】」，便可勝過負面情緒。於是，我和他談情緒，我鼓勵他：「情緒無分對錯」，喜怒哀樂乃人之常「情」，勉勵他放心分享心事；於是他握著我的手，弟兄間盡訴心中情。有成的人生在地上的日子不算長久，但我見證到上帝為他存留很多的恩典，祂的眼目沒有離開過有成。我以這節經文去為黎有成弟兄的生命讚美神：「你以恩典為年歲的冠冕，你的路徑都滴下脂油。」（《詩篇》65：11）

寧養院醫護同工不單只悉心醫治、看顧有成弟兄，也關顧他的家人。在有成弟兄安息禮拜當天，一位護士為黎詩敏姊妹寫了一封洋溢著主耶穌裡的愛和安慰的信。信末這樣寫道：

> 有成很勇敢地面對這場仗，由入院一刻、在他慶祝生日的房間，見過他的燦爛、開心笑容，見到他的自主，見到他的緊握每一刻可擁有的自由，出外，又或駕著電動輪椅在樓層穿梭，見到他的健談，也見過他的靜思、沉默後再展現的微笑、堅定。深深感受到他從信仰的幼苗成長，堅固地靠著主，主寸步不移，您也寸步不移。那令我想起這段經文，套用在有成身上：「那美好的仗我已經打過了，當跑的路我已經跑盡了，所信的道我已經守住了。從此以後，有公義的冠冕為我存留，就是按著公義審判的主到了那日要賜給我的，不但賜給我，也賜給凡愛慕他顯現的人。」（《提摩太後書》四：7-8）有成有您這位姊姊真好，您有有成這位弟弟也很美好。願主安慰您，陪伴您。我們會與有成天家再聚。You are in my thoughts and prayers! [41]

---

41 靈實司務道寧養院護士寫給S姊妹的信。筆者感謝S讓我讀到該信函。

誠然，靈實司務道寧養院以及基督教靈實協會的醫生、護士等同工們以及一眾服侍者牢牢秉承當年的精神，持守著「尊重生命・改變生命」的「全人醫治」使命，並且把這一珍貴傳統發揚光大。

五、小結

「靈實」一代、一代地把「尊重生命・改變生命」這優良傳統繼承下去，而且不斷發揚光大。每一代院長、醫生護士同工們，都全然沉浸在這個「以病人為本、全人治療」的服侍環境。院長方面：從早期的姜彼得醫生、林崇智醫生、高凌雲醫生、梁智達醫生、陳廣明醫生、徐德義醫生，等等；護士長方面：從司務道教士到黃茵若護士，等等，他們無分男、女，也不問中國籍、外國籍，統統都奉行「尊重生命・改變生命」為服侍病人的佳皋、鵠的。

回顧「靈實」過去六十年來在香港的社會關懷事業，我們看到「尊重生命・改變生命」乃其服侍人群的核心精神，而且始終如一，貫串「靈實」服務社會迄今的全歷史。今天，「靈實」已經發展成多元化社會服務（醫療、教育、復康、社區健康等）的非政府機構、兼備教會慈善和公營事業性質。其中，靈實醫院和靈實護養院等服務單位屬於公營事業部分；與此同時，「靈實」守住、珍惜自主經營的社會服務事業。正因如此，「靈實」才能夠比較敏銳於察覺人們在一個不斷發展、變遷的社會所遇到的種種新問題。針對這些問題及社會上隨之而來的新需要，「靈實」適切地作出回應，包括探討有關問題的深層次根源，從而提出解決方案，進而構思、推出新服務品種以滿足社會和人群所需。因此，「靈實」能夠真正做到與時俱進，成為一個日新又新的非政府機構。筆者認為：「靈實」之所以能夠達到這境界，乃基於其「尊重生命・改變生命」此一核心指導理念和精神。

The Amity Foundation: Christian Social Responsibility and Social Development in the Chinese Context

Philip L. Wickeri

Abstract

As the Amity Foundation in China (愛德基金會, founded in 1985) enters its thirty-second year, it is an opportune time to reflect on its approach to Christian social responsibility at the time of its founding. Against the historical background of Christian social service in China before 1949, this paper will examine the early sources of Amity's approach to social responsibility and its evolving conception of social development. Christian social service in the 19th and twentieth centuries was understood by most churches and mission agencies as a means of evangelism or an expression of Christian charity. The churches built up an extensive social service network, generally along denominational lines, of which the work of the Chung Hua Sheng Kung Hui (中華聖公會) may be taken as an example. In the early 1950s, the social service work of the churches was brought to a close and all social welfare programs came under the government of the People's Republic of China.

However, Christian social responsibility developed in the ecumenical world over the next decades, and this helped shape the creation of the Amity Foundation in 1985. The paper offers an interpretation of the early years of the Amity Foundation, drawing on published and unpublished resources and the author's own experience as a staff member of the organization (1985-1998). It briefly analyzes that social climate in China the made possible an organization such as Amity; the decision to launch Amity, on the part of

Chinese Christian leaders, especially Bishop K. H. Ting (丁光訓) and Mr. Han Wenzao (韓文藻); the response of overseas church organizations; early project initiatives; and differences between Chinese and overseas views of social development. Our aim is to better understand the learning as well as the misunderstandings that took place during the early years of Amity's work in China and its evolving movement from conception of Christian social responsibility.

Key Words: Amity Foundation, social responsibility, Chinese Christianity, social service, church organizations

「愛德基金會」：
華人情境下的基督教社會關懷與社會發展

魏克利

摘要

　　當「愛德基金會」（成立於1985年）邁入第三十二個年頭時，應是一個很好的時機，來回顧其成立以來進行的基督教社會關懷。以1949年以前基督教社會服務的歷史背景下，本文將先考察愛德基金會早期社會關懷的作法，及其後來對於社會發展觀念的變化。在十九世紀和二十世紀時，大多數的教會與宣教機構所理解的基督教社會服務，即是一種傳福音的手段，或是一種基督徒慈善的表現。教會一般是沿著宗派的路線，建立起廣泛的社會服務網絡，這可以用中華聖公會的工作當作案例。在1950年代初期，所有教會的社會服務工作，都被帶到中華人民共和國政府下一個緊密又全面的社會福利項目。

　　然而，在後來幾十年中，基督教的社會關懷在基督教的世界繼續發展，此促成了「愛德基金會」在1985年的創立。本文之寫作係依據已出版和未出版的史料，以及作者本身擔任該基金會工作人員的經歷（1985-1998）。本文將簡要分析：當時中國令此機構能夠成立的社會環境；決定發起「愛德基金會」的決心；中國基督教領導人的角色，特別是丁光訓主教和韓文藻先生；海外教會組織的反應；早期項目的推動；以及中國和海外在社會發展意見上的歧異。本文之目的，盼能更好的認識到「愛德基金會」在華成立初期的學習與誤解，及其對於基督教社會關懷觀念的演化。

關鍵詞：愛德基金會、社會關懷、中國基督教、社會服務、教會組織

Christianity is not the only religion that is concerned with social responsibility. All religions practice charity, social service, disinterested giving, social welfare work or philanthropy in some form. This is part of their religious teaching and doctrine, a compassionate response to suffering, poverty and human need. It may even be said that such giving is an aspect of religious life and practice in its most basic form. Religion is concerned not only with gods and the transcendent, but with human life in the here and now.

This paper considers the Christian-initiated Amity Foundation as an expression of social responsibility and social development in the Chinese context. We begin with a brief discussion of religion and social responsibility in China generally conceived, and then contrast this with the ecumenical experience of social development after the founding of the People's Republic of China in 1949.

The paper goes on to offer an interpretation of the early years of the Amity Foundation, drawing on published and unpublished resources and the author's own experience as a staff member of the organization (1985-1998). It briefly analyzes that social climate in China the made possible an organization such as Amity; the decision to launch Amity, on the part of Chinese Christian leaders, especially Bishop K. H. Ting (丁光訓) and Mr. Han Wenzao (韓文藻); the response of overseas church organizations; early project initiatives; and differences between Chinese and overseas views of social development.

Our aim is to better understand the learning as well as the misunderstandings that took place during the early years of Amity's work in China and its evolving understanding of Christian social responsibility.

I. Religion and Social Responsibility in China

In China, there has been a long religious tradition of charity, philanthropy and benevolence (慈善). Before the nineteenth century, Confucianism (whether or not we regard it as a religion), Daoism and Buddhism all practiced philanthropy and good works. Neo-Confucian scholars and merchants contributed to famine relief efforts in the Ming dynasty; Daoists provided free medical care and medicine for the needy throughout their history; and Buddhists contributed to the alleviation of human suffering through works of compassion, in the case of the monks and clergy, and through philanthropic associations usually organized by the laity. The most common form of traditional religious philanthropy, however, was that of highly localized popular religions. In traditional times and right up to the present, popular religious groups (民間宗教團體) have cared for the poor, the sick and the marginalized. They have established "halls of charity" (善堂), "societies of moral uplift" (德教會) and other organizations for this purpose.[1]

I mention this at the outset, lest it be thought that charitable work is an aspect of modernity that Christians have had a monopoly on. Religiously inspired charity, good works and social service have been around for quite some time. What Americans now like to call "faith-based initiatives"[2] and what might more accurately be termed religious-inspired charities have their equivalents in many social and cultural contexts.

The difference in the contemporary world is that religiously inspired charity has become highly institutionalized and global in nature. As religions became better organized and more prosperous, charitable activity moved from the local and the regional to the national and the global. Already in the

---

1 See Chapter 8 "Religious Philanthropy and Chinese Civil Society," in *Religious Life in China: Communities, Practices and Public Life*, ed. David Palmer, Glenn Shive and Philip Wickeri (New York: Oxford University Press, 2011).

2 I dislike the term faith-based initiatives (基於信仰的倡議). In attempting to be religiously inclusive, the term hides as much as it reveals. Some religions do not speak of faith all, Buddhism for example. Also, there are "faith-based initiatives" in the United States that are anything but charitable.

eighteenth and nineteenth centuries, Protestant and Catholic churches in the West, as well as the Jewish community, began to set up specialized organizations for charitable purposes. By the twentieth century, Jewish, Islamic, Buddhist, Hindu and other religious organizations all had well-organized international charities.[3]

II. From Christian Social Responsibility to Social Development

Christian social responsibility has been conceived in many ways throughout the history of the Church. In the Book of Acts it is recorded that the first Christians set aside "seven men of good standing" to serve the diaconal needs of the church (Acts 6: 1-6). This is the first instance in which the church addresses the social responsibility of the church, specifically to care for the widows. But even before this, we see that the people of Israel, the followers of Jesus and early Christians were deeply concerned with social justice and meeting social needs. Christian faith has nothing in common with the artificial distinction between body and spirit, the material and the spiritual. This is why Archbishop William Temple once termed Christianity the most materialistic religion in the world.

Throughout the history of the Church, there have been different ways in which Christians have reflected on issues of society and responded to social needs. Changes in society led to different Christian responses, but *diakonia* (or

---

3 There are many recent books on global charities, among them: Henry Garlepy, *Christianity in Action: The History of the International Salvation Army* (Grand Rapids, Eerdmans, 2009); Shawn Flanigan, *For the Love of God: NGOs and Religious Identity in a Violent World* (Sterling, VA: Kumarian Press, 2009); Gil Loescher, *Beyond Charity: International Cooperation and the Global Refugee Crisis A Twentieth Century Fund Book* (New York: Oxford University Press, 1996); Julia C. Hwang, *Charisma and Compassion: Cheng Yen and the Buddhist Tzu Chi Movement* (Cambridge: Harvard University Press, 2009); Jonathan Benthal and Jerome Bellion-Jourdan, *The Charitable Crescent: Politics of Aid in the Muslim World* (London: I. B. Tauras, 2009).

service) was always an important function of the church. Orthodox, Roman Catholic, Protestant and Anglican churches responded to society and engaged in social service in ways that were shaped by their faith and ecclesiology. With the Enlightenment, the separation of church and state and the growth of secularism, the impact of the Christian social thought and social service declined in Western societies. Still, churches found new ways of serving society and reaching out to the poor and the marginalized. Right up to the present day, churches from practically every Christian tradition continue to be involved in *diakonia*, both in their own countries and abroad.[4]

The idea that Christians must be involved in social service was extended to Asia, Africa and Latin America through the modern missionary movement, beginning in the 18th century. In China, Protestant missionaries debated the relationship between evangelism and social service. Anglican, mainline Protestant and some evangelical groups saw social service as an integral part of their mission. Social service was very broad. It included education, care for children, famine relief, attention to the needs of women, medical work, etc. Different mission agencies specialized in their approaches to social responsibility, but some churches kept them all together.

In the Anglican and Episcopal tradition in China, the mission societies organized their work around a three-pronged approach to church, education and social service. In Shanghai (under the Protestant Episcopal China Mission) and in Hong Kong (under the Church Missionary Society), churches were established, and then a school was built nearby, so that the two could work together. As things got going, the church might open a clinic, or a social service center. This three-pronged approach to mission was typically Anglican.[5] With the founding of the Chung Hua Sheng Kung Hui (中華聖

---

4 "Diakonia," *Dictionary of the Ecumenical Movement* (Geneva: WCC, 2002), pp. 305-310.
5 《步武基督：香港聖公會的社會服務》（香港：香港聖公會福利協會，2014）。

公會) in 1912, various boards centralized the church's missionary involvement, but Anglican schools, hospitals, and welfare centers operated locally as part of the Christian social service responsibility. Other denominational traditions in China had their own understanding of Christian social responsibility.

Already by the 1940s, there was a difference, in the church between charity, philanthropy and social service, on the one hand, and social development on the other. Christians have traditionally emphasized charity and work with the poor, but involvement with social development came later.

"If you give a man a fish; you have fed him for today. If you teach a man to fish; and you have fed him for a lifetime. " ("授人以魚不如授人以漁 "). This is supposedly a Chinese proverb, but I have not been able to determine its source. It captures the distinction I wish to make between charity and development in religious thinking. Development (or social development) emphasizes bringing people out of poverty, or, more accurately, helping poor people bring themselves out of poverty. Charity is both meaningful and well-intentioned, but it doesn't break the poverty cycle, and it doesn't challenge the existing socio-economic system. Charity presupposes an inequality in power relationships and at its worst may become patronizing.

I am not saying that religiously inspired charity is bad or somehow inadequate. Not all religious communities are concerned with development as such, even in the present day. Some religious groups, inspired by their teachings or scriptures, are content to do charity as a response to human need. Such groups as the (Protestant) Salvation Army and the Catholic Workers, and many Christian Mission organizations, Muslim Benevolent Associations, Buddhist Charitable Organizations, and Jewish Community Services are outstanding charities. They organize soup kitchens, offer shelter for the homeless, and collect donations for charitable work internationally. Some religious groups believe that development may be too "worldly," too "political" or too "secular."

However, there is an important distinction between "charity" and "social development." Social development, as opposed to simple charitable work, involves questions of strategy, assessment, planning, capacity building, accountability, requiring particular expertise and technical know-how as well as a high level of commitment, whether religious or not. Humanitarian aid organizations, NGOs and NPOs, as well as some religious groups are involved in social development, but they would not term such work charity, social service or social welfare.

The religious concern for what I am calling social development began in 1945, in the aftermath of World War II. Rebuilding and reconstruction efforts after the war; the emergence of new states (more than 50 new nations came into being between 1946 and 1970); new movements for social change, human and civil rights and economic progress – these are just some of the most important factors that encouraged secular organizations, Protestant and Catholic churches, Buddhists, Hindus, Jews and Muslims to concern themselves with development and societal improvement. They were not all engaged in social development to the same extent or in the same ways, however.

I define *social development as the promotion of human flourishing through social transformation, economic growth and political participation.* (社會發展就是通過社會進步、經濟發展和政治參與而促進物質、精神文明的繁榮) My definition is not ideologically or religiously specific, but it is drawn from the development experience of the ecumenical movement. In this essay, I will be focusing on social responsibility and social development in the ecumenical Christian community, in comparison to the early experience of China's Amity Foundation. This comparison highlights the very different approaches to charity and development in the international Christian community when the Amity Foundation was founded.

III. The Ecumenical Movement and Social Development

In the early 1950s, the social service work of the churches in China was brought to a close and all social welfare programs came under the government of the People's Republic of China.

However, Christian social responsibility developed in the ecumenical world over the next decades, and this helped shape the creation of the Amity Foundation in 1985. The general movement was from an emphasis on Christian service and social responsibility to social development. Social Development was seen as a movement away from charitable giving and Christian mission work as these had been traditionally understood. It emphasized the improvement of human life, not "benevolent giving" (charity) or "evangelism" (mission). Still, development came to be seen as a Biblical mandate for Christian churches. Its purpose was not to make more people Christian, but to contribute to human society and the fullness of life (John 10: 10) and to care for all parts of God's creation (Colossians 1: 16).

Christian mission agencies and development organizations from the historic Protestant Churches and the Orthodox world came to an "ecumenical" understanding of development in the 1940s, 1950s and 1960s through their participation in the World Council of Churches (WCC) and related bodies. The eventual institutional embodiment of this initiative was the Commission of the Churches' Participation in Development (CCPD), formed by the WCC in 1970. Under this commission, the debate about the purposes nature and processes of development became a focal point of the ecumenical agenda. Development, they believed, was not just a concern of governments and international aid agencies, but of every sector of society. Development, not charity, was needed to make the world a better place.

Ideas about social development were shaped by the politics of the Cold War. There were different understandings of development in the Communist and Capitalist blocs and among the non-aligned nations. Initially in the WCC, there was an almost implicit acceptance of Western (Capitalist) inspired views of development, emphasizing capital formation and a "trickle down" economy, ideas developed in Walter Rostow's important book, *Stages of Economic Growth*.[6] However, there was an increasing dissatisfaction with this approach through the 1970s. Gradually, the churches came to focus attention on non-economic factors in social transformation; people-centered development; partnership between the Global North and the Global South; a concern for justice and the environment. This shift in attention away from economic factors in development was, I believe, a mistake, albeit a well-intentioned one. It became a subjective way of speaking about development, one that was not easily measurable.

Within the World Council of Churches, this was summarized in a new understanding of development as struggle towards a "just, participatory and sustainable society." By the mid-1980s, around the time when the Amity Foundation was started in China, "solidarity with the poor," and "people's participation in development," and eventually "justice, peace and the integrity of creation" were the recurring slogans. These emphases came out of the experience of churches and peoples in the Third World, primarily in Asia, Africa and Latin America. There was a growth in the number of Christian inspired NGOs related to the Third World, with funding coming largely from state churches and development organizations in Europe.

It should remembered that in the 1970s, Cultural Revolution China was seen as a "model of development" in many parts of the world. Books appeared, meetings were held, and advocates suggested the China was a "model" of development for the Third World. This idea now sounds almost

---

6 This book went through many editions, and Rostow first introduced his ideas in the 1950s. The most recent edition, and probably the last, is W. W. Rostow, *Stages in Economic Growth: A Non-Communist Manifesto* (Cambridge: Cambridge University Press, 1991).

impossible to believe, and it was based on practically no quantitative study of China's rural experience. In the churches that were associated with the ecumenical movement, liberal Western and Third World Christians were enthusiastic about Cultural Revolution China, and it shaped their view of development.[7] "China the idea was more important than China the place" was a slogan that was popular in those days. It illustrates the romanticism involved in the idea of development then in vogue, but it shaped the way in which the Amity Foundation was initially understood by some.

To jump forward, the world had changed by the 1990s. There was no more Cold War, China had become a rising power, and there was a proliferation of aid organizations. The Chinese view of development had also undergone a fundamental change. Attention shifted to civil society and the so-called "third sector" in development work (as distinct from government and business). In the new millennium, churches (which were always part of the third sector) endorsed the United Nations "Millennium Development Goals."[8] At the same time there has been a decline of conciliar ecumenism, and with it, a decrease in resources that churches were committing to development. There has also been a rise in the work of secular development agencies and of new development initiatives like the Bill and Melinda Gates Foundation. Church-based development work today is not be as important as it once was. There has also been at least a partial return to denominationalism and bilateral exchanges, over ecumenical involvement. But we are getting ahead of ourselves.

---

7 This kind of thinking on China is characteristic of many of the essays presented at two conferences in the early 1970s. See the Lutheran World Federation and Pro Mundi Vita, eds. *Christianity and the New China* (South Pasadena: William Carey Library, 1976). For an assessment of China as a model of development in the late 1970s, see B. Michael Frolic, "Reflections of the Chinese Model of Development," Social Forces, 57:2 (December, 1978), accessed at http://www.jstor.org/pss/2577675 (21 September 2011).

8 For a good overview of the ecumenical approach to development, see Richard D. N. Dickinson, "Development," in *The Dictionary of the Ecumenical Movement,* 2nd edition, pp. 298-302.

The summary makes clear that even as ecumenical development work has shifted and perhaps declined, the ecumenical experience of social development had a much broader purview than Christian charitable works or Christian social service. Christian Mission in this sense was about justice, humanization and the embrace of the created world. This, in any event, was the world context in which the Amity Foundation was received.

IV. The Founding and Early Years of China's Amity Foundation

Against this background of international ecumenical development thinking, we turn to China in the period of "reform and openness" from the late 1970s onward, focusing on religion and development in the experience of the Amity Foundation. International thinking about charity and development had very little to do with the formation of the Amity Foundation, but it did influence how Chinese and foreign Christian leaders related to one another and how Amity was initially received internationally.

It was the Chinese reforms beginning in the late 1970s that created new possibilities for openness to the world and to Christian-initiated involvement in society. The Chinese Welfare Fund for the Handicapped (中國殘疾人福利基金) was set up in Beijing in March, 1984, and among the initiators were several religious personages, including the Buddhist leader Zhao Puchu (趙朴初), who was made an honorary Board member.[9] Deng Xiaoping's son Deng Pufang (鄧朴方), who had been paralyzed during the Cultural Revolution, became deputy director. The younger Deng had become a leading voice in reformist efforts to promote greater awareness of humanitarianism

---

9 See "The Chinese Welfare Fund for the Handicapped Set Up" (15 March, 1984), *China Study Project Journal*, 16 (April, 1984), p. 3.

and the need for social welfare programs. In one of his speeches published in *People's Daily*, he said that the China Welfare Fund for the Handicapped was socialist, humanitarian, patriotic and reformist, serving the people according to the new demands of the times. "Our work is one of humanism," Deng said, "that is to say we wish to raise the material and spiritual level of the people, so that everyone may feel useful, especially the physically handicapped, who are especially unfortunate."[10] He invited Mother Theresa to visit Beijing, and commended her for her spirit of sacrifice on behalf of the poor in India.[11] The younger Deng then went to Hong Kong, where he praised the activities of Christian voluntary organizations working with the poor, the elderly and the disabled. His was the traditional language of charity and social service, not development.

Shortly after the establishment of the China Welfare Fund for the Handicapped, Hu Qiaomu (胡喬木), a Party theoretician, began to encourage religious groups to undertake activities for social welfare. Specifically mentioning Buddhists and Christians, he said that "in the old society, religious believers did social work, and we should advocate this even more strongly today." Working for the betterment of society would bring religious believers and non-believers closer together and, according to Hu, undercut "wasteful superstitious activities." This would represent a new stage in the Party's relationship with religious groups and enhance their standing in society.[12] Social and political changes in China were creating a framework that

---

10 Deng Pufang, quoted in Geremie Barmé and John Minford, *Seeds of Fire: Chinese Voices of Conscience* (Hong Kong: Far Eastern Economic Review, 1986), p. 162. Also see Deng Pufang, "Let Us Contribute All Our Strength to Welfare Work for the Handicapped,"《人民日報》(*People's Daily*), 7 December, 1984.

11 See "Prejudice Against Humanitarianism," *China Daily*, 23 January, 1985. and "Mother Theresa Visits the Disabled," *China Daily*, 25 January, 1985.

12 Hu Qiaomu,〈引導宗教界辦社會公益事業〉("Lead Religious Circles to Run Enterprises for the Public Good"), 24 April, 1984,《新時期宗教工作文獻選編》(*Selected Documents on Religious Work in the New Period*)(北京：宗教文化出版社), pp. 105-106. Hu's proposal was not publicized at the time, but the fact that it was subsequently included in this collection of documents edited by the RAB and the CPC Central Committee

would make possible the increasing Christian activity in society that some Christian leaders hoped for. "The Decision on the Reform of the Economic Structure," approved by the Communist Party Central Committee in October 1984, called for the expansion of enterprise autonomy, which would include new initiatives coming from different sectors of society.[13] Taken together with the example of the China Welfare Fund for the Handicapped and Hu Qiaomu's proposal on religious involvement in social welfare, there was now both the political possibility and structural framework for the emergence of non-governmental voluntary organizations, including Christian-initiated ones.

The encouragement of religious charity by the government was an example of the secular recognition of the importance of religiously inspired charity for the benefit of society and it represented a political shift for China in the mid-1980s. Since that time, the government in China has increasingly encouraged religious organizations to be involved in social service. What it did not yet emphasize was a contribution to social development in the part of religious bodies.

In the 1980s, Chinese churches themselves had few resources of their own for any kind charitable of initiative, but Chinese Christians could draw on the support of churches in other parts of the world. Support for social welfare work had been an important aspect of Christian missionary work in China in the nineteenth and early twentieth centuries. Since the late 1970s, Bishop K. H. Ting had been re-establishing relationships with Christians and church groups overseas, and he was assisted by his deputy Mr. Han Wenzao.[14]

---

testifies to its importance.

13 "Decision of the Central Committee of the CPC on the Reform of the Economic Structure," *Beijing Review*, 27: 44 (29 October, 1984), pp. III-XVI. For a discussion of this decision, see Baum, "The Road to Tiananmen: Chinese Politics in the 1980s," The Politics of China: The Eras of Mao and Deng, ed. Roderick MacFarquhar, 2nd ed. (Cambridge: Cambridge University Press, 1997), p. 365.

14 I have analyzed this more fully in Philip L. Wickeri, *Reconstructing Christianity in China: K. H. Ting and the Chinese*

They were leading delegations of Chinese Christian groups all over the world, and receiving religious delegations at home. The two worked well as a team in those years, Ting as the leader, the thinker, the idea man, the visionary, and Han the doer, the administrator, the implementer and the man of action.

In late 1984, K. H. Ting and Han Wenzao spoke about this possibility, and their views are reflected in the informal statement, "On Contributions to China from Churches and Christians Overseas." [15] They now said more clearly than they had before that overseas contributions from religious bodies to non-religious programs and enterprises in China were welcomed, when given with due regard to Chinese national sovereignty, and out of a sense of Christian love in an open and above-board manner without any strings attached. They did not want to appear to be asking churches overseas for financial support, for there were rumors in Hong Kong that they were being pressured by the government to encourage foreign investment in China. These rumors were false. Ting was concerned that they not give the appearance of undercutting the principle of self-support in the church. Ting and Han elaborated these views over the ensuing months in various conversations and meetings. It is clear that they were thinking in terms of charitable contributions at this point, not Christian involvement in development.

Ting and Han were the leading spirits behind what became the Amity Foundation. By late 1984, they were already thinking of setting up a social welfare organization initiated by Christians.

Church (Maryknoll: Orbis Books, 2007), especially chapters seven and eight.

15 The statement was informal, because Ting and Han did not want to appear to be directly encouraging such contributions. "On Contributions to China from Churches and Christians Overseas" is based on an interview with this author in Nanjing on 4 December, 1984. It was initially published in *Bridge: Church Life in China Today*, 9 (January-February, 1985), pp. 3-5, with my interpretation, which reflected the idea of Bishop Ting. It was widely reprinted overseas. It was also translated and published internally in China, an example of "exportation for re-importation" (出口轉內銷)。

We expect that in time there will be more and different kinds of opportunities for making contributions to social service projects in China. In addition to existing non-Christian enterprises which are likely to increase in number, there may be other projects or welfare foundations in which Christians play a leading role. We are considering projects of the latter kind because, aside from making contributions to social modernization, they make way for more Christian presence and involvement in the people's common tasks and thereby change the image of Christianity among the Chinese people.[16]

Three weeks later, Ting sent a circular letter to twenty-nine friends in church institutions overseas, to solicit their opinion about the creation of such an organization. These friends were mostly from ecumenical churches, but they also included some prominent evangelicals.

The waning of ultra-leftism in China has now reached a stage when local and individual initiatives are encouraged so long as they work towards socialist modernization. We think this is a good environment within which Chinese Christians can not only do our share as citizens in nation building, but also make the fact of Christian presence and participation better known to our people, without in any way weakening the work of the church proper.[17]

---

16 "On Contributions to China from Churches and Christians Overseas," *Bridge*, p. 3.

17 K. H. Ting circular letter of 20 December, 1984. For one reflection on this letter see Rhea Whitehead, "Canadian Churches and Amity Foundation Partnership," *Growing in Partnership: The Amity Foundation, 1985-2005*, ed. Katrin Fielder and Liwei Zhang (Nanjing: The Amity Foundation, 2005), p. 180ff. Also see Ewing W. Carroll, Jr., Oliver Engelen and Beate Engelen, eds. *Amity's Founding: Recollections from Abroad* (Hong Kong: The Amity Foundation Hong Kong Ltd., 2010).

As he expected, the initial response from friends overseas was almost universally favorable. But they had different interpretations of what such a social service organizations would be. In any case, the nature and purpose of the Amity Foundation was not being decided overseas, but within China and for Chinese society.

A press conference announcing the forthcoming formation of Amity was held in Hong Kong on 21 March, 1985, taking advantage of Ting's and Han's presence in the territory on their return to China with a China Christian Council delegation that had gone to India. On 19 April, 1985, the Amity Foundation was established in Nanjing. The founding constitution of Amity, which may have been the first of its kind in China, stated its objective as follows:

> 本基金會由我國基督教界與其他各界人士組成，聯絡海內外同仁。在信仰互相尊重的原則下共同獻策出力，發展我國社會主義事業，開展同海外的朋友交往，促進世界和平，造福人群。[18]

The English language statement of purpose states that the goals of the Amity Foundation were threefold:

1. To contribute to the "Four Modernizations":
2. To serve as a channel for the ecumenical sharing of resources;
3. To make Christian presence and participation more widely known to the Chinese people.

These three goals were designed to appeal to different Amity constituencies

---

18 愛德基金會章程，1985.04.19.

and to spell out the general purpose of the foundation and its programs.

On January 1, 1987, Amity clarified its understanding of relationships with overseas organization, stating that (1) They should be in general sympathy with China's socialist modernization; (2) they should be willing to abide by the laws and customs of the People's Republic of China and operate in an open and aboveboard manner; and (3) They should respect the three-self principle of the Chinese churches. The document went on to stress that Amity was a "new form of Christian involvement in Chinese society," insofar as it was a Chinese initiative and because it emphasized co-operation between Christians and non-Christians.[19] This document was intended to clarify the service and development approach of Amity, as well as its nature as a Chinese initiative, for overseas organizations and sponsoring agencies.

The idea for Amity had come from both Ting and Han. Ting had the vision and the reputation in China and overseas; Han was able to develop the connections and get things done. As Overseas Coordinator, I became very much involved in Amity programs and relationships during its early years, and worked closely with Han and Ting for the next twelve years. For this reason, my narrative here will have a different tone than in many academic papers.[20] The full story of Amity's early history is beyond the scope of this paper, and so I will only touch on a few important points.

It was K. H. Ting himself who came up with the Chinese name for Amity, the two characters meaning love (愛) and virtue or moral power (德). He had briefly considered the name *Enlai* (恩來), which could be translated as "the grace which comes," and which also recalled the memory of Zhou

---

19 "Amity's Understanding of Relationships with Overseas Organizations," Amity Newsletter, 4 (Spring, 1987), p. 1.

20 This is based on my own notes and journals, the oral history that I did and records from the time. There are very few people still active who were there at the creation of Amity. The early years of the Amity Foundation, its formation in China and its international reception, would be a good subject for a doctoral dissertation in the area of religion and charity in contextual and global perspective. The Chinese context of Amity's foundation is in particular need of further study.

Enlai, but he rejected it because he knew there would be opposition in China and inevitable misunderstandings overseas. The characters 愛德 convey the sense of love and the power of love, as they do in Arthur Waley's translation of the 《道德經》 which was entitled *The Way and Its Power*.[21] 愛 and 德 also express Ting's sense of love as God's primary attribute and the dimension of Christian practice in society. The translation "Amity" was suggested by Janice Wickeri (魏貞愷) in late 1984 and this became the official English name.

Ting received encouragement for the idea of Amity from friends in the CPPCC and in the government in Jiangsu and Beijing, but questions about the new foundation were coming from other quarters in China. I have no record of these conversations and meetings, but I was informed of them in conversations and meetings with Bishop Ting. Objections centered on the possible involvement of overseas churches in China, and whether Amity would inadvertently subvert the Three-Self principle. In Beijing, Ting discussed Amity with senior officials from the Religious Affairs Bureau and the United Front Work Department (UFWD) who approved of the idea, but continued to raise questions throughout the 1980s. At one point in 1986, Xi Zhongxun (習仲勳), a veteran revolutionary and CPC Central Committee member who was then concerned with religious and cultural affairs (and father of the present Chinese leader 習近平), asked to see Ting about a proposed conference on international ecumenical sharing which was then in the planning stages. Xi wanted Ting's "clarification" on Amity's position on project funding and his assurance that the conference was not a fundraising event for the church.[22]

---

21 Arthur Waley, *The Way and Its Power: A Study of the Tao Te Ching and Its Place in Chinese Thought* (London: George Allen and Unwin, Ltd., 1965). The idea of translating *aide* as "love and the power of love" came from the late John Fleming, a Scottish missionary in China before 1949.

22 K. H. Ting to Philip L. Wickeri, Conversation Notes, Nanjing, China, 28 March, 1988.

In the 1980s and 1990s, there was no conflict or competition between the Amity Foundation and the Church, as their leadership overlapped. Start up funding for Amity came from the two national church bodies (兩會) in Shanghai. At the local level, church personnel or members often assisted in Amity programs. Amity was, in a sense, more like a Western European development agency, rather than a mission organization or a North American church body. It existed alongside the church and parallel to it, but the two did not overlap. Amity's programs and goals were development rather than mission oriented, and they would be evaluated in the same way that other development programs were evaluated, whether they were religious or secular in terms of their background.

In the Chinese social structure, Amity had to have a government or Party department to relate to and be supervised by. This is termed a "leading body" (主管部門). Amity was located in Jiangsu, and so its "leading body" became the Jiangsu UFWD. It still is. This choice worked to Amity's advantage, because it meant that Ting and Han, both well-respected leaders in the province, could draw on their provincial connections to get things done, rather than having to channel everything through Beijing. Because they both held prestigious positions in Jiangsu, it also meant that their decisions about Amity would be more readily accepted by the provincial government. It also meant that they would be able to cut through the bureaucracy more easily and quickly. This was essential to get the foundation going.

In order to demonstrate that Amity was a Christian-initiated, but not a church-sponsored organization, Ting and Han recruited both Christian and non-Christian board members. Three of the original fifteen board members were not from church circles, including Ting's friend and patron, Kuang Yaming (匡亞明), who had recently retired as president of Nanjing University. He became Amity's first honorary president. The Christian board members were senior TSPM/CCC leaders from Nanjing, Shanghai and

Beijing.[23] Ten of the original board members were members of the CPPCC, and several others were future CPPCC members.

Although an international Board of Advisors had been anticipated, Ting thought it unwise to proceed with this because of sensitivities about overseas involvement. Such a board has never been established, although a board of Amity advisors from Hong Kong was set up some years later. Ting became President of Amity, and Han Wenzao was named the General Secretary and the main person behind early programs and project initiatives.

Han Wenzao liked to say that Amity was "the result of the implementation of the consistent principles of Chinese Christians in a new stage."[24] By this he meant that Amity emerged out of the continuing commitment of the TSPM to contribute to Chinese society, a commitment that assumed a new organizational expression in the era of reform and modernization, one that drew on historic connections with Christian churches overseas. Through Amity, Ting and Han also hoped to make Christian presence more widely known in China, indirectly strengthening the witness of the Chinese church. Ting reasoned that Amity was a *praeparatio evangelica* that would help make Christian participation in nation building better appreciated and more widely accepted.[25]

In order to do this, Ting believed that Amity had to make an impact on

---

23　The original board of directors was composed by Kuang Yaming (匡亞明, honorary president), Ting Kuang-hsun (丁光訓, President), Fang Fei (方非), Li Shoubao (李壽葆), Chen Zemin (陳澤民), Wu Gaozi (吳高梓), Chen Suiheng (陳邃衡), Shen Derong (沈德溶), Shi Ruzhang (施如璋), Xu Guomao (徐國懋), Zheng Jianye (鄭建鄴), Luo Guanzong (羅冠宗), Xu Rulei (徐如雷), Zhao Fusan (趙復三) and Han Wenzao (韓文藻). In 1987, five more board members were added: Su Buqing (蘇步青), Wang Shenyin (王神蔭), Luo Zhufeng (羅竹風), Cai Wenhao (蔡文浩) and Shen Yifan (沈以藩). Chen Yuekuang (陳裕光) became Amity's second honorary president in 1986. Mr. Chen later donated his former university residence to Amity, and today it serves as the foundation's headquarters on Hankou Road in Nanjing.

24　"On the Amity Foundation," speech at the second orientation for Amity Teachers, 26 August, 1986.

25　K. H. Ting Circular Letter of 24 June, 1985. Also see, Philip L. Wickeri, "Development Service and China's Modernization: The Amity Foundation in Theological Perspective," *The Ecumenical Rveiew*, 41: 1 (January, 1989), pp. 78-87.

society and the church by serving as a channel of funding and personnel "for existing but inadequately-supported institutions."[26] With the idea of the China Welfare Fund for the Handicapped in mind, he assumed that these would include centers for the disabled and the mentally handicapped. In the early months after Amity was founded, Ting took foreign visitors to a number of hospitals and social welfare institutions in Nanjing. He wanted to support their work, but he did not enjoy these "promotional" visits, for they put him in the awkward position of being perceived as a benefactor. Some Amity board members, including Kuang Yaming, wanted Amity to initiate its own social welfare institutions, but Ting had to persuade them that this would not be possible or desirable in the present context. The teachers' project probably had the greatest initial impact overseas of any early Amity initiative, and Ting approved the plan in February, 1985. The following Fall, twenty-two teachers supported by churches with historic links with China came to teach at tertiary institutions, mostly in and around Nanjing. Ting said that they were to be language teachers, not missionaries, and they rendered outstanding service in this capacity.

It should be noted that in the early years of Amity, the projects were rather simple charitable initiatives involving contributions for social welfare and programs involving volunteer teachers and doctors. There was also the Amity Printing Company that would give priority to the printing of Bibles for the Chinese Church. This was the project that involved the largest amount of initial funding. However, the Printing Company was organizationally separate from the welfare and development work of the foundation. Because it is not directly related to the topic at hand, it need not be discussed at this point.

---

26 K. H. Ting Circular Letter of 20 December, 1984.

V. Amity Perspective and the Ecumenical Response

In the 1980s, voluntary, non-governmental organizations were new in China, and Amity was breaking new ground.[27] Amity was indeed a new Christian initiative in Chinese society. But the thinking behind Amity reflected Ting and Han's remembrance of things past: Christian social welfare institutions in the 1940s. They were aware of the pitfalls of missionary approaches to charity and social service, but they were not familiar with the ecumenical understanding of development, described in the first part of this paper. Still, despite a fairly traditional approach to religion and charity, Amity was new and open to learning.

Some leaders saw Amity's purpose as "pre-evangelistic" but others did not. From an ecumenical social development point of view, "pre-evangelistic" was a non-issue. As we have seen, development was not a way to evangelize people. At the same time, Amity leaders presupposed Chinese social development perspectives that were common in China in the 1980s, and this was largely a government initiative. Overseas churches had very little knowledge of the Chinese context, but they were open to working with Christian leaders.

Within China, a great deal of emphasis was placed on contributing to the "four modernizations" and exchanges with friendly organizations overseas. Amity, it was emphasized, was Christian initiated but not a church organization, and Amity did not do "religious" work. In China, there was both excitement about Amity, and with what the late Dr. Wenzao Han called an expression of "the implementation of the consistent principles of Chinese Christians in a new stage," but also a wariness about the intentions of some

---

27 For different reflections on Amity's development, see the essays and articles in Katrin Fielder and Zhang Liwei, eds. *Growing in Partnership: The Amity Foundation, 1985-2005.*

overseas Christian churches and potential some Amity partners.

Churches overseas had mixed responses to Amity. Many tended to be supportive, but they were often at a loss to know how they should respond. The historic churches and development organizations related to the ecumenical movement were eager to co-operate with Amity Foundation, for Amity was clearly something new, something with a potential to influence ecumenical thinking about development elsewhere, but also something they did not fully understand. In short, the ecumenical model of social development didn't quite fit, but nor did traditional religious perspectives on charity and social service.

The most positive response came from church based-development organization in Western Europe, especially from Germany and the Nordic countries, who saw Amity as a kindred organization.[28] They assumed that Amity had a similar orientation to their own, that Amity was not a mission organization, that Amity was not involved in proselytism and evangelism and that they could establish a partnership with Amity. In this respect, they were correct only in part, for there was as yet no Amity perspective on development. Many of the European partnerships that were formed in the first years of Amity have continued to this day. That is an impressive record for any development organization.

In contrast, some of the American-based conservative churches had no perspective on ecumenical social development and they were still operating on old-fashioned missionary ideas about charity, social service and mission. They wanted to send people to China and do projects as they did in other parts of the world, but they were, at least provisionally, willing to co-operate with Amity. An example was the (American) South Baptist Convention, an

---

28 Very soon after Amity was established, Christian Aid agencies in Europe founded the European Network of Amity Partners (ENAP), a network that continued for two decades. Some traditional mission bodies also took part, but the accent was clearly on development work.

organization with which Amity eventually severed ties.

In 1988, at the request of Bishop K. H. Ting, I wrote a short essay that was an attempt to clarify Amity's approach to development and service for overseas churches.[29] In that essay, I described Amity as a Christian-initiated expression of the "practice" orientation in Chinese society (實踐是檢驗真理唯一的標準). Amity was making a contribution to reform and openness, even as it was a response to reform an openness. I spoke about the need for working with people, regardless of their religious or political persuasion; about the structural dimension of Amity's work, which involved the question of accountability on all sides, and about the need for "ecumenical discipline" in relating to one another. These ideas reflected the thinking of Amity's leaders, but they were cast in the language of the European development organizations. It was an early effort to reinterpret Amity in development (not charity) terms.

Amity was not without its critics overseas. Those in the evangelical community who were opposed to the TSPM/CCC saw Amity as yet another government-sponsored initiative to undercut "true" Christian faith. Curiously, Hong Kong's Raymond Fung, then Evangelism Secretary of the WCC, voiced a similar concern. He suggested that Amity was a government initiative and "an attempt to control, if not the churches, at least the channels for ecumenical relationships with churches outside."[30] Ting was furious that this kind of response would come from the WCC, and he sent a sharply worded letter to Eugene Stockwell at the WCC.[31] Philip Potter, Ting's friend since the 1940s, who had recently retired as General Secretary, sent assurances that

---

29 The essay was published as "Development Service and China's Modernization: the Amity Foundation in Theological Perspective." *The Ecumenical Review*, 41: 1 (January, 1989), pp. 78-87.

30 Raymond Fung, "On the Amity Foundation in the Context of Ecumenical Relationships: An Assessment," unpublished report (July, 1985), p. 5. The report is in my personal files.

31 Letter of K. H. Ting to Eugene Stockwell, 18 May, 1986. A coy of the letter is in my personal files.

Raymond Fung did not speak for the World Council. Other voices in the WCC, especially Ninan Koshy and Kyung-seo Park, spoke up for Amity and the Chinese church, and the World Council would become one of the strongest supporters of Amity in its formative years. The CCC was yet not ready to join the WCC, but after this, relationships continued to improve.

A very different kind of critical response was coming from the left-leaning wing of the church that included many of Ting's closest Canadian friends. They were not only unsure about Amity, but sceptical about the whole direction China was moving under Deng Xiaoping. Ting sensed their alienation and sought to win them back. In a circular letter to those whom Ting called "time-tested friends of China," he praised them for their loyalty and commitment to justice, but also told them that times had changed.

> In recent years, to a great extent thanks to the foundation work our old friends have done, more of those in leading positions of the churches have come to show their friendliness towards China and their understanding and support of our Three-Self stance, including a growing number of evangelicals. Some of our old friends may regard their understanding of things as questionable theologically and politically. But we have no reason to reject their change and approach. What we are witnessing is a polarization phenomenon very much to our liking. Our policy of differentiation draws the line between those who take a hostile line and those who don't, not on other grounds. "All those who are not against us are for us," – that may be our motto.[32]

---

32 K. H. Ting Circular Letter of 24 June, 1985. Also see Jim Endicott, Steve Endicott, Katherine Hockin, Cyril Powles, Majorie Powles, Ray Whitehead, Rhea Whitehead, Don Wilmott and Theresa Chu to K. H. Ting, Letter of 22 October, 1985, in which they expressed their qualified support for Ting's position.

Ting was using the language of the united front in speaking to people whose friendship and support he deeply valued. He was also saying that changes in the international Christian situation held new promise and opportunities for China.

In sum, the international response to Amity was somewhat mixed. This was in part based on the mutual misunderstandings involved in China's early outreach to the world in the 1980s, but also based on the difference between charity and social development as a religious based response to human need.

VI. Conclusion

This paper has presented a case study of charity and development in the Chinese context and in global perspective. After clarifying the difference between these two types of religious response to human need, I have offered a brief survey of the shift in emphasis from religious-based charity to social development in the Christian ecumenical movement, in order to understand the founding and the different responses to the Amity Foundation in the 1980s and 1990s.

With the passing of the founding generation of Amity's leaders, the situation has changed. For one thing, its relationship with the two national Christian bodies is not as close as it once was, and there have even been tensions. Unlike in the past, Amity and TSPM/CCC leaders are no longer the same people. Religious bodies in China are now actively encouraged to become more involved in social service, and the TSPM/CCC has its own Department of Social Welfare. However, as we have shown, social welfare is not the same as social development.

In May, 2012, Amity hosted an international ecumenical conference, the first of its kind in mainland China. The theme was "Religion and Social

Development: Building an Harmonious Society." [33] The conference was co-sponsored by the School of Social and Behavioral Sciences at Nanjing University, an illustration of Amity's developing network of relationship with the Chinese academic world. The atmosphere for Amity's work in China has greatly improved since the 1980s, and especially since the February, 2011 statement jointly issued by six national government ministries, "Opinions about Encouraging and Regulating Charity Work Done by Religious Communities." In response, Amity has expanded its work of Christian social responsibility and development, and, as the 2012 conference shows, it has deepened its reflection on the meaning of social development in China, both theologically and social scientifically.

Today, the Amity Foundation is among the largest NGOs in China concerned with social development.[34] It also has a strong global presence and is connected with a variety of ecumenical and secular development networks. Its development perspective is clearer now than it was in the past. There is a new generation of leadership and a dedicated staff that is many times as large as it was when I was with Amity (up until 1998). Amity has a vastly greater number of projects than in the past emphasizing social development in its many manifestations. Amity has shared its experience within China and abroad, and Amity representatives have spoken about what it can contribute as well as what it can learn. Amity's response to social development has deepened and broadened over the past decades.

Amity is Christian-initiated but not a church organization. Its relationship to local Chinese churches has grown and not diminished, not only in Jiangsu but in many other parts of China. The General Secretary of Amity is Mr. Qiu Zhonghui (丘仲輝), a dedicated Christian who is President of

---

33 Theresa C. Carino, ed., *Christianity and Social Development in China* (Hong Kong: Amity Foundation, 2014). The book contains 18 essays on the conference theme by Chinese and foreign scholars.

34 For current programs see http://www.amityfoundation.org.cn (accessed 15 September, 2014).

the Jiangsu Christian Council. He succeeded Han Wenzao in this position some years ago, but he has been with Amity for more than two decades. Qiu is clearly aware of the problems China is facing, and sees Amity as making a contribution to social development by stressing its own sense of Christian social responsibility. Recently he has observed,

> People's choice of religion is associated with their exposure to religions and the compliance of their own values with the particular religion. Wholistic evangelism integrating the mission of preaching and social service is more acceptable in this land (China) of action culture. In modern China where education and rationality are increasing...social service is changing the attitude of both the church and secular society toward Christian faith. Today when the challenge of accountability is facing all charities and service providers, the tasks of Christian social service has to shoulder is to build up their credibility and capacity in quality service.[35]

In 2015, Amity celebrated its 30th anniversary. It has done much to contribute to a Chinese Christian sense of social responsibility. The challenge for the future is to face new challenges in areas as varied as ecological responsibility and work with migrants in the cities, as Amity deepens and broadens its work in Chinese society. This is not a question for academic study as much as it is a practical question for the future.

---

35 丘仲輝，〈讀聖言，行聖道：從愛德的聖經印刷事工與社會服務事工看當代中國的基督教〉，2014年8月，未刊報告。

【醫療事工】

Catholic Missions & the Ministry of Healing in China: With Special Reference to Health Care in Shandong

R. G. Tiedemann

Abstract

The 'ministry of healing' has been an integral part of the Christian religion, starting with Jesus, the "exorcist and healer". Or as Henry Sigerist, a historian of medicine, put it, "Christianity came into the world as the religion of healing, as the joyful Gospel of the Redeemer and of Redemption. It addressed itself to the disinherited, to the sick and to the afflicted, and promised them healing, a restoration both spiritual and physical." Caring for others and alleviating suffering was thus a Christian virtue that was promoted by both the Catholic and Protestant missionary enterprises. However, such work was not necessarily welcomed by all missionaries or for that matter by the majority of the Chinese people. Some Protestant ministerial missioners felt that medical work did not sufficiently promote direct evangelisation. By the 1920s more serious fissures began to appear within the classical or 'mainline' missionary movement, as conservative elements began to do battle with the 'modernists' and their 'social gospel' approach to mission. At the same time, there were those who rejected medical intervention and promoted 'faith healing' or 'divine healing' instead. As concerns Catholic missions, 'miracle healing' was an important characteristic even in the early twentieth century – not only at popular pilgrimage places such as Lourdes, but also in China. Here it is important to note that Catholic priests were not permitted to take part in direct medical work. Catholic hospitals and dispensaries were for the most part run by foreign religious sisters, some of whom represented female religious institutes specialising in hospital care. They dedicated their lives to ministering to the needs of the sick in alarmingly self-sacrificing ways. This paper examines some of the problems that arose in connection with Catholic low-level medical provision in Shandong in the late nineteenth and early twentieth centuries.

Key words: Catholic Missions, Ministry of Healing, Health Care, Shandong, the late nineteenth and early twentieth centuries

天主教福傳及其醫療事工：
以山東醫療關懷爲中心之探討

狄德滿

摘要

　　從耶穌的「趕鬼與治病」開始，「醫療事工」一直是基督宗教的一個主要部分。或如醫療史學者 Henry Sigerist 所說的，「基督教是以一個醫療的宗教到達世間，爲救贖與救贖者的喜樂福音。」它係針對那些弱勢的、病痛和受苦的人，應允他們在靈魂和肉體上得以痊癒。因此「關愛他人與減輕苦難」就成爲基督徒的美德，被提升爲天主教和新教傳教士的事業。然而，這樣的工作並不見得受到所有傳教士的歡迎，或是因此就被大多數的中國人民所接納。一些新教的傳教者認爲，醫療事工並不足以帶起直接福傳。到了 1920 年代，更嚴重的裂縫開始出現在古典或「主流」傳教運動中，保守勢力開始向「現代派」和他們的「社會福音」宣教方式開戰。與此同時，開始有那些排拒醫療治病，而代替以提倡「信心療法」或「神聖醫治」。如天主教會所關切的，「神蹟醫療」甚至在二十世紀初期就是一個重要特色，不只是發生在像露德那像熱門的朝聖點，也會發生在中國。這裡需要注意的是，天主教的神父都不被允許進行直接醫療的工作。大部分的天主教的醫院和診所，都是由外國修女所經營，其中一些人來自於專長醫院護理的女性宗教機構。她們以驚人的自我犧牲的方式，獻出生命來服事病人的需要。本文探討了在十九世紀末和二十世紀初，天主教在山東提供低層次醫療的狀況。

關鍵詞：天主教福傳、醫療事工、保健、山東、十九世紀末及二十世紀初

Among the means that are available to the Mission to approach [the people] and gain exposure, welfare and charitable assistance occupy a prominent place. One has to show the heathen that Christianity offers them a warm, compassionate heart. ...The Catholic Mission has since time immemorial made use of charitable works to influence the people – and that with complete devotion and often with heroic self-sacrifice.

Vitalis Lange 郎汝略 OFM (1929)[1]

The 'ministry of healing' 醫治的事奉 has been an integral part of the Christian religion, starting with Jesus, the "exorcist and healer".[2] Caring for others and alleviating suffering was thus a Christian virtue that was promoted by Catholics and Protestants alike. Indeed, much has been written about the contribution of Protestant medical missionaries to the introduction of Western medical procedures and 'scientific medicine', starting shortly after the arrival of the first Protestant missionaries on China's shores in the early nineteenth century. However, such work was not necessarily welcomed by other foreign workers or the Chinese people. Some fellow missionaries felt that medical work did not sufficiently promote direct evangelization. By the 1920s more serious fissures began to appear within the classical or 'mainline' Protestant missionary movement, as conservative elements began to do battle with the 'modernists' and their 'social gospel' approach to mission. Especially after 1900, there were those who rejected medical intervention and promoted 'faith healing' or 'divine healing' 神醫. At the same time, as a result of deeply entrenched suspicions fostered by a long tradition of fear of the outsider, most

---

1　Vitalis Lange, *Das apostolische Vikariat Tsinanfu. Franziskanische Missionsarbeit in China* (Werl: Verlag der Provinzial-Missionsverwaltung, 1929), p. 145.

2　See Amanda Porterfield, *Healing in the History of Christianity* (Oxford: Oxford University Press, 2005), Chapter 1: "Jesus: Exorcist and Healer".

Chinese sought to avoid contact with foreign medical personnel. These obstacles notwithstanding, in the early twentieth century medical missions developed rapidly and were spreading to all parts of the country, including its vast hinterland. Hospitals had been built at many major mission stations, staffed by specialized male and female physicians, surgeons and nurses. At the same time, Chinese Christians were increasingly being trained as doctors and nurses at major medical schools and colleges in China and abroad.[3]

In the Catholic China missions the approach to the care of the sick was quite different in significant ways and rather limited in scope. Although the Catholic missionary enterprise has a long history in China, in the modern era its medical missions never reached the level of sophistication of some of the Protestant endeavours. To be sure, 'miracle healing' was and continued to be an important characteristic of Catholic life in China and elsewhere.[4] The late Professor Erik Zürcher, for example, has provided details of such beliefs among Chinese Christians in the late Ming dynasty.[5] Such ideas were still strong in the early twentieth century, as can be seen, for instance, in the story of the healing power attributed to the Italian Sister Maria Assunta Pallotta FMM (1878-1905), who died of typhus after a short period of service in Shanxi.[6] However, although the modern beginnings of the Catholic

---

3 For a list of the major training facilities in China, see R. G. Tiedemann, "The Ministry of Healing," in: R. G. Tiedemann (ed.), *Handbook of Christianity in China. Volume 2: 1800 to the Present* (Leiden: Brill, 2010), p. 694. For a more detailed overview of Protestant medical missions in China, see R. G. Tiedemann [狄德滿], "The Development of Medical Missions in China: Controversies and Historiographical Considerations," in: Liu Tianlu 劉天路 (ed.), *Shen-ti, linghun, ziran: Zhongguo Jidujiao yu yiliao, shehui shiye yanjiu* 《身體・靈魂・自然：中國基督教與醫療、社會事業研究》 [Body, Soul, Nature: Research into Christianity in China and Medical Care, Social Works] (Shanghai: Shanghai renmin chubanshe, 2010), pp. 385-413.

4 The French town of Lourdes remains a popular pilgrimage destination for the sick and physically impaired. Georges Bertin. *Lourdes: A History of Its Apparitions and Cures* (London: Kegan Paul, Trench, Trubner, 1908), reprinted by Kessinger Publishing, 2004.

5 Erik Zürcher, "The Lord of Heaven and the Demons: Strange Stories from a Late Ming Christian Manuscript," in: *Religion und Philosophie in Ostasien. Festschrift für Hans Steininger*, ed. Gerd Naundorf et al. (Würzburg: Königshausen & Neumann, 1975), pp. 359-375.

6 Henrietta Harrison, "Rethinking Missionaries and Medicine in China: The Miracles of Assunta Pallotta, 1905-2005,"

missionary enterprise in the Chinese Empire date back to the late sixteenth century, significant differences existed with regard to regular medical practice. Most notably, according to the old Canon Law (before 1936), priests were not permitted to practise the art of medicine, especially when cutting or burning (cauterization) was involved. They were only able to transmit medical knowledge, give good advice and provide first aid. For priests in the missions there existed special dispensations, but medicine was not allowed to be their main occupation. Thus, in case of necessity and where danger to life was not involved, clerics could "practise medicine through pity and charity towards the poor, in default of ordinary practitioners". The Sacred Congregations in Rome did on several occasions grant permission to priests to make and distribute medical confections, and allowed priests who had formerly been physicians to practise the art, but with the clause

"gratis and through love of God towards all and on account of the absence of other physicians.... In cases where a cleric had formerly been a physician, he may not practise medicine except through necessity, without obtaining a papal indult, which is generally not granted except for an impelling cause.... The main reason why clerics should not practice medicine arises from the danger of incurring the irregularity which is caused by accidental homicide or mutilation. Even accidental homicide induces irregularity if the perpetrator be at fault."[7]

Although the regulations concerning medical practice were somewhat relaxed in mission countries, priests were nevertheless required to be "skilled in the art of medicine and prescribe their remedies gratuitously. They must also abstain from cutting and burning (*citra sectionem et adustionem*)."[8]

Journal of Asian Studies 71.1 (2012), pp. 127-148.

7 See William Fanning, "Medicine and Canon Law," *The Catholic Encyclopedia*, Vol. 10 (New York: Robert Appleton Company, 1911). <http://www.newadvent.org/cathen/10142a.htm> (accessed 19 September 2014).

8 Ibid.

I. The Old Catholic China Missions

Given these restrictions, virtually none of the Catholic priests who came as missionaries to China in the sixteenth to eighteenth centuries were permitted to act as physicians or surgeons. "From the viewpoint of the Catholic Church, the science of medicine constituted a rather secular and corporal part of the over-all concept of human salvation, and exercising medical treatment was strictly forbidden for priests including, of course, missionaries."[9] In their pursuit of a policy of accommodation, the early Jesuits paid considerable attention to the indirect apostolate of arts, crafts and sciences. It was part of their policy of adaptation to the life-style and etiquette of the influential Confucian elite of literati and officials. In other words, their approach to evangelization was 'from the top down', albeit primarily in Beijing rather than in the provinces. As is well known, many of the Jesuit priests were based at the imperial court, the centre of the Chinese ruling class. As we shall see, at times European medicine did play a special role in this interaction between imperial power and foreign expertise. Although priests could not proceed like secular surgeons, some missionaries nevertheless acted as physicians and pharmacists. That is to say, the Jesuits – and subsequently also the Franciscan friars – relied on specialized European lay brothers (修士) who had been trained as physicians, surgeons and pharmacists.

It is, however, important to keep in mind that in early modern China – as well as in the modern period – Chinese medicine had reached a comparatively high level of effectiveness. Whereas the early Jesuits were able to attract the attention of the scholar-official class in connection with their propagation of European scientific knowledge, these 'scholars from the West'

---

9 Claudia von Collani, "Mission and Medicine in China between Canon Law, Charity and Science," in: Staf Vloeberghs (ed.), *History of Catechesis in China* (Leuven: Ferdinand Verbiest Institute, K.U. Leuven, 2008), p. 38.

were less successful when it came to medical knowledge. In other words, medicine in the Chinese context constituted a special challenge for the missionaries. To be sure, more advanced surgical techniques and anatomical knowledge had been developed in Europe, "but traditional Chinese medicine had a rich and ancient body of knowledge about plants and the functions of the human body, permitting a very effective treatment."[10] In theory, therefore, a meaningful exchange of knowledge could have taken place, but this did not happen in any significant way. Each side felt that its own techniques were superior. Moreover, the unusual approaches in Chinese medicine were regarded as being superstitious and strange by the foreign priests. Chinese scholars, on the other hand, were not attracted to the science of anatomy.

As transmitters of scientific and other knowledge between the East and the West, members of the Society of Jesus did produce translations of Western medical texts into Chinese as well as Chinese works into European languages. The German Jesuit Johannes Schreck, also known by his Latinized surname of Terrentius 鄧玉函 (1576-1630), was the first to introduce Western medical knowledge in his *Taixi renshen shuogai* 泰西人身說概 [Abstract of the Western theory of the human body] in 1625 or shortly afterwards. Schreck was an outstanding scholar, scientist, astronomer as well as a trained physician who had studied medicine at several prominent European universities *before* entering the Society of Jesus. Further translations by other Jesuits in the early China mission, especially of anatomical texts, followed.[11] At the same time, they introduced Chinese medical knowledge to Europe, especially those concerned with pulse diagnosis. The Polish Jesuit Michał Piotr Boym 卜彌格 (1612-1659) was no doubt the most important transmitter of information on pulse diagnosis as well as descriptions of various plants and animals in the

---

10 Ibid.

11 For details, see Ursula Holler, in: Nicolas Standaert (ed.), *Handbook of Christianity in China. Volume One: 635-1800* (Leiden: Brill, 2001), pp. 787-791.

Middle Kingdom, with short annotations concerning their medical qualities and effects.[12]

Although medicine was well developed in China, the missionaries nevertheless stressed the importance of a successful medical engagement. The Italian Franciscan Giovanni Francesco Nicolai (Giovanni Francesco da Leonissa 余宜閣; 1656-1737) strongly recommended medicines as an important element of the missionary enterprise of the Friars Minor. "He mentioned various remedies and medical secrets, plasters and ointments to heal wounds and external illnesses, also theriac from Venice for and against everything, pointing out that all these remedies could be helpful at various occasions."[13] Here we may digress and point out that the mention of theriac of Venice is indicative of the pre-scientific nature of medicine in Europe at this time. Theriac or theriaca, especially that produced in Venice (known as Venice Treacle in English) was a medical concoction which had been in use since ancient times until the middle of the eighteenth century. It contained up to 60 different potions, tonics, plant and animal parts was touted as a generic antidote and cure-all. Any failure of these products to achieve the desired therapeutic result was attributed to defective composition or manufacture.

As this example shows, during the early modern period European medicine still left much to be desired – at least according to our modern understanding. Nor can it be said that the practice of Chinese medicine was always convincing and successful. The European discovery of the New World (the Americas) had a significant impact not only in Europe but also in China.

---

12 Ibid., pp. 795-797. For a more comprehensive account, see Reinhard Wendt, "Des Kaisers wundersame Heilung. Zum Zusammenhang von Mission, Medizin und interkontinentalem Pflanzenaustausch," in: Reinhard Wendt (ed.), *Sammeln, Vernetzen, Auswerten. Missionare und ihr Beitrag zum Wandel europäischer Weltsicht* (Tübingen: Gunter Narr Verlag, 2001), pp. 23-44.

13 Claudia von Collani, "Healthcare in the Franciscan Far East Missions (17th-18th Centuries)," *Archivum Franciscanum Historicum* 107 (2014), p. 96.

In the medical field, the administration of quinine (奎寧 or 金雞納) is particularly noteworthy. Of course, the scope of this kind of missionary medical practice was rather limited, because it mainly concerned, as is well known, the successful treatment of the Kangxi Emperor himself. In 1693, the Jesuit priests Jean-François Gerbillon 章誠 (1654-1707) and Tomé Pereira 徐日昇 (1645-1708) treated him with quinine for an attack of fever. In consequence, the Emperor was well-inclined toward missionaries with medical skills. In 1709, the Jesuit lay brother Bernard Rhodes 羅德先 (1645-1715) treated him twice: once for severe palpitations and again for a growth on the upper lip.

The Kangxi Emperor had already by 1685 indicated his wish to have European physicians at the court. Isidoro Lucci 盧依道 (1671-1719) SJ and the barber-surgeon and Macaense-born João Baptista de Lima (1659-1733) were the first to arrive in Beijing in response to the emperor's request.[14] As Ursula Holler has pointed out, the Kangxi Emperor also instructed Joachim Bouvet 白晉 (1656-1730) and Gerbillon to set up a chemical laboratory to manufacture the required medicines.[15] Afterwards, the Jesuits in Beijing became more involved in practical medicine, involving Rhodes and several other lay brothers. It is reported that one of them, lay brother Manuel de Matos (1725-1764), a competent surgeon, declined ordination as a priest in order to continue his medical work. Two Chinese Jesuit priests, Aloysius Gao 高類思 or 高仁 (1732-1780) and Stephanus Yang 楊德望 or 楊執德 (1733-1798?), were sent to Paris for medical training. After their return to China in 1766, they practiced medicine – presumably after the Society of Jesus had

---

14 Beatriz Puente-Ballesteros, "Isidoro Lucci S. J. (1661-1719) and João Baptista Lima (1659-1733) at the Qing Court: The Physician, the Barber-Surgeon, and the Padroado's Interests in China," *Archivum Historicum Societatis Iesu* 82 (2013), pp. 165-216. For a more comprehensive study of medical issues during the Kangxi reign, see Beatriz Puente-Ballesteros, "De París a Pekín, de Pekín a París: La misión jesuita francesa como *interlocutor médico* en la China de la era Kangxi (r. 1662-1722)." Doctoral dissertation, Universidad Complutense de Madrid, 2009.

15 Holler, p. 794.

been disbanded.

Whereas the Jesuits, accustomed to working with the Chinese ruling class, devoted much effort to the transfer of scientific knowledge, the Franciscans paid particular attention to the well-being of the soul and the body of ordinary folk. Moreover, the Spanish friars who entered the Middle Kingdom from the Philippines focused on the poor and needy – and especially the sick – to whom they preached the Christian message in an immediate fashion.[16] Although Belchior Carneiro Leitão 賈尼勞 (1516-1583), the Portuguese Jesuit missionary bishop and administrator of the diocese of Macau, had in 1569 built the first European hospital on Chinese soil, along with an asylum for lepers, it was the Franciscans who were able to establish a hospital on the mainland. In 1673 they were able to gain access to the house of the Prince of Pingnan 平南王 (Shang Zhixin 尚之信; 1636-1680) at Canton (廣州). In the 1670s the city was holding out as a Qing fortress in the midst of rebel-held territory. At this time, the friars served Shang Zhixin as musicians, architects, mechanics and clock-makers and in return were permitted to acquire terrain at Yangrenli 揚仁里 outside the city wall in 1677. There they built a church and an infirmary which functioned until its confiscation in 1732.

Three Franciscan lay brothers were noted for their art of medicine and pharmacy at Canton – and after 1732 at Macau: Blas García 艾腦爵 (1625-1700), Antonio de la Concepción 安多尼 (ca. 1666-1749) and Martín Paláu (1720-1788). Here we should not forget that one important function was to provide care for ill friars.[17] Indeed, even in the modern era many missionaries

---

16 The first Franciscan to arrive on the Chinese mainland was the Spaniard Antonio Caballero (in religion: Antonio de Santa Maria 利安當; 1602-1669). A member of the Order of Discalced Friars Minor (Alcantarines, Discalced Franciscans), he entered Fujian from the Philippines via Taiwan in 1633. He was later based in Shandong. Later, from 1684, Italian Franciscans sent by Propaganda Fide also established missions in various parts of China.

17 For examples from the Yangrenli hospital and the Franciscan *infirmeria* in Macau, see Claudia von Collani, "Healthcare in the Franciscan Far East Missions (17th-18th Centuries)," *Archivum Franciscanum Historicum* 107 (2014), pp. 98-

received some basic instruction in medical care to help fellow priests in mission territories that did not have proper medical facilities. It is this more general ministry of healing to not only fellow missionaries but also to ordinary Chinese, including to lepers, that is particularly noteworthy.

This compassionate aspect of the Catholic approach is perhaps best exemplified by the founding of a religious order dedicated to health care. The 'Order of the Ministers of the Sick' (靈醫會), now commonly known as Camillians, was founded by Camillio de Lellis (1550-1614) in Italy in 1584. Its members dedicated themselves 'before anything else to the practice of works of mercy towards the sick' and ensured that 'man is placed at the centre of attention of the world of health'. They professed the vows of chastity, poverty and obedience and consecrated their lives 'to service to the sick poor, including the plague-ridden, in their corporeal and spiritual needs, even at risk to their own life, having to do this out of sincere love for God'. Faithful to this undertaking, hundreds of Camillians in early modern Europe died serving people who had the plague. Although the Camillians did not come to China until 1946[18], a similarly sacrificial approach to health care can be observed among missionaries – and especially among Catholic sisters – in the nineteenth and early twentieth centuries.

---

106. Further details on the Franciscan medical work in East Asia are found in Severiano Alcobendas, "Religiosos médico-cirurjanos de la Provincia de San Gregorio Magno de Filipinas," *Archivo Ibero-Americano* 34 (1931) to 37 (1934).

18 It should, however, be noted that two Camillian priests, Giacomo Giordani and Stefano Signorini, were sent by Propaganda Fide to China as "Apostolic Missionaries" in the early part of the 18th century. With extreme difficulty, they were able to work for some years as 'optometrists' at the court in Beijing. But the initiative, too isolated, soon came to an end. The first priest died after ten years and the second went back to Italy in 1739. The Camillian presence at Zhaotong in Yunnan in the late 1940s was of equally short duration. They were expelled by the Communists in 1952. During their brief sojourn, they had served in the St. Joseph Hospital, which was run by the Franciscan Missionary Sisters of Graz. The Camillians concerned themselves in particular with lepers.

II. The Ministry of Healing in Modern China

As mentioned already in the introduction, when the first Protestant missionaries arrived on the coast of southern China in the early decades of the nineteenth century, they quickly recognized the value of medical missions in the evangelization process. Not only did many of the early missionaries acquire some basic medical skills before leaving for the Middle Kingdom, but the sending societies also appointed fully trained medical doctors, some of whom were also ordained ministers[19], to the mission field. As the Protestant missionary enterprise spread slowly from the treaty ports to inland locations, the various missions built well-staffed modern hospitals in towns and cities across the vast empire where 'scientific medicine' was practiced. In time several medical colleges were also established. This concern with improving and preserving the lives of others was, of course, an integral part of what would later be called the 'social gospel' approach of 'mainline' Protestant missionary societies.

Although the Catholic China missions had started their healing programmes some two centuries earlier, they could not attain the Protestant level of medical sophistication in the nineteenth century. For one thing, Canon Law continued to impose constraints on the type of health care that could be provided. Moreover, it should not be forgotten that Chinese Catholicism had retreated into remote rural refuges in China's vast hinterland following the century of prohibition since 1724. It would take several decades before institutional facilities could be established in major urban centres. Still, even in the twentieth century it proved very difficult for a variety of reasons to attract secular medical doctors to inland mission stations. While secular

---

19 We are, or course, familiar with the first medical missionary to China, namely the Rev. Dr. Peter Parker (伯駕; 1804-1888), a skilled American surgeon and opthalmologist who sailed for Canton in 1834.

medical facilities were available in the treaty ports, in the late nineteenth century it would take three or more weeks for sick priests in the interior to reach foreign hospitals and properly trained medical doctors in the cities on the coast. Sick priests had to rely, therefore, on the care of their confreres. It is one of the reasons why it was important for a missionary to have at least some knowledge of medicine. Going through the late Father Richard Hartwich's chronicle account of the Society of the Divine Word (SVD) in the Vicariate Apostolic of South Shandong, it becomes shockingly clear that a large number of priests died from typhoid fever and other deadly diseases over the years. In such situations, the carers would also be exposed to the contagion. If a Protestant missionary doctor was nearby, Catholic priests could avail themselves of his services. Thus, when Josef Freinademetz[20] was dying from typhoid fever at the SVD station of Daijiazhuang 戴家莊 (Shandong) in early 1908, Dr. Charles Hodge Lyon 李嘉理 (1874-1946) attended him several times from the nearby American Presbyterian Mission at Jining.[21] In a few cases, when no European nursing care was available, desperate foreign priests visited Chinese doctors.

Medical treatment was available not only for Catholic priests but primarily for the local Christians and non-Christians. Such treatment was often combined with prayers, the dispensation of the sacraments, especially baptism, and Christian amulets, and was considered to be the spiritual way to overcome illness. In this regard it should be pointed out that looking after the corporal as well as spiritual needs of women posed a particular problem in Chinese society on account of the strict segregation of the sexes. To some extent this problem was overcome by employing female catechists (*nü*

---

20 Josef Freinademetz 福若瑟 (1852-1908) SVD, canonized in 2003, was from the Ladin-speaking part of South Tyrol, at the time part of Austria; now in northern Italy.

21 Fritz Bornemann, *Der selige P. J. Freinademetz 1852-1908. Ein Steyler China-Missionar. Ein Lebensbild nach zeitgenössischen Quellen* (Bozen: Freinademetz-Haus, 1977), pp. 505-506.

*chuanjiao xiansheng*女傳教先生) and Catholic Virgins (*tongzhen* 童貞; also *zhennü* 貞女, i.e. 'chaste women'). Especially during the years when Christianity was proscribed and very few European and Chinese priests were able to operate clandestinely in China, the task of preserving the faith in the Catholic *chrétientés* often fell to these dedicated women. Besides propagating the faith among women and instructing girls, they also went out to administer baptisms. It was not only widows who were used as baptizers (*quanxi xiansheng* 權洗先生)[22], by the late eighteenth century the Virgins[23] also assumed this task. Because it was usually combined with administering medication to sick people, these women usually had some rudimentary medical knowledge. The baptism of infants *in periculo mortis* took on particular significance. In view of the fact that the victims of famine, sickness, and infanticide were more likely to be girls than boys, Catholic Virgins were obviously very much involved in saving the souls – and even the lives – of these unfortunate youngsters. A Jesuit missionary based on the Haimen peninsula of Jiangsu noted in this regard: "If I [am able to] send two hundred and fifty children to heaven in [a period of] six months, it is principally the zealous virgins to whom I owe this good fortune. They are constantly seeking out these small creatures; the cost of a few hundred cash does not frighten them."[24] Indeed, throughout the modern missionary era women were sent out as so-called 'medico-baptizers'.[25] They carried a supply of 'medicines' to give

---

22 *Quanxi* 權洗 refers to baptism administered by a lay person in case of necessity.

23 On the phenomenon of Catholic Virgins, see R. G. Tiedemann, "Controlling the Virgins: Female Propagators of the Faith and the Catholic Hierarchy in China," *Women's History Review* 17.4 (September 2008), pp. 501-520. Because of the protracted nature of getting this article into print, I subsequently produced another article on this topic: R. G. Tiedemann, "A Necessary Evil: The Contribution of Chinese 'Virgins' to the Growth of the Catholic Church in Late Qing China," in: Jessie Gregory Lutz (ed.), *Pioneer Chinese Christian Women: Gender, Christianity, and Social Mobility* (Bethlehem: PA: Lehigh University Press, 2010), pp. 87-107.

24 Théobald Werner to his sister Philomène, Haimen peninsula, 20 Oct 1847, *Annales de la Propagation de la Foi* 21 (1849), p. 324.

25 In South Shandong the Steyl Missionaries (SVD) baptized some 50,000 infants "in danger of death" during the first ten years of their work in China. Bornemann, *Der selige P. J. Freinademetz*, p. 600 note 40. For the year 1894 the

them the pretext to surreptitiously baptize moribund children.[26]

Given the long tradition of kidnapping scares in China, the activities of the 'medico-baptizers' inevitably produced ugly rumours. In Hainan island, for instance, it was said that the Catholic 'healer' took out the eyes of sick children to make "detestable drugs": from the aqueous humour [of the eye], water was made to chase away the devil; from the white of the eye false silver was produced which it was impossible to distinguish from the real [silver]; the 'healer' then "opens the children's abdomen, takes out the gall, liver, heart and bone marrow to make drugs from them", which were then sold at an exorbitant price.[27] More generally, in the Chinese mind Western medicine had, of course, long been associated with certain potions used to convert women and then to seduce them. Barend ter Haar asserts that "During the nineteenth century Western missionaries, and their associates, came to be identified as the primary suspects in cases of kidnapping, organ-snatching and foetus-theft, largely replacing earlier scapegoats, such as travelling [Chinese] beggars, monks and other outsiders."[28]

What we may call the 'irrational forces' at work in some of the anti-missionary agitation were conditioned by the widely held Chinese belief that foreign missionaries engaged in atrocious practices, immoral licentiousness, sorcery and kidnapping of children. Christian orphanages and hospitals, in

---

figure was 10,568, and in 1900 it was 11,000. Richard Hartwich, *Steyler Missionare in China. I. Missionarische Erschliessung Südshantungs 1879-1903. Beiträge zu einer Geschichte* (St. Augustin: Steyler Verlag, 1983), p. 259, 440. In 1940 the baptisms of moribund infants still represented rather sizable number in the vicariates and prefectures apostolic of China. Lazaristes du Pétang (Peking), *Les Missions de Chine. Seizième Année (1940-1941)* (Shanghai: Procure des Lazaristes, 1942).

26 Writing from the Vicariate Apostolic of Southeast Zhili in 1860, the Jesuit missionary Prosper Leboucq described in some detail how the baptizers proceeded to perform such surreptitious baptisms. Leboucq, 336th letter in *Lettres des nouvelles missions de la Chine* (Paris, 1841-1872), vol. 3, p. 174.

27 Charles-Pierre Amat to the prefect apostolic of Guangdong, Philippe-François-Zéphirin Guillemin 明稽埒 MEP (1814-1886), Hainan island, 26 April 1855, *Annales de l'Oeuvre de la Sainte-Enfance* 10 (1858), p. 197.

28 Barend J. ter Haar, *Telling Stories: Witchcraft and Scapegoating in Chinese History* (Leiden: Brill, 2006), especially Chapter 4: "Westerners as Scapegoats", here p. 154.

particular, aroused Chinese suspicions and were the targets of some of the most serious anti-missionary incidents in China. This Catholic missionary preoccupation with dying youngsters easily gave rise to wild rumours which were readily believed, not only by the uneducated masses, but even by the elite. Evidence of the misrepresentation of Christianity is even found in Wei Yuan's *Haiguo tuzhi* (魏源《海國圖志》). The work contains the following comment on the Catholic religion: "New converts are made to swallow a pill .... Male and female followers are known to spend the night together in church. And followers, once deceased, have their eyes gouged out by their mentors."[29] Such preposterous notions about foreign practices became deeply ingrained in the minds of many Chinese and persisted at least to the middle of the twentieth century. In the second half of the nineteenth century, lurid tales and an incendiary pictorial literature flourished, such as *Death Blow to Corrupt Doctrines: A Plain Statement of Facts*. Published by the Gentry and People. Translated by missionaries of Dengzhou, Shandong. (Shanghai, 1870). A rather more vicious pictorial work was reproduced by missionaries as *The Cause of the Riots in the Yangtse Valley. A "Complete Picture Gallery."* (Hankow: [Hankow Mission Press], 1891). The anonymous Western compiler translated the texts on the Chinese prints and added annotations. The Chinese author of this graphic pictorial work was said to be Zhou Han 周漢, an expectant *daotai,* and a native of Ningxiang (寧鄉) in Hunan.[30]

Given the general anti-Christian climate in China during the second half of the nineteenth century, the work of the ambulatory Virgin baptizer was clearly not without danger. At the same time, the foreign priests who were joining the missionary enterprise in greater numbers at this time

---

29 Tam Pak Shan, trans., "Selections from An Illustrated World Geography by Wei Yuan," *Renditions: Chinese Interpretations of the West* No. 53-54 (Spring and Autumn 2000), pp. 14-15.

30 For further details concerning Zhou Han's activities, see Stephen R. Platt, *Provincial Patriots: The Hunanese and Modern China* (Cambridge, Mass.: Harvard University Press, 2007), pp. 64-67.

objected to the Chinese Virgins' relative independence, religious initiatives and weak corporate identity and began to insist on increased surveillance and appropriate training. To this end, European sisters were invited to – among other things – exercise spiritual control over the Virgins. However, the arrival of foreign women religious would also have a significant impact on missionary health care. It now became possible to conduct the ministry of healing in a more systematic fashion, especially after the arrival of dedicated hospital sisters. This was, however, a protracted process. Although the first two groups of foreign sisters had reached the China coast in 1848,[31] several decades would pass before the convents of women religious could be established in, for example, the interior of Shandong. It was primarily the new railways that opened up the hinterland to several female congregations, many of them newly-founded missionary institutes. Thus, the first six Franciscan Missionaries of Mary (瑪利亞方濟各傳教女修會) arrived in Ji'nan, Shandong's provincial capital, in 1909.[32] The first Missionary Sisters Servants of the Holy Spirit (聖神婢女傳教會), on the other hand, did not have such an easy journey in 1905. The journey by rail from Qingdao to Ji'nan was comfortable enough, but the journey by boat up the Yellow River to their destination at the rural village of Poli 坡里 (Yanggu *xian*) was anything but comfortable. Although later that year some of the sisters, after basic language training and acculturation, transferred to the central station at the prefectural city of Yanzhou 兖州, this, too, involved a fatiguing journey in Chinese carts. Moreover, it would take several more years before the railway reached that city. In 1906 a second group of Holy Spirit Sisters, having landed in

---

31 They were the Sisters of St. Paul of Chartres 沙爾德聖保綠女修會 who established their first base in Hongkong. In the same year the first Daughters of Charity of St. Vincent de Paul 仁愛修女會 arrived in Macao, but the obstructive Portuguese authorities forced them to transfer to Ningbo in 1852.

32 The Franciscan Missionaries of Mary established their first convent in China in the Shandong treaty port of Yantai 煙台 [Chefoo 芝罘] in 1887 as well as in the leasehold territories in Qingdao 青島 (1902) and Weihaiwei 威海衛 (1908).

Shanghai, made the slow, fatiguing journey to Yanzhou on the Grand Canal.[33]

Such inconveniences notwithstanding, the presence of European women religious, reinforced over the next two or so decades by other communities of women religious in Shandong, mainly from the United States, as well as the founding of Chinese sisterhoods, made it possible to establish more effective and coordinated medical services in the various vicariates and prefectures apostolic of Shandong. The foreign sisters' initial contact with Chinese patients occurred during consultations at their respective mission stations. As the annual statistics indicate, the missionary sisters had a steady stream of visitors — and not just from Chinese women but also from men. They also went out to visit sick people in their homes. As the Franciscan friar Vitalis Lange 郎汝略 (1880-1934) noted, they would wash and feed the poorest in their "miserable and dirty Chinese hovels".

> The deep impression this selfless charitable activity makes on the heathen population cannot be described. At the beginning the people cannot get over it that strangers — and foreign ladies at that — minister to their needs in their misery, to show them the love which they do not receive from their relatives. And all this without remuneration, and all with the greatest kindness and with the greatest love and self-sacrifice![34]

Lange alludes once more to the disorder and uncleanliness in Chinese habitations to emphasize the sacrificial lives these sisters were leading. They were exposed to many disgusting, repulsive and dangerous diseases, not to mention the soars as a result of "unbelievable filthiness", as well as smallpox,

---

33 Richard Hartwich, *Steyler Missionare in China. II.Bischof A. Henninghaus ruft Steyler Schwestern 1940-1910* (Nettetal: Steyler Verlag, 1985), pp. 227-228.

34 Lange, p. 148.

typhoid fever and cholera. He adds that the Chinese are aware of the contagiousness of these diseases and are, therefore, appreciative of the sisters' selfless work. He points out that two sisters make these visits together, one foreign and one Chinese. This makes it easier to win the confidence of the non-Christians. More importantly, from his perspective, these charitable activities among the impoverished sick people formed an integral part of and were combined with Christian evangelization.[35]

The danger of contagion as a result of contaminated food and water became evident during the typhoid fever epidemic in Yanzhou in 1907. Several priests, lay brothers, foreign sisters and Chinese Virgins were affected. The inadequate and unhealthy accommodation of the foreign sisters seems to have contributed to the sad state of affairs. Bishop Augustin Henninghaus 韓 甯鎬 (1862-1939) stated that this epidemic was particularly severe in the Yanzhou mission residence during the great North China Famine of 1906-1907.

> All the sisters and a large number of priests were affected by the plague. They are difficult times when the deadly fever is lurking out here. Medical help and sensible nursing are rare and difficult to secure.... With a heroic sense of self-sacrifice the sisters in particular have done their duty in these sad days. Three of twelve, among them our able pharmacist Sr. Liboria (5.12.07), and the first directress of the small family, Sr. Dolorosa (27.12.07), fell victim to the disease.[36]

Although dispensaries had already been set up at various mission stations and staffed by Chinese Virgins in the late nineteenth century, this component

---

35 Ibid., pp. 148-149.
36 Hartwich, II, pp. 321-322. Sr. Liboria (Antonia Ruhrort; 1876-1907); Sr. Dolorosa (Luise Schottenröhr; 1876-1907).

of the missionary enterprise was expanded as the number of foreign sisters increased. At these places the sisters – and to a lesser extent the priests and lay brothers – could diagnose illnesses and dispense the appropriate medication.[37] (For details concerning the locations in Shandong, see the table at the end of this paper). It was, however, more challenging to establish Catholic hospitals in the interior of the province and only a small number were actually built in the province during the missionary era. The first such initially rather rudimentary facility was opened at Yanzhou on 16 November 1906. In time it would develop into a sizable medical facility. The German Franciscan Mission in Ji'nan had to wait until 1931 before the newly arrived Hospital Sisters of St. Francis of Springfield, Illinois (方濟醫院服務修女會) were able to open the modern St. Joseph's Hospital in the western suburb of the city. Usually the missionary sisters were in charge of the hospitals and a somewhat limited medical service could, therefore, be offered. However, from time to time fully qualified secular doctors who could carry out surgical intervention were available. Thus, when the Yanzhou hospital was opened in 1906, the German administration at Qingdao sent the naval surgeon Dr. Dörr to assume control. But he stayed only for a few months: the excessive costs and differences with the sisters led to his recall.[38] The hospital was henceforth managed by lay brothers of the Society of the Divine Word. The most prominent among them was Heinrich Pötter (in religion: Brother Rudolf 盧德福; 1872-1952) who, after some rudimentary training in nursing and pharmacy, had arrived in Shandong in 1898.[39]

Although Catholic hospitals did not offer a full range of medical services,

---

37 Interestingly, one source states that the Steyl Mission had 40 such places in the South Shandong Mission, some of them staffed by male and female Chinese doctors (大夫). Fritz Bornemann SVD (ed.), "Br. Rudolf, Heinrich Pötter 1872-1952," *Analecta SVD* 34 (Romae: Apud Collegium Verbi Divini, 1977), p. 143.

38 Ibid., pp. 264-266.

39 Bornemann SVD (ed.), "Br. Rudolf, Heinrich Pötter 1872-1952," pp. 142-158.

the dedicated male and female missionaries, along with Chinese sisters and Virgins, were nevertheless popular with needy people. This was especially the case during the turbulent republican era. The frequent warlord confrontations brought destruction of life and property, irregular exactions and looting. The loss of central authority aggravated collective violence and fostered the growth of more severe banditry. Only the mission stations remained relatively safe havens to which rich and poor, Christians and non-Christians, flocked in times of impending danger. The mission compounds not only protected the people but also offered sustenance and medical aid to the starving and sick. Wherever warlord armies came to blows, wounded soldiers of whatever faction were treated in mission hospitals. Such missionary interventions occurred in hundreds of cities and towns all over North China during the turbulent 1920s.

In some parts of China, the greatest threat to missionary benevolence came from the revolutionary movements after 1927. Foreign mission stations became principal targets of the Communist revolutionaries who held missionaries for ransom, confiscated medical supplies, and on several occasions killed foreign priests. Here we may mention just one example, namely the Catholic leper asylum at Moximian 磨西面 (泥頭) in western Sichuan (or Xikang). Such asylums were rather sensitive establishments at the best of times. At Moximian several Franciscan friars and brothers, along with some Franciscan Missionaries of Mary, had taken on the task of looking after the unfortunate lepers. On 29 May 1935 Communist forces on the 'Long March' invaded the village and apprehended the Franciscan friars and brothers. It is said that they were interrogated by Mao Zedong himself. All except two were subsequently released. The "Communist hordes" did not molest the sisters but roughly handled the lepers. "There were more than 30,000 Reds in the band, including a large number of women. They ransacked the village, carrying away everything movable and edible, and now the people of the district are without means of subsistence. The lepers are in the same plight."[40] The two captives – the Italian friar Epifanio Pegoraro 畢天爵 (1898-1935) and the Spanish brother Pascual Nadal Oltra 陸 (1884-1935) – were beheaded at Lianghekou 梁河口 (Sichuan) on 25 December 1935.[41] This was by no means an isolated case. In the final analysis, it is probably fair to say that the Chinese Communists would not tolerate any competition for the goodwill of the people.

With the outbreak of the Anti-Japanese War (1937-45) the foreign missionaries once again had the opportunity to meet the needs of the suffering Chinese people. During the destructive Japanese assaults at the beginning of the war, they were able to resume their by now customary role in times of conflict, offering shelter, food and medical aid, as well as spiritual relief amidst indiscriminate bombing, raping and killing.[42] In spite of the great dangers, many missionaries decided to stay with their flocks. It was an opportunity to show the reality of their faith and sincerity of their love for the people who were suffering all around them. After the initial assault of the Japanese invasion had passed, the rural districts behind enemy lines were once more plunged into chaos by various contending military forces, the resurgence of banditry and the recrudescence of semi-religious self-defence forces[43]. The confusing state of affairs made missionary life increasingly difficult. Especially in contested areas, such as the mountains of central Shandong, they had to

---

40 "Abducted Franciscans Still Missing," *Malaya Catholic Leader* (31 August 1935).

41 *Necrologium Fratrum Minorum in Sinis. Et orent pro defunctis...*, comp. Daniel Van Damme OFM. (Hong Kong: Printed by Tang King Po School, Kowloon, 1978), p. 191.

42 One account states that the Society of the Divine Word (SVD) mission in south Shandong looked after some 120,000 refugees during the first year of the war. Johann Kraus, *P. August Hättig, S.V.D., ein Kämpfer für Gottes Reich im Reiche des Drachen; gefallen 1942 in China* (Kaldenkirchen: Steyler Verlags-Buchhandlung, 1957), p. 197.

43 On the various local defence groups in the Central Shandong Massif, see Wang Yu-chuang, "The Organization of a Typical Guerrilla Area in South Shantung," in: Evan F. Carlson, *The Chinese Army: Its Organization and Military Efficiency* (New York: Institute of Pacific Relations, 1940), pp. 94-100, 104-106; David M. Paulson, "National Guerrillas in the Sino-Japanese War: The 'Die-Hards' of Shandong Province," in: Kathleen Hartford and Steven M. Goldstein (eds.), *Single Sparks: China's Rural Revolutions* (Armonk, NY: M. E. Sharpe, 1989), pp. 128-150.

deal with unpredictable Nationalist and Communist guerrilla forces as well as sporadic Japanese incursions. The level-headed Swiss Catholic priest Alois Regensburger 郏振波 (1907-1992), for example, adapted well to the ever changing local situation at his isolated mission station of Jingwangzhuang in Mengyin *xian* 蒙陰縣井旺莊. When Japanese soldiers entered his village, he would put on a white European coat to welcome them; when Nationalist forces came, he would dress in a fine long silk robe (*daguazi*) "to prove that I honoured the troops"; when the Communists arrived, he met them in the shabbiest *daguazi*, "for one had to act like a proletarian".[44] In this way he was able protect the local people and even look after some wounded soldiers that had been left behind by the Guomindang's 40th Army.[45]

III. Conclusion

As this brief outline has indicated, the Catholic approach to medical missions was in significant ways quite different from the Protestant one. The many Catholic women (and not so many men) who came to China to staff the hospitals and dispensaries dedicated their lives to ministering to the needs of the sick in self-sacrificing ways rather than to introducing innovative medical techniques or building impressive institutions. However, by the early part of the twentieth century certain voices came to the fore, agitating for the proper training of religious missionary personnel, men and women, as physicians and surgeons. Among the first to raise this issue was Dr Agnes McLaren (1837-1913), a Scottish physician and former Protestant missionary in India. She had converted to Catholicism in 1898 and afterwards began to train women doctors for Catholic missions.[46] One of her pupils, the Austrian

---

44 Alois Regensburger SVD, *Sie nannten mich Donner. 21 Jahre in China* ([Kaldenkirchen:] Steyler Verlag, 1972), p. 96.
45 Ibid., pp. 99-100.
46 Katherine Burton, *According to the Pattern: The Story of Dr. Agnes McLaren and the Society of Catholic Medical*

doctor Anna Maria Dengel (1892-1980), founded the Society of Catholic Medical Missionaries (or Medical Mission Sisters) in Washington DC in 1925. These religious sisters were professionally trained to provide full medical care to the poor and needy in mission territories.

Another advocate of modern health care for needy people around the world was Dr. Paluel Joseph Flagg (1886-1970), an anaesthesiology resident at St. Vincent's Hospital in New York. In 1912 he founded the Catholic Medical Mission Board. The board sent British-born and trained Dr. Margaret Marion Traill Lamont (nee Christie; 1867-1931), also a convert to Catholicism, and her family to China in 1914.[47] She was the first medical missionary to answer Dr. Flagg's call to service. In Germany some years later, in 1922, the Medical Mission Institute (MI) was founded in Würzburg by the Salvatorian priest Christopher E. Becker (1875-1937) to train mission doctors and sisters. But it was not until 1936 that the Canon Law preventing members of religious orders practicing medicine in its full extent was finally removed. On 11 February 1936, the Sacred Congregation of the Faith issued an instruction to religious institutes of women which not only confirmed the pioneer efforts of the Medical Mission Sisters for the medical relief of women and children in the missions but also extended this apostolate to other religious communities.

These important decisions led to the recognition of Anna Dengel's Medical Mission Sisters as a religious congregation, with the sisters making public profession of vows. It soon spread to other countries and continents. In her Directives to the Medical Mission Sisters, Anna Dengel conveyed the new spirit in the medical apostolate that combined compassion and scientific medicine, as expressed by the pope:

Missionaries (New York: Longmans, Green, 1946).

47 Margaret Lamont, *Twenty Years Medical Work in Mission Countries* (Shanghai: Chung Hwa Book Company, 1918).

They (the sisters) must see in the patient the suffering Christ claiming their love and sympathy. Since love expresses itself in sacrifice, the sisters will do whatever is necessary for the patient without counting the cost to themselves. Let them follow the instructions of Pope Pius XI: 'Love your sick and care for them with devotion. Look after them intelligently and scientifically.... Proceeding in this natural order, you will inspire the confidence and trust which will prepare the mind for higher and supernatural things.... The people must never get the idea that conversion and Baptism are necessary to reward your devoted care, your sincere and unselfish Christian charity and zeal. Use all means at your disposal to make them experience in themselves that your religion is good and truly inspired by self-sacrificing love.' [48]

Unfortunately these changes came too late in the China missions where dramatic political developments soon heralded the end of the missionary era.[49] Here many selfless priests, brothers, sisters and Virgins, committed to the ministry of compassion, kept up the struggle to bring comfort and relief to thousands of suffering Chinese.

---

48 Quoted in Sister M. Regis Polcino, "The Medical Mission Sisters, Their Founder, Mother Anna Dengel, M.D., and Their Role in the Historical Evolution of the Medical Mission Apostolate," *Transaction & Studies of The College of Physicians of Philadelphia* 35.1 (July 1967), p. 5. On Dengel, see also Angelyn Dries OSF, "American Catholic 'Woman's Work for Woman' in the Twentieth Century," in: Dana L. Robert (ed.), *Gospel Bearers, Gender Barriers: Missionary Women in the Twentieth Century* (Maryknoll, NY: Orbis Books, 2002), pp. 134-136.

49 Besides the Camillians mentioned above, the Brothers of Mercy of Our Lady of Perpetual Help (or Trier Brothers) had been involved in medical care at the Catholic hospital at Lanzhou in Gansu province since 1933.

Acronyms and Abbreviations used in the table below:

OFM   Order of Friars Minor (Franciscans) 方濟各會；方濟會

SVD   Society of the Divine Word (Steyl Missionaries) 聖言會

ASC   Sisters Adorers of the Most Precious Blood 寶血會

Aux.   Auxiliaries in the Propagation of the Faith (Chinese)

FMM   Franciscan Missionaries of Mary 瑪利亞方濟各傳教女修會

Josephines Sisters of St. Joseph 若瑟會 (Chinese)

Oblates   Oblates of the Holy Family (Yenchow) 聖家會 (Chinese)

OSF (D)   Franciscan Sisters of the Holy Family (Dubuque)

OSF (L)   Franciscan Sisters of Luxemburg (Hospitalschwestern von der
            Hl. Elisabeth vom III. Orden des Hl. Franziskus)
            盧森堡方濟第三會仁愛會

OSF (S)   Hospital Sisters of St. Francis (Springfield)
            方濟醫院服務修女會

SMIC   Missionary Sisters of the Immaculate Conception of the Mother
            of God 聖母無原罪傳教修女會

SSpS   Missionary Sisters Servants of the Holy Spirit (Holy Spirit
            Sisters; Steyler Missionsschwestern) 聖神婢女傳教會

Catholic Hospitals and Medical Services in Shandong 1940

Vicariate or Prefecture Apostolic / Missionary Congregation	Hospitals			Dispensaries			Leprosy Asylums		
	No.	Principal Locations	Religious Community in Charge	No.	Principal Locations	Religious Community in Charge	No.	Principal Locations	Religious Community in Charge
V. A. Chefoo / French OFM 煙台代牧區	3	Yantai 煙台 (1 European hospital; 2 Chinese hospitals)	FMM	5	Yantai (2) 煙台 / Fangzi (1) 坊子	FMM / FMM	1	Xishan 煙台西山	FMM
V. A. Chowtsun /American OFM 周村代牧區	0			5	Huimin 惠民 / Qiuliuzhuang 浦台縣邱李莊 / Zhoucun 周村 / Zhangdian 張店 [淄博]	ASC / OSF (D) / OSF (S) / OSF (S)	0		
V. A. Ichowfu / German SVD 沂州府代牧區	2	Wangzhuang 沂水縣王莊	SSpS	8	Linyi 臨沂 / Feixian 費縣 / Mengyin 蒙陰 / Wangzhuang 沂水縣王莊	SSpS / SSpS / SSpS / Aux.	0		
P. A. Idubsien [Qingzhou 青州] / French OFM 益都縣代牧區	0			2	Yidu 益都 [青州]	FMM	0		
P. A. Lintsing / Chinese secular clergy 臨清代牧區	0			3	Shierlizhuang 十二里莊 / Daguhang 臨清達古巷	SMIC / Josephines	0		
V. A. Tsaochowfu / German SVD 曹州府代牧區	6	Heze 荷澤 / Shanxian 單縣 / Yuncheng 鄆城 / Caoxian 曹縣	SSpS / SSpS / SSpS / Oblates	24	Heze 荷澤 / Shanxian 單縣 / Yuncheng 鄆城 / Caoxian 曹縣 & other places	SSpS / SSpS / SSpS / Oblates	0		

V. A. Tsinanfu / German OFM 濟南代牧區	1	Ji'nan 濟南	OSF (S)	10	Ji'nan 濟南 Hongjialou 濟南洪家樓 Taian 泰安	FMM SMIC OSF (S)	0		
V. A. Tsingtao / German SVD 青島代牧區	1	Qingdao 青島	FMM	7	Qingdao 青島 Jiaozhou 膠州 Gaomi 高密 Jimo 即墨 Zhucheng 諸城	FMM FMM SSpS Oblates Oblates	0		
P. A. Weihaiwei / French OFM 威海衛監牧區	2	Includes 1 hospice		5	Weihaiwei 威海衛 Weihaiwei 威海衛	FMM OSF (L)	0		
V. A. Yangku / Chinese secular clergy 陽穀代牧區	0			7	Poli 坡里 and other places	SSpS Aux. & Oblates	0		
V. A. Yenchowfu / German SVD 兗州府代牧區	4	Ziyang 滋陽 [Yanzhou 兗州] Jining 濟寧 Caoqiaokou 濟寧曹橋口	SSpS SSpS SSpS	20	Daijiazhuang 戴家莊 Ziyang 滋陽 [Yanzhou 兗州] Ziyang 滋陽 [Yanzhou 兗州] Jining 濟寧 Caoqiaokou 濟寧曹橋口 Lincheng 臨城 Zaozhuang 棗莊	SSpS SSpS Oblates SSpS SSpS SSpS SSpS	1	Guanzhuangpu 滋陽官莊鋪	SSpS

Source: Lazaristes du Pétang (Peking), *Les Missions de Chine. Seizième Année* (1940-1941). (Shanghai: Procure des Lazaristes, 1942), pp. 110-146.

二十世紀前期《使信月刊》中的臺灣：
以英國長老教會傳教士的事工爲中心*

張勤瑩

摘　要

　　《使信月刊》（*The Messenger*）創刊於十九世紀中葉，是英國長老教會發行的機關刊物。隨著海外傳教事業的拓展，該刊逐漸出現福爾摩沙的消息，可視為是當時在臺傳教士的發聲平台。

　　本文根據《使信月刊》在二十世紀前期的報導內容，探討傳教士在臺實踐的福音事工及其實踐的社會關懷面向，藉此闡明該刊的特色及其宣傳功能。其一，該刊介紹不少醫療傳教士在臺見聞，積極展現福音與醫療結合下的成果；其次，報導者致力於描繪臺灣的人情風土，激起基督徒讀者的同理心，以利響應海外事工的需求。

　　《使信月刊》保存了自十九至二十世紀中葉以前的臺灣生活片段，但報導內容及其解釋，多呈現以福音觀點的報導題材與宣傳策略。此外，傳教士從醫療活動中，觀察一般民眾在臺灣社會的生活難題，同時藉此彰顯出傳教士以福音改良社會的理念。

關鍵詞：《使信月刊》、英國長老教會、傳教士報刊、二十世紀前期臺灣

---

* 本文修改過程中，承評論人吳學明老師、王成勉老師以及匿名評審專家的寶貴意見，筆者在此致上誠摯謝意。

一、前言

　　過去探討新教傳教士在海外落實的具體事工，多是關注在傳教士從事福音事工的成效上；似較少從英文報刊傳播的取向，關注傳教士身兼報導海外宣教工場的角色。在電子網路時代來臨的百年前，長期駐守海外傳教工場的英國傳教士，究竟如何邀請英國讀者，一同關注並支持傳教士在異地的遭遇，及其實踐的社會關懷，特別是福音與醫療相關的宣教活動？[1]

　　以英國長老教會（Presbyterian Church of England）的機關刊物《使信月刊》（*The Messenger*）為例，該刊涉及不少以「福爾摩沙」（Formosa）為名的報導。[2] 令人好奇的是，當時英國長老教會傳教士，究竟採取怎樣的視角，來報導他們在臺灣的見聞及當地民眾的生活與道德情境？又，撰寫文字報導的傳教士，如何引導英國社會的讀者，解讀海外宣教工場的社會現象，及其背後代表的實質問題？[3]

　　1865年，首位英國長老教會醫療傳教士馬雅各（James Laidlaw Maxwell, 1836-1921）抵臺後，自此陸續有英籍與加拿大籍的傳教士

1　為傳播福音而遠赴海外生活的傳教士，其遭遇到的挑戰與難題，可從報刊中獲得相關訊息。例如前往中國的英國長老教會傳教士，必須在離國前接受培訓，包括語言、語音學以及中國宗教等方面的學習；了解中國人的社會、心理，還有中國歷史、地理與文學等等，亦是課程範圍。抵達傳教工場後，亦須留意生活中可能伴隨而來的生命威脅，包括地震、飢荒、瘴疾、熱病或死亡等等。"Dr. Mott's Canton Conference," *The Messenger* (April 1914), p. 131; Dr. F. W. Heyworth, "Missionary Life as It is," *The Messenger* (Oct. 1924), p. 154. 事實上，傳教士能否在海外執行任務，健康因素相當關鍵，即使是專業的醫療傳教士，如蘭大衛醫師（David Landsborough III, 1870-1957），在二十世紀初亦曾飽受彰化地區傳染病的威脅，染上痢疾與瘴疾。因反覆患病而被迫辭呈，後來身體逐漸康復，且在委員會力勸下打消此念。"Formosa: Work in Taichu (Chianghoa)," *The Messenger* (Dec.1902), p. 326; "Formosa: The Chianghoa District," *The Messenger*, (Feb. 1900), p. 44; "Dr. Landsborough," *The Messenger* (Oct. 1908), p. 353. 關於英國長老教會傳教士駐臺者（1864-1945），參見賴永祥長老史料庫：http://www.laijohn.com/missionaries/1864-1945-EP.htm（檢索日期：2014/08/01）。

2　筆者按：為行文方便，下文改以臺灣稱之。

3　筆者按：2006年教會公報社發行一套橫跨1850年至1947年份的精裝版《使信全覽》及光碟，是由臺南基督長老教會歷史委員先將《使信月刊》進行數位化建檔，並從臺灣神學院教會歷史資料中心及英國長老教會的典藏中補齊原件闕漏後，重新印行，本文撰稿即據此套史料而成。此外，本文採用《使信月刊》的中文譯名，是依循賴永祥在《教會史話》第四輯中的譯名。關於《使信月刊》從溫哥華運回臺灣，並典藏在臺灣基督長老教會歷史資料館的經過，參見賴永祥，《教會史話第四輯》（臺南：人光出版社，1997），頁11-14。

出現在臺灣的土地上，並活躍於淡水、彰化、臺南、高雄與東部臺灣的鄉間，其中尤以隸屬於英國長老教會的傳教士，佔據多數。[4] 這些傳教士無分男女，遠渡重洋傳播福音，並在早期物質條件不佳的臺灣環境中生活多年。有趣的是，傳教士勤於記錄日常生活中經歷的事物，並發表在其機關刊物《使信月刊》上，類型涉及傳教事工，包括醫療、教育與社會救助等相關紀錄，還有傳教士個人相關動態、旅行經驗、與本地信徒互動的情形，或是介紹日本官方治臺政策，以及開發地方教會的經過等等。

對於二十世紀前期，在臺經營傳教事業的英國長老教會傳教士而言，透過《使信月刊》此一宣傳媒介，有效縮短海外宣教工場與母國之間存在的遙遠距離。相對而言，當時身處英國社會的基督徒，亦可利用《使信月刊》取得臺灣相關訊息。至於這些身處海外，且肩負報導工作的英國長老教會傳教士，將選取什麼樣的報導題材，讓母國讀者可以藉助閱讀與想像，一同參與這跨越國界的社會關懷計畫及其改造過程？從傳教士的角度觀之，疾病與道德之間又產生什麼樣的關聯？相對而言，透過《使信月刊》的傳播，是否也影響英國讀者對臺灣的想像，進而支持傳教士在當地的事工？上述問題有待從《使信月刊》中相關報導進行釐清。

回顧華文學界探討二十世紀前期英國長老教會在臺活動，研究成果多著墨在具體事工的活動與成就方面；或是以傳教士留下的文字紀錄作為具體史料，來建構宣教史論述。[5] 其中，《使信月刊》的報

---

4 作為首位抵臺的醫療傳教士馬雅各，其先於1863年12月抵達中國，而後經長老教會指派下，於1865年轉往臺南宣教。"Dr. Maxwell's Missionary Jubilee," *The Messenger* (June 1914), p. 195. 此外，早在馬雅各抵臺前，英國長老教會駐廈門的杜嘉德牧師（Carstairs Douglas, 1830-1877）與駐汕頭的金輔爾牧師（Hur Libertas Macjebzie, 1833-1899）已於1860年中訪問北臺灣，此後更鼓吹臺灣宣教事宜，奠定日後醫療傳道。參見賴永祥，《教會史話第一輯》（臺南：人光出版社，1990），頁273-278；鄭仰恩，《定根本土的臺灣基督教——臺灣基督教史研究論集》（臺南：人光出版社，2005），頁261。

5 臺灣基督教史的研究成果中，涉及諸多與英國長老教會在臺活動的相關議題：首先，以臺灣長老教會為首，探討基督新教在臺灣的發展史與各地區的教會歷史。參見臺南基督長老教會總會編，《臺灣基督長老教會百年史》（臺南：基督長老教會，1965）；黃茂卿，《太平境馬雅各街紀念教會九十年史》（臺南：太平境教會，1988）；林治平主編，《基督教與臺灣》（臺北：宇宙光，1996）；鄭仰恩，《定根本土的臺灣基督教——臺灣基督教史研究論集》。從十七世紀荷蘭傳教士抵臺傳教，直到戰後臺灣基督

導，有助於佐證英國長老教會的研究論題，顯見其重要的史料價值。[6] 本文擬鎖定二十世紀前期《使信月刊》的相關報導，來介紹英國長老教會傳教士在臺耕耘福音，及其實踐社會關懷的做法。透過與醫療傳教事工相關的報導題材，包括醫療傳教士蘭大衛醫師等人，抵臺後之見聞與醫療活動；亦有助於解釋以福音改良社會，乃報導者所欲彰顯之價值。[7]

二、《使信月刊》的性質、特色與宣傳功能

自十九世紀中葉發行以來的《使信月刊》，是英國長老教會提供給英國本土與海外宣教委員會（Foreign Mission Committee），刊登基

教的發展概況：參見林金水，《臺灣基督教史》（北京：九州出版社，2007）。關於教會史料與各地區教會歷史，參見賴永祥，《教會史話第一輯》；臺灣教會公報週刊編輯，《臺灣古早教會巡禮》（臺南：人光出版社，1996）；陳梅卿，《宜蘭縣基督教傳教史》（宜蘭市：宜蘭縣政府，2000）。其次，以臺灣長老教會的社會關懷面向為主，包括神學詮釋、教育、醫療等相關研究。例如：李欣芬，《基督教與臺灣醫療的現代化：以彰化基督教醫院為中心之探討（1896-1936）》（臺師大歷史研究所碩士論文，1989）；張妙娟，《開啟心眼：《臺灣府城教會報》與長老教會的基督徒教育》（臺南：人光，2005）；吳學明，《臺灣基督長老教會研究》（臺北：宇宙光，2006）；蔡維民，《基督漫步於福爾摩沙：基督教在臺灣》（臺北：五南出版社，2009）；張妙娟，〈日治前期臺灣南部長老教會的主日學教育（1896-1926）〉，《興大歷史學報》，第22期（2010），頁79-103；陳慕真，〈日治末期的臺灣基督長老教會：以《臺灣教會公報為中心》〉，《臺灣史料研究》，第37期（2011），頁32-49。由於相關討論眾多，筆者暫不一一列載。其三，知名傳教士的傳記與傳教貢獻。幾位著名的新教傳教士的傳教貢獻與其著作、日記，不斷被編輯重印與翻譯，諸如馬偕（George Leslie Mackay, 1844-1901）、巴克禮（Thomas Barclay, 1849-1935）、甘為霖（William Campbell, 1841-1921）等人在臺灣具體的活動與事蹟。其四，關於臺灣原住民的基督教信仰及其文化等等。

6 例如，在《看見十九世紀臺灣──十四位西方旅行者的福爾摩沙故事》一書中，介紹李麻夫人（Mrs. Hugh Ritchie, 1828-1902）對於臺灣女子教育的貢獻，採用1878年份的《使信月刊》，並節錄出數篇相關報導，以便向讀者介紹李麻夫人在臺灣的事蹟。顯示《使信月刊》中的報導，其實隱含著許多傳教士在臺灣的活動。費德廉（Douglas L. Fix）、羅效德編譯，《看見十九世紀臺灣──十四位西方旅行者的福爾摩沙故事》（Curious Investigations: 19th-Century American and European Impression of Taiwan）（臺北：如果出版社，2006），頁220-224。

7 時至1930年，蘭大衛生日之際，許多當地人包括曾經就診的病患與學生，紛紛前來祝壽，並感念其在臺灣三十六年來的醫師生涯。"A Shoka Anniversary," The Messenger (April 1930), p. 235. 此外，關於梅監霧與蘭大衛二人在中部地區傳教經過的報導，參見"Formosa: The Chianghoa District," The Messenger (Feb. 1900), p. 44; "Chianghoa, Formosa," The Messenger (July 1901), p. 191. 另外，任英國長老教女宣道會（Women's Missionary Association, WMA）主席的貝爾女士（Mrs. Bell），於1910年代訪視臺灣之際，特別參訪彰化醫館。甚至傳達其終於能夠理解，蘭醫師為何能夠掌握臺灣民眾的心。Mrs. Bell, President W. M. A., "A Visit to the Mission Field," The Messenger (June 1912), p. 183.

督教訊息的重要園地。隨著傳教士邁入亞洲的腳步頻仍，促使該刊內容逐漸出現來自亞洲地區的相關宣教事蹟，包括來自福爾摩沙、印度、孟加拉、中國、澳門、日本、新加坡、馬來西亞以及菲律賓等地的報導訊息。該刊也成為當時讀者關注英國長老會在海外傳教發展的重要媒介，且不乏出現臺灣的相關報導，此皆當時派駐臺灣的英國長老教會傳教士，筆耕不懈下的成果。

　　自十九世紀晚期以來，這些英籍傳教士紛紛透過文字與照片，建構出以實際經歷為主的生活見聞與圖像敘事，使得當時臺灣的風土民情，可以藉由文字印刷與報刊傳播的力量，映入英國基督徒的眼簾，無形中縮短了英國社會與臺灣之間的遙遠距離。倘若從媒體理論，來檢視英國長老教會傳教士在《使信月刊》中對於臺灣的報導，可以發現當時居住在臺灣的傳教士，可謂是透過此一刊物，向英國基督徒讀者進行「轉譯」（transition），並以此造就出一個融貫基督信仰、旅行探險與異文化風俗的「福爾摩沙」；而「轉譯」的素材來源，多以實際生活經驗為主，且不乏醫療、教育與社會救助等等工作面向。至於形式上則以文字描述居多，搭配圖像或是照片為輔。[8]

　　經由《使信月刊》的報導與宣傳功能，位處遠東傳教區域的臺灣，不再是英國讀者眼中的不知名的蠻荒之境，特別是經由英國長老教會傳教士等先鋒「開拓」下，成為一個值得重新以基督信仰，期待改革進步的新世界，使得母會以及英國本土的基督徒讀者，能夠持續關注臺灣民眾的屬靈情形。不僅如此，就連派駐到其他世界各地的傳教士們，也能從《使信月刊》刊登的報導，反思不同區域之間的事工經營與具體成效。[9] 下文將透過《使信月刊》的性質與特色，解釋遠

8　媒體理論學者麥克魯漢（Herbert Marshall McLuhan, 1911-1980）指出：「媒體能把經驗逐譯成新的形式，就這股力量而言，所有媒體都是積極活躍的隱喻。……利用翻譯的手段，將立即的感官經驗轉化成有聲的象徵符號，於是一整個世界都可以在任何時刻，瞬間地召出、擷取。」麥克魯漢（Marshall McLuhan），《認識媒體：人的延伸》（*Understanding Media: The Extensions of Man*），鄭明萱譯（臺北：貓頭鷹出版，2006），頁92-93。

9　1913年《使信月刊》轉載一則向傳教士邀稿的訊息，內容是關於《宣教：國際評論》（*International Review of Missions*）的編輯，徵求海外傳教士的來信，希望他們能夠提供目前遭遇最迫切的問題，並列舉

赴海外的傳教士，除了傳教使命之外，更身兼報導者的宣傳角色。

（一）《使信月刊》的性質與特色

　　《使信月刊》自十九世紀中葉創刊以來，發行時間長達百年之久，歷經過二次大戰的戰火，直至第二次世界大戰結束後正式停刊。長年來，該刊刊名歷經多次沿革，但仍維持月刊發行的形式，其刊名沿革如下。

表 1 《使信月刊》名稱沿革

年代	《使信月刊》名稱
1845-1867	*The English Presbyterian Church*
1868-1878	*Messenger and Missionary Record of the Presbyterian Church of England*
1881-1884	*Outlook*
1884-1885	*Presbyterian*
1885-1891	*Presbyterian Messenger*
1891-1906	*Presbyterian*
1906-1907	*Monthly Messenger of the Presbyterian Church in England*
1908-1947	*Presbyterian Messenger*

資料來源：賴永祥，《教會史話》第一輯（臺南：人光出版社，1990），頁 248。

　　根據該刊刊載的報導，大致上多與英國國內或是海外的基督教動態密切相關，多元題材也反映當時英國基督徒讀者的閱讀興趣。據統

幾個值得的討論方向：一則，向非基督徒民眾宣傳福音的做法；二則，解釋基督徒理想對個人及社會的影響，以及前者與社會習俗的關係；三則，教會在傳教區域的指導與組織；四則，建立學校或是醫院；最後，來自任何層面的困難或困惑等等。"Problems of the Mission Field," *The Messenger* (June 1913), p. 201. 這些討論方向並未針對特定傳教區域，反映出傳教士在海外宣教過程中面臨的實際問題，亦可視為普遍性的現象。

計，《使信月刊》在1908年前半年的流通情形，達一個月四千本以上的銷售量。[10] 以1913年《使信月刊》的廣告為例，其介紹該刊專欄特色時，區分成如下幾種類別：包括「宗教儀式實踐、藝術與圖像訊息、長老教會的具體事項、文學專欄、個人消息、國內及海外的傳教士動態、正面且有價值的報導……等等」，內容多涉及基督教事工在英國社會的實踐情形。[11] 此外，培育英國兒童靈命，亦成為該刊專欄的訴求之一，顯見《使信月刊》的編輯亦積極開闢兒童讀者群。[12]

《使信月刊》的報導題材中，亦包括傳教士應奉行的準則與任務，以及前往海外生活的準備事項等等。[13] 此外，伴隨著十九世紀英國福音運動的浪潮，造就不少知名傳教士，相關報導亦出現在《使信月刊》當中。例如，出身劍橋大學的史達德（C. T. Studd）亦是其中之一。[14]

透過規模盛大的集會與活動，亦是凝聚英國基督徒關注海外傳教工場的做法之一。1925年，曼徹斯特召開「學生基督徒運動」（The Student Christian Movement）大會，會議長達六日。《使信月刊》亦

---

10 "The Circulation of the Messenger," *The Messenger* (June 1908), p. 200.

11 "The Presbyterian Messenger in 1914," *The Messenger* (Nov.1913), pp. 346-347.

12 以兒童為主體的報導，其訴求大致可以區分成兩類：一種是以兒童的靈性教育為主："Children's Portion," *The Messenger* (1896), p. 41; "Children's Missionary Meeting," *The Messenger* (May 1904), p. 149; "For the Children: Heaven, the Work of Little Hands," *The Messenger* (July 1908), p. 227; "The Summons of the Children," *The Messenger* (July 1908), pp. 249-250; "For the Children: Wings or No Wings," *The Messenger* (Jan. 1909), p. 10; Miss E. Gallienne Robin, "For the Children: The King's Army," *The Messenger* (Feb. 1909), p. 48; "Home Religion: Teaching the Children to pray," *The Messenger* (July 1911), p. 238; "Work Among Children," *The Messenger* (Sep. 1917), p. 206; "Edinburgh House Press Publications for Children," *The Messenger* (Dec. 1927), p. 208. 另一種則是引導兒童關注海外傳教區域的情形："Our Own Missions- Formosa to be the Children's Mission," *The Messenger* (Mar. 1896), p. 105; "Home and Field Notes: A Children 's Missionary Exhibition," *The Messenger* (Mar. 1909), p. 102; "Mission Books-Children of Africa and Arabia," *The Messenger* (July 1910), p. 260; "Missionary Books: Children of Japan," *The Messenger* (Jan. 1911), p. 28; "Miscellaneous- Missionary Presents for Children," *The Messenger* (Dec. 1925), p. 230.

13 《使信月刊》亦曾宣傳利文斯頓學院（Livingston College）提供實用醫療保健課程，可供傳教士、探險者、公職人員，或者其他計畫準備前往熱帶國家者進修。"Preservation of Health in Tropical Climates," *The Messenger* (May 1913), p. 94; "Livingstone College," *The Messenger* (June 1914), p. 196.

14 1885年史達德連同其他六位成員，由內地會（China Inland Mission）遣往中國，此即著名的「劍橋七傑」（The Cambridge Seven）。史達德強調讓福音傳遍世界是英國的責任，並闡述傳教士的工作及使命，參見"Mr. C. T. Studd," *The Messenger* (July 1908), p. 244.

特別報導，擁有多年在臺宣教經驗的梅監霧牧師（Rev. Campbell Moody, 1865-1940）等人，亦前往曼徹斯特會場發表演講，向學生們呼籲臺灣與中國的屬靈需求，藉此吸引更多基督徒青年男女投身海外宣教事業。[15]

藉由海外傳教士在《使信月刊》報導上描述親身經歷，或是親自向英國本土觀眾演講宣傳海外傳教工場的情況，有助於更多的英國基督徒認識，並且關注這些在海外奉獻的傳教士及其成果；同時也讓國內更多物力與人力，匯聚到海外宣教工場。

（二）《使信月刊》的宣傳功能與海外傳教事工的推廣

前述指出，為了吸引英國讀者的目光，並響應英國長老會在海外的福音事業，《使信月刊》提供一個宛如訊息交流的平台，讓更多的海外傳教士，可以向英國讀者宣傳與分享基督教信仰在異文化環境中的進展情形。因此，英國長老會莫不將《使信月刊》視為是宣傳事工的重要媒介。關於該刊的報導類型及宣傳要點，下文列舉數例說明之。

首先，宣傳英國長老教會在臺宣教的進展，並提供傳教士一個投書寫作的園地，介紹與傳教相關的活動或著述。[16] 梅監霧牧師不只是親身向英國的基督徒講解臺灣的傳教情形之外；亦經常投書《使信月刊》，籲請更多人協助海外傳教工場，好讓異教徒早日完成自立的目標。[17] 此外，更有人撰文呼籲《使信月刊》的讀者，協助在英國籌設

---

15 據《使信月刊》報導，此一深具國際性的「學生基督徒運動」，創始自1895年，其宗旨是為招募具理想性且有熱忱的青年男女，一同致力於神國事工；成員來自全球40多個國家，2,700所大專院校，約有25萬名學生。該年度與會者，計有1,600名來自不同國家的青年男女，齊聚一堂共同關注基督教會的普世任務，英國長老教會成員自是身列其中。Rev. James Adamson, "The Student Christian Movement-Great Conference at Manchester," *The Messenger* (Feb. 1925), p. 281. 筆者按：梅牧師因熱病發作，於1924年返英療養，返英期間出版多部著作，至1931年因健康關係而退休。鄭仰恩，〈英國乞丐？臺灣保羅？——梅監霧牧師小傳〉，《新使者》，第60期（2000年10月），頁25-26。

16 英國長老教會海外宣教委員會祕書麥菲爾（W. M. Macphail），巡視東亞傳教區域期間，特地前來參加福爾摩沙大會的經過，向讀者宣傳英國長老教會長期在臺灣福音耕耘情形。Rev. W. M. Macphail, "A Visit to the Mission Field," *The Messenger* (May 1913), pp. 89-90.

17 Rev. Campbell N. Moody, "The End of Foreign Missions," *The Messenger* (Dec. 1927), pp. 209-210.

「傳教士圖書館」，希望讓更多人能夠清楚地理解傳教士在海外的需求，是故，英國長老會著手蒐集有關傳教領域的書籍，期使更多民眾透過圖書館的館藏，涉獵傳教領域的著作，包括「事實、方法、成就以及傳教工作的問題等等」。[18] 由此可知，透過知識的力量，期待英國基督徒能夠激發奉獻熱忱，支持傳教推展；此點也展現英國長老會對海外工場的重視程度，畢竟光是透過傳教士進行不定期的演說，能夠激起的影響有限。

其次，運用圖像、照片的宣傳力量，向英國民眾傳達傳教士在海外的具體活動。傳教士除了透過寫作，增加海外傳教事工在《使信月刊》版面上的能見度外；亦經常運用新的攝影技術，來記錄並呈現海外傳教生活實況。

事實上，自十九世紀晚期以來，透過照相技術的應用，使得《使信月刊》刊登不少珍貴的歷史照片。此法不但取代過去的圖繪方式，更寫實地再現福音在異地傳播的艱辛過程；同時也為傳教區域，保留許多歷史影像。例如，《使信月刊》中保存不少二十世紀前期臺灣的中、南部風土景象，呈現出當時傳教士所接觸到的臺灣民眾生活，甚至包括當時臺灣社會遭逢天災的景象。[19]

此外，英國長老會亦運用新的影像技術，將傳教士在海外拍攝的景象，製作成幻燈片擇地放映。透過此一技術，英國民眾不只是藉由文字描述；亦可搭配新的影像技術，來認識臺灣風土。遂有醫療傳教士在二十世紀初期，將其在臺的傳教影像製成幻燈片後，在英國幾大城市，如利物浦、新堡等地巡迴放映；《使信月刊》也會不定期公告

18 George L. Brander, "The Missionary Library," *The Messenger* (Feb. 1923), p. 332.

19 《使信月刊》中，保存不少日治時期臺灣社會的老照片，除了介紹臺灣的景觀與物產，以及教友的活動之外，亦有助於我們觀察相關的傳教細節。諸如在鄉間傳教的傳教士除了步行之外，他們在當時可使用的交通工具，遠比現在所能想像為多。馬雅各曾撰文描述，在二十世紀初期，從臺南到安平，四英里長的距離中可見的交通工具：包括馬車、推車、轎子、黃包車、騎馬、到安平乘船、牛車等等。J. L. Maxwell and B. S. Lond, "Travelling in Formosa," *The Monthly Messenger* (Feb. 1904), pp. 40-43. 此外，透過照片可以留意，傳教士在《使信月刊》中選取出什麼樣的角度，讓臺灣「如實地」顯影。

幻燈片放映地點及演講訊息，歡迎有興趣的民眾參加。[20]

其三，為了培育新的基督徒讀者群，一同關心福音在海外的發展，兒童讀者群也成為《使信月刊》關注的對象之一。至少在十九世紀末葉的《使信月刊》中，已出現鼓勵英國兒童關注臺灣傳教事務的訊息。隨著英國長老會傳教士在臺灣的步履，英國兒童也曾被鼓勵去留心此地的福音進展。例如，青年教育委員會（Instruction of Youth Committee）提議，在兒童主日學的課程主題中，增設關於福爾摩沙的部分；此外，《使信月刊》的編輯，亦曾發動英國兒童為臺灣民眾募書；或是呼籲英國兒童捐款支持北港教會的籌建等等。[21]

透過《使信月刊》作為媒介，海外傳教委員會與傳教士，共同建構一個「翻譯異文化」的文本空間，而英國的兒童讀者，顯然也被邀請進入這個閱讀與想像的連結中。[22] 於是，以臺灣為主體的青少年讀物也應運而生，向英國兒童介紹臺灣風土與傳教動態。例如，蘭大衛醫師的夫人連瑪玉（Marjorie Landsborough, 1884-1984），在1920、30年代為英國兒童撰述關於福爾摩沙的著作，吸引英國兒童認識臺灣之餘；也為後世留下歷史見證。[23]

---

20 "Mission Lantern Slides," *The Messenger* (Nov.1911), p. 369; "Mission Lantern Slides," *The Messenger* (Nov. 1912), p. 335.

21 Rev. Richard Roberts, "Work among the Young – New Plans for Our Sunday Schools," *The Messenger* (Jan. 1912), p. 5; "Mission Collecting Books," *The Messenger* (Feb. 1912), p. 53; "Formosa: Mission Notes – The Chianghoa Gospel Tent," *The Messenger* (Oct. 1913), p. 326; Rev. Richard Roberts, "Work among the Young – New Plans for Our Sunday Schools," *The Messenger* (Jan. 1912), p. 5.

22 "Formosa to be the Children's Mission," *The Messenger* (1896), p. 105. 梅監霧牧師亦撰文呼應此說，重申「讓福爾摩沙成為兒童的傳教區域」。"Young People's Missionary Meeting – Mr. Campbell Moody," *The Messenger* (June 1901), p. 171.

23 一般論及蘭大衛、蘭大弼（David Landsborough Ⅳ, 1914-2010）父子二人的醫療奉獻時，偶會介紹連瑪玉女士「切膚之愛」的事蹟，卻少著墨在連瑪玉扮演傳教、母親與作家的多元角色上。在連瑪玉的著作中，除了描述臺灣的生活景象，並側寫臺灣基督徒的生活故事之外，亦反映出當時在臺的外籍傳教士，對於日本政府治臺政策的評價。例如，日本政府為貫徹其理蕃政策，而大力推行的吳鳳「殺身成仁」的故事。當時臺灣民眾立廟祭祀吳鳳，以及乩童治病行為，亦呈現在其書中。此外，連瑪玉還提到蘭大衛夫婦倆親訪霧社後，對於日人治理原住民政策的印象。Marjorie Landsborough, "Gaw Hong," *Stories from Formosa* (Presbyterian Church of England, 1924), pp. 223-237. 相隔數年卻爆發霧社事件。此外，馬雅各亦曾為英國兒童讀者撰述在臺佈教之經過，作為主日學的教材。參見 Dr. James L. Maxwell, "Missionary Letters to the Boys and Girls of the Church- Formosa," *Sunday Schools Lesson for March 24,1912*, Presbyterian Church of England Foreign Missions Archives (PCEFM)/ H-10/ No.1938.

英國長老會運用《使信月刊》的版面，向英國讀者介紹海外傳教的具體進度，此舉不但有助於英國讀者拓展其眼界，從閱讀經驗中，汲取傳教士在海外工場的相關知識訊息；進而提升宣教區域在讀者心中的能見度，連帶引起讀者關注海外宣教工場的需求。[24]

至於讀者們對於英國長老教會在海外傳教事業的響應情形，同樣也可從《使信月刊》的報導中獲得印證，包括透過捐款、供應物資，或是直接投身傳教行列等等。就臺灣作為一個傳教區域，英國讀者願意以行動表示支持，包括捐贈書籍畫報、醫療藥品，或是捐款等等。[25]

根據1925年英國長老會勸募的建築基金，就「海外傳教委員會」鎖定的區域而言，是以臺南、汕頭、孟加拉與印度等地區為主；建築項目則列有傳教人員的住所、醫院、學校與其他設施等等，光是興建臺南長老教學校（即現今的長榮中學）校舍的經費，已達1,350英鎊。[26] 除了建築用的經費之外，海外傳教委員會亦懇請母會協助，彌補收入赤字，亦期能提高傳教士子女的教育補助。[27]

為了刺激英國民眾捐款，增加海外傳教基金的收入，《使信月刊》不定期公布傳教基金總額。例如，1913年11月份的《使信月刊》，公布近三年的基金款項。[28] 抑或列舉英國其他差會的年度收入，包括內地會（China Inland Mission）、或是倫敦會（London Missionary Society）的情況。推其用意，目的或與刺激讀者捐款有關。[29]

---

24 安彼得醫師（Dr. Peter Anderson）介紹二十世紀初高雄醫館的病床設備是以竹床為主。且因夏天之際將與蘭大衛醫師前往臺南，基於人手不足，故高雄醫館暫不開放，希望英國長老教會能再派傳教士前來協助醫療工作。"Takow Hosipital," *The Messenger* (Oct. 1908), p. 352.

25 《使信月刊》向讀者宣傳，日本當局願意讓捐贈給教會醫院的物品，予以免除關稅的優惠；呼籲讀者以實際行動響應。"Gifts for Formosa," *The Messenger* (Dec. 1913), p. 384; "Goods and Gifts for Formosa," *The Messenger* (Mar. 1914), p. 90. 除了藥品之外，英國讀者亦捐贈書籍、畫報給臺南新樓醫院，提供院內的病人翻閱。"The Tainanfu Hospital: Difficulties," *The Messenger* (Aug. 1900), p. 212.

26 "United Missionary Building Fund – Schedule of Buildings Urgently Required," *The Messenger* (Feb. 1925), p. 284.

27 Duncan Macgregor, "The Foreign Mission- Pressing Needs," *The Messenger* (May 1925), p. 381.

28 "Home and Field Notes – The Mission Fund," *The Messenger* (Nov. 1913), p. 351.

29 經《使信月刊》報導，內地會在1911年的收入達63,000英鎊，其中還包含來自美國與澳洲的捐助。相較

表 2 英國長老教會海外傳教基金款項

年份	月份	基金總額
1913 年	1-9 月	5,878 英鎊
1912 年	1-9 月	5,844 英鎊
1911 年	1-9 月	6,577 英鎊

資料來源：*The Messenger* (Nov. 1913), p. 351.

　　總之，透過《使信月刊》的報導，體現英國長老會在國內的發展方針，不少來自海外的宣教訊息，更是清楚呈現基督福音在異文化環境中的扎根過程。憑藉此一刊物的傳播功能，使得當時英國的基督徒讀者可以透過閱讀，一同見證臺灣的福音事蹟，包括1895年中日戰爭以降，關於傳教士眼中所見的臺灣的信仰、經濟、社會、治安等相關情形，以及當時傳教士實踐其傳教使命的社會關懷面向。[30] 然而，當時駐臺的傳教士採取什麼樣的宣傳策略，以便將其耕耘的社會關懷事工，更清楚地傳遞給英國讀者？與醫療相關的報導，又將如何證實福音的重要性？

三、宣揚福音‧改良社會──傳教士視角下的社會關懷事工

　　根據《使信月刊》的報導，撰文向英國母會以及讀者呈報傳教動態，成為派駐海外的傳教士的職責之一。不過，擷取異文化生活經驗，仍須考慮到何為重要，且易於引發英國讀者的共鳴？換言之，身

之下，1911年1至9月，英國長老教會海外傳教基金總額為6,577英鎊。"China and the Gospel," *The Messenger* (Dec. 1912), p. 369; "Home and Field Notes – The Mission Fund," *The Messenger* (Nov. 1913), pp. 351-352.

30 《使信月刊》提供不少涉及日本治臺政策的評論。諸如向英國讀者描述，日本政府在臺的壟斷事業，包括鐵路、鹽、鴉片與樟腦等等。據1909年《使信月刊》的報導，樟腦貿易為日本殖民政權賺入一年30萬英鎊的收益。"Formosa Camphor," *The Messenger* (Aug. 1909), p. 296.

兼報導者的傳教士，固然以傳教為宗旨，但其擇別報導題材的立場，以及當時英國讀者看待海外傳教事工的閱讀興趣，亦值得留意。十九世紀以來英國基督徒理解福音事業在海外傳播的角度之一，乃是以社會進步的論調，來看待傳教士在非基督教地區的事業，並視其為有助於改善當地社會秩序。[31]

透過社會進步意識，來關注傳教士在海外實踐的具體成效，包括引導民眾接受福音，進而改善生活，打造一個信奉基督教的靈性生活與社會環境，是當時英國社會普遍接受的論調。值此，傳教刊物中的報導內容，遂提供讀者們用來印證基督福音的題材。然而，當臺灣被納入英國長老會的海外傳教事業之一環時，傳教士亦須透過此一以社會進步為主的報導框架，來描繪臺灣民眾及其生活。[32]《使信月刊》固然為吾人保存了十九至二十世紀中葉以前的臺灣生活片段，但報導內容中涉及的觀點及其解釋，則呈現出傳教士帶有信仰觀點的報導策略，特別是傳教士對於異文化社會持有的關懷立場，及其報導時的側重方向。

《使信月刊》報導臺灣的部分比例有限，不過題材五花八門，本文無法一一兼論，但將選取幾種題材，包括與福音進展有關、傳教士的奉獻以及醫療工作的情形等，檢視傳教士在臺實踐攸關社會進步的社會關懷面向，藉此指陳傳教士報導背後具備的社會進步論調。此外，儘管醫療事工只是諸多傳教事業中的一環，在醫療傳教士的筆下，福音與醫療之間具有密不可分的關聯性，亦成為二十世紀前期《使信月刊》介紹臺灣醫館貢獻的主調。[33]

---

31 "Missions Promoting A New Social Order," *The Messenger* (Aug. 1899), p. 219.

32 其中有不少涉及臺灣的報導，直接以「進步」為題。"Formosa: Progress," *The Messenger* (Mar. 1896), p. 100; "Formosa: A Review of Progress," *The Messenger* (Feb. 1905), pp. 43-44; S. W. Carruthers, "Progress in Formosa: on the Takow-Kelung Railway," *The Messenger* (Aug. 1906), pp. 210-211; "Formosa – Progress at Giok-Li," *The Messenger* (Nov. 1918), p. 183; "Progress in Formosa," *The Messenger* (Dec.1921), p. 285.

33 臺南新樓醫館於1900年竣工，相關討論參見臺灣基督長老教會總會歷史委員會主編，《臺灣基督長老教會百年史》（臺南：臺灣基督長老教會，2013年三版），頁109-110。

（一）以福音觀點「再現」福爾摩沙

自十九世紀中葉以降，福爾摩沙島上福音傳佈的經過，開始躍上《使信月刊》的版面後，使得這座島嶼逐漸成為英國讀者關注的新興傳教區域，該刊也不定期宣傳傳教士的傳教進展。

為了標榜臺灣作為一個宣教工場的重要性，《使信月刊》的報導，提供諸多素材，有助於將臺灣建構成一個重要的傳教工場，便於向讀者描繪傳教士在海外經營福音事工的進展，及其具福音視域的生活見聞。

1. 報導策略之一：傳教士在臺生活紀實

關於英國長老教會傳教士長年耕耘臺灣中、南部的福音進展，可從《使信月刊》的相關報導中獲得例證，無論是涉及教育、慈善或是醫療等面向，其報導基調多與改善臺灣社會有關。1923 年，一篇介紹遠東傳教工作的文章，用有限的報導篇幅，突顯出臺灣的醫療需求與醫療傳教士在臺灣經營的成果，包括醫療傳教士在彰化醫館（今彰化基督教醫院前身）與臺南醫館的耕耘，讓英國讀者對照當時中、南部兩地醫館的經營情況。[34]

臺灣的報導雖多與傳教訊息相關，但題材包羅萬象，舉凡傳教士抵臺、婚配、出版著作、傳教見聞，甚至是辭世消息，皆可從中獲

---

34 該文主要介紹檳城、新加坡、廈門與臺灣等地，值得注意的是，臺灣的報導篇幅較其他地區為多。就報導者搭乘火車所見的臺灣景象，是一個較中國開化，且鄉間種植大量稻米的豐饒之地。不過，以彰化醫館而言，醫館設備老舊有待修繕，儘管目前已規劃在市郊外籌建新的醫館，但彰化醫館卻面臨專業人手不足的問題，尤其是當醫館內護士離職結婚後，讓缺乏專業護士協助的蘭大衛醫師，工作更顯疲累；相較之下，臺南醫館經由馬雅各二世（Dr. James Laidlaw Maxwell Jr., 1873-1951）主事與周惠憐醫師（Percy Cheal）的協助下，不僅館內設備汰舊更新，復有兩名能幹的本地護士以及一些本地助手，讓當地病人能夠得到妥善照顧。"Our Work in the Far East," *The Messenger* (Feb. 1923), p. 330. 關於蘭大衛在臺期間行醫的器物、照片與文件記錄，可以透過彰化基督教醫院院史館的典藏進行深入研究。彰化基督教醫院院史館網站：http://www2.cch.org.tw/history/page.aspx?oid=2（檢索日期：2013/9/28）。此外，1923 年《使信月刊》公告馬雅各醫師辭職的消息，感謝他在臺南醫館服務將近二十三年期間，為臺南醫館奠定諸多現代化基礎；並為其預備前往上海就任中國醫療傳教士協會（China Medical Missionary Association）擔任執行祕書一事祝賀。"Missionary Notes- Dr. Maxwell," *The Messenger* (July 1923), p. 68.

悉，有助於英國讀者從基督教的視野來理解臺灣的風土民情。[35] 例如，華森夫婦（Mr. and Mrs. Watson）曾在彰化地區傳教兩個月，藉此比較基督徒村落與非基督徒村落間的差異。[36] 此外，巴克禮夫人（Mrs. Barclay, 1858-1909）身為第一位抵達臺灣東部的英國婦女，同時也是巴克禮的妻子，曾解釋臺灣的風俗，包括鄉間社會買賣女嬰的情形，以及「童養媳」處境等等；亦曾透過《使信月刊》，發表其獨自在南部鄉間施藥治病，以此說服婦女信主的經過。[37]

奉行街頭傳教的梅監霧牧師，經常深入鄉里傳道，以敲鑼打鼓的方式，吸引臺灣民眾前來聆聽福音，一般民眾也能夠透過梅牧師的講道，理解基督教義的良善之處，且樂於與之交往。[38] 另一方面，梅牧師亦經常呼籲讀者捐款籌建教會，積極響應英國長老教會在臺灣的建設，讓更多臺灣民眾聆聽福音。[39]

不過，看似如實介紹其在遠東傳教工場的見聞，也可視為是利用報導版面，向英國讀者強調，醫療傳教士在臺灣經營醫館的成效與困難，除了提升醫療品質的需求，包括醫療設備更新、專業護理人手、擴建醫館規模等等，這些都是有待解決的要項；亦讓讀者們認識臺灣社會亟待改善的問題，期待更多英國基督徒伸出援手響應經費與人手

---

35 報導中經常可見傳教士前往遠東的訊息，包括汕頭、廈門、臺灣等地，例如，連瑪玉女士（Miss Majorie Learner），與馬雅各醫師夫婦一同抵臺。"Our Missions in the Far East," *The Messenger* (Nov. 1909), p. 332. 此外，隨著傳教士的步伐，亦見識深富在地特色的情景。曾有傳教士前往高雄南部的漁村宣教，適逢該村漁民於上午捕獲一頭鯨魚，但四處卻瀰漫陣陣惡臭。報導還提到漁民捕鯨方法，及當地漁獲，包括成堆的新鮮鯊魚。"Formosa: A Whaling Station," *The Messenger* (April 1915), p. 140.

36 "Chianghoa," *The Messenger* (Sep. 1907), pp. 249-250.

37 "Itinerating in Formosa," *The Messenger* (Sep. 1898), pp. 235-238; "Formosa: Among the Southern Stations," *The Messenger* (Nov. 1902), pp. 288-290. 關於巴克禮夫人辭世的消息，當年亦公布在《使信月刊》上。"Mrs. Barclay," *The Messenger* (Sep. 1909), p. 332.

38 梅監霧牧師不忘打趣地描述：彰化民眾甚至疑惑，蘇格蘭人也說中文？然而，對於梅牧師而言，傳教難題並不在語言溝通上，而是一般臺灣民眾其實無法輕易接受罪與救贖的觀念，呼籲應該擺脫對異教徒所持有的刻板印象，並重新反思傳教方法。相關討論參見 Kazue Mino, "Campbell N. Moody's Reflections on the Christian Mission," *International Bulletin of Missionary Research* Vol. 38, No. 3 (July 2014), pp. 135-138.

39 Campbell Moody, "Chianghoa: 'I Cannot Take it in'," *The Messenger* (Feb. 1906), p. 44; "Rev. Campbell N. Moody, M. A.," *The Messenger* (July 1907), pp. 196-197; "Formosa: Mission Notes – The Chianghoa Gospel Tent," *The Messenger* (Oct. 1913), p. 326. 此外，梅牧師亦出版著作，描述福爾摩沙傳教經過，《使信月刊》刊登書介。"Missionary Books – The Heathen Heart," *The Messenger* (Sep. 1908), p. 316.

不足的問題。

　　無論是聚焦在臺灣島內各地的具體傳教事工，或是從英國長老教會在遠東的傳教佈局檢視臺灣，《使信月刊》的編輯、撰文者與身處海外的傳教士，無非希望透過訊息的流通，讓英國讀者能夠獲悉傳教士在臺灣面臨的需求與處境。

　　例如，在臺南醫館服務的安彼得醫師（Dr. Peter Anderson）及其夫人，為求順利請款20英鎊，為臺南醫館添購100床的蚊帳，遂在《使信月刊》上撰文強調瘧疾乃經由蚊子作為傳播途徑，強調添購蚊帳的必要性，懇請英國讀者捐款添購設備，讓臺灣民眾可以享有更好的醫療資源。[40] 此外，當臺南醫館發生屋頂漏水，安醫師亦透過《使信月刊》，詢問有無任何讀者願意提供省錢的建議，不無間接暗示捐款之意。[41] 由是可知，《使信月刊》乃是在臺傳教士向英國讀者展示其傳教進度與需求的平台，其重要性不可或缺。

2. 報導策略之二：宣揚英國長老會在臺宣教的重要進展

　　1911年冬天，三十位分別隸屬於南部英國長老教會與北部加拿大長老教會的傳教士，首度在臺召開為期三日的聯合會議。該會議的目的，主要探討以適切方法在臺灣建立神的國度。相關報導刊於1912年的《使信月刊》，報導者向讀者強調，臺灣群眾接受福音程度，遠高於其他地區，並期待臺灣的傳教前景。[42]

　　此外，拓展福音傳播對象，亦是備受重視的議題。臺灣群眾被區分為幾大特定群體：包括學有專精的人士，諸如學生、教師、醫生、

40　"The Tainanfu Hospital," *The Messenger* (Feb. 1901), p. 41. 十九世紀英國熱帶醫學的研究成果發現，瘧疾是寄生蟲疾病，且蚊子與瘧疾傳播有關，此一發現過程與印度的英國殖民醫官羅斯（Ronald Ross, 1857-1932）和倫敦的熱帶醫學專家萬巴德（Patrick Manson, 1844-1922）之間的合作有關。參見李尚仁，〈萬巴德、羅斯與十九世紀末英國熱帶醫學研究的物質文化〉，《新史學》17: 4（2006年12月），頁145-194。安彼得提出兩點看法兼顧醫療與傳教的雙重任務，一則，以限制病人數目為前提，由醫師個別向病人談道；訓練本地駐守，使其成為本地的醫療傳教士。參見魏外揚，〈基督教在臺早期的醫療宣教〉，收錄於林治平主編，《基督教與臺灣》，頁284-285。

41　"The Tainan Hospital," *The Messenger* (Dec. 1908), p. 418. 其用意或有引導英國讀者關注並募款之意圖。

42　"Formosa: A Union conference," *The Messenger* (April 1912), p. 124.

銀行與公司行員等，以及，推估約有12,000名的高山族，分別被視為是有待深耕的兩大群體。多數群眾則介於這兩個群體之間，如農夫、漁民、郵差、警察、商人、木匠、泥水匠、工人等等，傳教士認為他們對福音更保有開放態度，顯示福音工作大有可為。[43]

隔年，遂於彰化舉行第二次聯合會議。英國讀者可再度從《使信月刊》的報導中，獲悉該次會議的討論，當時英國長老教會與加拿大教會在臺經營的成果相當豐碩，建立神學院、男校、女校與醫院等等，皆證明分駐南北的傳教士們，無分差會，皆共同致力於教育與醫療事業，期能提升臺灣民眾的靈性生活。[44] 不僅如此，傳教士對於臺灣這個傳教工場的前景普遍持有樂觀態度，這點也可從《使信月刊》當時的前後報導中，得其梗概。

原則上，派駐臺灣的英國長老教會傳教士，每四年會全面調查全臺出席教會禮拜的人數（見表3、4）。

對照表3、4所示，統計數據與項目，當是為了讓英國母會與讀者，更確切了解臺灣民眾信主人數增長情形。例如，1923年臺灣基督徒總數增長至29,560人，相較於1918年統計的基督徒為28,507人，反映全臺基督徒人數呈現出增長趨勢，相距五年共增加1,053人。此外，據統計，當時臺灣基督徒人口總數中，幾乎有三分之一的人口具備羅馬拼音字讀寫的能力。總結上述，不具名的撰文者，乃將

表3 1898年至1914年臺灣民眾參與週日禮拜儀式的人數

	1898年	1902年	1906年	1910年	1914年
上午出席人數	3,969	5,885	6,496	6,905	9,033
下午出席人數	3,577	5,567	6,435	6,662	8,766
受洗兒童人數	1,368	1,808	2,211	2,901	3,924

資料來源："Census of Formosa Mission Church," *The Messenger* (Nov. 1914), p. 365.

---

43 "Formosa: A Union conference," *The Messenger* (April 1912), pp. 125-126.
44 "The Synod of Formosa," *The Messenger* (Jan. 1913), pp. 20-21.

表 4 1923 年臺灣民眾參與週日禮拜的人數及其他統計數據

統計項目	臺灣民眾人數
上午出席人數	14,166 位
下午出席人數	11,678 位
基督徒總數	29,560 位
羅馬拼音字讀者	9,126 位
漢字讀者	1,844 位

資料來源："Census of Church Attendance in Formosa," *The Messenger* (Mar. 1924), p. 306.

福音在臺灣的發展，視為是領先中國教會之冠。[45]

　　此外，駐臺的傳教士亦透過《使信月刊》，解釋及評論日本的治臺政策，包括鴉片專賣及其衍生的走私問題等等；以及日人統治對於教會事業的影響。[46] 事實上，從諸多關於臺灣的訊息中，不少標題揭示當時傳教士對於臺灣社會的具體關懷面向，舉凡解決醫療需求、改善教育環境以及生活條件等等；最重要者，莫過於提升臺灣民眾的靈命。

---

45 "Census of Church Attendance in Formosa," *The Messenger* (Mar. 1924), p. 306.
46 據二十世紀初期的《使信月刊》顯示，日本殖民政府當時對於基督教，持相對寬容的態度，而且日本官員對臺灣基督徒的印象及信任，普遍高過非教徒。此外，諸如治安的改善、禁止纏足以及島內交通設施的進步等等，皆贏得馬雅各、梅監霧與蘭大衛等人稱許。"Rev. Campbell N. Moody, M. A.," *The Messenger* (July 1907), pp. 196-197; "Chianghoa Hospital," *The Messenger* (Oct. 1906), p. 277. 相對而言，傳教士也不吝評論日本的統治政策。例如，在臺灣吸食鴉片者須領有牌照，且不得隨意轉賣牌照。據日本政府統計數字，臺灣登記有案的抽鴉片人口，自1900年至1908年，呈現逐年下降趨勢。"Under the Japanese Flag," *The Messenger* (Mar. 1904), p. 74. 不過，傳教士卻發現隱藏在數字統計下的非法行為。因為領有牌照的人，會將鴉片私下轉賣給煙行；甚至走私大陸的情況亦有之，導致售出的總值並未減少。也有鴉片吸食者改由購買自印度進口的鴉片，價格甚至比原本從中國進口的鴉片更昂貴。"Formosa-After Fifty Years," *The Messenger* (Aug. 1916), pp. 252-253; "Opium Smoking in Formosa," *The Messenger* (Aug. 1909), p. 296. 事實上，日本當局的部分政策的確牽制教會事業的權益。1899年總督府醫學校創立後，日人拒發執照給教會醫院系統培育的醫學生。換句話說，學生必須通過總督府醫學校的訓練始能領有執照；不僅如此，日人廣設學校的作法，也讓不少早先在鄉間辦學的教會學校受到衝擊。此外，教會租地契約不得超過一百年；1902年《使信月刊》的報導指出，日本當局在臺南執行的開路計畫，影響到神學院的建地。"Tainan High School," *The Messenger* (Jan. 1902), p. 15; "Under the Japanese Flag," *The Messenger* (Mar. 1904), p. 74; Formosa-Tainan Hospital Chapel," *The Messenger* (April 1902), p. 105.

身兼報導者角色的傳教士，藉《使信月刊》作為宣傳媒介，向英國讀者解釋其事工的重要性，並利用有限的報導篇幅，展現社會關懷與福音傳播的結合。下文欲進一步聚焦在醫療報導上，凡是涉及臺灣醫館的運作，及病人形象描繪的報導，均有助於解釋傳教士如何運用報刊作為宣傳媒介，強化醫療與福音結合的重要性。

（二）疾病與福音的結合：從醫療相關報導看傳教士在臺實踐的福音事工

早期臺灣中、南部一帶，不時出現傳染病，進而影響民眾生活。日本政府為了消除臺南當地的流行疾病，作法之一則是強制清潔，包括清洗屋舍，但外國人則不在此強制命令的規範內。[47] 於是，關於疾病問題與醫療需求，亦成為《使信月刊》介紹臺灣的常見主題。醫療傳教士因堅信醫療工作，有助於改善當地民眾對於基督教的觀感，遂經常描述醫療傳教士與當地民眾互動的情形，並且將他們的醫療工作與經驗公布在《使信月刊》上，期待英國讀者也能從報導內容，一同見證醫館對於福傳的影響。至於相關的疾病問題與民眾就診情形，亦可從中取得線索。

1911年抵臺的戴仁壽醫師（Dr. George Gushue-Taylor, 1883-1954），曾公布一份有關其在臺南新樓醫館的醫療相關數據（見下表）。[48] 當時抵臺時間不過年餘的戴仁壽，相當關注臺灣南部的疾病問題，並透過《使信月刊》，公布1912年7月至9月間，臺南醫館的診療情形。其中，患有眼疾的病人，有相當高的比例已近全盲；甚至

---

[47] 由於日本警察的處置相當嚴厲，一旦不合規定，動輒毀壞民眾的家當，但此舉易於引發民眾不滿情緒。"Formosa – The Plague," *The Messenger* (Jan. 1900), p. 16; "Takow, Formosa," *The Messenger* (June 1908) , p. 204. 關於日本總督府的防疫調查、措施與衛生活動，參見范燕秋，〈新醫學在臺灣的實踐（1898-1906）〉，收錄於李尚仁主編，《帝國與現代醫學》（臺北：聯經，2008），頁28-46。

[48] 因創立「樂山園痲瘋療養院」而聞名於臺灣醫學史的戴仁壽醫師，其相關討論參見王文基，〈痲病園裡的異鄉人：戴仁壽與臺灣醫療宣教〉，收錄於林富士主編，《宗教與醫療》（臺北：聯經，2011），頁433-451。

表 5 臺南新樓醫館醫療工作紀錄

醫療工作類型	人數統計
門診病人（初診與回診）	3,153 人
午後門診	751 人
手術（眼疾與牙疾）	331 人
初次住院病患	514 人
訪視病患	5 人

資料來源：Dr. Gushue-Taylor, "Early Impressions Formosa," *The Messenger* (Jan. 1913), p. 22.

從發病至全盲的速度不到一週。[49]

　　以醫館作為傳播福音的重要中介，戴仁壽不僅強調多數因診治而獲重生的臺灣病患，有助於發揮宣傳福音的影響力；更呼籲英國讀者，一同為臺灣的醫療事工代禱。

　　彰化曾是瘧疾盛行的地區，當時主持彰化醫館的蘭大衛醫師，面對看診壓力，一日多達400位病患；儘管醫務繁重，仍不忘耐心地向病人傳教。[50] 蘭大衛醫師向英國讀者解釋，當時臺灣民眾前來醫館就診的病因，不只是瘧疾，包括心臟與其他器官易位、痲瘋病、眼疾、外傷、骨折、動物造成的傷口，以及戒除鴉片煙癮等等，亦是常見的類型。[51] 為求順利進行難度較高的外科手術，蘭醫師在彰化醫館以及大社醫館看診期間，已使用氯仿（chloroform）為病人麻醉（見下

---

49 針對此一現象，戴氏提出幾點解釋：包括大量灰塵傷到眼角膜所致；或是當地民眾習於採用本地的民俗療法，導致病情惡化。Dr. Gushue-Taylor, "Early Impression Formosa," *The Messenger* (Jan. 1913), p. 22. 關於1912-1916年間臺南醫館男女病患（含門診與住院）的具體數據，可參見"Tainan Hospital Statistics," (Nov. 1912-Oct. 1916), PCEFM/ H-10/ No. 151.

50 連瑪玉轉引蘭大衛醫師的書信指出，「除了禮拜天之外，我每天都要看四百個以上的門診病人。住院病人也超出床位的數量，一百三十個到一百四十人擠在七十五張床上。這些人之中有些是病患的親友前來充當護士，不少病人遠道而來，我只好安排他們住院。」連瑪玉，《蘭醫生》（*Dr. Lan*），劉秀芬譯（彰化：財團法人彰化基督教醫院，2005），頁148-151。

51 Nielson, "Formosa：Work in Taichu (Chianghoa)," *The Messenger* (Dec. 1902), p. 326; "Formosa: Some Medical Notes," *The Messenger* (July 1903), pp. 192-193. 關於彰化醫館的開刀手術及福音相關工作的介紹，參見 *Shoka Christian Hospital, Formosa, 1926-1927*, PCEFM/ H-10/ No. 152-153.

表 6　彰化醫館以及大社醫館相關紀錄

	彰化醫館	大社醫館
住院病人人數	80 人	93 人
外科手術 /（使用氯仿進行麻醉）	130 人 / 11 人	83 人 / 10 人

資料來源："The Chianghoa Hospital," *The Messenger* (Feb. 1901), p. 41.

表）。[52]

1. 從接受醫治到接受福音：《使信月刊》報導中見證的臺灣病人

　　醫療傳教士與臺灣病人間的相處，可謂是建立病人對醫館信任關係的第一步。以醫療傳教士的使命，除了醫治身體疾病之外，最終目的乃是希望能夠引導臺灣民眾領受福音之良善。因此，取得臺灣病患對於教會醫院的信任感，顯得格外重要。[53] 例如，二十世紀初期，中部地區的福音事工，是由梅監霧與蘭大衛合作下，分別透過街頭傳教與醫療工作的進行，讓民眾逐漸打破對西方宗教的偏見；而長年經營彰化醫館的蘭醫師，更是與當地民眾建立起深厚情感。蘭大衛醫師解釋前往鹿港教會禮拜人數逐漸增加的原因。

> 　　據鹿港的傳道人回報，有數位前來教會禮拜的民眾，曾是我之前的病患，而且現在的鹿港民眾，對這個新宗教（基督教）的態度較友善。醫療工作無疑傳播了這點，或許也與治癒鹿港知名商人的傷寒重症密切相關。[54]

52　"The Chianghoa Hospital," *The Messenger* (Feb. 1901), pp. 40-41.

53　楊念群指出，從醫學人類學角度，解釋現代醫療體系中的「委託制度」，與傳統基督教生活方式密切相關，具有隱密的特點，但這也導致西方傳教士在中國遭受誤解，特別是十九世紀教案中，因民眾無法分清教堂與醫院的真實區別，遂將其視為是「神祕空間」，引發不少謠言。楊念群，〈「地方感」與西方醫療空間在中國的確立〉，收錄於李尚仁主編，《帝國與現代醫學》，頁 377-382。

54　David Landborough, "Chianghoa Hospital," *The Messenger* (Oct. 1906), p. 277. 早在十九世紀末，蘭大衛醫師就已經注意到醫館內有不少來自鹿港一帶的病患。此外，隨著鐵路開通，便捷的交通方式，以及病患之間

此外，其夫人連瑪玉女士亦強調，醫館有助於擔負福音工作，可為門診病患安排早禱，甚至連病人候診時也有教理可聽，讓數以千計前來求診的病人，在等待醫治的過程中聆聽福音。除了門診病人之外，彰化醫館亦安排頻繁的病房巡視，也為住院病人安排早、晚禱；平時也針對住院療養的婦女安排課程。[55]

醫療工作不僅吸引中部一帶的在地民眾認識基督教，臺南醫館的傳教士亦提供相關例證，證實醫館是傳播福音的重要中介。一名小販因前往臺南醫館治療眼疾，康復後便改宗基督教；日後，此人無論去到何處，皆致力向當地民眾傳福音。另有案例顯示，臺南醫館內有羅馬拼音字的教學活動，可供病患及病患家屬學習閱讀《聖經》，以此增加福音傳播的機會。[56]

2. 福音觀點詮釋下的醫療與道德

回顧二十世紀前期傳教士在臺灣的醫療活動，特別是透過《使信月刊》提供的報導訊息，可以發現不少在臺的醫療傳教士，忙碌於救治病患的工作之餘；亦經常在《使信月刊》上，描繪其對臺灣病患的觀察，特別是關於非基督徒病患，最後願意接受福音的過程，並採取福音與醫療的結合，來詮釋其落實社會關懷具體實踐面向。然而，關於醫療技術專業層面，卻非其報導中的敘事重點。有趣的是，綜合醫療傳教士提供的報導，內容富有故事性，易於激起讀者的惻隱之心。

1879年抵臺至1910年退休的安彼得醫師，促成醫療工作在南部

的口耳相傳，有助於基督教在彰化地區的傳播，也是促使病人願意前來彰化醫館求診的原因之一。"New Stations in Chianghoa, Formosa," *The Messenger* (May 1899), pp. 126-127; "Chianghoa, Formosa," *The Messenger* (July1901), pp. 190-192.

55 Mrs. David Landsborough, "The Joy of Return," *The Messenger* (Jan. 1920), pp. 5-6. 此外，連瑪玉曾描述日治時期的彰化醫館，不僅人滿為患，更是彰化鎮上最忙碌的地方；兩層樓的建築是當時彰化及中部地區的特殊地景，隨時都有來自各地的病患包圍住蘭醫師。Marjorie Landsborough, *In Beautiful Formosa* (Taipei: Ch'eng-Wen Publishing reprinted, 1972), pp. 98-109.

56 Dr. Gushue-Taylor, "Early Impressions: Formosa," *The Messenger* (Jan. 1913), p. 23; "Tainan Hospital," *The Messenger* (July 1928), p. 94; "Tainan: An Operation and its Results," *The Messenger* (Dec. 1928), p. 205. 該文提到當地一名有錢的老婦，在醫生協助下割除囊腫；其女則在醫館內由女傳教士Miss Barnett教導下，學會以羅馬拼音閱讀《聖經》，而後進入婦女聖經學校就讀。

地區的進展，讓不少在地群眾對教會醫院的醫療措施產生信任感。不僅如此，安彼得醫師透過與病患的互動，遂將其見聞發表在《使信月刊》上。例如，南部有一婦人前來醫院動手術，卻因丈夫吸食鴉片，不事生產，只好典當手鐲飾品支付住院費用；另有一名等待出院的婦女，其夫則因無照吸食鴉片，故遭日本政府判刑；還有少婦因病無法餵養女嬰，寧可讓其出養。但也有一些舉目無親且窮苦的民眾，基於期待康復的心理，表示只要病症能治好，就願意敬拜上帝。[57] 經其觀察，這些非基督徒的病患，其家庭成員或多或少有道德上的問題，特別是吸食鴉片造成生活困頓與無奈。

根據安醫師對於臺灣病人的觀察與詮釋，使讀者接受的訊息，並非以醫治病人的專業知識為主，而是從道德層面去檢視，這些飽受疾病之苦的人們，其背後隱藏的家庭與道德問題，尤以弱勢的臺灣婦女之處境為甚。[58]

經《使信月刊》的報導可知，醫療傳教士詮釋下的「疾病」，不只是病人身上外顯的病徵而已；從基督教的立場，這也反映出異教環境中的道德與生活問題，有待以福音改善之。換言之，一旦傳教士透過醫療措施，助使病患康復後，即有機會以福音開導助其悔罪，藉此改善當地民眾吸食鴉片、賭博等道德問題。

提供西式醫療服務的教會醫院，除了收費低廉，且願意救治窮苦者之外；良好的醫療成效，也成為臺灣病人願意親近基督教信仰的開端，甚至成為福音的見證人。與此同時，醫館也會安排同工，教導病患禱告。彰化醫館的護士與傳道人，會利用每週一次的機會，訪視過去曾至彰化醫館求診的病患，並且邀請他們週日參加教會禮拜前，先提早來閱讀《聖經》。讓這些願意參加教會活動的民眾，學習禱告、

---

57 "The Tainan Hospital," *The Messenger* (Dec. 1908), p. 418; Dr. Anderson, "Takow, Formosa," *The Messenger* (June 1908), p. 203.

58 從性別角度來看，二十世紀初，無論是前往彰化醫館或是大社醫館的病患多屬男性，依照1900上半年的統計數據，共有1,602位病患前往就診，其中有350位是婦女；大社醫館的紀錄則是有1,013位病患，其中有240位是婦女。由於筆者目前尚無法掌握到更多數據，來探討二十世紀前期臺灣女性病患前往教會醫院的情形，期能於未來作進一步分析。"The Chianghoa Hospital," *The Messenger* (Feb. 1901), pp. 40-41.

覆誦《聖經》與讚美詩等等。[59] 基於此，在臺的醫療傳教士透過《使信月刊》進行宣傳時，傾向將醫館的功能，描述成一個可以讓這些因病悔罪的民眾接受福音的環境；此一空間更成為傳教士奉獻其傳教使命的所在。在臺行醫多年的安醫師，更自詡其工作是「為身處異教黑暗地區的男女，帶來光明與希望」。[60]

綜合《使信月刊》中關於臺灣醫館的報導，可知二十世紀前期臺灣中、南部地區由教會醫院所建立起的醫、病關係，包括當時醫療傳教士從專業角度提升臺灣醫療環境的經過、民眾前往就診的病因，以及病患個人的家庭情況及其與地方教會醫院的互動情形等等，皆有助於吾人從該刊報導中，深入認識傳教士對於地方社會的關懷與具體實踐。然而，對於當時依賴《使信月刊》取得海外傳教工場新資訊的英國讀者而言，不難從醫療傳教士的敘事中，想像臺灣病人的鮮明形象。一旦從報導中了解異教徒的處境以及傳教士的犧牲奉獻，遂可能增加響應海外傳教事工的機會，這也達到《使信月刊》的宣傳效果。

不過，《使信月刊》提供的報導訊息，仍有其侷限性。其一，報導內容多來自於傳教士個人的紀錄或隨筆，探討問題的角度未能深入核心；其次，受限於報刊的篇幅形式，報導的訊息易於流於零碎。其三，報導視角的選取，主要是以基督教福音為基調，以此詮釋非基督徒的生活、疾病等問題時，往往可能擴大至道德層面的解釋，並未深入說明醫療的具體措施。儘管如此，《使信月刊》仍舊為後世讀者，保存二十世紀前期來臺的英國長老教會傳教士之生活動態與相關紀錄。

四、結語

隨著英國長老教會在海外傳教工場的拓展，作為英國長老教會機

---

59 "Work in Shoka and Tainan: The Annual Reports," *The Messenger* (Feb. 1931), p. 275. 關於彰化醫館內傳道人的福音工作，參見吳學明，《臺灣基督長老教會研究》（臺北：宇宙光，2006），頁51-56。
60 "The Tainan Hospital," *The Messenger* (Dec. 1908), p. 418.

關刊物的《使信月刊》，逐漸出現以福爾摩沙為名的報導。促使英國讀者開始關注這個位處遠東傳教工場的臺灣及其住民接觸福音的過程。透過《使信月刊》作為媒介，為英國讀者與地處亞洲的福爾摩沙，建立起一個特殊的想像連結，使得英國讀者可以透過傳教士移動的步伐，認識異文化的風土民情，進而以福音傳播達成社會進步的報導立場，激起英國讀者關注臺灣民眾屬靈發展的興趣。

本文以《使信月刊》的報導，介紹該刊的特色，說明英籍傳教士自十九世紀晚期，至二十世紀前期，不斷透過文字與照片，向英國讀者建構出豐富的臺灣見聞與生活圖像。此外，當時傳教士透過社會進步的視角，報導福音事工在臺的進展情形，其中，以醫療方面為例的相關報導，正提供一幅具宗教視野的社會關懷圖景，投射在傳教士耕耘的臺灣土地上。

具體而言，《使信月刊》的宣傳功能有二： 其一，為了吸引英國讀者的目光，進而重視福爾摩沙，在臺的傳教士透過文字與影像的宣傳力量，向英國讀者描述當地的傳教進展。並引導讀者建立其與福爾摩沙之間的連結，無論透過捐款、物資或是加入傳教行列，來關注島上人民的生活與屬靈情形。

其次，身為報導者的傳教士，其敘事模式主要以福音傳播為基調，以此詮釋他們在海外傳教工場的生活與見聞，特別是與臺灣民眾的互動過程。醫療傳教士樂於將臺灣病人的形象，塑造成西方醫療技術的受惠者，未來更可化身成福音的傳播者，以此強化福音傳播與醫療行為的關連性，有助於吸引更多英國讀者，願意響應英國長老教會在臺灣的傳教事業與需求。

總的而言，發行年代跨越百年的《使信月刊》，其中攸關臺灣的報導訊息，有助於認識當時英國長老教會傳教士旅臺期間的日常生活，以及為了刻劃海外傳教事工的成就，所採取的報導策略。藉由《使信月刊》的報導，有助於觀察英國長老教會傳教士的報導者身分。其宣傳以傳教為宗旨的社會關懷，目的之一應是為讓更多基督徒讀者願意響應海外傳教工作，協助推動與社會關懷相關的措施。

除了本文運用的醫療相關報導之外，《使信月刊》尚提供諸多豐富報導訊息，有助於讀者認識二十世紀前期的臺灣社會。惟其內容龐雜，基於本文篇幅有限，故未能全面介紹之。或待來日學界先進更發揮《使信月刊》之研究價值，繼續探論該刊中涉及臺灣醫療、教育、社會救助與慈善活動等等面向的議題。

（本文曾刊登於《華神期刊》第七期 [2015 年 11 月]，頁 37-71）

民國時期農村的醫療與衛生：
以基督教人士之相關言論為主的分析

皮國立

摘要

　　十九世紀末，中國興起了各方面的衛生論述，但直到二十世紀二
〇年代末期，知識份子與醫生、傳教士等群體才慢慢了解到：鄉村的
土地、生活與環境的重要性與獨特性，有別於城市，與民族國家之生
計更加密切相關；而基督教人士也注意到：如果要實現中華歸主的理
想，只注重城市是不夠的，而要將目光轉往廣大的中國鄉村，破除迷
信、拯救苦難。

　　本文主要先梳理整個鄉村衛生問題在近代中國受到重視的起源，
以及基督教對中國農村社會的觀察，內容涉及了二〇年代初至三〇年
代相繼興起的平民教育與鄉村建設運動，以及各教會大學、基督教人
士與團體在農村的一些具體觀察與作為，包括完成諸多醫療衛生事工
之情形，主要著眼於環境衛生與醫療方面的相關史實整理和論述。
1920 年代末，南京國民政府也開始致力於農村衛生工作，希望將醫
藥衛生之權力收歸於中央，當時的衛生專家認為，鄉村衛生不能和宗
教慈善事業混為一談，但卻因為國家在農村衛生力量的缺乏與不健全
因子，使得基督教還是發揮了有別於國家醫療的角色。此時基督教的
社會力量並沒有完全退去，而是成為一個輔助的角色。全文補充了過
去學界對基督教人士在農村衛生工作方面的不足，可以彰顯基督宗教
的鄉村衛生論述與工作事蹟在民國史上的特色與地位，也是近代基督
教在社會慈善工作上的重要貢獻之一。

關鍵詞：基督教、中國農村、衛生、醫療、慈善、疾病

一、前言

　　根據1933年的一份資料，與基督教相關的醫療衛生救濟非常多。整體有關西方天主、基督教的慈善事業，據1931年徐家匯王守璇司鐸的統計：天主教多設孤兒院、安老院、施診所、瘋人院等等；新教則主要在培養醫護人員和機構上努力，有醫院212所，還有盲人學校、孤兒教養院、慈幼協濟會、華洋義振會、痲瘋救濟會、國民拒毒會等等。[1] 另一報導指出，在設立醫院、禁鴉片、廢纏足與盲人、瘋人學校等慈善事業，「耶穌教在華所經營之醫藥事業十倍於天主教所為者也」。[2] 對於近代中國的基督教而言，建立醫院和醫學校，培養醫藥從業人員，就是一種慈善事業，特別是對中國這樣衰弱的國家而言。[3] 故有謂基督教在華建設傳教事業，「其所造就之利益，最為顯著者，蓋無有過於醫藥一道。」[4] 而教會也致力於改善中國的衛生教育與工作，例如在北京高等學院中，從1921年夏季開始了一個由北京教會醫學聯合會指導，北京大學附設的執行委員會領導的衛生教育運動。當時有北京協和醫學院的兩個學生在42個暑假學校中進行關於公共衛生的講課，推展現代醫療。[5] 1922年5月在蘇州則成立了一個公共衛生聯合會，並獲得員警當局的批准。還在6月舉行了一個衛生展覽，同時開展了熱烈的運動。在夏季的月份裡，在青年會大會中開辦了一個免費醫療診所，由青年會與一些其他的中國教會組織參與了這項工作，它充分顯示教會融入中國社會慈善醫療的脈絡，而且與後來國民政府的夏令衛生工作可能有極大的關係。[6]

1　〈天主耶穌兩教在華慈善事業〉，《申報年鑒》1933年刊，頁T3-T4。補充參考：周秋光、曾桂林，〈近代西方教會在華慈善事業述論〉，《貴州師範大學學報（社科版）》，第1期（2008），頁6-13。

2　〈耶穌教在華之事業〉，《申報》，1920年12月19日，第19版星期增刊。

3　渠達成，〈教會新聞：武陽漢教會事業（湖北）：傳道之外教育醫藥慈善事業甚多〉，《通問報：耶穌教家庭新聞》，第17、18期（1936），頁14。

4　〈耶穌教在華之事業〉，《申報》，1920年12月19日，第19版星期增刊。

5　中華醫學會編，《中華醫學雜誌》，1921年，頁122、161、275；《中華醫學雜誌》，1922年，頁87；《中華醫學雜誌》，1924年，頁497；《中華醫學雜誌》，1930年，頁744。

6　酈順利撰，《中華醫學雜誌》，1923年，頁122。

而有關近代中國慈善歷史的研究，成果相當豐碩，但針對農村之衰弱疾病之救濟情況，特別是學界對基督教在農村這方面的慈善事業之研究，仍有不足之處，在劉家峰教授的開創性研究《中國基督教鄉村建設運動研究（1907-1950）》中，已經很好的將民國時期基督教在鄉村建設的工作與背景進行梳理了，[7] 本文在這個基礎上，主要再針對整個鄉村衛生問題在近代中國受重視的起源，以及基督教對中國農村社會的觀察，並探討民國時基督宗教對農村的關注及其進行的醫療衛生事工，主要著重於環境衛生與醫療方面的相關史實。

其次是教會在農村工作所遇到的種種轉型與困難。南京的哈奇森醫師曾論述〈鄉村中的醫院〉，希望把訓練良好的中國醫生與外國醫生置於同等的位置，以便將來完全可交由中國人管理和支持，這其實和當時教會本土化的運動是一致的，教會醫生希望有更多的中國西醫來接手這些工作，這也促進了中國西醫的本土化。[8] 但是，教會還是要顧及傳教，又要在政府衛生力量的權力空間內周旋，找到可以努力的空間。那麼，教會的困難在何處？他們進行了哪些鄉村衛生的工作等等。最後，礙於一篇文章所能處理的問題有限，故本文主要鎖定的資料，是以民國時期出版的各式刊物為資料主體，包括新教（天主教確實較少）教徒及其團體。全文補充基督教人物的相關衛生論述，以彰顯基督教衛生論述在這個時代中的特色與地位，[9] 補充基督教會對近代中國鄉村衛生工作之關注。

二、農村問題被重視的開端

整個農村破產與衰弱的問題，早在清末民初時就被陸續提出，但

---

7 劉家峰，《中國基督教鄉村建設運動研究（1907-1950）》（天津：天津人民出版社，2008），頁63-86。

8 中華醫學會編，《中華醫學雜誌》，1920年，頁416-451及補遺；《中國醫學雜誌》，1920年，頁1-4。

9 關於鄉村建設的資料介紹，可參考劉家峰，《中國基督教鄉村建設運動研究（1907-1950）》，頁2-10，本文將補充期刊的資料，除教會本身外，還有部分醫療期刊。

未持續受到關注，一直到民國之後才漸漸被加以重視。李入林指出：農村民眾人數佔全中國85%以上，在這優勝劣敗的世界，若不能使全國大多數的民眾「具有銅筋鐵骨之身體，和衝風冒雨之精神，何能內求治安、外御強權？」[10] 而這大多數的人，指的就是生活在農村之民眾。還有人指出：「據犯罪學家的統計和考察，犯罪行為是和體質有莫大關係的，即就生理和病理學上考察，這話也有相當的根據。」所以農村也要重視優生學。[11] 九一八與一二八事變後，京滬各大城市經濟一片蕭條，政府也慢慢感受到稅收之不足，經濟之凋敝與不堪一擊，其根源就在於農村經濟的破產。[12] 三〇年代成立的農村醫藥改進社則言：「我國農村醫藥，素患飢荒，衛生知識，不得灌輸於農民腦蒂，病夫載道，死亡累野，此實天殤民族元氣之最大禍機，加以近年農村經濟急趨崩潰，大多數農民生活尚不能自給，有病非乞哀求憐於泥塑木雕之下，即聽憑疾患之自然變化，因此死於非命者，不知凡幾，人口日在喊退過程中，誠屬眼前最嚴重之國家問題。」[13] 種種跡象都顯示，農村問題逐漸成為中國今後能否健全發展之核心課題。一位中醫朱殿指出：「我這次回到故鄉——江陰，在農村看到許多可悲的事實，在我未到的前兩天，後村一位農夫叫王德才，患了極重的濕溫症，他是一個在經濟破落下的勞農，有一妻和一位六歲的小孩，平時生活苦得很，替人家做做田工，尋幾個錢，家裡麥飯一天吃兩頓，還不得飽，今年收到幾斗豆子，賣了好久賣不掉，生了這慢性病，別說請醫生診治買藥吃，連柴米都沒有來源，他的老婆和兒子，整天睜著眼睛，餓著肚皮朝他哭，不幾天，這位悲慘境遇中的王德才，竟不耐煩的一命嗚呼了，他遺下來的寡婦孤兒，只得各自分途去掙扎自己的生命。」[14] 可見農村破落與貧病的慘況。

---

10 李入林，〈農村衛生之管見〉，《醫潮月刊》，第1卷第3期（1947），頁4。

11 何克林，〈農村衛生問題〉，《通大醫刊》，第1卷第1期（1936），頁22。

12 章之汶，〈基督徒與農村運動：南京基督徒學生聯合會秋令會講稿之一〉，《農林新報》，第11卷第1期（1934），頁4。

13 〈農村醫藥改進社〉，《申報》，1933年3月4日，第13版。

14 朱殿，〈如何救濟農村病夫〉，《現代國醫》，第2卷第5期（1932），頁2-3。

而基督教人士也注意到這類現象，顏福慶在1937年也指出，教會最大的計畫應放在農村，基督教醫院應考慮設在農村，而非城市，他明確指出教會醫院在農村開展的工作還不夠，足見考究民初基督教的農村衛生關注點，不能單從醫院來看，而應該先著眼於教育與建設工作。[15] 而有關振興農村的運動，因中央政府之衰弱，無暇他顧。故民間之鄉村相關建設與教育，開展於二○年代，比中央政府更早。而這些早期投身於鄉村工作的領袖，其實都與基督教關係密切，包括晏陽初、陶行知、李景漢、陳志潛、謝扶雅等，皆為知名的基督徒。[16] 例如1927年陶行知的中華教育改進社創設南京試驗鄉村學校影響較大。[17] 另一方面，14歲即受洗的晏陽初，則於1921年開始提倡平民教育，1924年轉向鄉村，他主持的「中華平民教育促進會」，在直隸保定展開平民教育。該會一開始也沒有很重視農村衛生問題，而是先從教育著手，再轉向農業，最後再往衛生邁進。衛生之事，顯示平教會運動希望加強該會與中央及地方政府領導的關係，建立起與他們的合作，在某種意義上發揮輔助政府的角色。[18] 1928年，民間的鄉村建設運動陸續展開。[19] 至1931年，鄉村教育已和鄉村調查與建設合流，梁漱溟在山東鄒平展開的鄉村建設實驗，即將教育與建設合而為一，至於定縣的平民教育，在該年也開始進行公共衛生的相關工作；而牽涉鄉村教育與建設之問題，多少都與衛生有關。[20]

　　南京國民政府比基督教晚，於二○年代末三○年代初才開始注意農村問題。1933年成立的農復會可為代表。同年8月，內政部下令在

---

15 劉天路編，《身體・靈魂・自然：中國基督教與醫療、社會事業研究》（上海：上海人民出版社，2010），頁288。

16 羅偉虹主編，《中國基督教（新教）史》（上海：上海世紀出版集團，2014），頁560。

17 張玉法，《中國現代史》（臺北：東華書局，民84）下冊，頁556-557。

18 陳志潛原著、端木彬如等譯，《中國農村的醫學——我的回憶》（成都：四川人民出版社，1998），前言，頁65。

19 本文僅就與醫療衛生有關的部分論述，其他方面與實際個案的研究，可參考劉家峰，《中國基督教鄉村建設運動研究（1907-1950）》，第四、五章。

20 張玉法，《中國現代史》下冊，頁558。

省府管轄下成立「實驗縣」，從事農村復興工作，[21] 當時農復會就有設立醫院的計畫，可惜直到中日戰爭前都沒有付諸實行。[22] 不過，其實政府對整個農村醫療衛生之重視，還是與基督教有莫大的關係。北京著名的協和醫學院在 1921 年由洛克斐勒基金會遠東代表蘭安生（Dr. John B. Grant）開始組織公共衛生教學，該基金會於 1913 年創立，其創始人老約翰·洛克斐勒（John D. Rockefeller Sr.）本身就是虔誠的浸禮教徒，在基金會還未成立之時，他就將醫療作為慈善事業的重點，努力捐助，造福人類。他的精神來源於喀爾文教派的中心思想，亦即「從事發明創造，不斷地收穫、節約和捐贈，表現出一種獲得上帝認可的意義與價值模式」，基督教精神是一種道德力量，而理性與科學則是社會變革之原動力，二者相加則可化腐朽為神奇。[23] 至1928 年初，該會與協和醫學院合作，選擇河北定縣晏陽初開辦的平民教育促進會，進行社區的衛生實驗。陳志潛於 1930 年初被邀請擔任定縣平教會農村衛生處的主任，和晏陽初合作。晏在一次世界大戰時，曾做為一名基督教青年會的助手來處理華工事務，他體驗到底層平民未受教育的痛苦，回國後才致力於平民教育。1928 年，晏陽初開始覺得單靠教育無法幫農民填飽肚子和保衛生命，故開始致力於建立衛生制度；同年，晏陽初任命姚尋源醫師為平民教育運動鄉村衛生處首屆主任，蘭安生也同意，姚尋源本身就受過傳教士培訓和教會醫院的薰陶，但他仍傾向用醫院模式來進行鄉村衛生之改善，他離開後，陳志潛就接了他的位置。1929 年，晏陽初曾說，對待定縣的工作：「你需要一個科學家的頭腦和一個傳教士的心靈。」[24] 陳志潛從1932 至 1937 年在定縣設立第一個社區衛生實驗區，他是蘭安生的學生，更是後來的顧問與同事。陳志潛並舉家搬到定縣，等於是和晏陽初合作，堪稱近代中國醫學史上最早的醫學教育研究和促進地方衛生

---

21 張玉法，《中國現代史》下冊，頁 519。
22 何克林，〈農村衛生問題〉，《通大學刊》，第 1 卷第 1 期（1936），頁 23。
23 陶文釗、梁碧瑩主編，《美國與近現代中國》（北京：中國社會科學出版社，1996），頁 317-345。
24 陳志潛原著、端木彬如等譯，《中國農村的醫學──我的回憶》，頁 77-80。

的一項探索。[25] 陳志潛認為，要在農村建立起「社區醫學」的概念，必須依靠治療技術的醫學，該體系也不是醫生對病人、單對單的模式，而是一種治療與預防結合，納入流行病學、生命統計和衛生行政的模式。[26] 這使得鄉村衛生的內涵更加豐富，調查、人員的配置都較醫院來得複雜。1937 年的日本侵華戰爭，使定縣經驗過早夭折，要到1950年之後才有更多的進展。[27]

以上是與基督教有關的醫療事業機關所做的努力，但比較為人所忽略的，反而是基督教人士本身延伸出來有關醫療慈善的鄉村關懷。例如華北基督教農村事業促進會，是華北各教會和幾個學校組織的團體，專門幫助各地農村的服務工作。其工作包括了衛生、農事、合作等。[28] 從大背景來看，整個教會的醫療在民國時期逐漸有本土化的現象，一些從西方學習歸國的西醫發現，他們很難打進原來的教會醫學體系，故1915年他們成立了本土的中華醫學會。該學會的成員發現，教會醫生自己有醫學會，而且有排擠現象，故他們自己成立了醫學會，反而及時吸收了教會醫學會的一些醫生，[29] 所以可以說後來中國的西醫化，其實也是基督教本土化的一種映照。該醫學會的調查指出，教會醫學在現代公共衛生上取得了重大進步，現在應該要有中國本地的西醫力量進入。在二〇年代中期，還沒有國家級、省級或市級的公衛組織，不難想見農村衛生的惡劣程度，一直要到南京國民政府成立後，才逐漸將精神放在現代衛生行政改進上，城市衛生當然是優先的，農村問題比較不被重視。李入林曾指出：「民國成立以來，公家對於農村衛生，殊少注意。除一二農村衛生實驗區外，衛生設施大部分集中於都城大市，殊為失計。」[30] 而教會的農村事業，教育與衛生兩方面是不可分割的，衛生與現代生活需要被教導，所以衛生觀念

---

25 陳志潛原著、端木彬如等譯，《中國農村的醫學——我的回憶》，前言，頁3。
26 陳志潛原著、端木彬如等譯，《中國農村的醫學——我的回憶》，緒論，頁1。
27 陳志潛原著、端木彬如等譯，《中國農村的醫學——我的回憶》，中文版序，頁2。
28 〈教會大事：江西基督教農村服務聯合會〉，《田家半月報》試刊（1934），頁6-7。
29 陳志潛原著、端木彬如等譯，《中國農村的醫學——我的回憶》，頁22。
30 李入林，〈農村衛生之管見〉，《醫潮月刊》，第1卷第3期（1947），頁4-5。

常被包括在教育事業中。早在南京國民政府未成立的二〇年代初，已有不少教會人士同意將傳教工作放在到農村去，而且有不少的教會團體開始注意此事。當時教會的教育事業，包括中國基督教全國協會，逐步推動辦理全國公民教育運動，希望能培養平民有愛國、救國的責任感，其中，衛生與慈善之調查事業都在教會的規劃名單中。[31] 1926年，已有聯合改進農村生活之結合，有中華職業教育社、中華教育改進社、中華平民教育促進會、東南大學農科教育科合設「聯合改進農村生活董事會」，也推陶知行為主席，其下就有箴言：「基督教教育宗旨，造就健全國民，發展共和精神，培養職業知能，更以基督之犧牲服務精神，完成其高尚人格。」[32] 雖然教育工作已經開展，但衛生工作還有實際施行的層面需要去調查與理解，然後才能展開行動。1935年，毛吟搓曾寫《基督教的農村事工》，這本書是他應中華監理公會的青年團契大會在杭州開會時，該會主任希望毛吟搓撰寫的。他分析了中國農村衰弱的近因與遠因，包括了外國和本土的不良因素。他認為中國的農村廣大，即使是生在農村，都不見得了解全國的狀況。而對於農村事業的調查與統計，向來沒有開展；政府不重視，當然屬於農村的事業團體也非常少。這些都導致了農村經濟破產，洋貨充斥、農民的國貨慘賠，盜匪橫行、教育落後等等問題。基督教會對此問題的關懷，將在下一小節分析。[33]

三、基督教對農村事工與醫療衛生之描述

依報刊的資料顯示，中國的基督教會於二〇年代初開始重視農村問題，1922年有人指出，教會將城市點作為佈道的主力是大錯特錯的，應該轉往農村。若希望基督教能夠中國化，有一天能中華歸主，

---

31 〈青年會公民教育運動之籌備〉，《申報》，1924年4月27日，第14版。
32 〈聯合改進農村生活之消息〉，《中華基督教教育季刊》，第2卷第2期（1926），頁96-97。
33 毛吟搓，《基督教的農村事工》（上海：文瑞印書館，1935），頁1-12。

就必須重視農村的佈道。[34] 還有人舉耶穌對農村的重視：「耶穌走遍加利利，在各會堂裡教訓人，傳天國的福音，醫治百姓各樣的病症。」[35] 周博夫則指出：「近來高唱『自傳』、『自養』、『自立』和什麼『本色的教會』，這些目標何時能達到呢？以我看非待農村基督化之後不可。農村基督化之日，就是本色教會實現之時。」[36] 1924年，王鑰東指出，整個「中華歸主」的運動當時皆以城市為中心，似乎有些空洞。中國大部分的人口都住在鄉村，所以「中華歸主必以農村教會為前提」，必須要打破過去教會領袖專注於城市的舊觀念。王指出，現在具體做法是要先展開對農村的風俗、人情、土地等問題之考察，才能了解什麼是農村最需要進行的事工。細部的不說，如果能在農村開辦醫院，使農民不受庸醫愚弄，又能與病人講道，實比蓋城市醫院更加事半功倍；也可以舉辦滅蠅會、禁賭會，抑或是創辦慈善機關，處理包含養老、育嬰等事。[37] 可惜，多數醫生都居住在大城市中，為謀自己的發財，不願往農村去，毛吟搓認為這就像耶穌說的：「我餓了，不給我吃，渴了不給我喝，作客旅不留我住，我赤身，不給我穿，病了，坐監，不來看顧我。」[38]

在進入實際農村工作前，要先進行一些調查。早期的農村調查與鄉村建設、教育等有密切關係，通常結合調查與實驗等步驟，多由教會大學的知識份子和基督教團體合作而展開。[39] 例如1928年平教會成立了統計調查處（後改為社會調查部），知名社會學者李景漢即被平教會聘為調查處（部）主任，健康衛生當然是調查的項目之一；他同時也擔任燕京大學教師，指導學生一同展開調查工作，是教會大學

34 謙，〈農村佈道主義〉，《興華》，第19卷第13期（1922），頁3-9。

35 何鳳智，〈基督教對於農村婦女的責任（續上期）〉，《希望月刊》，第11卷第3期（1934），頁7。

36 周博夫，〈農村教會底將來〉，《真光》，第23卷第7期（1924），頁35。

37 王鑰東，〈農村教會應興辦的事工〉，《興華》，第21卷第22期（1924），頁4-8。

38 毛吟搓，《基督教的農村事工》，頁31。毛自述引《聖經》之《馬太福音》第25章第31至40節。

39 費正清等編著，《劍橋中華民國史1912-1949》（北京：中國社會科學出版社，1993）下冊，頁400-401。

鄉村調查的典範之一，其他教會大學的調查工作也相繼展開。[40] 又如 1919年北京華洋義賑會、[41] 金陵大學（如金陵大學農經系）於1928 年開始進行之農村調查都是顯例。後者早於1922年就設有農業專修 科和鄉村師範科，但多偏重於教育；[42] 至1928年始分出農業與教育 兩組，當時就設有實習活動課，包含農業的生產與地質調查等課程。 在衛生方面，該科設有兩類學校，一類為農村小學，一為農民服務 社，後設有「衛生股」，其初擬之組織有：農村衛生所、衛生運動、 嬰兒保育會和農村浴室等，其他如教育、娛樂等事項，也都有專股負 責，除調查外，也進行一些實際的農村工作。[43]

當然，這些工作都是在摸索中逐步前進的，隨著農村逐漸被重 視，有更多的描述與觀察文字出現。當時基督徒一方面進入農村、另 一方面進行調查與描述，以求在傳教工作上發現可著力之處，這就與 教會大學的社會調查不完全相同，因為它通常與傳教工作更直接相 關。一本由上海廣學會編纂的《農村建設討論會報告書》，可能是之 前工作的討論報告。它揭示在農民教育上，兒童教育固然重要，但農 村多是青年、成年人，對其「補充教育」，也是很重要的。救濟農村 的積極目的是要改良農村，在醫藥衛生方面，除了教育父親要為家庭 成員的健康負責外，母親的角色也很重要，因為母親的角色，往往與 家庭的清潔與整齊更有關係，而且負責兒女疾病的預防和診治工作， 也和母親的角色相關；至於青年，則要導引其鍛鍊體格，增強身體； 當然，其他方面也很重要，多與基督教的信條有關，例如愛情的清 潔、婚姻的神聖等等。[44] 章之汶則認為，農村可以進行的事工，例如 「傳福音給貧窮的人」、使「瞎眼的看得見」，只讓文盲得見真理； 至於要讓「受壓制的得自由」，指的是肉體的壓制，便要用「衛生」

---

40 黃新憲，《基督教教育與中國社會變遷》（福州：福建教育出版社，1996），頁226-227。
41 民國時期組織災害救濟的中國紅十字會、華洋義賑會等，組成人士多為基督徒。當災害發生時，這些團 體也會和教會合作，一起賑濟災民。參考羅偉虹主編，《中國基督教（新教）史》，頁557。
42 張玉法，《中國現代史》下冊，頁519-521。
43 周恢，〈金大農村服務專修科概況〉，《中華基督教教育季刊》，第4卷第4期（1928），頁115-117。
44 以上轉引自毛吟搓，《基督教的農村事工》，頁42-43。

來解決，章認為這和定縣的四大教育是相同的，也是基督教可以努力的地方，當然，衛生需要有人和醫院來幫忙，也是不爭的事實。[45]

當時對農村環境與衛生的描述，大概有以下諸端。農村本有其衛生之條件，如恬靜自然、空氣好、環境清幽、人口少等等。所缺乏的只是醫療資源，如醫生、藥品之不足，還有現代衛生觀念之不足，所以通常農民只能乞求郎中和穩婆。[46] 各種迷信問題是基督教最為關注的，毛吟搓就指出「農民無智」，他說：「害了病，往往在初起不肯延醫服藥，只在求籤問卜，一旦病重，心慌意亂的瞎請醫生，結果人財兩失。」[47] 所以一方面教會應設立農村醫院，也應該要取締庸醫，徹底隔除農村惡習，並宣傳普遍的衛生觀念。[48] 教會人士指出：要根除舊有思想，和根除舊中醫、建立新衛生觀是一體的。施中一則指出：「鄉間都存有『天意』的思想，對於衛生，素不注意。近來鄉友的衛生習慣已漸漸養成起來了。譬如：刷牙的本來可說百不得一，現在已佔到十分之一、二了。宴會的時候也有許多鄉友用公共筷防傳染病了，用蠅拍打蒼蠅的已很普遍。其餘對空氣的流通、衣服的潔淨、路上牛糞的掃除、生水的不喝，也有不少在實行的了。」過去生病常靠「仙人」和「女巫」，不肯真正承認自己的病。當西醫觀念慢慢進入農村，等於舊迷信將被革除，他說：「我們現在看到『硫磺油膏』、『金雞納霜』、『阿基路而』等新藥得以在本鄉推行，並且日廣一日，信鬼神的風氣得以漸却。」[49] 周博夫則認為，農民本身就有敦直、樸素、服從、富於信仰心的特質，但通常都被低劣宗教所牽制，基督教應趁此時機進入，帶給農民光明。[50] 而這也是基督教可以進入農村的意義──消除迷信、促進衛生。宗教色彩過於濃厚，信鬼

---

45 章之汶，〈基督徒與農村運動：南京基督徒學生聯合會秋令會講稿之一〉，《農林新報》，第11卷第1期（1934），頁3-7。

46 衣旦，〈農村衛生事業推進的先決條件（續）〉，《申報》，1937年3月9日，第16版。

47 毛吟搓，《基督教的農村事工》，頁13。

48 何克林，〈農村衛生問題〉，《通大醫刊》，第1卷第1期（1936），頁21-23。

49 施中一，《舊農村的新氣象》（蘇州：蘇州中華基督教青年會，1933），頁38-39。

50 周博夫，〈農村教會底將來〉，《真光》，第23卷第7期（1924），頁32-33。

神不信醫藥，這點是中西醫一致認為農村衛生的大問題，中醫也不諱言指出，如在農村辦理醫藥事業，必定要指導民眾一般醫藥衛生的常識和醫藥、衛生和疾病之間的關係。[51] 雖然有中醫指出，西醫就是靠教會的力量排除中醫、入侵農村，[52] 但其實真正的實情可能為農村醫療資源不足，有些基督徒在農村衛生問題上是希望整合中西醫療資源的，其中西折衷的言論，是認為農民的頭腦還沒有完全的開通，只靠西醫的方法和藥物，無法滿足農村的需求。若實地考察就可以發現，農民認為傳統醫藥還是獨一無二的，所以折衷的辦法就是先請一個中醫，先滿足農民的急需後，再請西醫，使農民能了解西醫的便利功效，這樣農民比較容易信服。而且這不是一朝一夕能成的，必須花費功夫，並且長期實行，邵雯光同樣也提到養老院、育幼院的興辦，和其他農村事業的問題。[53] 雷鳴遠神父認為，能治病的醫生就是好醫生，中國醫理雖講不通，但能治病卻是事實，又說：「他（中醫）不動刀，不割，成績比動刀的好」，並說自己的胳膊也是靠中醫，才免了開刀之苦。[54]

又，針對農村環境與衛生問題，毛吟搓還指出，農村之自然環境，雖有自然可愛之處，但汙濁骯髒之環境，還是處處可見。首先就是「坑廁」，是沿路擺滿的，甚至把廁所蓋在家中。毛形容：如無錫、常州、湖州等處的大城市中，亦是廁所林立，都是為了「糞博利益」。而這些「坑廁」，既沒有蓋子，又必待滿坑，才能取出宿糞尿，臭氣熏天、滋生蚊蠅，這就是傳染病的源頭。農民以為有利，其實害處更大。[55] 濟南齊魯大學附設龍山鎮基督教「農村社會服務處」，撰寫暑期工作的經過時指出：該區域有二十多個村莊，「居民既未受教育，又無衛生習慣，農民之生活簡單而困難，故欲使其生活

---

51 丁少侯，〈建設農村醫藥的入手三策〉，《國醫公報（南京）》，第4卷第2期（1936），頁18-19。

52 朱殿，〈急需抵抗外醫侵入農村〉，《醫界春秋》，第74期（1932），頁4。

53 邵雯光，〈農村教會應興辦的事工〉，《青年進步》，第79期（1925），頁21-23。

54 以上引自〈雷鳴遠司鐸訪問記：暢談慈善農村國醫各種問題〉，《磐石雜誌》，第3卷第1期（1935），頁45-46。

55 毛吟搓，《基督教的農村事工》，頁33。

狀況求合於衛生之道，實所難能。故該地之居民，均茅屋數間、人畜同處，牛溲馬勃遍地，便溺載道，雨則道途泥濘，晴則塵土遍野，門前灰糞纍纍，臭氣難當，蚊蠅成群，為害最烈，瓜果小賑，零星食物叫賣者，衣服襤褸、袒背跣足，蒼蠅率集其上，令人作嘔，朝發傳染病，夕即可普遍全村，與言衛生之道，亦不之聽。」[56] 其次是養豬、牛等畜牧行為，一樣有累積糞便的風俗，而且更骯髒，因為積的糞便比人的更不好清理，加上怕牲畜被偷，所以發展出一種「人與牲畜居處比連」的居住文化；而且房屋都是「暗房亮灶」，不合於衛生，應該要多開天窗或窗戶，就可以通氣，合於衛生了。[57] 何克林指出：「就復興農村教育言，普及農民教育，自為主要措施之一。然而對於農村教育的效果，也應特別注意；教育的效果是興教者及受教者的體格，有極大的關係，而教者和受教者的體格，當然與其四周的環境衛生完備與否有密切關係，即是有完備的衛生環境，才可造出健康的體格；有健康的體格，才可增加教育的效率，所以復興農民教育，也應注意到農村衛生。」[58] 在傳染病預防法上面，農民更是非常需要。[59] 毛總結農民沒有衛生與預防之習慣，有幾個面向：第一是不知隔離、病人與常人之用具，不肯分開；其次是吃喝的殘餘，不肯丟掉，病人的器具，也不知消毒；而親友探視病人、死後往弔，必吃吃喝喝，以致釀成普遍的傳染病。這些衛生的呼籲與行動，對農民而言，本身就是「一個新運動」，是救濟工作的一環，也是推行現代醫學的效力。當醫生還未到農村之前，這些衛生知識的灌輸，就是行救濟，要靠傳教人來實行。[60] 三〇年代政府的力量雖逐步進入農村，但教會是不完全滿意的，他們認為教會與政府的最大差別，就在於政府派去農村的人要「位置」，反而變成吸血鬼了，不如教會做的傳教與慈善事

---

56 鄭子修，〈龍山三月記〉，《青年進步》，第109期（1928），頁90。
57 毛吟搓，《基督教的農村事工》（上海：文瑞印書館，1935），頁33-34。
58 何克林，〈農村衛生問題〉，《通大醫刊》，第1卷第1期（1936），頁22。
59 這種論述非常多，參考李廷安，《中國鄉村衛生問題》（上海：商務印書館，1935），頁39-55。
60 毛吟搓，《基督教的農村事工》（上海：文瑞印書館，1935），頁32-33。

業。[61]

　　那麼，有什麼衛生工作是可以進行的？陶知行說：「農民不知衛生，吐瀉、瘧疾、寄生蟲病、皮膚病等都是農民所常犯的。所以醫生到鄉下去是農民所最歡迎的，我在上海做過一次小試驗，我與幾個同學帶了一點藥，跑到鄉下去，藉藥的介紹，農民就和我們做了好朋友。有了友誼，以後就幫助他們辦學。……一個醫生，在城市工作，不過是湊了熱鬧就是了。城市中的太太小姐也有許多醫生要在那裡服事，何況他們的病多數是咎由自的取呢[62]。醫生不願下鄉，應當歸咎于醫學教育之不良。」[63]可見農民非常需要醫藥之救助，又，毛吟搓認為今後辦理的救濟農村事工，應該分為：增加生產、調劑金融法、提倡醫藥衛生、普及教育以及心靈改造等五種，乃救濟農村的基本事業。[64]下一節來分析有關農村醫藥衛生的問題。

四、農村衛生事業之開展

　　農村中醫療衛生事業如何開展、有何成果，實耐人尋味。教會方面曾認為，基督教的醫院和教會應該有更密切的關係，而不是像過去互不聯絡、漠不關心，應該有整體之計畫。以中國如此之大、人口之多，整個中國的西醫院只有500所，基督教醫院也只有231所，發展醫藥事業非常迫切。[65]但事實就是，設備好的醫院對農村而言是遙不可及的資源，農村衛生，需要更多元的辦法才有可能開展。

　　何鳳智指出，在1912年，有一位哈維夫人在美國密蘇里州的一個小農村辦理農村教育，教導婦女如何操持家務、注重清潔衛生，並

---

61 章之汶，〈基督徒與農村運動：南京基督徒學生聯合會秋令會講稿之一〉，《農林新報》，第11卷第1期（1934），頁5。

62 原引文如此，但實際文意應為「咎由自取的呢」，感謝審查委員提出。

63 陶知行，〈全國團契大會紀錄：農村問題與社會改造〉，《中國基督徒學生運動特刊》，第12期（1933），頁107。

64 毛吟搓，《基督教的農村事工》（上海：文瑞印書館，1935），頁14。

65 上海檔案館藏 U120-0-23-8「1936年中國基督教運動概況」，頁10。

請教員來講習罐頭、蔬菜等等的保存法，還講解嬰兒的健康清潔與保育等方法，村人都說：「聽了這種講習以後，家中的幼兒從不生病了。」已顯示教會這種服務、改良與救濟合一的精神。[66] 早在1920年，報紙就說明：「西部偏僻之省分，除基督教會所設之醫院外，不復有醫藥之便利矣。」[67] 但這些「偏遠」之處，還不完全是指農村的意義。1922年，基督教全國大會假上海市南京路市政廳開會，當時反對基督教的力量已不小，教會認為，不要去批評這種反對聲浪，而應該確信自己做的對社會有益，故謂「吾等可自信、任何設施、決不致以損害社會為前提」，當時也希望透過集會來凝聚教會的力量，故會上也討論了鄉村教育、城市衛生等問題，並謂：「中國各地，無論其為鄉村為城市，無不見有禮拜堂塔尖之矗立；換言之，則均為吾教徒所當服務之地。惟我等觀察所得，城市教育，勝於鄉村，而因人口繁密之故，污濁殊甚，以致疾疫屬行。至鄉村地方，鄉野空氣殊潔，於個人生活，其為暢利、惟因我國社會貧乏之故、青年子弟泰半失學。」當時會議的結果，一致主張，利用教堂本身之經費，來提倡教育及衛生，已開始重視鄉村衛生。[68] 1925年，邵雯光指出，教會中的農村人才必定要從農村中出來，才了解農村，具有犧牲精神，能長期為農村服務。[69]

在醫藥衛生工作開展的實際層面上，主要是將衛生教育推展到農村去。毛吟搓認為，要促進農民的醫藥衛生知識，須重視幾點：首先是農民對疾病的本質不明瞭，所以生病了就以為是「鬼祟」，生病不求醫，就會去燒香、求籤，所以要向農民解釋：解釋病由，使農民知道疾病怎麼來的，病菌怎麼傳染？腸胃如何不舒服？在破除迷信方面，毛吟搓有一妙喻，他認為，服藥應如何「靈驗」？如瘧疾服用金

---

66 何鳳智，〈基督教對於農村婦女的責任（續上期）〉，《希望月刊》，第11卷第3期（1934），頁9。

67 〈耶穌教在華之事業〉，《申報》，1920年12月19日，第19版星期增刊。

68 〈基督教今後在華發展之方向：鄉村教育、城市衛生〉，《申報》，1922年5月13日，第14版。

69 邵雯光，〈農村教會應興辦的事工〉，《青年進步》，第79期（1925），頁18。

雞納霜，一服即效，比求籤更有效，說明清楚，就能破除迷信。[70] 在中華基督教青年會出版的一本書中就指出：前幾年瘟疫很熾，幸好有鄉事領導大家去打防疫針，「事後大家又都預備了十滴水」，否則死亡一定很可觀。[71] 教會剷除迷信、打倒神像引來了村民的惡感，但是「這小小的醫藥工作已經大殺了求神延巫的風氣」，可以用來改造社會，破除迷信。[72] 毛吟搓則指：「衛生是現在社會上的一種共同運動」，認為教會可做的促進農民衛生的舉措有：放幻燈片，可到農村中去作衛生運動，促進農民的衛生知識，用幻燈片可以啟發農民的思想，也可以聚集人潮。其次可利用各種「畫片」，因為農民不識字，無法用文字宣傳，必須用口傳和圖畫。若能將圖畫解釋給農民聽，再將圖送給他們，宣傳效果必定很大。[73] 也有人建議，多在鄉村醫院內掛人體解剖圖，可以解釋病情，又可以讓病人逐漸信仰西醫。[74]

　　基督教大學的學生，則是運用拜訪、遊行、介紹書報、演講和寄宿等方式來貼近農民生活，了解農民的需求。在提倡衛生方面，這些學生在演講時會特別強調衛生的問題，例如講述飲食、睡眠、居室衣服以及沐浴休息等事，並講述如何消滅蚊蠅、預防傳染病與微菌等。不過，他們也坦承：「農民實行者則絕少，然此亦生活困難，有以致之，誰之咎哉？」[75] 可見這樣的工作非常不容易，而且非常需要一些技巧。甚至，毛吟搓後來悲觀的指出：「多數農村教會裡的教友，都是有名無實，關閉教堂，停歇工作，不在他們心上，平時所稱為教友者，亦無非支撐場面而已。到今日真要上場工作呢，他們要連自己也不承認是教友了，至於以前的工作人員呢？在農村間，天天覺得空閒，上好守本分的，作宿堂內，終日無事，到了禮拜日，才要捧經一

70 毛吟搓，《基督教的農村事工》，頁35-36。
71 十滴水的歷史，可參考皮國立，〈中西醫學話語與近代商業論述——以《申報》上的「痧藥水」為例〉，《上海學術月刊》（2013），頁149-164。
72 以上兩小段引文引自施中一，《舊農村的新氣象》（蘇州：蘇州中華基督教青年會，1933），頁40。
73 毛吟搓，《基督教的農村事工》，頁36。
74 劉紹周，〈鄉村開業醫應負的使命〉，《社會醫藥》，第2卷第9期（1935），頁4。
75 鄭子修，〈龍山三月記〉，《青年進步》，第109期（1928），頁92。

講，次之坐茶館、著著棋、吃吃茶、講講空話，再次之營副業作生意，更不興的，還有吃吃老酒，……就是教會中也坐好一個老魔鬼，卻沒有耶穌基督在內了。」[76] 此語道出了教會農村工作的困難與阻礙。即使如此，毛依舊認為：「一位鄉村牧師，在新村中間，不要抱經成聖，應當趕到民間去，不要化大資本，只須自己先研究農民的需要而實施，就可作合乎農民需要的工。」[77] 一本主張農民解放的書也指出，農村工作應適度學習一些醫藥知識，「能夠治療醫些簡單的，而又是農村中最常有的疾病，更需要利用極廉價的土藥，如像豬油、硫磺油膏治療癬，使君子治蛔蟲，常山治瘧疾等。只要隨時留心有關的書籍和經驗。」[78] 可見懂一些藥理對農村事工可能非常有用，江浙基督教鄉村服務聯合會的施中一就曾觀察到農村一位村幹事用西藥治好農民的「走馬牙疳」，農民送上一隻大公雞給他做為謝禮。[79] 在天津，天主教的一位神父雷鳴遠也發表議論，因為「能少用農民一個錢，就少用他一個錢。」要從小事做起，不能空談大理想。[80] 農民除了「窮」這個因素沒辦法看醫生之外，其實富農也沒有「延醫服藥」的習慣，他們大多認為生了大病才要延醫，所以小病小痛、日常衛生，都沒有加以注意。要救濟農村，就要從農民的健康問題上著眼；[81] 又，一般農村沒有醫生和藥鋪，但這兩者卻是最基本的。所以農民生病只能往城裡跑，很不方便；或請一位醫生到農村看病，同樣不方便，所以農民當然沒有延醫看病的「習慣」。這要怎麼解決呢？首先，就是要設立定期化的診療所，而這種診療所，站在宗教者的立場，是不能收費的，因為是救濟的本質；而如果跟農民收藥費，那他

---

76 毛吟搓，《基督教的農村事工》，頁46。
77 毛吟搓，《基督教的農村事工》，序言，頁1-2。
78 吳紹荃，《到農村去》（生活書店，民36），頁61-62。
79 施中一，《舊農村的新氣象》，頁38-39。
80 〈雷鳴遠司鐸訪問記：暢談慈善農村國醫各種問題〉，《磐石雜誌》，第3卷第1期（1935），頁45-46。
81 毛吟搓，《基督教的農村事工》，頁20-30。

們寧願等病慢慢好，這就不是救濟的本義了。[82]

除了醫藥衛生外，教會也比較重視傳教之間的關係，例如提到了農村婦女在鄉村的地位與力量，和日常衛生的種種關係：如果一家的婦女肯信教，那麼通常全家也都會信教，因為她可以感動男人的鐵石心腸。[83] 並且教會也對農村婦女有些責任，因為農村許多生產、家務都要靠婦女，而他們的衛生卻令人擔憂，例如不事洗浴，所謂只洗頭足，終身不曾洗浴全身的人比比皆是，也不知如何處理妊娠、月事等生理事務；農村女子也知道梳妝打扮、塗粉、穿耳，但這些與衛生毫無關係，故生病者不知凡幾。而且，婦女不知清潔衛生，當然兒童的死亡率就高了。[84] 在這些衛生論述中，當然也有針對農村環境而制定的策略，如毛吟搓就說：消滅蚊蠅的運動，在大城市中早已展開，但在農村中卻未曾聽說，故農村間蚊蠅就非常多。而滅蚊比滅蠅更難，因為滅蠅他已有經驗，就是到農村中送農民每戶一支捕蠅拍，農民都很願意去撲滅蒼蠅的。至於蚊子，較難驅除，因為中國南方都是水田，容易儲水，易生蚊蟲，只好教農民盡量避蚊。[85] 對於傳染病的預防，除衛生知識外，宗教的關懷與心靈的療癒，恐怕也是一種無形的力量。[86]

在機關團體方面，以基督教慈善救濟的工作而言，1934年統計了一份〈基督教在華所辦主要慈善事業調查表〉中顯示，孤兒院的數目還是比較多的，安老院病人也有不少，但臨時的施診所確實比較少，也沒有特別標出哪些是屬於農村的工作。[87] 在政府尚未設立普遍

---

82 毛吟搓，《基督教的農村事工》，頁30-31。

83 邵雯光，〈農村教會應興辦的事工〉，《青年進步》，第79期（1925），頁20。

84 何鳳智，〈基督教對於農村婦女的責任〉，《希望月刊》，第11卷第1期（1934），頁8-9。

85 毛吟搓，《基督教的農村事工》（上海：文瑞印書館，1935），頁37。

86 本文找到的是一則瘟疫的禱告文，內容是：「全能的上帝，凡人的生死有病無病都屬於主，我們因了犯罪，所以主降時疫懲治我們，伏求主施恩垂聽我們禱告，懲治的時候，求主記念主的憐憫垂顧我們有重罪的人，今我們遭遇時症，求主施恩消除這災禍，主責罰我們如同父親責罰兒女，我們既受這責罰，願各人心中都能覺悟自己身體的懦弱，年壽短促，盡心學習天道，至終得享永生。這是靠著我主耶穌基督，阿們。」引自〈時疫禱文〉，《聖公會報》，第19卷第16期（1926），頁24。

87 〈基督教在華所辦主要慈善事業調查表〉，《時事月報》，第11卷第3期（1934），頁105-106。

的醫療院所之前，基督教的農村醫療大部分採用的是一種施醫佈道的模式，這類施行者多是有學醫背景的教徒。[88] 但這看在學習過現代公衛的學者來說，仍顯不足。當然，站在基督教的立場，中國幅員廣大，中央政府是無法面面俱到的；而且農村人民對政府派來的官員，還是不太信任，毛吟搓就指出：「可惜的！現在一般有權有錢的大老，正在大聲疾呼的，喊著救濟農村，開會討論，研究、調查、報告，忙得不得了，其實都是足未涉農，毫不知道農村是何物的門外漢，或者請了幾個留學生，做了專家，戴上一副外國農家的眼鏡，來看中國的農村，也是有學識無經驗的來胡說一大堆，騙騙幾個大人老爺的不懂，於實際的生產上是不見成效的。」[89] 故凡醫療衛生未完備之處，各種教會團體還是努力進行農村醫療的工作。

舉例來說，如福建協和學院的農村服務工作，據1933年的報告，已進行了約九年的歷史。該校學生除開辦小學、主日學外，也提倡衛生協助施藥等工作。也有教會的牧師會主動捐助從事這類工作的學校，用以發展鄉村服務之用。[90] 湖南的教會，如芷江內地會設有農村分會26處、福音醫藥房3處。[91] 一些教會醫院，也持續和教會合作，進行農村的醫藥衛生改進工作。[92] 當時有些中醫，也參與了鄉村衛生的實際工作。例如武進的一位名醫叫錢今陽，除了擔任中央國醫館支館施診所主任，及創辦光華平民施診所外，一些地方的施診所，也都會請錢擔任醫生。這類醫者多會涉入農村醫療事務，例如他就曾擔任普濟局和東鄉名山施診所的醫生，實際參與農村醫療。[93] 而相對的，負責農村醫療衛生的人，例如省立鄉村衛生實驗區的主任朱雲

---

88 段友德，〈旺清門基督教自立會近聞（奉天）：施醫佈道之先聲〉，《通問報：耶穌教家庭新聞》，第844期（1919），頁7。

89 毛吟搓，《基督教的農村事工》，頁21。

90 〈基督教學校新聞：福建協和學院農村服務工作擴張計畫〉，《中華基督教教育季刊》，第9卷第4期（1933），頁109。

91 郭彼得，《通問報：耶穌教家庭新聞》，第1718期（1936），頁15。

92 毛吟搓，《基督教的農村事工》，頁20-30。

93 〈本社撰述委員錢今陽服務農村醫局〉，《壽世醫報》，第1卷第9期（1935），頁15。

達，就是錢今陽的老朋友，這種網絡關係，對農村醫療的開展是有助益的。[94]

　　雖然教會的農村慈善醫療和政府希望建立之常規農村衛生制度還是有所差別，而政府總希望將衛生與醫療之事「收歸國有」，但三〇年代以後，政府其實是希望和教會合作的，[95] 而教會方面也有和政府合作的聲音，希望教會醫院能參與到政府的計畫之中，這樣教會醫院就會變成基層醫院，而能幫助訓練農村的醫療人員。[96] 陳志潛也想和教會合作，他沒有排斥教會的工作，只是覺得衛生制度的建立恐怕比發展慈善或一時的熱忱來得更長遠有效，他說：「教會和北京第一衛生所，當時均肩負著一些健康教育工作。該所訓練助產士和為學校教師提供健康教育。在其總目標中強調個人衛生，……然而，我們的目的是想具有更大的規模，並影響更多的聽眾。介紹醫學科學的基本概念，而不是教他們一些專門技術。教會已經成立了一個健康教育委員會，它的計畫包括對教師的培訓、衛生現狀的調查和組織在街上進行衛生宣傳活動。而且希望盡一切可能，將其健康教育活動與教會傳道計畫結合進行。」但陳認為這種對大眾宣傳的工作只有暫時性的效果，很快就被人們忘記了。[97] 不過，中央政府還是抱持正面態度的，1935年內政部衛生署專員胡美，在蕪湖召開全安徽省教會醫院院長的聯席會議。胡美在會議上說，他奉衛生部劉瑞恆部長的請託，已在湘、贛、浙三省召開教會醫院會議，目的就是希望各教會醫院能和各地省縣政府，進行公共衛生的合作，鄉村衛生教育與宣傳工作也在其中。在場的教會醫院領袖，也指出教會在歷次天災、瘟疫時都會進行救濟，所以應當支持政府，並認為這樣的會議還要持續進行。[98] 華北基督教農村事業促進會山東支部的常年大會，在山東齊魯神學院舉

94　〈省立鎮江鄉村衛生實驗區主任過常回籍〉，《壽世醫報》，第1卷第9期（1935），頁15。
95　教會大學與政府之合作，見羅偉虹主編，《中國基督教（新教）史》，頁562。
96　劉天路編，《身體‧靈魂‧自然：中國基督教與醫療、社會事業研究》，頁291。
97　陳志潛原著、端木彬如等譯，《中國農村的醫學──我的回憶》，頁52。
98　〈全省教會醫院院長聯席會議〉，《衛生半月刊》，第2卷第10期（1935），頁40。

行，會上該大學醫院公共衛生主任姚尋源醫師也針對教會如何與政府合力提倡公共衛生事業，進行專題演講。[99] 當然，這種趨勢是本文可以指出的，但實際工作的開展，還是無法證實，因為中日戰爭很快爆發了。

戰後，仍有不少有心人士努力於農村衛生工作。1948年，當時基督教青年會會長是顏福慶，有鑑於體育人員之缺乏，特別發起體育事工，並請上海衛生局張維局長擔任導師並演講，其他局處長也擔任講員，讓全國青年會派員參加，課程內容除體育外，另有健康教育、個人衛生、公共衛生、公共安全等四個科目申請，可惜農村衛生的項目，已沒有被強調。[100]

五、結論

民國時期的農村醫療衛生事業之開展，有各種包括基督教會或與衛生相關的團體力量進駐，二〇年代末，南京國民政府的力量也加入，一方面希望將醫藥衛生之權力收歸於中央，當時的衛生專家認為鄉村衛生不能和慈善事業混為一談，[101] 但又因為諸如農村衛生力量的缺乏與不健全因子，所以仍必須與原有教會的力量進行合作，原來教會的力量並沒有完全退去，而是成為一種輔助。1934年，定縣發展出一套農村衛生的體系，並為中央政府推薦給全國採用，「在設計第一個系統的農村衛生保健組織時，我們盡力避免單純抄襲傳教士們在中國農村已經做了的工作，我們確信那樣將可能是一個嚴重的錯誤。教會醫學畢竟是在那些和中國農村非常不同的條件下發展起來的，它主要是私人開業行醫及以醫院和門診部行醫來滿足那些與西方社會具有某些共同之處的有特權的城市名流們的需要，並未重視廣大

99 〈華北基督教農村事業促進會山東支部聚年會〉，《田家半月報》，第2卷第11期（1935），頁8。
100 上海檔案館藏Q400-1-1926「上海基督教青年會」。
101 李廷安，《中國鄉村衛生問題》，序，頁1。

農民群眾。」[102] 陳志潛這段話其實是對教會的農村醫療衛生工作的性質有所誤解，因為教會進去農村的力量，不是整個醫學或衛生體系的模式，而是慈善和教育的本質，在資源不足且落後的中國農村，各種力量的整合，雖說多是政府的責任，但對貧苦的農村民眾而言，慈善力量應該是多多益善為宜的。可以說「農村」（鄉村）這個地方，多多少少是大家競逐醫療與衛生話語權的場域。

不可諱言的是，即便有所開展，但整體來說民國時期的農村衛生運動還是失敗的，「到民間去」、「到鄉間去」、「服務農村社會」，固然是民國時髦之高調，但「言之非艱，行之時艱」，非常不容易。[103] 1947年的一場農村景象回顧，仍非常慘烈，農村「千里之內，無一防病事業」、「散步農村，舉目四望，一般農民十之八九，形容憔悴、面現菜色。」[104] 可見農村醫療還是不如人意的，從教會的言論也可看出，當時傳教的重心，似乎還是在城市，而且這裡面還存在資源排擠的效應，例如：「監理公會的宗教事工，本來城鄉互相工作的，照數量計算起來，鄉間的教堂，比之城市底多，只是近年來為了維持經濟關係，把農村間的教會，逐漸裁撤，城市的教堂還能夠照樣維持，鄉間的教堂，不久恐將全部裁併，這是因經濟所促成的教會不景氣，是覺得非常的不幸。」[105] 這樣的觀察反映了1935年左右的狀況，當時鄉村教會可能是失敗的，政府投入的資源與人力，還是不及都市的多，經濟上的無法持續支援，是農村事業的致命傷。雖然當鄉村成為一個好的衛生或慈善救濟之間的實驗場域，但都遇上經濟資源匱乏、無利可圖的問題。

1923年在上海舉行了博醫會醫學會議，會上福勒醫師曾宣讀一篇報告是關於〈教會醫學政策〉的文章，該文曾經充分加以討論：

---

102 陳志潛原著、端木彬如等譯，《中國農村的醫學——我的回憶》，前言，頁65-66。
103 鄭子修，〈龍山三月記〉，《青年進步》，第109期（1928），頁92。
104 李入林，〈農村衛生之管見〉，《醫潮月刊》，第1卷第3期（1947），頁4-5。
105 毛吟搓，《基督教的農村事工》，頁45。

我們主張，在中國的每一個教會醫院應當有優質人員和設備，成為高效率的內科及外科模範，從這裡應當向人民散佈出醫學和衛生知識，它應當成為宣傳基督福音的中心。可以認為，許多現存的組織並沒有達到這個標準。向國內的教堂發出的呼籲並沒有結果，小醫院的處境是可悲的。問題是在於，究竟中國人能被吸引來從事、支援這些工作，以致使中國人得以自給自足到怎樣一種程度。另外一點是，教會應該佔領更多的地盤，還是把精力集中於一些能做得更好的工作上，而同時又盡可能幫助中國人自己幫助自己。究竟那一種做法更聰明一些？[106]

二〇年代後，教會對醫療傳教工作是充滿分歧的，一方面認為教會應該繼續藉醫療來擴張勢力，另一方面又強調教會應該放手讓過去醫療傳教的工作交給中國人來做，但對這種教會醫院的本土化，各差會或不同的醫學傳教士仍持不同之意見，其實代表了某些外籍教會人士對教會醫院完全移交給華人的擔憂。[107] 幸好，換一種角度來思考，在南京國民政府成立後，衛生署雖然將醫療衛生的工作收歸國有，但基督教的力量、洛克斐勒基金會的支持、鄉村教會在各地的工作，仍對鄉村衛生工作發揮了一定程度的正面力量；而且，三〇年代後的趨勢，政府還是希望與教會保持合作的關係，教會一樣也可以在農村衛生上發揮作用；只可惜，政府似乎沒有思考如何好好整合宗教團體的力量，開展農村的事務，而且中日戰爭太早開打，這種合作關係沒有能激盪出另一種更完整的模式。即便是定縣經驗，也不過就是小小的實驗區，很難撼動全國農村衰弱的情況。李入林曾有一段深刻的評論，時值1947年，國共戰事逆轉的一年，他說：「本年六月一日，我同敝科防盲主任李波到江寧衛生院參觀一切，看見十九位窮苦農民來院割治眼疾，號金、診金、藥金、手術費一概免收，該院醫生

---

106 中華醫學會編，《中華醫學雜誌》，1923年，頁246。
107 李傳斌，《條約特權制度下的醫療事業：基督教在華醫療事業研究（1835-1937）》（長沙：湖南人民出版社，2010），頁81-82。以及羅偉虹主編，《中國基督教（新教）史》，頁530。

護士招侍此等勞苦農民，體貼周全之至，我因之有感對馬龍瑞院長說：政府一切事業皆具此等精神，共產黨可以自行消滅。馬院長說，任何黨爭都可以沒有了。」[108] 他的話，顯示出農民的需求，這已非新聞，長久以來的老問題並沒有得到解決，可以說國民政府在農村的工作確實失敗了，他們並沒有成功整合或尋求更多和教會合作的機會，這也可作為觀察近代中國變遷態勢的一種輔助性視角。

---

108 李入林，〈農村衛生之管見〉，《醫潮月刊》，第1卷第3期（1947），頁5。

【特殊事工】

一戰時期「華工基督教青年會」的再評估

李宜涯、王成勉

摘要

　　雖然近年學界開始注意到第一次世界大戰華工的研究，但是對於照顧他們的「華工青年會」卻缺少研究，多是一筆帶過，是以學界迄今仍對「華工青年會」之貢獻有著衝突的看法。究其原因，乃是學者們在接觸到華工或教會史料時，往往會有意無意地避開史料中的宗教層面，以致難以全面了解或正確的評估「華工青年會」的工作與影響。從青年會會徽英文的 Spirit, Mind, Body 即可顯出，其「德育」不僅是字面的道德意涵，更有著基督教教理中身、心、靈的全面關懷。有鑑於此，本文將檢視與討論「華工青年會」的「德育」工作，以補過去在此方面研究之不足。本文特別著重當時「華工青年會」針對華工發行的《華工週報》來研究，論述「華工青年會」如何來推展「德育」的觀念，同時檢討其「德育」的成效。

關鍵詞：華工青年會、《華工週報》、德育、華工、第一次世界大戰

一、前言

一百年前，第一次世界大戰爆發，中國也捲入這場以歐洲為主的
戰爭。中國對當時歐戰最主要的貢獻，就是有十四萬多名的中國工人
被招募前往歐洲戰地為協約國工作。[1] 這些華工解決歐洲勞力欠缺的
窘境，也為自己掙得一份不錯的工資。[2] 原本這些華工所受學界關注
極少，近百年來只有一些零散的作品。而因第一次世界大戰百周年將
屆的關係，有大量的各式紀念及慶祝活動，而學術會議與書刊出版亦
現高潮，其中亦有一些針對華工的研究與活動。[3] 可以說華工對於一
戰協約國的貢獻得到各方學界的肯定。

而當年讓華工能盡心工作，又能適應歐洲生活的原因，則首推在
法國成立的「華工青年會」。這是英、美的基督教青年會見到華工初

---

1 關於在歐洲或法國華工的人數，一直眾說紛紜，範圍從135,000至200,000之間。法國當時的一位青年會
　工作者 G. H. Cole稱，法國華工總共約有140,000多人。見 G. H. Cole, "With the Chinese in France," p. 12.
　(n.d., preserved at The Kautz Family YMCA Archives of the United States, Minneapolis, Minnesota，以後簡稱美
　國青年會檔案)。Chen Ta提出的數字是150,000人（100,000名在英國部隊營地，40,000名在法國部隊與
　工廠，還有10,000名則為美國部隊服務）。見 Chen Ta, *Chinese Migrations, With Special Reference to Labor Con-
　ditions* (Washington D.C.: Government Printing Office, 1923), pp. 143-144. Thomas LaFargue認為英國部隊有華
　工150,000名，而華工的總數量為200,000。見 Thomas LaFargue, *China and the World War* (Stanford: Stanford
　University Press, 1937), p. 151. 陳三井教授認為在英、美、法政府下工作的華工有140,000人；根據在華盛
　頓中國使館所接獲的報告，包括在法國、埃及、美索不達米亞、巴勒斯坦等地的華工，在1918年10月
　的人數總共約有175,000人，故可推論為協約國工作的華工總人數當在175,000至200,000人之間。見陳三
　井，《華工與歐戰》（臺北：中央研究院近代史研究所，1986），頁34-35。新近出版的研究在數字上
　比較接近，如 Paul J. Bailey稱法國有135,000名華工。Paul J. Bailey, *Reform the People: Changing Attitude towards
　Popular Education in Early Twentieth-Century China* (Vancouver: University of British Columbia Press, 1990), p. 234.
　而徐國琦認為「華工總人數保守數字大約為14萬人」。徐國琦，《文明的交融：第一次世界大戰期間的
　在法華工》（北京：五洲傳播出版社，2007），頁59。Xu Guoqi, *Strangers on the Western Front: Chinese work-
　ers in the Great War* (Cambridge, Mass.: Harvard University Press, 2011).
2 當時中國普通工人薪資一天是兩角，而當時法國招工，根據惠民公司的合同每日工資為五法郎（折合國
　幣約一元七角八分），雖是法國工人的二分之一或三分之二，但較國內所得高八、九倍。陳三井，《華
　工與歐戰》，頁95。事實上華工在法國工作時，也會因為工作性質不同與工作獎金之故，有更高的加
　給。
3 如第一次的「一戰華工國際學術研討會」於2008年9月於山東威海召開，後來出版了論文集：張建國主
　編，《中國勞工與第一次世界大戰》（濟南：山東大學出版社，2009）。第二次的華工國際學術研討會
　（International Conference of Chinese Workers in the First World War）於2010年5月於法國的Boulogne-sur-
　mer和比利時的Ypres兩地召開，該會議的法文版論文集也已出版。Li Ma (ed.), *Les travailleurs chinois en
　France dans la Première Guerre mondiale* (Paris: CNRS, 2012)

到歐洲難以適應的困狀，積極的在華工中推展青年會的各項活動項目，在穩定華工的身心上成就卓越。可是學界對於「華工青年會」的評價並不完全，也不一致。如一些學者抱著失敗的觀點來看「華工青年會」的貢獻，因為華工回到家鄉後，既沒有導致山東地區基督徒數量的增加，也沒有證明那裡公民道德的提高，更沒有方法在中國的情境運作出工會意識；而華工史淪為現今公關活動，或被誇大為中國參與一戰的意義。[4] 而另一些學者則對「華工青年會」的教育項目有諸多的肯定。[5] 基本上，學者多傾向用青年會的四育精神來了解青年會。但是有趣的是，對於「華工青年會」的「德育」卻是避而不談，更談不上研究。例如研究歐戰與華工的資深學者陳三井，在出版《華工與歐戰》一書後，還特為文補足「華工青年會」的重要性，但是〈基督教青年會與歐戰華工〉一文只有兩行提到德育：「青年會四元目標之一的德育活動，本以宗教活動為主，透過星期日之佈道、宗教演說、信徒集會暨查經祈禱會等，傳佈福音，勸人為善，藉此禁絕不良嗜好。」[6] 同樣的，徐國琦在研究華工的專書中，有一章專門提到青年會與華工（Chapter 8: The Association Men and Chinese Laborers），可是只有一頁多的地方提到青年會的德育工作，而且常是引用報導的資料，而多非「華工青年會」的史料。[7] 也就是說這些接觸到華工或教會史料的學者，在研究時會有意無意地避開史料中的宗教層面。這

---

4 持這樣觀點的作品可以參見Nicholas John Griffin, "The Use of Chinese Labor by the British Army, 1916-1920" (unpublished Ph. D. dissertation, University of Oklahoma, 1973) and Judith Blick, "The Chinese Labor Corps in World War I," *Papers on China*, Vol. IX (1955), pp. 111-145；Paul J. Bailey, 〈第一次世界大戰中的華工：一段被忽視的插曲,中國外交政策與現代勞工史的演變〉，魏格林、朱嘉明主編，《一戰與中國：一戰百年會議論文集》（北京：東方出版社，2015），頁477-493。

5 採正面觀點的作品可以參見陳三井，〈基督教青年會與歐戰華工〉，《中央研究院近代史研究所集刊》，第17期上冊（1988.6），頁53-70；Nicholas John Griffin, "The Use of Chinese Labor by the British Army, 1916-1920" (unpublished Ph. D. dissertation, University of Oklahoma, 1973) and Margo S. Gewurtz, "For God or for King: Canadian Missionaries and the Chinese Labour Corps in World War I," in Min-sun Chen and Lawrence N. Shyu (eds.), *China Insight: Selected Papers from the Canadian Asian Studies Association Annual Conference Proceedings, 1982-1984* (Ottawa: Canadian Asian Studies Association, Carleton University, 1985), pp. 31-55.

6 陳三井，〈基督教青年會與歐戰華工〉，《中央研究院近代史研究所集刊》，第17期上冊（1988.6），頁59。

7 Xu, *Strangers on the Western Front*, pp. 194-195.

樣的做法與心態，很有可能會造成研究上的不足或不平衡，不但讓學界難以全面了解其工作與貢獻，更無法正確的評估「華工青年會」的事工與影響。

有鑑於此，本文將檢視與討論「華工青年會」的「德育」工作，以補過去在此方面研究之不足。[8] 全文將分成三個部分來討論，第一個部分是「華工青年會」的背景、成立與運作；第二個部分是「華工青年會」如何來推展「德育」的觀念；第三部分則是檢討其「德育」的成效。在史料上，主要是依據「華工青年會」專門為華工所發行《基督教青年會駐法華工週報》（以下簡稱《華工週報》）[9]，另外輔佐以當時的一些教會史料、個人傳記及近年研究成果。

二、「華工青年會」與《華工週報》

「華工青年會」的成立，係因歐戰華工無法適應歐洲的工作與生活。一戰時期由於協約國嚴重的人力短缺，所以積極向外招募工人，以解決勞動力不足的問題。而中國勞工成為一個主要的招募對象，共有 14 萬多人前往歐洲。但是要有效運用這些勞動力卻不是一件容易的事。一方面是華工大概百分之八十以上為文盲，[10] 他們對歐洲及其語言一無所知，過去也從沒有機會了解歐洲文化，以致因巨大的文化和語言屏障產生了許多誤解。[11] 另一方面協約國軍方管理不當及軍官

---

8 本文之初稿"Beyond Simple Charity: A New Appraisal of the YMCA Service to Chinese Laborers in World War I"，曾在第42屆 International Conference of the International Society for the Comparative Study of Civilization (ISC-SA) 上發表（DeVry University's Crystal City (Arlington) campus, Washington D.C., June 6-9, 2012），感謝與會學者提供諸多意見，此稿現已經過重大修正。

9 有關《華工週報》之介紹，請參見李宜涯，《聖壇前的創作——20年代基督教文學之研究》（臺北：秀威資訊科技，2010），〈第六章：文學的社會服務——《華工週報》個案研究〉。

10 G. H. Cole, "With the Chinese in France," p. 20.

11 R. M. Hersey, "General Statement Regarding The Y.M.C.A. Work for the Chinese laborers in France," (March 1919), p. 7. (YMCA Archives); Michael Summerskill, *China on the Western Front: Britain's Chinese Work force in the First World War* (London: Michael Summerskill, 1982), p. 150; Blick, "The Chinese Labor Corps in World War I," pp. 124-125; Chen Ta, *Chinese Migrations, With Special Reference to Labor Conditions*, p. 147. 陳三井，《華工與歐戰》，頁123。

對華工的種族歧視，以致在華工營引起了許多衝突、罷工及反抗。[12]

　　雖然宗教有著撫慰人心的功能，但是英法軍方卻對傳教士與教會組織保持距離，以免他們影響到軍中的管理，無法讓華工充分的被利用。例如英國軍方在招募華工時，主張用傳教士在中國受到尊敬的地位，來幫助他們招募勞工。但是又篩除掉在政治上太自由、進步或持和平主義的傳教士。[13] 當華工到達法國時，英國的青年會提議願意照料華工的生活，提供娛樂，卻被軍事當局以擔心「鬆弛紀律」而拒絕。[14] 同樣的，法國當局相當懷疑青年會的工作，認為青年會的幹事會傳播罷工理念與無政府主義，將會干涉他們對華工的管理。[15]

　　可是到1917年底到1918年初時，許多華工營每幾日就發生暴動或衝突，而有青年會私下進行輔導的卻平安無事。[16] 這終使英法軍方求助於教會，而英美的基督教青年會積極接受這項邀請，號召「中華基督教青年會」與歐美的中國留外學生一起加入這項照顧華工的行動，組成了「華工青年會」。[17] 通過北美基督教青年會國際委員會的動員，有109名青年會幹事為華工服務。其中有74名中國學生幹事。其中，29人直接來自中國，39人來自美國，5人來自英國，1人是在法國留學的中國學生。[18]

　　北美基督教青年會對於籌組「華工青年會」上扮演很重要的角色。首先它派遣北京青年會的幹事艾德敷（Dwight W. Edwards）到法

---

12 1916年至1918年，華工營中發生了25起騷亂，包括4起暴亂，2起勞工之間的爭鬥，3起違反連隊制度案，以及2起陰謀案。Blick, "The Chinese Labor Corps in World War I," pp. 128-129.

13 Griffin, "Chinese Labor and British Christian Missionaries," p. 290.

14 Blick, "The Chinese Labor Corps in World War I," p. 126; Cole, "With the Chinese in France," p. 14; Charles W. Hayford, *To the People: James Yen and Village China* (NY: Columbia University Press, 1990), p. 24.

15 Peter Chen-main Wang, "Caring Beyond National Borders: The YMCA and Chinese Laborers in World War I Europe," *Church History: Studies in Christianity and Culture*, vol. 78, no. 2 (June 2009), p. 329；亦見吳相湘，《晏陽初傳：為全球鄉村改造奮鬥六十年》（長沙：岳麓書社，2001），頁20。

16 Blick, "The Chinese Labor Corps in World War I," pp. 126-130.

17 R. M. Hersey, "General Statement Regarding The Y.M.C.A. Work for the Chinese laborers in France," (March 1919), p. 7. (YMCA Archives). "Y.M.C.A. Chinese Section, Report of Conference of Workers held at Peronne on 23/24 July 1919," p. 31. (YMCA Archives of the USA.

18 關於「華工青年會」的組成經過，請參見：陳三井，〈基督教青年會與歐戰華工〉，《中央研究院近代史研究所集刊》，第17期（1988.6）；與 Wang, "Caring Beyond National Borders."

國的華工營調查人員與當地情況。他發現還需要有 127 名青年會幹事加入對華工的服務。他特別強調,所需的中國幹事要有以下的特徵:1. 有良好的基督徒品格;2. 能夠講北京官話和英語;3. 具有不干涉軍事紀律的機智;4. 具有做好工作又堅定信仰的經驗。[19] 雖然不能說華工青年會所有的中國幹事都具有這樣的美德,但是至少這是北美基督教青年會在號召與選取中國幹事的重要考量之處。的確當時被號召來的留美學生,許多是一時之選,如晏陽初剛從耶魯大學獲得學士學位的第二天就啟程前往法國,其他的留美學生如史義瑄、林語堂是哈佛大學的學生,傅葆琛是耶魯大學研究生,蔣廷黻剛從歐柏林學院獲得大學學士,芝加哥大學的碩士生桂質廷、傅智,剛自 Hamline University 獲得大學學士的程其保等。而當時積極配合北美基督教青年會呼籲的中華基督教青年會,其所派到法國的 29 名幹事,也都是熟悉青年會事工,又有與外國幹事一起推動工作經驗的人,包括上海青年會幹事陳維新、北京青年會幹事石葆光等。[20]

以 109 名幹事組成的青年會來服務 14 萬華工,當然在人手上嚴重不足。即使部分青年會幹事用巡迴的方式以一人來照顧幾個營區,估計還是有三分之一的華工始終沒有機會得到青年會的服務,甚至發生華工因而抗議的事件。[21] 服務華工的青年會幹事必須在非常艱苦與辛勞的情況下來服務,而且必須隨華工營隊的變化而調動。

青年會工作可以分成三類:教育、消遣和宗教。教育功能包括教授各類課程,如中文、英語、法語、歷史、地理和數學。許多關於公共事務、公民的職責和權力、健康和衛生以及戰爭意義的演講,已安排在勞工回國後進行。晏陽初關於識字的富有經驗的教學是個很大的成功,他創辦的《華工週報》是個很有用的工具,激起了勞工的學習

---

19 Edwards, "The Chinese Labourer in France in Relation to the work of the Young Men's Christian Association," p. 16. (YMCA Archives of the USA).

20 此方面的中文資料與報導非常多,直接的幹事報導,請參見:陳維新,《駐法華工青年會紀要》,《中華基督教會年鑑》,第 6 期(1921),頁 208-210。

21 Xu, *Strangers on the Western Front*, p. 182.

興趣，把現代世界展現給了他們。至於消遣活動，雖然許多勞工在歷經十個小時的體力勞動後對體育活動不感興趣，但他們中有些人喜歡足球、室內壘球、籃球和排球，有些則下象棋、放風箏或玩其他遊戲，還有些華工以戲劇自娛娛人。在宗教方面，這些青年會幹事提供佈道、禮拜服務，講解《聖經》，舉行禱告會甚至洗禮。儘管有些華工營不允許有宗教服務，但青年會幹事仍試圖從個人層面施加基督教的影響。除以上活動，青年會幹事代寫家書也大受華工歡迎。[22]

籌辦《華工週報》的晏陽初（1893-1990），就是在這背景下，剛自耶魯大學畢業後就登船前往歐洲。晏陽初抵達法國後，立即開始忙碌的為華工代寫代讀家信。在服務過程中，他發現勞工們資質不差，其為文盲多係過去因貧窮而未受教育。故如能授以簡單文字，便其自寫家信，則遠比代寫讀家信，要更有意義。所以他自字典、報刊與口語中選取一千餘字作為基礎，編成教材。經過第一班40人的學習，其中有35人可以完成課業，對青年會與華工而言，均是相當振奮之事。

晏陽初和青年會的幹事既發現華工們對識字讀書的濃厚興趣與潛力，故一方面開辦識字班，加強他們讀、寫能力，另一方面則計畫使他們回國後能發揮新力量，影響社會。因此便在青年會的宗旨下，積極推行另一計畫。即是出版一份週刊，先用毛筆寫在大張的紙板上，然後刻板石印，初期每期印10,000本。[23] 這樣一來可以增加其流通量，二來也能擴充內容，達到影響效果，並成為識字班的輔助教材。

《華工週報》從1919年1月15日創刊第一期，到1920年1月1日完成最後一期，共計發行了45期。在絕大部分的期數中，都是維持兩位編輯一起工作。第1期至第17期，主編為晏陽初，傅智（即傅若

---

22 Blick, "The Chinese Labor Corps in World War I," pp. 126-128; Summerskill, *China on the Western Front*, pp. 170-174；陳三井，《基督教青年會與歐戰華工》，頁53-70。

23 根據編者自己的描述，其印刷方法為，「巴黎無中國印字器具，本報之創辦者，費盡心力，方得下法：1. 寫成大字，2. 照相將原稿縮小，3. 電鍍師雕鉛版，4. 法人印刷。」〈本報周年之回顧〉，《華工週報》，第45期，1920年1月1日。

愚，1893-1984）為副主編；第18期至第38期，主編為傅智，陸士寅擔任事務編輯；第39期至第45期，主編為陸士寅（1889-?）。晏陽初在完成階段性任務後，就在1919年6月返美，進入普林斯頓大學就讀。傅智原也是美國留學生，在赴法為華工同胞服務近一年後，於1919年11月左右，返美至芝加哥大學，續攻社會學碩士。當時同是留美學生的陸士寅，曾任中華民國駐美國西雅圖總領事館領事，後赴法服務華工。

　　《華工週報》由於定位清楚，其讀者群是特定的對象，為一群知識程度不高的華工，因此，晏陽初在第1期的篇首，以「本報特告」方式說明該報的編輯方針：「本報是特為開通華工的知識、輔助華工的道德、聯絡華工的感情辦的。」[24] 在這方針下，以後每期的內容，頭條皆是主編針對華工身心靈做論述，約一千字左右，其餘輔以固定的專欄，如「歐美近聞」、「祖國近訊」、「華工近況」等，並間雜以「歐戰小史」、「名人傳略」、「世界奇聞」、「中國歷史撮要」等專欄。一些半文言的小笑話與圖文並茂的小漫畫也不時出現。在晏陽初的編輯策略下，《華工週報》受到華工的歡迎。週報編輯自己寫稿與翻譯，整理來稿與編輯，並自刻鋼版，銷售量最高時達到15,000份，可謂是對華工影響很大的一份刊物。[25]

　　《華工週報》的編輯方式為：一頁分上下兩欄，每欄橫排30行，直行20字，每欄含標題有600字，一頁可容1,200字，每期4頁8欄，所以一期的稿量約4,000餘字（扣除標題）。沒有標點符號，而是用傳統中文古書圈點的方式斷句，如有重要文句，或是用連續的圈點，或是字體形式與油墨加重，以顯示重要性。嚴格來說，就編輯技巧而言，《華工週報》並無突出的技巧可言。但在1910這個年代，《華工週報》根據當時流行的樣式，上下對排，採用石印，而在文句

---

24 〈本報特告〉，《華工週報》，第1期，1919年1月15日。在週報的最後一期，編者在回顧時，再度提出這個宗旨，「本青年會因此創辦週報，聯絡華工的感情，增進華工的智識，輔助華工的道德。」〈本報周年之回顧〉，《華工週報》，第45期，1920年1月1日。

25 徐國琦，《文明的交融：第一次世界大戰期間的在法華工》，頁138。

重要表達處，線條顏色會加深加重，以示突顯，晏陽初的編輯意識已可謂很強。

《華工週報》在基督教青年會的支持下創辦，內容自會以青年會的精神「德、智、體、群」來培養現代的工人，而且受到了華工的歡迎。[26] 可是到底在《華工週報》中間有無「德育」的教導？有無基督教的精神？如果有的話，那週報編輯在面臨軍檢與不得傳教的勞工約定中，是如何在字裡行間透露與傳遞這樣的信息？最後，華工得悉了這樣的訊息嗎？這些問題的探究不僅使我們能更加了解這一份極有意義的週報，更可以做為檢視「華工青年會」在「德育」方面的教導。

三、《華工週報》的關懷與福音

相較於一般的刊物，《華工週報》有一些特殊性與優勢。首先，《華工週報》的發行對象非常清楚。它是辦給這些在一戰被招募來歐的華工。它不需考慮外面的市場或外界對它的觀感。第二，《華工週報》就是由華工青年會的幹事在負責編輯，所以它的編輯策略簡單又清楚。只要通過英軍檢稿官的檢查，就不會有多大的干擾。而英軍檢稿官所重視的，是華工的安定與不可涉及政治事務。[27] 故基本上，雖然其不能成為一份教會刊物，但是基督教青年會的「德、智、體、群」基本觀念是可以被接納的。第三，《華工週報》所佔的優勢，就是其成為晏陽初所辦「千字課」的輔助教材。其不但被廣泛的閱讀，而且是被仔細地閱讀。[28] 第四，也由於晏陽初以《華工週報》作為

---

26 關於《華工週報》中有關基督教青年會精神的發揚，請參見：李宜涯，《聖壇前的創作——20年代基督教文學之研究》，〈第六章：文學的社會服務——《華工週報》個案研究〉。

27 《華工週報》對於英軍檢稿擴大範圍，甚至限制華工的愛國言論，有其難言之隱。一直到了最後一期，《華工週報》的編者提到經營週報的幾項主要困難時，才言明其中之一為「檢稿嚴屬」：「本報每期原稿，均須英軍檢稿官批准後，方能付印。諸君時惠稿件，鼓吹僑胞，熱心愛國，往往不見登載者，蓋在此也。譬如山東問題，西藏交涉，輿論反對的。」〈本報周年之回顧〉，《華工週報》，第45期，1920年1月1日。

28 不只是晏陽初自己用《華工週報》當輔助教材，其他營區亦是如此。如《華工週報》刊載：「白龍青年會的漢文班，自從本報出版以來，即用之為課本，教導工人，此事已著成效，近得劉君自梅夫來信說，

「千字課」的輔助教材，所以其在用字選擇上是與課本配合，特意不用艱澀的文字，更不採用文言。[29] 雖然乍看之下該刊物過於淺俗，但這正是能為華工接受之處。所以在分析《華工週報》的基督教訊息時，這些特殊性與優勢應該作為重要的參考。

在面對這些百分之八十以上是文盲，又多來自鄉野的下層民眾，如何傳遞基督教的訊息是一個很好的考驗。《華工週報》的確沒有講述基督教的教理，也沒有直接傳佈基督教。但是若從間接傳教的角度，這份刊物無疑是借用基督教與基督徒的「社會關懷」來見證基督教。晏陽初在《華工週報》連載四期的〈革心〉這篇長文，就是最直接與最具代表性的作品。

〈革心〉一開始先點出中國今日的問題是在於人心。文章表示中國不富不強的原故，是因為私心的人太多，中國人的心壞了。正如樹根爛了，樹枝不能發葉結果。民心壞了，國家自不能富強。故當今全國人民急需革心。「有新心而後有新人，有新人而後有新社會，而後有新國家。」[30] 晏陽初認為，醫心病必須要經由宗教，但是中國舊有的儒、釋、道、回等教，雖然世代相傳，信眾數以兆計，卻無法達到正心、齊家、治國的境界，故「千年以來，人心愈趨愈下，私心愈久愈大！」[31]

這時候晏陽初以美國為例，提出了解決之道。他指出美國今日富強，就是因為公心人多，私心人少。而這並非是美國人生來就比中國人好，而是：

該處青年會亦將仿效辦法，以週報為課本云。」〈週報課本〉，《華工週報》，第13期，1919年5月14日。

29 例如《華工週報》所辦的徵文比賽，即要求用白話。後來還刊登啟事：「在前報我們已經說得清楚，所有的一切論著，必須要用普通官話。但是此次寄來的論說，十居八九，都是用文話，你們都知道，工人中讀書識字的不多，通文理的更少，若把文話登在報上，實在是廢工廢錢了，我們也說過，著作不得過六百字，此次寄來的論說，有九百有一千的，自此以後若寄來的論說，有用文話的，或是過了字數的，無論你著得如何的美好，我們都不讀你的論說，你若不尊規矩，是你自己吃虧咯。」〈特告注意〉，《華工週報》，第7期，1919年3月12日。

30 晏陽初，〈革心〉，《華工週報》，第11期，1919年4月30日。

31 晏陽初，〈革心〉（一續），《華工週報》，第12期，1919年5月7日。

> 美國人請了治心革私的良醫把他們的心治好了，所以他們國民
> 的公共心大、愛國心深，他們的國家也一天天的富強。……美
> 國人的神醫，就是耶穌基督。……受了他醫治的人，無論男
> 女、無分種族，他心是公的。不單是愛自己，也是愛他人。[32]

也正因為如此，才會有這麼多美國傳教士長途跋涉遠赴中國，為中國
人辦醫院、開學堂。

這篇長文到了最後，晏陽初以「華工青年會」的中國幹事作為例
子，來呼應前面的論述，也見證耶穌醫治的功用。他表示這些中國在
外留學的青年：

> 把學業擱起，冒潛水艇的危險來為華工作公僕，……是因為他
> 們各個人的心，都是為神醫耶穌改革過，醫治過的，因此他們
> 有公德心，有愛同胞的心，做愛同胞的事。所以各位應當理
> 會，耶穌是外國人的神醫，能改革外國人的心，也能改革中國
> 人的心。……所以我愛國的同胞呀，若我們要祖國富強，非人
> 人有公德心不可，若要人人有公德心，非急請神醫耶穌基督革
> 心不可。[33]

〈革心〉這篇長文連載了四週，就好像一篇宣教的講章，先講出
人類的問題，然後進一步提到其他宗教的無助，然後提出耶穌能夠改
變人心的大能，最後以自己這批正在為華工服務的青年會幹事作為見
證。無論在文章的前後呼應，或是在感性訴求上，都顯得很有力量。

在《華工週報》第8期有一篇與〈革心〉互相呼應的文章，就是
晏陽初對於「華工青年會」總幹事柯和璧（G. H. Cole)的介紹。晏陽
初在〈柯和璧先生〉一文中，仍然是沿用這種以關懷行動來見證耶穌

---

32. 晏陽初，〈革心〉（二續），《華工週報》，第13期，1919年5月14日。
33. 晏陽初，〈革心〉（三續），《華工週報》，第14期，1919年5月21日。

改變人心，以及以關懷來把愛傳遞出來的說法。晏陽初在文章的一開始就提到「柯和璧先生，坎拿大人氏，基督教徒」，因其為見到「我國國大人多，但是國人無知識的大多，稍有知識的人，又缺公德心，以致國弱民貧，幾乎到了亡國的地步」，故在大學時候，就立志要來幫助中國、教育人民和改革人心。[34] 柯和璧大學畢業後就履行其志願，在1905年到天津辦青年會，後來受邀到上海全國總會演講部任職，在全國各地演講，讓數以萬計的中國同胞受惠。

晏陽初特別指出柯和璧持續對華人的關懷。當一戰爆發，柯和璧本來擔任坎拿大軍事青年會的教育部部長。可是見到華工語言不通，風俗不熟，喫虧受苦，即辭了他教育部長的職分，來法國為華工開辦青年會。

> 各位看看柯先生愛我華人的心，是如何的大，如何的深，先生自任駐法華工青年會總幹事以來，白天夜晚少有一點閒時，不是為這樣事籌畫，便是為那樣事勞心，一月半月的又要到這裡去調查華工的情形，又要到那地方去開設青年會，無日無時。[35]

到了文章的結尾，晏陽初巧妙的歸結到，柯和璧的這些關懷，其實都是來自於基督教的愛。他說：

> 柯先生不是中國人，他愛中國的心，比我們更深更切。……是因為他是基督徒，有了基督的普愛在他心裡。……除了基督教外，什麼教能出這樣有博愛有公德心人，如柯和璧先生呢？[36]

雖然晏陽初在全文一點都沒有傳教，也沒有呼召華工參加教會、

---

34 晏陽初，〈柯和璧先生〉，《華工週報》，第8期，1919年3月26日。
35 晏陽初，〈柯和璧先生〉，《華工週報》，第8期，1919年3月26日。
36 晏陽初，〈柯和璧先生〉，《華工週報》，第8期，1919年3月26日。

或是研讀《聖經》。但是對於身受青年會照顧的華工來說，縱使不對基督教產生好感或興趣，也不致敵視基督教。

在45期的《華工週報》中，有這種直接提到基督教的文章並不多。週報的主編用不著談論基督教的教義，也用不著去講述青年會德智體群的道理。因為德智體群的項目已經在華工營中實施，而青年會的幹事也身體力行的落實他們對於華工的關愛。所以要驗證他們的成效，當以華工感受的角度來看。

隨著戰爭的結束，有越來越多的青年會幹事離開，此時許多華工都藉此機會表達他們對於幹事們的感激之情。在《華工週報》中至少有二、三十則這樣的簡短通訊，其中可以看出他們對於青年會幹事的感念，也有一些看出他們知道基督教的精神在其中。現摘記幾則如下：

> 王長泰先生，久任阿本科地方青年會幹事，為人和藹可親，辦事認真熱心，該地第一百二十九隊華工弟兄們，念先生服役之功，近來特製金牌一面贈之，牌上刻有「愛人如己」四字。[37]

> 全紹武先生，自希成，直隸北京人，向在奴埃兒地方辦理華工青年會，成績卓著，近日調回巴黎任職。奴埃兒工人，感全先生平日恩愛，有銘詞一首寄來如下，功不再誇，真幹則成，名不在沾，有事則憑，事我幹事，維其德馨，真光滿胸露，塵土入臉青，談笑皆可意，往來無定程，可以傳真理，講聖經，無片辭之可摘，無辭辛之苦聲，救主十字架，提反石頭刑，全君云，何懼之有。[38]

> 伯勒司本會幹事正樂德陳維新二君，錶上所刻者，有「推己及人」與「愛人如己」等字樣。[39]

---

37 〈華工近況〉，《華工週報》，第15期，1919年5月28日。

38 〈華工近況〉，《華工週報》，第22期，1919年7月16日。

39 〈華工近況〉，《華工週報》，第39期，1919年11月19日。

幹事王鴻恩回國，華工第一百三十六隊感激其德，於臨行之際，特製錦廉一幅贈之，本孔孟之大法，信主有道，鎔歐亞於一治，德我無疆。[40]（以上內文之底線皆依原文）

從「愛人如己」、「真光滿胸露，塵土入臉青」、「傳真理，講聖經」、「信主有道」等用詞，可以知道華工了解到青年會幹事的服務，同時能引用教會的語句來表達他們對幹事的敬意。

四、「華工青年會」的歷史意義

雖然北美青年會在號召中華基督教青年會與當時留學北美的中國青年前去幫助華工時，認為這有人道關懷、宣教與傳佈西方文明的三大意義。[41] 但是要衡量14、5萬人的華工受到何種影響，是否成為文明的大使回到鄉土去發揮影響，是一件不可能評估的事，但是這並不影響「華工青年會」的重要性。「華工青年會」至少有四點重要的歷史意義。

第一、就基督教在華發展史來看，這是中國基督徒第一次回應了國際基督教的運動，以人力、財力參與這場照顧華工的工作。無論是中華基督教青年會，或是參與「華工青年會」的幹事，注意到萬里外華工的苦況與需要，熱情的放下自己的工作、課業與時間前去照顧，不但讓數以萬計的華工受惠，讓協約國得到幫助，也贏得當時英、美、法軍方的敬佩。這代表中國基督徒的成熟，能夠以關懷的心去看社會與自己的同胞，參與這場規模宏大的愛心計畫，這是難能可貴

---

40 〈華工近況〉，《華工週報》，第41期，1919年12月3日。
41 北京青年會幹事艾德敷（Dwight W. Edwards）被北美青年會派往法國調查華工情況後，他提出八個為華工開展工作的理由，共可以歸納為三點。第一，華工在社交、身體和心理上都遭受創傷，急需青年會去改善他們的條件；第二，從長遠來看，這種情形給傳教事業提供了機遇，該機遇不僅對華工有利，也有利於基督教在中國的發展；第三，這是一個使華工對西方產生良好印象的黃金機會，他們回國後將可向同胞傳播西方文明。並啟動青年會服務華工的工作。Edwards, "The Chinese Labourer in France in Relation to the work of the Young Men's Christian Association," pp. 2-6.

的。

第二、就基督教會宣教史的角度來看，「華工青年會」的時機也是深具意義。基督徒在華一直是少數中的少數，在十九世紀下半葉才經歷眾多的反教，即使到二十世紀初，中國還是屬於宣教區，不但經費上多未能夠自立，在教務上也多為宣教士主政。所以這時中華基督教青年會能夠積極參與國際事工，是難能可貴的。換個角度來說，如果當時中華基督教青年會規避這項行動，不但失去見證自己信仰的機會，也會被宣教士所鄙視。更進一步來說，服務華工不見得是一件光榮的事，也不會讓這批青年會的幹事有參與世界大戰，站在勝利者一方的感覺。但是當關懷的感動到來時，有沒有站出來服事的意願，有沒有對自己所信仰的神負責，有沒有對《聖經》中關懷弱勢的教導去回應，這是宣教史所注重的地方。

第三、無論就基督教史或是就教育史來看，這是中國平民運動的源頭。由於「華工青年會」在識字教學上的成功，當時中華基督教青年會全國會總幹事余日章即思在國內也來推行識字教育，以解決眾多文盲的問題。[42] 余日章認為中國民主之不彰，在於文盲之比例太高。由於國民多數不能讀寫，不具備現代國之基本知識，即不會察覺做為公民之權利與責任，也就不會去注意國家之福利。[43] 故其氏思考將華工青年會成功的識字教育用於國內。於是余氏在晏陽初、傅若愚回國之時，延攬他們到青年會，擔任新在智育部下成立的「平民教育科」的正、副主任，以從事推動平民教育之工作。當時青年會的中西幹事都給予晏氏許多意見，而晏氏他們也訪問各地、查考資料，根據在法國教授華工的經驗，重新編輯出「平民千字課」四冊。[44] 實行的前兩年中，在長沙、煙台、嘉興、杭州四地試辦平民識字教育，都有相當

---

42 有一資料表示當時華工識字率達百分之三十八。Garrett, p. 156.

43 David Z. T. Yui, *Character, China's Hope* (NY: Foreign Division, YMCAs of the United States and Canada, 1924), p. 3.

44 Garrett, pp. 159-165. 有關晏陽初辦平民教育之理想，可見其中英文之傳記，吳相湘，《晏陽初傳》；Hayford, *To the People*；另可見晏陽初著，詹一之編，《晏陽初文集》（成都：四川教育出版社，1990）。

理想的效果。[45] 這吸引了不少國內教育家的注意。後來在1923年夏於北京開中華教育改進會年會時，一些教育家同時開了平教會議，成立了「中華平民教育促進會總會」，並聘請晏陽初為總幹事。而晏陽初則邀請另一位「華工青年會」的幹事傅葆琛出任平教總會的鄉村教育部主任，在各地推動鄉村平民教育。

雖然晏陽初被禮聘他去，而且另外已成立專門的全國性平民教育機構來推動此事，可是青年會並未就此停止其平民教育的理想。余日章一方面以傅若愚接任青年會平民教育科主任之職，一面視國內各地的情況，或者由青年會單獨主持，或者與平教會合作辦理，繼續積極進行平民教育。據傅若愚在1935年時統計，青年會所教過的平民學生人數當在25萬人左右。[46] 而後余日章更將「平民運動」進一步推展到「公民運動」，以改革政治與人心。[47]

第四、「華工青年會」的意義不限於其對於華工、青年會、平民運動的影響。參與「華工青年會」的幹事自己也受到這場運動的洗禮。他們在關懷的行動中看到華工的純樸與可塑性，自己也深受感動，進而改變自己人生的方向。晏陽初的例子是最多人所了解和引用的。後來晏陽初曾向賽珍珠提到他為什麼要推動平民教育運動。當他在巴黎發行《華工週報》時，有一天，他收到了一封信，這封信出自一位經過讀寫訓練的勞工之手，其內容大致如下：

> 晏先生，尊敬的先生：自你主辦的報紙問世以來，我開始了解天下發生之每件大事。但是，你的報紙價格十分便宜，每份才

---

45 這四次測試的情況都稍有不同，但測試及格率均在六、七成。傅若愚，〈平民教育運動〉，《中華基督教會年鑑》，第8期（1925），頁128；Garrett, p. 161; Herman C. Liu and Daniel C. Fu, "The Association and Citizenship Training," in Publication Department, National Committee YMCA's of China, *The Young Men's Christian Association and the Future of China* (Shanghai: Association Press of China, 1926), p. 63.

46 傅若愚，〈青年會對於平民教育之貢獻〉，《中華基督教青年會五十周年紀念冊》（上海：基督教青年會全國協會，1935），頁48。

47 關於余日章推動公民運動，請參見王成勉〈余日章與公民教育運動〉，《教會、文化與國家》（臺北：宇宙光出版社，2006），頁41-76。

售一生丁，我擔心它會由於虧本而停刊。茲寄上 365 法郎，請收下，這是我在法國當三年勞工積攢下來的錢。[48]

晏陽初告訴賽珍珠：

這件事使他深受感動，他決心用自己畢生的精力去充實他們的生活……從那天起，晏陽初對自己的抉擇毫不動搖，他決心回到中國去，把自己的畢生精力和才智奉獻給祖國的平民百姓。[49]

華工所以飄洋過海，辛辛苦苦地在戰地作勞工，就是為了掙點錢回鄉。但是這位勞工願意將三年所存下來的錢全部捐給《華工週報》，可以了解到《華工週報》在華工眼中的分量有多大，以及晏陽初內心的衝擊有多大。

事實上，不只晏陽初受到感動。在 1919 年 7 月「華工青年會」的幹事大會中，許多幹事分享了自己的感觸。有一個曾在教會學校畢業的幹事說，他以前因為十九世紀外國對中國的侵略，所以一直很反對傳教士和傳教工作。但是當他到法國與外國青年會幹事一起工作後，看到傳教士在工作上的關愛與犧牲，因而徹底改變了過去的態度。[50]也有留美的幹事分享，他透過與外國青年會幹事一起工作，發現了自我的意義。他到法國起先不是為同胞服務，而是努力「發現自我」。在法國服務一年後，他非常開心，因為他「可以自信地宣稱找到了自我——不是通過他個人的能力，而是通過他與英國和美國青年會幹事一起工作。」[51]

---

48 賽珍珠，《告語人民》（桂林：廣西師範大學出版社，2003），頁 266。1 法郎等於 100 生丁（centimes）。

49 賽珍珠，《告語人民》，頁 266-267。

50 "Y.M.C.A. Chinese Section, Report of Conference of Workers held at Peronne on 23/24 July 1919," p. 31.

51 "Y.M.C.A. Chinese Section, Report of Conference of Workers held at Peronne on 23/24 July 1919," p. 31.

可以看出「華工青年會」是一個相互感染與相互影響的交集處。華工在這兒感受到這些幹事、青年會以及基督教，華籍的幹事從華工與外籍幹事的身上也得到感動、協約國的軍方與宣教團體也肯定了青年會的工作與幹事。這種多方面的意義應該是關懷事工的特色。

五、結語

研究教會史時，有一個需要注意的地方。就是衡量教會的某一事件、運動或發展時，不宜用一般社會的指標。過去對於「華工青年會」的負面看法似乎有些道理，就是既然華工主要來自山東，可是華工回去後山東的基督徒人數並沒有增加；又如，既然華工被給予了工人集體的觀念，可是後來中國的工會並沒有因此興起。同樣的，既然他們處在西方社會，又受到青年會以德智體群的陶冶，他們是否成為北美青年會所寄望的西方文化的大使？這些質問似乎有所見地，但教會人數多少、教堂多少、工會有沒有增加，以及傳遞西方文化與否，並不是基督教發展一定的成果，或者說在一定的時間內就要看得到的發展。要衡量教會，應當用教會所看重的，或是用教會的特色來衡量，這樣才能了解教會的價值所在。

換個角度來說，「華工青年會」的意義超過了時間、空間、人數的衡量標準。雖然我們無從得知有多少人因為這些幹事而相信基督教，但是那並不是這些幹事們所關切的。因為他們是在聽到遙遠的歐洲有同胞需要關切，心中有了感動，就放下自己手上的工作去幫助他們。他們教導與幫助十幾萬幾近文盲的華工，毫無名利、金錢可求。雖然他們好像一無所得，但是基督教的社會關懷就是這樣的教導。基督徒是否回應這樣的教導，才是衡量他們的標準。在幾十年或是幾近一百年後，檢視「華工青年會」的史料，還是讓人感受到這股關懷的力量，這就是那批青年會幹事的信仰見證。

一種歌唱的關懷：
以《民眾聖歌集》（1931）爲例

陳睿文

摘要

　　1931年，時任燕京大學宗教學院院長的趙紫宸（1888-1979）與燕大音樂系主任美國傳教士范天祥（Bliss Wiant, 1895-1975) 共同為中國普通基督徒民眾編撰《民眾聖歌集》一本。該讚美詩集無論是從文本角度、抑或是從音樂層面，都可謂是1930年代初中國讚美詩處境化程度之反映。與此同時，該讚美詩集也因貼合民眾、強調為普通百姓所用之特點，表述出在華基督教的社會關懷性。本文即希望通過對《民眾聖歌集》文本的具體解讀，來窺看中國處境化讚美詩如何表述其社會關懷，以此為推動中國基督教的發展作出自我獨有的貢獻。

關鍵詞：《民眾聖歌集》、趙紫宸、讚美詩、處境化、社會關懷

1931年，時任燕京大學宗教學院院長的趙紫宸（1888-1979）聯合燕大音樂系主任美國傳教士范天祥（Bliss Wiant, 1895-1975）為中國普通民眾基督徒編撰《民眾聖歌集》一本。此前不久，兩人已共同翻譯、編輯了《團契聖歌集》（1931），內含124首讚美詩，由趙以文雅之譯辭譯出，范天祥選取世界知名讚美詩曲調為該集編配曲調，以供燕大團契所用，反響良好。在此情形之下，趙、范二人又擬出版貼合民眾、言辭簡潔、運用中國曲調之讚美詩一集，以回應當時基督教「到民間去、到鄉村去」之趨勢。故由趙親自作詞，范選取中國曲調進行譜曲，編輯出《民眾聖歌集》一冊，從文本、音樂方面皆反映出1930年代初中國讚美詩處境化之具體程度，也因其貼合民眾、強調為普通百姓所用之初衷與特點，表述出在華基督教社會關懷之特性。本文即希冀通過對《民眾聖歌集》文本的解讀，來窺看中國處境化讚美詩集所蘊含的關懷特徵。文章第一部分將對撰寫《民眾聖歌集》之緣起進行論述；第二部分將通過分析趙紫宸的作詞十原則，觀測文本創作的處境化及其中所體現的關懷民眾、以民眾為基的特點；第三部分則旨在從上帝論、基督論角度對《民眾聖歌集》文本的處境化進行探索；結論部分將對中國處境化讚美詩與基督教社會關懷之關聯進行探討。

一、「一種創作的試驗」：《民眾聖歌集》之緣起

　　早在1921年，時任教於蘇州東吳大學的趙紫宸即已開始對處境化聖詩創作有所興趣，並親身嘗試翻譯聖詩多首，「但他不懂音樂，不知道他所翻譯的詩能否配合音樂的抑揚頓挫。」因而在1925年，當趙聽聞燕京大學正由年輕的美國傳教士范天祥擔任音樂系主任之時，即致信范天祥，表達自己對翻譯聖詩的志趣，希望邀約他一同合作。[1] 他寫道：「我和范天祥先生通信，約他和我合作，批評我的譯

1　黃永熙，〈燕京大學與〈普天頌讚〉──范天祥與范天祥夫人〉，范燕生，《穎調致中華──范天祥

詩的音節。」[2] 次年，趙應燕大聘請赴該校任教。1927年，又被任命為燕大基督教團契崇拜主任。他在1931年時寫道：「連任至今，已經四載，我遂有機會試用我所譯的聖歌。所譯的詩斷斷續續地油印出來，合成一冊，共七十七首；其中有二十餘首不合用。」[3] 趙所提的這本聖歌集，是指他與范天祥在1931年為燕大團契所編的《團契聖歌集》，由趙翻譯、編輯歌詞，范天祥選擇曲譜，「集中各譜，源流不一。」[4] 出版不上十六個月，就已告罄。應同道者擬購函索，趙紫宸再譯若干首，以為增補。[5] 對於歌集皆為西方聖歌之現象，范天祥寫道：「也許有人要問，在現代的中國，為中國基督徒運動製作聖歌集，何以不採用中國的音樂？對於這個問題，我們有兩個答覆。第一：本集所收入的樂譜，多係基督教古今名著，是世界所公有的，並不是一國一族所可私佔的……。第二：譯詩者與我正計劃將已採集的中國調子，譜入四聲，再寫新詩，另為一集，以補本集的不足。兼收並蓄，諒亦為同道們所樂聞。」[6] 而這本中國調子的詩歌集，即是其後由范趙共同編著的《民眾聖歌集》。

趙紫宸在1931年敘述《民眾聖歌集》的創作緣起時寫道：

> 本年一月底，范天祥教授與我將團契聖歌集全部付印後，就打算再同著這本民眾聖歌集。范先生擔任將所收集的民歌調子，

傳》（香港：基督教文藝出版社，2010），頁x-xi。

2 趙紫宸，〈序一〉，《團契聖歌集》（北平：燕京大學基督教團契，1933），頁1。

3 趙紫宸，〈序一〉，《團契聖歌集》，頁1。。

4 對此，趙紫宸寫道，「三年之前（指1928年），我和范天祥先生協定同著一本聖歌集，我獨任譯詩輯文的工作，他獨任選譜校樂的工作。他是音樂專家，選譜校律，諧音協律，悉係精擅，有他至誠般的協助，我的心願，就更加熱切了。」趙紫宸，〈序一〉，《團契聖歌集》，頁1；范天祥，〈序二〉，《團契聖歌集》，頁6。

5 對此，趙紫宸寫道：「此聖歌集出版不上十六個月，已經告罄了。而同道者擬購函索，猶繼踵而來。於是范天祥先生催我再譯若干首，以為增補的再版。我因身病國難，了無情緒，竟耽誤了半年多。茲因例假在即，這重公案不能不了；故增譯改作，六天竣其事。工作既成，便可付梓。其他種種，皆范天祥先生負責。」趙紫宸，〈再版序一〉，《團契聖歌集》，頁4。

6 范天祥，〈序二〉，《團契聖歌集》，頁5。

譜入四聲，我擔任按譜作詩。[7]

　　對於創作的緣由，他指「我為民眾作這聖歌集的緣故，第一是要為民眾作一點極微細的貢獻，第二是自己願意做一種創作的試驗。」[8] 另又特別指出《民眾聖歌集》與《團契聖歌集》在適用對象上及創作方法上的不同：

> 團契聖歌集是為學生作的，文字樂譜，都偏於深雅。民眾聖歌集是為民眾——尤其是農村的民眾——作的，文字應當極淺顯，調子應當極普通。[9]

　　這裡即強調了對如何作民眾為之所用的讚美詩的考量。與此同時，趙又提到《民眾聖歌集》及《團契聖歌集》在文本、音樂內容、形式上所呈現的不同之處：

> 團契聖歌集的詩是翻譯的詩，樂是西方的樂。民眾聖歌集的詩歌是創作的詩歌，音樂是中國民間原有的音樂。[10]

　　此外，兩者完成的時間、速度也不一樣：

> 團契聖歌集是積年工作的成績，有歌一百二十四首。民眾聖歌集是一月之內完成的工作，只有五十四首讚美詩。[11]

　　對於創作速度之快，趙對此自己有所補充：

---

7 趙紫宸，〈序一〉，《民眾聖歌集》（北平：燕京大學宗教學院，1931），頁1。
8 趙紫宸，〈序一〉，《民眾聖歌集》，頁1。
9 趙紫宸，〈序一〉，《民眾聖歌集》，頁1。
10 趙紫宸，〈序一〉，《民眾聖歌集》，頁1。
11 趙紫宸，〈序一〉，《民眾聖歌集》，頁1。

我自有生以來，直到一個月之前從不曾做過一首民眾可用的詩歌。我也明知我的試作，並沒有什麼優點。只有一點，還可以自信，就是所著的歌不算不通順罷了。我作這本歌集，好像從樓上投石到樓下，石頭越近地越落得快：前禮拜五下午晚上，作了十首，禮拜天下午三點鐘之內，作了六首，於是五十餘首詩，完全脫稿。[12]

談及《民眾聖歌集》的創作，趙指「這些創作的民眾聖歌是一種嘗試，也許是毫無成功的。但因朋友們的鼓勵，我就大膽做去。」對於作詞的方法，趙紫宸指：「我作歌與今人填詞一樣，並不知道音樂，只知道按空格填字。填好之後，由同事范先生彈琴，同學鄭少懷先生試唱，將不合節奏的地方一一指出來，然後修改好。」[13]

上述篇幅反映出，趙紫宸與范天祥所編輯的《民眾聖歌集》，有別於《團契聖歌集》。在緣起及文本創作上，與《團契聖歌集》相比，有一定的關聯，但又絕不相同。是趙范新的嘗試，也是當時音樂處境化的典範。

二、「適合民眾的需要」：《民眾聖歌集》與作詞十原則

趙紫宸親自為《民眾聖歌集》作詞訂立了十條原則：「在作歌之前，我為自己規定了十個原則。」[14] 這十條原則，不僅是一種歌詞上的處境化詮釋，也充分表達出對普通民眾信徒的一種社會關懷。

首先，趙紫宸指出：「民眾的聖歌必須是具體的。民眾嘴裡唱歌，心裡應能看見一幅圖畫。」他認為：

像團契聖歌集裡「在永默中跪覲真神／以愛解悟真契」那一類

---

12 趙紫宸，〈序一〉，《民眾聖歌集》，頁1。
13 趙紫宸，〈序一〉，《民眾聖歌集》，頁6。
14 趙紫宸，〈序一〉，《民眾聖歌集》，頁1。

的話，不但是太抽象，並且是太奧妙了。在民眾聖歌中，應當有「看小鳥飛上又飛下啊，看田園裡那百合花，也不種，也不收，也不會紡紗，天父尚且養活他，何況咱？」這樣的詞句來幫助百姓理解。[15]

在此，趙紫宸乃指讚美詩的具體性能幫助普通民眾看到自己活在耶穌基督裡。

其次，他認為，「民歌要簡單淺白才好。簡單淺白的歌，是老少咸宜，雅俗共賞的。」他指寫歌詞要像「白樂天做詩，要吟詠給老嫗聽」，認為「我們做民眾的聖歌，尤其應當如此。」即強調所作的詞須幫助民眾較易地理解其間的內涵。然而，趙又強調，「不過簡單淺白，極不容易。我初次試作，在這一點上，恐怕還不會達到深造。」[16]

第三，趙紫宸又提到：「但我們不必完全遷就民眾，有時候，倒也要想法子提高民眾的思想與觀感。」對於如何提高民眾的思想觀感，他首先提出「竭力要極淺白的文字，含帶詩意」，並以〈天恩歌〉中的歌詞「他是春風我是草／讓他吹」為例來說明此點。在此，趙將上帝比作春風，將人們比作草，意含春風的吹拂能促進草木的生長，正如上帝的恩典增進民眾的靈性一般。簡言之，趙希冀借詩性的語句來表述上帝的恩典。除此之外，趙又嘗試用中國詩詞的韻律來幫助民眾理解讚美詩的意蘊。他用〈四時歌〉舉例：

　　許多白藕如春雪，一片青苗得太陽。

在此，「許多」與「一片」、「白藕」與「青苗」、「春雪」與「太陽」相對應，以幫助民眾理解與記憶，如趙所言：「大約是民眾所能明白的。」他又以運用〈如夢令〉所作的〈聖靈歌〉為例：「但

---

15 趙紫宸，〈序一〉，《民眾聖歌集》，頁1-2。
16 趙紫宸，〈序一〉，《民眾聖歌集》，頁2。

願聖靈同在，好像太陽光彩，照透我心肝。教我深深崇拜，神愛，神愛，廣大過於洋海。」另有「調寄浪淘沙，花月吟，鳳凰臺思美人等歌，都用原詞音節。」趙指出：「民眾應當享受美。本集中的試作，非常注重這一點。」[17] 其間的關懷意味不言自明。

對於第四條原則，趙紫宸指出：「民眾的歌，應當含帶中國民族性中最好最重要的成分。據我看來，中國人的生活是與自然打成一片的。中國人要見上帝，必在人生裡，也必在自然裡。」[18] 關於這點，他在其作品中也常常提到中國人與自然的關係，例如他寫道：

> 中國人對於自然有特殊的態度。在中國的思想史上，自然與人兩個概念，非常融合。……人在自然裡見人道，在人生裡見天道；人最高的生活就是法自然。……我國沒有發展科學，卻發明了人與自然融洽的道理……我國天人一貫之說，實為我國根本的思想。自然與人，其道一貫……人是自然的一份子，自然是人的本性。自然與人渾然一體。[19]

在〈陶詩中的宗教〉一文中，趙又間接地闡述了自然與中國宗教的關係：

> 我又以為無論陶淵明的宗教觀或教義如何，他已經瞻見了「真意」，已經與自然的靈魂——上帝——作了深密的神交。……這個真意，不是東籬的菊花，不是南山的佳氣，也不是相與飛翔的山鳥——乃是超乎言詮的神化的感應。既知而可辨，欲辯而無言。其中有不可臆度的平安，有超乎言說的聲明。此等境界，我無以名之，名之曰宗教！[20]

---

17 趙紫宸，〈序一〉，《民眾聖歌集》，頁2。
18 趙紫宸，〈序一〉，《民眾聖歌集》，頁2。
19 趙紫宸，〈基督教與中國文化〉，《真理與生命》（1927年6月），頁252-255。
20 趙紫宸，〈陶詩中的宗教〉，《真理與生命》（1929年4月），頁16。

在此，自然與宗教相融合，自然表達了宗教，宗教的含義也通過自然表述出來。因而，兩者相融合。如趙所指，在《民眾聖歌集》中，就「常有引人欣賞自然的句子。」他舉例：

> 如晨更歌裡的「東方太陽紅，頭上天色藍」；清晨歌裡的「天高飛鳥過，地闊野花香」；一日歌裡的「清晨起來太陽紅，背了鋤頭去作工，路旁有古松，灣曲像老龍，上接白雲一重重」。[21]

上述段落描繪出太陽、天空、飛鳥、花朵、松樹等的自然景物，反映出趙對於自然與宗教的神學解讀。又如〈清晨歌〉，乃基於詩篇「太陽如同新郎出洞房，又如勇士歡然奔路」（19: 5），趙以相似的詞句將《聖經》經文與文化闡釋融合於一體：「清晨起來看，紅日出東方，雄壯像勇士，美好像新郎」即是一例。內容對自然景觀多有描繪，也期以直觀的實相、具體的描繪來幫助民眾理解。

在第五點中，趙紫宸指出：「民眾有深懇的宗教經驗，做歌的人，應當揣摹描擬，為之宣洩。」[22] 關於宗教觀念這一點，他在其著作中也闡述得較為清楚：

> 我們也要了解信教的人有了深遠幽邃的宗教經驗，洶湧迴盪於胸中，便藉著他們的藝術，造廟宇，建儀節，創音樂，作詩歌，立佛像，圖諸天，以為他們經驗的象徵。[23]

在此，趙不單單視經文、教義、實踐為宗教的核心，另強調了宗教經驗的重要性，指讚美詩能藉以表述民眾宗教經驗，宣洩其宗教感情。在其〈基督教與中國文化〉一文中，他亦特別闡明宗教經驗、神

---

21 趙紫宸，〈陶詩中的宗教〉，《真理與生命》（1929年4月），頁2。
22 趙紫宸，〈陶詩中的宗教〉，《真理與生命》（1929年4月），頁3。
23 趙紫宸，〈基督教與中國文化〉，頁257。

祕經驗與中國文化的相關性：

> 中國文化中第四種有勢力的傾向是中國人的神祕經驗。……將
> 來在中國，基督教若能根深蒂固，在神祕的宗教經驗有深邃的
> 得獲，即少數人亦足以像一粒芥子，一勺酵頭。祇要有少數有
> 經驗的虔信的人存在，宗教即有存在，基督教即有存在；基督
> 教即有存在，無論怎樣受抨擊，受迫害，也不能損其毫髮。教
> 會的組織是重要，但終沒有個人的得到宗教經驗與信仰那麼重
> 要。[24]

在《民眾聖歌集》中，他以下述段落舉例說明該集中的讚美詩如
何幫助民眾表述其宗教經驗：

> 例如祈禱歌中「主啊，惟你知道我，何等軟弱何等窮」，晚禱
> 歌中「有時要心焦，有時要打算，心上愁雲難打消，父知道，
> 恩比愁雲更加高」，尊主歌中「耶穌最慈悲，耶穌最有情，他
> 能感化我，除我鐵石心」，試探歌中「耶穌救主可憐我，教我
> 祈禱勝惡魔，教我罪心像死井，永遠不會起風波」，那一類的
> 話，都是為民眾發洩宗教情緒的。[25]

趙紫宸另提到《民眾聖歌集》中又考慮到「至如勇敢，喜樂，仁
愛，和平，等經驗」。[26] 比如，「耶穌最勇敢，耶穌最聰明，捨生救
贖我，與我一同行」（〈尊主歌〉，第20首）一句，突出耶穌人性
上勇敢、聰明的特性，以及與信徒同行的特點；「主的教訓比蜜甜，
主的誡命勝黃金，我願萬事跟從主，歡喜與主永相親」（〈祈禱

---

24 趙紫宸，〈基督教與中國文化〉，頁258、259。
25 趙紫宸，〈序一〉，頁4。
26 趙紫宸，〈序一〉，頁4。

歌〉，第30首）則表述出主訓寶貴以及作為基督徒的快樂。[27] 宗教
經驗作為一個寬泛的詞，趙在其作品中的強調也是多元的。

在第六點中，趙紫宸強調了在民眾讚美詩中表述讚美的重要性：
「民眾的聖歌應當是讚美詩。只有心向上帝的讚美，能夠使人心有高
山景仰的感想。」他以〈聖父歌〉為例：「例如聖父歌：『大慈大悲
聖天父，我們抬頭見恩光，見你榮耀像日月，見你仁慈像海洋。』」
在此，趙以佛教的語言「大慈大悲」來表述對聖父的景仰。[28] 又如在
〈靈修歌〉中，「我心所相信，被殺的羔羊」，「我心所仰望，聖子
主耶穌」，「我心所敬愛，基督耶穌名」等句亦充滿頌讚意味。[29]

在第七點中，趙紫宸指出：「民眾的詩歌自應與民眾的日常生活
有密切的關係。詩歌裡若能將生活寫出來，不甚好麼？」[30] 對此，
〈種田歌〉即具體直觀地反映出該點的內涵：

> 戴上涼帽，背上鐵鋤，到田裡去，讚美耶穌！
> 插秧拔草，苗長草枯，盼望收成，讚美耶穌！
> 種瓜種豆，瓜大豆粗，靠天吃飯，讚美耶穌！
> 春天撒種，不亦樂乎，摩拳擦掌，讚美耶穌！
> 夏天太陽，好像火爐，仍舊作工，讚美耶穌！
> 秋天雨水，滿江滿湖，仍舊作工，讚美耶穌！
> 冬天收藏，全家歡呼，克勤克儉，讚美耶穌！

在此，趙紫宸用具象的語言，描繪出一年四季農民勞作之景象，
正如其自己所言：「種田歌有十節，語句極簡單，是依從這一條原則

---

27 趙紫宸、范天祥，〈祈禱歌〉，《民眾聖歌集》，頁30。
28 趙紫宸，〈序一〉，頁5。趙的這種佛化的寫作風格，在其《團契聖歌集》的翻譯作品中，有更多反
　映，用中國本土更為熟知的佛教、地方宗教言辭，來表述基督教的一些概念，是趙詩歌翻譯的慣用手
　法，也是其處境化創作的重要表徵。
29 趙紫宸、范天祥，〈靈修歌〉，《民眾聖歌集》，頁31。
30 趙紫宸，〈序一〉，頁5。

的。」[31] 在這裡，趙通過對不同季節、情景的描述，嘗試將民眾日常生活寫入讚美詩中。貼近民眾、關懷民眾、從民眾出發，皆詮釋而出了。

另一例子為〈農事歌〉（第48首），亦細緻描繪了民眾的日常生活與作工：

> 深深雨露蓬蓬雪，紅紅太陽光華，春天撒種在田中，長青苗，
> 種菜蔬，種豆得豆，種瓜得瓜，汗流千點不徒勞。
> 養豬養羊養牛馬，都得肥壯繁盛，養蜂得蜜最清甜，得暢銷，
> 養雞鴨，養魚滿池，種竹成林，養蠶做絲像銀條。[32]

〈主召歌〉（第33首）則是這一原則的另一反映。在此，趙將耶穌描繪成與民眾共同作工的人：

> 耶穌召我跟他行，召我與他同作工，我耕田地看見他，與我同
> 在勞苦中，我趕集我看見他，挑擔推車兩相從。
> 耶穌召我拜天爺，虔心祈禱依靠他，清早與主同出門，晚上與
> 主同回家，救主名是我榮名，主光即是我光華。[33]

趙自己指出：「在主召歌裡，生活與宗教，說明是冶於一爐，不能分開的。」[34] 他另在〈耶穌基督〉一文中亦指出，「生活是生長的，寬廣的，建設的，創造的，活潑潑而充滿了生趣的，並無需乎戰戰慄慄地去執圭執玉！耶穌要給人的生活，是一種新人的生活，其中有上帝的動盪，所以能有中心，能自由，而浩然長往。」[35] 在這些與

---

31 趙紫宸，〈序一〉，頁5。
32 趙紫宸、范天祥，〈農時歌〉，《民眾聖歌集》，頁48。
33 趙紫宸、范天祥，〈主召歌〉，《民眾聖歌集》，頁33。
34 趙紫宸，〈序一〉，頁5。
35 趙紫宸，〈耶穌基督〉，《耶穌基督：燕京宗教時論》（北平：燕京大學宗教學院，1934），頁30。

民眾日常生活密切相關的讚美詩中，趙的創作暗示出在基督徒的生活中，俗世並不會與宗教世界分離。

除了描繪作工的讚美詩，另有讚美詩反映出民眾生活的多方面，如〈喜慶歌〉（第51首）、〈家庭歌〉（第52首），〈小孩歌〉（第53首）以及〈喪事歌〉（第54首）等，均涉及到社會倫理。如趙所寫：

> 中國人是最重倫常，最重人生的，因此本集中有四時歌中的「常將好處分兄弟，閒把經文教子孫」，感恩歌中的「我有好朋友，我有好鄰家，家裡有親人，門前有好花」等等話。至於人情深切，悱惻纏綿，民眾雖不文，其感覺實有較幽遠悠長於文人者，至情至性，都在民間！我做本集，不能表彰此情於什一，慚也何如，慚也何如！[36]

在〈喜慶歌〉中，趙紫宸描繪了夫妻關係，須是「男婚女嫁成家庭，偕白頭，到老，相親相愛結同心」。又道：「一夫一婦快樂深，彼此相敬更相幫，到永遠，好合，有福同享苦同當」。在〈家庭歌〉中，他定義了「家庭好」與「好家庭」兩對概念。對於建立家庭的好處，趙指出：「夫婦相敬無煩惱，福同享，苦同當，相親相愛好偕老」。怎樣才是一個好的家庭？那即是「早晨晚上拜真神，讀聖經，做禱告，一家都與主相親」。而成立一個好家庭的結果則是：「親骨肉，好子孫，兄弟姊妹共一門，你體諒，我幫助，大家和睦受天恩」。在此，趙紫宸通過讚美詩文本，向民眾闡述了簡樸的倫理，最為直接地呈現出《民眾聖歌集》的關懷特性。

在論述第八條原則時，趙紫宸寫道：「民眾詩歌，也應當幫助民眾關心社會國家世界的生活。」[37] 他以〈晚禱歌〉（第3首）為例，

---

36 趙紫宸，〈序一〉，頁3。
37 趙紫宸，〈序一〉，頁5。

指：「本集晚禱歌的末節可以代表這個意思：『人生多難多辛苦，求主可憐有病人，安慰孤與寡，救度苦與貧，引導國家得和平，更加恩，教我們做好國民。』」[38] 此外，另有〈社會歌〉（第19首）及〈立功歌〉（第47首）表達出這一原則。趙在其著作中，也提及耶穌對於社會的關注，如他所寫：

> 耶穌並沒有直接講論社會問題。他所講的大都是人生的改革；因為人生有了向上的變化，社會不能不跟著變化。[39]

在〈社會歌〉中，我們可以讀到下述耶穌關於社會擔當、以及應建設何種社會的語句：

> 耶穌救主到世上傳福音，教人悔改相信天父得新心，窮苦的同胞應當快快聽，瞎眼能夠見光明，世界上應該有公平，同胞要相親，奴才們都要得解放，一切都要新，天國離人不遠，要儆醒，因為禧年快來臨。[40]

也有反映如何改革社會的詞句：

> 耶穌引導我們同去傳揚，平等自由救世福音大亮光，改良社會叫他變做天堂，叫人不再有悲傷，大家要作工，要相幫，有苦大家嘗，有福同享有難同當，志向要堅強，打破一切不平。[41]

與此同時，〈立功歌〉中對社會建設、社會關懷則有更清晰的表述：

---

38 趙紫宸，〈序一〉，頁5-6。
39 趙紫宸，〈耶穌基督〉，頁34。
40 趙紫宸、范天祥，〈社會歌〉，《民眾聖歌集》，頁19。
41 趙紫宸、范天祥，〈社會歌〉，《民眾聖歌集》，頁19。

我們作工雖勞碌，勤苦之中得真福，織新布，做衣服，耕地種田五穀熟，靠天父，衣食足，又為社會謀幸福。

我們作工不落空，一年春夏又秋冬，家庭裡，社會中，民生全靠我工農，用愛心，成大功，天父恩德真無窮。[42]

在此，趙希望通過自我進步、努力工作、自律、遵守社會規則等建立起一個良好的社會。有學者指出：

> 趙指出了華人神學中的一個關鍵問題。這種在傳統內的尋索不是空想主義。對於趙而言，就如陶淵明一樣，從不摒棄對於社會倫理的追尋。也因此，自由主義神學的「社會福音」對趙是如此重要，因為這證明了相似的倫理關懷，通過跟隨耶穌將救贖與人類的自我實現相關聯。趙對於在社會內的價值實現是儒家傳統的核心，這是中國文化意識的極大一部分，如果拒絕儒家文化，就是拒絕這一種倫理關懷。[43]

在第九條原則中，趙紫宸寫道：「民眾詩歌，應當根基於聖經，尤其是聖經故事。本集中，這一類的歌占一大部分。我們若能用聖歌使民眾學習聖經，當然是一件好事情。例如浪子回頭歌，撒種歌，十童女歌，葡萄樹歌等都是屬於這一類的。」[44] 在此也可窺見華人基督教對於《聖經》的重視。

對於第十條原則，趙則提出：

> 每首歌，須是一篇說教的講章。這一點應於民間的宣教師，很有幫助。在唱詩之前，宣教師可以講所要唱的一首，逐句逐節講一遍，一方面可以叫民眾完全瞭解詩的意思，長期來，不致

---

42 趙紫宸、范天祥，〈立功歌〉，《民眾聖歌集》，頁19。

43 Bob Whyte, *Unfinished Encounter: China and Christianity* (London: Fount Paperbackes, 1988), p. 181.

44 趙紫宸，〈序一〉，頁6。

於隔膜，一方面也可以使宣教師有宣講的材料和機會。本集的詩歌都是應當這樣用的。宣教師先講，會眾然後唱，是一個最適宜的辦法。[45]

在此原則中，趙將讚美詩視為講道，鼓勵牧師對讚美詩的文本進行闡釋，以更好地幫助民眾理解。

趙紫宸嘗試以上述十條原則來為《民眾聖歌集》作詞，並將詩歌視為動人的藝術，以幫助闡釋基督信仰及塑造人格。[46] 趙為《民眾聖歌集》所撰寫的文本將基督信仰植入中國本土文化，嘗試用處境化的文本來傳達豐富的《聖經》形象及靈性內涵。如他所言，「我做這些歌的時候，不但要適合民眾的需要，也想加增民眾對於聖教的認識，提高民眾日常生活的興趣。」[47] 上述十原則旨在想民眾所想，以簡潔、具體之文本，傳達民眾倫理、表述宗教情感，其內在關懷性已表露無遺。與此同時，它們亦是趙紫宸歷來創作詩歌的生命經驗的反映與表述。如前所述，趙在創作《民眾聖歌集》之前，已有翻譯《團契聖歌集》的經驗。雖有自我寫作與翻譯從形式而言不盡相同，然而，從對於處境化的追求來看，則帶有相同的目的。因而，《民眾聖歌集》文本可謂是趙紫宸生命經驗、宗教經驗、處境化詩歌經驗共同積累後的表達。

三、 基督論與上帝論：文本的另一種處境化

早在第四及第五世紀，基督教早期神學家及教會領袖即對基督論和上帝論建立了標準的模式，這些模式也為東西方所接受，並在所有的文化中重新進行了詮釋，這在《民眾聖歌集》中即有所體現。從涉及上帝的文本來看，《民眾聖歌集》中共有四首：〈聖父歌〉（第4

---

45 趙紫宸，〈序一〉，頁6。
46 趙紫宸，〈序一〉，頁4。
47 趙紫宸，〈序一〉，頁5。

首）、〈三一歌〉（第5首）、〈天恩歌〉（第6首）、〈感恩歌〉
（第7首）。

在趙早期的上帝論詮釋中，他指出其中一個他所著重的原則，乃
是上帝的人格。如他所寫：

> 基督教的根本是上帝，上帝是人格，是靈；故基督徒的宇宙
> 觀，是以精神為萬物之本的觀念。我們幾乎可以說，人和人格
> 是宇宙的雛形，人的宇宙是人格的居廬。我們環身的事物，都
> 是聖的，美麗，而且可愛。[48]

在此，趙強調了上帝透明的人格以及他與人類的關係。趙在描繪
上帝時，傾向於運用兩種表述：上帝是人格，上帝是愛。在〈耶穌的
上帝觀〉一文中，「人格」與「愛」在趙的神學理解中相互融合。
「上帝有人格」是指上帝對於人類的所需是有「知」、有「感」的
（《馬太福音》6: 32）。[49] 換言之，在同情及愛裡，上帝對人的需
求和願望有所認同。

在上述四首讚美詩中，即反映出上帝有「知」、有「情」的一
面。首先，根據趙所言，上帝是有「知」的，能夠滿足人的需求，
〈天恩歌〉的相關語句如「天上的父親大慈悲呀，賞我吃穿樣樣都全
備」，「不憂愁今天穿什麼呀，不憂愁今天要吃什麼，我天父，他知
道」，即反映出這點。[50]〈感恩歌〉（第7首）的相關語句如「讚美
聖天父，恩典無限量，賞賜我衣服，又賞我口糧，保養我身體，感化
我心靈，白天勤作工，黑夜得安寧」，也表達出相似的含義。指出上
帝愛我們，知曉我們的所需，為我們預備日常及四季所需，反映祂的

---

48 趙紫宸，〈基督與我的人格〉，《宗教與人生問題討論課本》（上海：青年協會書報社，1925），頁
6。
49 趙紫宸，〈耶穌的上帝觀〉，《生命》（1921年9月），頁5。
50 趙紫宸、范天祥，〈天恩歌〉，《民眾聖歌集》，頁6。

有「知」。[51]

與此同時，趙又指出上帝是「有情」的，祂有「愛人之德」。在耶穌眼裡，上帝有人格，「因為人格裡面，情與知同為要素」。[52] 對此，〈天恩歌〉有所表述：

> 請看小鳥飛上飛下呀，請看田園裡那百合花，也不種，也不收，也不會紡紗，天父尚且養活他，何況咱。[53]

此段是趙對於上帝有愛人之德的反映。祂不僅愛天上的飛鳥，更愛人。上帝愛世界，對此充滿情感。愛以及上帝與人共情的結合是趙在其讚美詩寫作中有關上帝的一個顯著特徵。

除了有知有情外，趙紫宸指出耶穌所指的上帝的第二個原則是：上帝是人類的父親。如趙寫道：

> 上帝為父這一層意思中，含蓄基督教一切精神與教理，因為耶穌的人生觀，社會觀，都以上帝為父一理為基礎，而這一理從字義與事蹟雙方看，都是以道德為指歸的。……上帝與人既為父子，其關係自然是道德的，倫常的了。這個關係，不待說明，而自然彰顯著。[54]

在〈三一歌〉（第5首）中，即指出上帝作為父親的特徵：「唱聖哉聖哉聖哉神啊，大慈大悲廣大權能啊，管天地，愛世人，做人老父親。」[55] 這在趙紫宸〈耶穌的上帝觀〉一文中已表達出來：「上帝想要人類與祂有真正的父子（女）關係。」[56]

---

51 趙紫宸、范天祥，〈感恩歌〉，《民眾聖歌集》，頁7。
52 趙紫宸，〈耶穌的上帝觀〉，頁6。
53 趙紫宸、范天祥，〈天恩歌〉，頁6。
54 趙紫宸，〈耶穌的上帝觀〉，頁7。
55 趙紫宸、范大祥，〈三一歌〉，《民眾聖歌集》，頁5。
56 趙紫宸，〈耶穌的上帝觀〉，頁14。

這種父子關係的比喻在趙之前許多的神學家與基督徒亦有用過。在趙看來，這種父子關係是兩層的。一是玄學的，以上帝為因，為造物主，為造人類的本原；一是倫理的，以上帝為父，人類為子，而父子之間相通於愛。同時，趙認為玄學的意義可以隱而不提，倫理的意義才是要訓。[57]

除此之外，趙指出，耶穌的上帝觀中的第三點是：上帝是人類唯一的救贖主。[58] 這是基督教的基本原則。趙在〈聖父歌〉（第4首）中寫道：「大慈大悲聖天父，你救苦難你哀憐，你的審判最公道，你的救法最完全」，表明上帝是我們唯一的救贖主。[59] 正如趙所寫：

> 上帝救贖人，因為祂希望人能像祂一樣完美。……罪惡成為了阻礙，分離了上帝與人，因而上帝必須除掉罪，將人從罪中拯救出來。總而言之，上帝想要讓人離開罪，且走向祂。[60]

在這裡我們可以看到趙對上帝的詮釋有獨特的著重點：上帝的人格、有知有情、作為父親的上帝以及救贖的上帝。這些思想對趙並不陌生，自新約時代以來就被不斷發展。趙在其神學寫作中進一步更為豐滿地發展了上帝的教義，這在他《民眾聖歌集》出版前後的寫作中亦有體現。在此，趙的貢獻在於，他在簡單的讚美詩中表述出對於上帝的觀點，且能較易地被普通民眾所接受。

從基督論來看，《民眾聖歌集》中的〈聖子歌〉（第8首）、〈好牧人歌〉（第9首）、〈救世歌〉（第10首）、〈尊主歌〉（第20首）以及〈愛主歌〉（第26首）均從一定程度反映出趙早期的基督論。

在這些讚美詩中，反映出耶穌「人而神」的特點，這是趙紫宸早

---

57 趙紫宸，〈耶穌的上帝觀〉，頁7。
58 趙紫宸，〈耶穌的上帝觀〉，頁13。
59 趙紫宸、范天祥，〈聖父歌〉，《民眾聖歌集》，頁4。
60 趙紫宸，〈耶穌的上帝觀〉，頁14。

期基督論中的重要一部分，如他所寫：

> 然而這一天將很快來到，沒有什麼能夠阻止西方「神而人」的
> 耶穌成為中國人「人而神」的耶穌。中國人將通過祖先所發現
> 的真理來理解這位耶穌以及他的教導。[61]

在此，趙紫宸講述的是一位中國耶穌，以中國文化及哲學為進路
的耶穌。值得注意的是，趙將西方「神而人」的耶穌與中國「人而
神」的耶穌區分開來，並且趙將耶穌視為有血有肉的人。

〈尊主歌〉即對耶穌「人而神」的特點有所反映：

> 耶穌最慈悲，耶穌最有情，他能感化我，除我鐵石心。
> 耶穌最勇敢，耶穌最聰明，捨生救贖我，與我一同行。
> 耶穌最體諒，耶穌最溫柔，與我同受苦，一同背軛頭。
> 耶穌最清潔，耶穌最公平，創造新生活，領我進天城。[62]

在此，趙用「慈悲」、「有情」、「勇敢」、「聰明」、「體
諒」、「溫柔」、「清潔」、「公平」描繪作為人的耶穌，反映了趙
早期神學思想中將耶穌視為人的特點。在趙眼中，耶穌是「捨生救贖
我，與我一同行」的耶穌，也是「與我同受苦，一同背軛頭」的耶
穌。祂亦是「與我朋友相稱呼」（〈愛主歌〉，第26首）的耶穌。[63]
如趙在1933年所寫：

> 耶穌並不是因為他是上帝或上帝的兒子而吸引我。相反，引起

---

61 T. C. Chao, "Our Cultural Heritage," in *China Her Own Interpreter: Chapters by a Group of Nationals Interpreting the Christian Movement*, ed. Milton Stauffer (New York: Missionary Education Movement of the United Stateds and Canada), p. 19.

62 趙紫宸、范天祥，〈尊主歌〉，《民眾聖歌集》，頁20。

63 趙紫宸、范天祥，〈愛主歌〉，《民眾聖歌集》，頁26。

> 我注意、引發我興趣的，乃是因為他是一位徹徹底底的人。
> ……當耶穌宣稱自己是人子時，不管這個術語意味著什麼，我
> 都感到高興。因為我確切地知道他所教導的都是真實的，因為
> 他是人。[64]

　　這是趙強調耶穌作為歷史的人的一個個人的確切表述，也同樣對於中國文化的重要性進行了著墨。同時，也反映出耶穌與人的平等性。正如趙紫宸所指，普通人和耶穌的宗教經驗也是相同的，只不過是量上的區別。因而，耶穌與人是平等的。[65]

　　除此之外，在關於耶穌的讚美詩中，趙紫宸另突出了耶穌其他方面的人格。〈救世歌〉中指「狐狸有洞鳥有巢，耶穌飄零真可嘆」。[66] 趙在〈耶穌基督〉一文中已表達過相似的意思：「耶穌的人格是圓滿的，豐富的……耶穌可以處貧賤，居卑下；空中的鳥有巢，地上的狐有洞，人子沒有枕首的地方。」[67] 因而該讚美詩反映出耶穌人格的圓滿性。又有如〈聖子歌〉中所描寫的：「仁愛耶穌度苦難，醫治疾病救窮人」、「仁愛耶穌做榜樣，也愛朋友愛仇人」等，突出耶穌仁愛的特點。[68] 在基督教及中國文化中，仁愛均是考量的因素。根據趙所言，仁愛在作為人子的耶穌身上得到了真正的體現。耶穌的仁愛表現在對一切人的平等性上，這是基督教的一個明顯的貢獻，也是趙的神學及其讚美詩寫作中對於「人而神」的耶穌的觀點的中心點。

　　趙也同時在歌詞中強調了效法耶穌這一點。在〈聖子歌〉中，他寫道：「仁愛耶穌可憐我，教我永遠會跟從，背著寶架做見證，引人到主愛光中」以及「仁愛耶穌做榜樣」。正如趙所寫：

---

64 T. C. Chao, "Jesus and the Reality of God," in *Truth and Life*, March (1933), pp. 1-2.

65 趙紫宸，《基督教哲學》（上海：中華基督教文社，1926），頁239。

66 趙紫宸，〈救世歌〉，《民眾聖歌集》，頁10。

67 趙紫宸，《耶穌基督》，頁22。

68 趙紫宸，〈聖子歌〉，《民眾聖歌集》，頁8。

> 他引導著，我們跟隨著……耶穌救我們，我們救自己。……
> 耶穌將道路示我們，使我們都走努力勇進、奮鬥而得生命的道
> 路。[69]

他又道：

> 因為上帝在道成肉身中所啟示的，正是在於我們要親自跟隨
> 他，以他的人格為模範。耶穌從上帝裡出來，垂示法身（佛家
> 用語），在我們人類中做一份子，使我們躬親他的訓誨與行
> 為。他是人類與人類的本原，連合統一的模範。[70]

因而，在〈好牧人歌〉中，趙紫宸寫道：

> 獨有主耶穌，發出慈悲聲，自己前頭走，羊群後面跟，領到水
> 邊，領到草場，獲得安寧。
> 只要依靠他，跟他往前走行，走到山頭上，太陽放光明，天高
> 地厚，主恩無窮，你儘管放心。[71]

此兩段即表達出以耶穌為模範，跟隨耶穌的重要性。[72]

在上述篇幅中，可以看到，《民眾聖歌集》有關耶穌的讚美詩反映出他早期基督論的一些特點。首先，反映了耶穌與上帝的關係；其次，反映出「人而神」的耶穌這一特點，通過歌詞將耶穌建構成一個

---

69 趙紫宸，《基督教哲學》，頁239。
70 趙紫宸，〈更大的工作〉，《生命月刊》，1926年3月，頁3。
71 趙紫宸，〈好牧人歌〉，《民眾聖歌集》，頁9。
72 以耶穌為模範，是趙紫宸基督論中的一點，即強調耶穌是人的模範，為人類做了榜樣：「（耶穌）足以做我們的模範。他來宣傳天國，重估人與人的關係和價值，使我們知道做人應當維持什麼，創造什麼；所以他垂示了我們做人的目標。最緊要的，是他自己經過一切，制勝一切，得大神通，具大神力，使我們知道人格的能力有無盡藏的根源。他怎麼得權能，我們也可以怎樣地得權能。」趙紫宸，〈基督與我的人格〉，《宗教與人生問題討論課本》（上海：青年協會書報部，1925），頁20-21。

真正的人，幫助民眾更好地認識耶穌。同時，也反映出耶穌與眾生平等的形象，以及仁愛的一面，強調人需跟隨耶穌。這些文本並非完整全面地勾勒趙的早期基督論，但卻從一個清晰的角度折射出他的思想是適合於普通民眾這一受眾的，連同描繪上帝的處境化文本，表達出三〇年代中國讚美詩本對於普通信徒的關懷。

四、歌述關懷：處境化讚美詩與基督教社會關懷

「社會關懷」是基督教的一個重要特色。舉凡基督教所到之地，無不顯示教會（包括傳教士、信徒與教會機構）對於當地社會之關懷，形成教會與社會密切的互動關係。讚美詩處境化，即是以藝術的形式，來表達基督教對於社會之關懷。早在十九世紀，西方傳教士如蘇慧廉（William Edward Soothill）等即注意到西方聖詩對於中國信徒的晦澀性，因而極有必要發展處境化聖詩以幫助中國信徒更好地理解讚美詩，以促進其基督信仰，這即從一定程度表達出基督教社會關懷的屬性。

至二十世紀初，這種對於中國讚美詩處境化的關注開始由西教士向華人轉向。在這之中，趙紫宸與范天祥的合作可謂獨辟先河。趙氏與范氏首先合作《團契聖歌集》一冊，趙氏以極其文雅之語句，對120首西方聖詩進行了處境化的翻譯，其譯文運用含帶佛教、道教意味的詞語譯出，在燕京大學基督教團契中引起很大反響，以至很快告罄。這一適合知識界層面的讚美詩集編撰也帶動了其後《民眾聖歌集》的編撰，從對當時燕京大學基督教團契的關懷，進一步向中國普通民眾延伸。不同於此前翻譯之歌詞，在《民眾聖歌集》中，趙氏以簡潔之文本，旨在幫助普通民眾理解基督教之深意，這即體現出一種文本語言上的基督教關懷。對於如何作詞，趙氏的作詞十原則從多方面作出解答。除了強調最為直觀的簡潔明瞭性，《民眾聖歌集》的文本另強調讚美詩與自然描繪（即宗教與自然）的關係、與民眾日常生活的關係、與社會倫理的關係等等。文本所呈現的上帝論與基督論反

映出趙紫宸早期上帝論與基督論的特點，也折射出趙所強調的基督教與中國文化相融合的精神。此時期的趙，對於中國文化的看法，與早年不同。他不再對傳統文化進行否認，以顯示基督教的貢獻，而是多多尋求傳統思想與基督教教義之間的關聯。[73] 在《民眾聖歌集》中，我們可以看到他對於中國文化的反思。例如，自然與上帝，在趙的定義中，與中國文化相關，而這點也在其讚美詩歌詞中反映出來，表現出趙所強調的「在生活、自然中見上帝」。[74] 此外，《民眾聖歌集》的內容也多反映民眾日常生活、倫理關係，展現中國文化傳統的另一些方面。正如趙所寫：「（中國文化）第二個有勢力的傾向是倫理的傾向。……倫理之極致，便成了宗教。」[75] 在上述的討論中，我們可以看到《民眾聖歌集》的內容涉及中國民眾的日常生活、家庭、鄰里關係，傳達出「中國人是最重倫常，最生活的」這一概念，也反映出「從深切的宗教經驗中鞏固倫理基礎」這一思想。[76] 此外，鑒於趙紫宸強調藝術是「中國文化的第三種趨勢」，我們可以說，趙運用讚美詩這一具體的藝術形式來促進中國民眾對於基督教的理解。[77] 正如趙自己所寫：「假使基督教要在中國人心血裡流通，她必要在美藝上有貢獻。」[78] 他又有補充：「宗教不是一種方式所能表顯，所以必有事乎象徵。有事乎象徵，故必借重美術。凡有宗教，必有儀式，必有建築，音樂，繪畫，文章以傳遞其生活的豐富。」[79] 從這一點觀之，趙的處境化讚美詩正是表述中國普通民眾宗教生活的一種象徵。范天祥指趙紫宸希望大多數基督徒能夠用能表述其宗教生活的語言和形式來進行崇拜。這即涉及到這些處境化讚美詩的功能。[80] 與此同時，中

---

73 T. C. Chao, "The Appeal of Christianity to the Chinese Mind," *The Chinese Recorder* (May 1918): 288-296. Bob Whyte, *Unfinished Encounter: China and Christianity*, p. 179.

74 趙紫宸，〈基督教與中國文化〉，頁252-255。

75 趙紫宸，〈基督教與中國文化〉，頁255。

76 趙紫宸，〈序一〉，頁6。

77 趙紫宸，〈基督教與中國文化〉，頁256。

78 趙紫宸，〈基督教與中國文化〉，頁257。

79 趙紫宸，〈基督教與中國文化〉，頁257。

80 Bliss Wiant,"Oecumenical Hymnology in China," *The International Review of Missions* 35 (1946): 429.

國民眾的神祕經驗，是趙所指出的另一種影響中國文化的趨勢，這也被表述在這些處境化讚美詩中。此外，一些讚美詩以中國詩歌的韻律寫出，則是中國文化與基督教融合的另一表現形式，旨在幫助民眾理解。

因而，《民眾聖歌集》的內容表達，首先是語言表述貼近百姓；其次是內容上容易為民眾所理解，如其對上帝與耶穌的表達，即反映出趙早期上帝論與基督論的種種，如強調上帝是有知有情的上帝，是人的父親。耶穌具有「人而神」的特點，是仁愛、平等的耶穌。這種處境化文本，不但是趙紫宸自我神學思想的體現，亦是貼合民眾，從民眾出發，為民眾所想的文本，即體現出基督教在藝術上所展示出的一種對於中國社會、信徒的關懷。

此外，我們也需提到，《民眾聖歌集》選用中國曲調作為讚美詩的旋律，其曲調含括中國傳統民歌、中國宗教音樂及學堂樂歌等多方面。這種採集中國歌曲調子的做法，從十九世紀開始便為傳教士所用。如有一名傳教士如此描述他採集中國樂曲的場景：「這些年來我一直在零散地記錄下一些中國的旋律。我在中國的寺廟，鄉村以及城市的街道上等地方聆聽中國曲調。……在我的記錄本上記錄著一些我認為非常值得保留的曲調。其中有一首北方的愛國歌曲，這首歌我只聽過一次，是一位北京姑娘從她的學者父親那裡學來的。她在一條小船上為我演唱了這首歌，我在月光下匆匆將旋律記下來。這真是一個奇妙的時刻，在眾多的中國歌曲中這首曲子顯得極不尋常。」[81] 在此值得一提的是，在處境化讚美詩追尋過程中，傳教士們在發現西方的聖樂體系並不能為中國教徒所接受時，他們則反過來從中國音樂本身入手，開始不斷追尋中國本土化聖樂的發展。一方面，傳教士歷來對中國音樂本身的系統性及科學性存在質疑；另一方面，又不得不反過來在根本上從中國音樂入手，運用中國音樂體系來進行傳教，這種聖

---

81 Eleanor Macneil Anderson, "Chinese Melodies and Christian Worship," *The Chinese Recorder* (February, 1934): 107-108.

樂處境化過程所展示的，實際上是一種向中國音樂尋求靈感的局面。
這種局面的鋪陳將中國音樂從原本界定的西方音樂體系標準下脫離開
來，從一個平等對話的角度來觀測中西音樂交流，從而為原有的「歐
洲中心論」主導下的中西音樂交流的不平等性提供了相關駁論。這即
是音樂傳教在史學及音樂學層面為我們展示的一種新的重要的分析圖
景。而《民眾聖歌集》音樂上的特點，則可以看作是對追求處境化中
國讚美詩之路的一種傳承，但亦有更多突破、以及新處境下的新因
素。如〈謝恩歌〉（第50首）的曲調「宣平調」，原來是一首孔教
的旋律。另有採自佛教的曲調，如〈禮拜歌〉（第28首），取自佛
教頌歌「普陀調」。還有如〈靈修歌〉（第31首），曲調來自中國
民歌「江上船歌」，是一首在長江勞動的船夫搖櫓所唱的歌曲。另有
「孟姜女」調的〈慈悲聖父歌〉等。音樂上的處境化可謂從《民眾聖
歌集》中極為具體、直觀地反映出來，表達了創作讚美詩所帶來的社
會關懷。

　　與此同時，《民眾聖歌集》的出版亦是對於當時中國基督教處境
化的一種回應。一方面，隨著高漲的愛國情愫，中國教會開始重思與
西方教會的關係，其對於自立和變革的訴求日益強烈。[82] 如杭州中華
基督教教會提出脫離西差會、教權自主、行政獨立、經濟獨立、打破
自由五點。[83] 全國教會皆紛紛響應，以其各自的方式，來回應對自立
的訴求。如趙紫宸所評價：「中國信徒謀求教會自立，雖所走的路徑
不同，所持的理由不同，或因內部有中西的糾紛，或因環境有齟齬的
困難，然其所達到的目標則大略相同。北至蘭州、南至廣州、東至溫
州、西至貴州，教會的情形，境遇，宗派，組織，差殊極遠，而所設

82 Sumiko, Yamamoto, *History of Protestantism in China: The Indigenization of Christianity* (Tokyo: Tōhō Gakkai, 2000), p. 143. Also, see, Daniel H. Bays, "The Growth of Independent Christianity in China, 1900-1937," in *Christianity in China: From the Eighteenth Century to the Present*, edited by Daniel H. Bay (Stanford, CA: Stanford University Press, 1996), pp. 307-316.

83 葉運隆，〈杭州基督徒獨立運動結果成立杭州市中華基督教會〉，《中華基督教年鑑》，第10卷（1928），頁23。轉引自段琦，《奮進的歷程：中國基督教的本色化》（北京：商務印書館，2004），頁377。

立的自立教會，沒有一個是以公會定名的，也沒有一個是以『中華基督教會』定名的。『中華基督教會』之上，冠以地名以為分別，頗可以見教會心理的一致。凡有教會之地，無不感受人才經濟兩相匱乏的痛苦，然而痛苦自痛苦，進行自進行，獨立奮鬥，直叫人歡喜無量，踴躍三百。」[84] 一些報紙、雜誌如《聖報》、《文社月刊》等，也紛紛登文鼓吹自立。[85] 與此同時，另一方面，中國教會開始進一步關注在神學、禮儀方面上的去西方化，旨在將中國文化的因素植入進去。作為力主建立中國本色教會的一員，趙紫宸指出一個新的普世中國教會應該是獨立，而不附屬於任何宗派或傳教團體。他指出「中國基督教想要創造自我的信條，建立他們自己的宗教，一方面傳承西方教會的古老傳統，一方面在基督教基礎上融入其文化最好的因素，從而建立一個中國人身心都可以接受的基督教。」[86] 他又強調：「中國基督徒開始意識到建立本色教會體系的必要性，並日思夜想地尋求如何建立中國基督教文學。」[87] 鑒於趙在二〇年代即積極參與本色基督教文學的創作，因而其對於中國讚美詩的創作不只是個人興趣，也含括在當時的基督教文學創作框架之下。[88] 也因此我們可以說，對於處境化讚美詩的關注，不僅僅是從讚美詩本身出發的社會關懷，更是更廣泛層面中國基督教處境化框架下所呈現出的關懷。

---

84 趙紫宸，〈風潮中奮起的中國教會〉，張西平，《本色之探：20世紀中國基督教文化學術論集》（北京：中國廣播電視出版社，1998），頁317。

85 段琦，《奮進的歷程：中國基督教的本色化》，頁377。

86 T. C. Chao, "The Chinese Church Realized Itself," *CR* (May-June 1927): 305.

87 Chao, "The Chinese Church Realized Itself," 308.

88 Sumiko Yamamoto, *History of Protestantism in China: The Indigenization of Christianity* (Tokyo: Tōhō Gakkai, 2000), 90. Other description of Chinese Christian literature work during this period could be seen Wang, Chen Main,"Contextualizing Protestant Publishing in China: The Wenshe, 1924-1928,"in *Christianity in China: From the Eighteenth Century to the Present*, edited by Daniel H. Bay (Stanford, CA: Stanford University Press, 1996), pp. 292-306. 王成勉，《文社的盛衰——二〇年代基督教本色化之個案研究》（臺北：宇宙光出版社，1993）。

五、結語

　　《民眾聖歌集》是「中國基督徒意識到自我文化、文明價值」的一個例子。[89] 同時，在非基運動之後，三〇年代開始，在國際基督教的影響下，中國教會開始關注地方區域及鄉村的事工（1928年在耶路撒冷所舉行的國際傳教會議上，即強調了對於農村地區基督教發展的關注。）[90]《民眾聖歌集》的出版，即是一種對地方民眾的關懷，趙紫宸「有意地選擇形式簡單、意義明瞭的詞句，並將它們融入到中國曲調中」，幫助中國民眾體味。[91]

　　總而言之，《民眾聖歌集》代表三〇年代早期中國處境化讚美詩集編撰的一個重要貢獻。范天祥在1931年致其朋友的一封信中這樣寫道：「全國基督教協會深感鑒於中國是一個以農業為主的國家，鑒於基督教是一個全人類的宗教，如果要讓基督教成為在華的永久生命，我們需要去做更多的事來贏得普通民眾的心。（民眾聖歌集）這一讚美詩集正是為回應這一需求而出版，我們在此祈禱上帝對此滿有祝福。」[92]

　　對於《民眾聖歌集》的出版，范這樣評論：「讚美詩集的出版是極其成功的，這一讚美詩也傳遍了中國。」可見該讚美詩集受歡迎的程度。[93] 它也直接影響了1936年《普天頌讚》的編撰。在《普天頌讚》中，內含中國曲調讚美詩62首，其間從《民眾聖歌集》中選取9首。更為重要的是，在《民眾聖歌集》出版後，特別是在1934年、1935年《普天頌讚》出版前，國內湧現出大量對於處境化讚美詩的

---

89 Chao, "The Chinese Church Realized Itself," 307.

90 Kenyon L. Butterfield, L. L. D., "Christianity and Rural Civilization," *The Christian Mission in Relation to Rural Problems: Report of the Jerusalem Meeting of the International Missionary Council March 24th-April 8th, 1928* (London: Oxford University Press, 1928), pp. 3-31.

91 Wiant,"Oecumnical Hymnology in China," 429.

92 "Bliss Wiant's letter to friends," July 1, 1931, United Board for Christian Higher Education in Asia (hereafter cited as UBCHEA) Archives, Series IV, Reel 194, 364-5620.

93 Wiant,"Oecumenical Hymnology in China," 429.

探討，內容涉及翻譯、詞曲的創作內容、語言的表述等等，為《普天頌讚》的成書以及其間對處境化讚美詩的選編及創作奠下了不可複製的理論及實踐基礎。而就讚美詩出發的社會關懷，也從十九世紀傳教士的嘗試至二十世紀華人自身的探索，在《民眾聖歌集》的出版後達到了一個高峰，為讚美詩所呈現出的社會關懷寫下了濃墨重彩的一筆。

天主教聖言會的社會服務事業：
以新店大坪林德華女子公寓爲例（1968-1988）[*]

吳蕙芳

摘要

　　德華女子公寓為天主教聖言會於1960年代在新店大坪林設立的女工宿舍，當時基於該地區工廠林立，且普遍雇用大量來自全臺各地之年輕女性，故如何解決女工們的住宿問題成為當務之急。該女子公寓名稱源自當時擔任大坪林聖三堂主任司鐸、負責規劃及籌建該宿舍的天主教聖言會會士萬德華神父（Fr. Edward J. Wojniak, SVD, 1909-1983）。屬波蘭裔美籍的萬德華神父曾服務於中國河南省，1940年代因中共政權建立，驅逐教會勢力，萬德華神父被迫離華返美。1960年代其自願至臺灣，首先將新店大坪林之教堂聖三堂修建完成，接著投身該地區的其他工作，德華女子公寓即為其最受矚目的社會服務事業。該女子公寓之構思起於1965年，次年為籌措龐大建築經費，萬德華神父赴歐美等地募款數月，並邀請蔣夫人宋美齡女士為公寓籌建之名譽主任委員，以號召更多中外力量的投入與協助，1968年公寓第一期工程完成開始營運，甚獲各界好評，其後陸續完成各棟建築，持續嘉惠來自臺灣各地離家工作之年輕女子，惟後來因主客觀環境之變化，營運長達二十年的德華女子公寓終於1988年正式停業。本文即針對該女子公寓的創建與發展作一個案研究，以為當代天主教會投身社會服務事業之實例說明。

---

*　本文為行政院科技部專題研究計畫案（編號NSC102-2410-H-019-004-MY2）補助下之部分研究成果；文章撰寫期間，承蒙聖言會中華省會會長柏殿宏神父（Fr. Francis Budenholzer, SVD）與會士柯博識神父（Fr. Jac Kuepers, SVD）、美國芝加哥聖言會檔案館（Robert M. Myers Archives）專員Peter Gunther先生、德華女子公寓管理員袁嬤嬤女士、美國艾琳達博士（Dr. Linda Gail Arrigo）等人之提供相關資料及協助解讀資料，謹此致上誠摯謝意。

關鍵詞：職業婦女公寓、女工宿舍、萬德華神父（Fr. Edward J. Wojniak）、通用器材公司、工業化社會、社會關懷

一、前言

聖言會（Society of the Divine Word，簡稱SVD）為天主教傳教修會之一，由德國閔斯特（Münster）教區聖楊生神父（Fr. Arnold Janssen, 1837-1909）於1875年（清光緒元年）創立於荷蘭史泰爾（Steyl）村中。該修會以向教外地區宣揚天主教信仰為主要目的，其首個工作區即為中國山東；1882年（清光緒8年）於陽穀縣坡里莊建立據點，日後逐漸擴及甘肅、河南、青海、新疆、北京等地。[1] 1949年中共建政後驅逐教會勢力，聖言會士紛紛從中國撤出，其中，光令才神父（Fr. Bernhard Kolanczyk, 1903-1983）與司文德神父（Fr. Joseph Stier, 1911-1979）曾於1948、1949年間短暫來臺視察，然未能立下長久發展基礎，直至1954年，因原負責陽穀教區、後派駐嘉義之牛會卿主教（1895-1973）的邀請，三位聖言會士——賈德良神父（Fr. Leo Kade, 1903-1981）、紀福泰神父（Fr. Aloysius Krieftewirth, 1904-1990）、陶賀神父（Fr. Aloysius Tauch, 1909-1987）——來臺協助傳教工作，開啟聖言會在臺灣的福傳事業，並因三人之關鍵性報告，終令聖言會羅馬總會於1959年正式設立聖言會中華區會（China Region, 1975年改為中華省會China Province），並先後派遣諸多聖言會士來臺拓展相關工作，持續該修會在華之福傳活動迄今。[2]

學界有關聖言會在華傳教活動的探究，前人已有部分成果，如1970年代即有柯博識（Jac Kuepers）專門探討聖言會在山東的傳教事業 *China Und Die Katholische Mission In Süd-Shantung 1882-1900*，[3] Fritz

---

1 狄剛，〈聖言會在華傳教簡史〉，收入《聖言會在華傳教一百周年紀念特刊（1882-1982）》（新莊：輔仁大學聖言會，1982），頁16-20；〈聖言會在華傳教工作簡史〉，收入羅光主編，《天主教在華傳教史集》（臺南：徵祥出版社，1967），頁203-243。

2 Anton Weber, "Across the Strait to Taiwan," *The Word in the World* (1990/1991), pp. 65-69；溫安東，〈聖言會在臺灣的過去與現在〉，收入《聖言會的軌跡：創會125周年紀念講座手冊》（臺北：財團法人天主教聖言會，2000），頁13-27。

3 Jac Kuepers, *China Und Die Katholische Mission In Süd-Shantung 1882-1900* (Steyl, Drukkerij Van Het Missiehuis, 1974)；又柯博識於2013年亦撰有相關聖言會任魯南發展之專文，見柯博識，"A Case of Cultural Interaction between the German Catholic Mission and the Population of South Shandong in Late Qing China"（中國清朝

Bornemann則有聖言會於各地之福傳工作成果*A History of the Divine World Missionary*，其中有數章涉及在華傳教內容；[4] 2000年後有Karl Josef Rivinius關注聖言會於義和團時期的傳教活動及其影響，[5] 吳伯（筆名）專研聖言會於1920年代以來在甘肅、河南的傳教事業，[6] 而柯博識、袁小涓、施珮吟則撰有關於聖言會與北平輔仁大學發展之專書、專文等；[7] 惟前述成果主要呈現該修會於1949年以前在中國大陸的活動情形，至於聖言會來臺發展的相關研究，相對而言似較為欠缺；其中，柯博識曾撰有聖言會士蔣百鍊神父（Fr. Richard Arens, 1912-1990）對輔仁大學在臺復校之貢獻，[8] 而筆者本文則欲透過德華女子公寓之創建及發展歷程，說明聖言會於1960至1980年代在新店大坪林地區的社會服務工作，以為該修會在臺福傳事業之一實例。

二、美籍神父的中國情緣（1937-1947）

德華女子公寓的創建者為波蘭裔美籍的聖言會士萬德華神父。1909年9月28日出生於芝加哥的萬德華神父在家中四兄弟裡排行最小，由於雙親（Casimir & Frances Dycsknewski Wojniak）均為虔誠天主教徒的家庭教育背景，奠定其深厚的宗教信仰基礎。[9] 1922年9月離家至聖言會芝加哥會院所在地的泰克尼（Techny）開始初學階段，

　　末年德國天主教傳教士和山東南部的人民：一個文化交流的個案〉，《輔仁歷史學報》，第31期（新莊，2013.09），頁143-202。

4 Fritz Bornemann, *A History of the Divine Word Missionary* (Bozen, Freinademetz-Haus, 1977), pp. 287-320.

5 Karl Josef Rivinius, "Mission and Boxer Movement in Shandong Province with particular reference to the 'Society of the Divine Word'", 收入《義和團運動與中國基督宗教》（新莊：輔仁大學出版社，2004），頁259-295。

6 吳伯，《華夏遺蹤：聖言會甘肅、河南福傳史（1922-1953）》（臺北：光啟文化出版社，2006）。

7 柯博識（Jac Kuepers）著，袁小涓譯，《私立北京輔仁大學1925-1950：理念、歷程、教員》（新莊：輔仁大學出版社，2007）；袁小涓，〈1949-1950年北京輔仁大學控制權的爭奪——以校務長芮歌尼為中心的討論〉，《輔仁歷史學報》，第22期（新莊，2009.01），頁307-331；施珮吟，〈試論芮歌尼主校初期（1946-1948）輔仁大學的發展〉，《史學研究》，第23期（新莊，2010.05），頁111-164。

8 柯博識，〈聖言會士蔣百鍊神父與輔仁大學在臺復校的關係〉，《輔仁歷史學報》，第29期（新莊，2012.09），頁35-66。

9 Fr. Schmitz Bartley, "Father Edward Wojniak, S. V. D.," May 31, 1984, unpublished, pp. 1-2.

就讀於小修院與神哲學院，經過數年的養成教育，於 1931 年 8 月 15 日首次發願，1937 年 3 月 7 日正式被祝聖為神父。[10]

萬德華神父的首個傳教工作即在中國，1937 年 10 月與何神父（Fr. Arthur Haines, 1908-1985）一同抵達上海與舊識米幹神父（Fr. Thomas Meagan, 1899-1951）會面後不久，即前往山東兗州府的戴家莊學習中文，1938 年 6 月萬德華神父至河南新鄉開始正式福傳工作。當時新鄉監牧區由米幹神父領導，由於長期戰亂與頻繁天災的破壞，大量難民無所適從，米幹神父即要求所有會士在各自傳教站開設救濟中心提供保護與賑濟，因此天主教會獲得人們普遍的支持與信任。

然 1941 年底珍珠港事件爆發後不久，河南新鄉的美籍聖言會神職人員即被日軍拘禁在方濟會（Order of Friars Minor，簡稱 OFM）靈醫女修會的王大夫醫院中；1943 年 3 月，再移居至山東濰坊基督教長老會（Presbyterian Church）的中學；同年 8 月，透過代表教廷的蔡寧主教（Baptist Mario Zanin, 1890-1958）之努力交涉，日軍又將天主教傳教人員轉移到北平，關押在方濟會開辦的語言學校中，直至 1945 年 8 月日軍投降後，美籍會士們才回到新鄉重啟傳教事業。[11]

惟 1945 年 9 月，由劉伯承（1892-1986）率領的共軍突襲新鄉監牧區西部的幾個堂口並捉走若干聖言會會士，為此，萬德華神父曾親自到修武與共軍談判。其後因國共雙方在美國協調下簽訂停戰協定，於 1946 年 1 月至 1947 年 3 月間實維持一相對平靜之局面，因此美籍聖言會士得被釋放，新鄉監牧區可持續在米幹神父領導下穩定發展；而亦在此時，萬德華神父被派往共軍佔領的沁陽，期望尋找與共軍和平相處的有效方式，以維持在地的教會工作，然努力數月未成，終於 1947 年返美，結束在中國的傳教工作。[12]

---

10 有關萬德華神父的早年經歷係據聖言會檔案紀錄而來，而臺灣報紙的相關刊載亦來自檔案資料的部分內容中譯文；參見："Divine Word News Service T-6630," 1969；"Divine Word News Service T-7303," January 16；"Fr. Edward Wojniak, S. V. D.," November 14, 1983；〈蔣夫人極關切改善女工生活特在美接見萬德華司鐸垂詢興建女工宿舍計畫〉，《中央日報》，1966.08.25，第 2 版。

11 昊伯，《華夏遺蹤：聖言會甘肅、河南福傳史（1922-1953）》，頁 73-75。

12 昊伯，《華夏遺蹤：聖言會甘肅、河南福傳史（1922-1953）》，頁 96。

綜觀萬德華神父在中國的首次福傳經歷，時間雖然只有十年，卻與中國人民、中國民間社會結下不解情緣，在往後歲月中其不時回顧這段經歷，據 Raymond Kunkel 神父（1918-2003）的觀察：「1947年回到美國後的萬德華神父，會驕傲地告訴願意聽他說話的每一個人——他曾經在中國傳教，那是他有關認同與榮耀的來源，在此後的傳教工作中。」[13] 又 1957 年萬德華神父撰寫《原子彈使徒：米幹神父》（*Atomic Apostle: Thomas M. Megan, S. V. D.*）一書紀念 1951 年過世的米幹神父時，在該書扉頁中他明白記載：「米幹神父是我此生最偉大及最好的朋友，經由那幾年艱困的傳教生涯我被啟發及導引，且在十年的快樂與悲傷歲月中，我能夠深層地了解中國。」[14]

回到美國的萬德華神父服務於賓州匹茲堡教區的一間醫院，十一年後（1958），因聖言會正式接受臺灣為其傳教區，燃起萬德華神父心中的中國情緣，他主動申請到臺灣來傳教，等待兩年後終於獲准。於是，1961 年秋，在其福傳生涯邁向第 25 周年之際，亦將啟程出發接下新工作之時，他撰文說明自己的抉擇，該文除追憶他在中國傳教的過去，也展望他到臺灣傳教的未來；關於前者，他說：「我福傳生涯與中國發生關係實始於 1926 年，當我仍是伊利諾州泰克尼的學生，那時，我與米幹神父已建立深厚的友誼」；至於後者，他宣稱：新的福傳工作是他的「首愛」（First Love），尤其，「來自中國大陸各省數百萬的難民，現在聚集在福爾摩莎這個相對小的區域內，……就某種程度而言，當傳教事業從中國被埋葬，現在中國又再度展現於傳教事業前」。[15] 從文中可知，曾在中國傳教十年的萬德華神父，始終未忘懷與米幹神父的深厚情誼，及當年在河南共同開創福傳事業的刻骨銘心歲月；且其將 1949 年以後的臺灣（Formosa 福爾摩莎）視為

---

13 Fr. Schmitz Bartley, "Father Edward Wojniak, S. V. D.," p. 5.

14 Edward Wojniak, *Atomic Apostle: Thomas M. Megan, S. V. D.* (Techny, Divine Word Publications, 1957), "Acknowledgments".

15 Edward Wojniak, "Formosa Today China Tomorrow," *Divine Word Missionaries*, Vol. Ⅲ , No. 3 (Autumn 1961), pp. 2-5.

另一個中國（Free China自由中國、Young China年輕中國），[16] 一個需要他幫助的中國，所以，他決定到臺灣來接續當年他在中國被迫中斷的傳教工作，此舉實繼續其對中國的「舊情」，亦結下與臺灣的「新緣」。

1961年11月22日，萬德華神父抵達臺灣基隆港時，同屬聖言會士的田耕莘樞機主教（1890-1967）已從羅馬回到臺灣，且被任命為臺北教區總主教，兩人於臺北見面後，萬德華神父得到的首個任務是：將聖言會在大坪林準備成立的新堂區建築作出改善，因當時土地上有數棟日式平房，分別規劃為聖言會根據地、樞機主教居所、聖堂，而萬德華神父即負責建出正式教堂以取代原來的聖堂。[17]

自1962年1月起，萬德華神父全心投入大坪林堂區的教堂建築工作，他請其河南舊識林慎白神父（Fr. Friedrich Linzenbach, 1904-1981）協助設計可容納約300至400人的教堂，自己則不斷想方設法地籌措各項經費；至1964年11月22日教堂落成並由田耕莘樞機主教祝聖而正式啟用為止，不到三年時間裡，萬德華神父持續寫信向美國芝加哥會院報告財務吃緊狀況，或在其自創的教堂刊物 *Formosa High Lights* 上仔細說明相關事務；如1962年1月18日信中請求省會提供美金1,000元，以協助聖堂的屋頂修繕，並提及教堂的建築經費估算至少需要美金20,000元，另外新購置的兩塊土地則需美金7,500元。[18] 而1964年11月底，教堂已正式啟用，但萬德華神父自德國訂製，將安置於教堂側邊的四大扇彩繪玻璃窗，及祭臺後方牆壁上的馬賽克聖三圖像、魚群圖像仍未抵達，且相關經費尚欠缺近美金10,000元。[19] 事實上，直到1965年9月，即教堂已建成並使用近十個月後，萬德華

---

16 萬德華神父言及臺灣時往往以"Formosa", "Free China", "Young China"之名稱呼，參見：*Divine Word Missionaries*, Vol. Ⅲ, No. 3 (Autumn 1961), p. 2; *Formosa High Lights*, December 8, 1965, p. 1; Edward Wojniak, "New approach to evangelization in Taiwan," *Catholic Mission*, (December, 1970), p. 25.

17 大坪林地區原本供教友望彌撒之聖堂為一日式平房，並非具教堂形式之建築，真正出現教堂形式之建築即1964年落成之聖三堂。

18 "Letter from Fr. Edward Wojniak to Fr. Francis Kamp," January 18, 1962.

19 *Formosa High Lights*, December 1, 1964.

神父仍為無法付清的款項甚為煩惱。[20]

　　然即使教堂建築工作如此艱困，相關經費籌措如此令人費心，萬德華神父卻對堂區的福傳工作充滿信心與希望；早在來臺後的第一個月（1961年12月），他即寫信給任職於義大利羅馬總會會長秘書的好友 Fr. William Hunter 表示：「目前教會在福爾摩莎的未來是非常光明的，我會毫不猶豫地稱這兒為傳教工作的黃金時代（Golden Age）」；[21] 又1962年1月18日寫信給美國省會芝加哥會院時，他明確向省會負責人 Fr. Francis Kamp（1920-2011）表示：「我希望你及全世界都知道，在我一生中從未感覺像現在及在這個地方工作得如此快樂」；[22] 而觀察萬德華神父與人交往之書信資料，其每每在信紙書寫日期位置之上方加註「Paradise Of Formosa」數字，[23] 可知其對臺灣福傳事業前景之看好及對新店大坪林堂區角色扮演之重視。

　　此外，這段期間，他因教友人數日益增加而開心不已，並不斷期許更高目標的達成，如其在1962年聖誕節出刊的 *Formosa High Lights* 上言：今年的聖誕節有20多人領洗，令本堂的教友人數超過40人；[24] 到1965年復活節出刊的 *Formosa High Lights* 上則說：目前有30人參加慕道班，今年應該有50人可以領洗；而且，我班上有8位婦女，她們的孩子加起來共31個，如果這些母親願意領洗，那麼孩子們全部都可能接受洗禮。[25]

　　同時，自1961年底開始，萬德華神父亦委請與聖言會早有合作關係之女修會——聖家獻女傳教修會（Missionary Sisters Oblates of The Holy Family，簡稱OSF，以下中文簡稱聖家會）的兩位修女協助兒童

20 "Letter from Fr. Edward Wojniak to Mr. Art Pape," September 2, 1965.

21 "Letter from Fr. Edward Wojniak to Fr. William Hunter," December 10, 1961.

22 "Letter from Fr. Edward Wojniak to Fr. Francis Kamp," January 18, 1962.

23 此類書信可參見："Letter from Fr. Edward Wojniak to Fr. Francis Kamp," December 16, 1963; "Letter from Fr. Edward Wojniak to Mr. Art Pape," August 8, 1964; "Letter from Fr. Edward Wojniak to Fr. Francis Kamp," March 21, 1965; "Letter from Fr. Edward Wojniak to Fr. Francis Kamp," February 11, 1968.

24 *Formosa High Lights*, Christmas, 1962.

25 *Formosa High Lights*, Easter, 1965.

福傳工作；[26] 事實上，至萬德華神父來臺後的第三年，即1964年的聖誕節——當時教堂已落成並使用，其便著手堂區中診所與小學的籌設事務；[27] 再至1965年的復活節，他更為數年努力而在堂區中逐一出現的教堂、診所、圖書室、遊戲室、籃球場等設備而滿懷感恩，[28] 惟前述各項規劃中的設立小學一事，後來卻因土地無法順利取得被迫擱置，改以興建女子公寓替代之。

三、女子公寓的創建歷程（1960年代）

萬德華神父有關女子公寓興建之構思早見於1965年12月8日出刊的 *Formosa High Lights* 上，當時他觀察到堂區附近快速工業化帶來的社會轉變及新的生活需求，所以撰文指出：

> 年輕中國的工業化非常快，工廠如蘑菇般地到處都是，……在我堂區的附近有超過1,300個工廠女子被一打的工廠雇用，有些工廠是屬於美國的資金。大量的工廠工作者移入這個地區造成嚴重的房屋短缺，1,300人中的大部分女子被雇用在座落於嚴重擁擠及欠缺衛生環境的工廠裡，她們約10人到12人分享一個榻榻米（日本式家庭用的床），如果一個女子感冒，或者更糟，染上肺結核或其他疾病，可以想像可能的風險。廁所和洗澡設備是很原始及幾乎是不存在的，這些女子大部分沒有能力擔負個人的床位及其他「舒適的家」，她們一週工作六天，月薪美金12至15元，此一刺激令我想到，也許我可以有些作為去填補這個令人哭泣的需要。[29]

---

26 "Letter from Fr. Edward Wojniak to Fr. William Hunter," December 10, 1961.

27 *Formosa High Lights*, December 1, 1964.

28 *Formosa High Lights*, Easter, 1965.

29 *Formosa High Lights*, December 8, 1965, pp. 1-2.

因此他覺得：解決住宿問題在目前而言是應該優先於建立小學的計畫，故其刻不容緩地促使當月底即將來臺、曾規劃聖三堂建築事務的林慎白神父，再次擔負起相關工作——設計出可容納500人的全新樓房式女子公寓之藍圖。[30]

若將萬德華神父於1960年代觀察到的新店地區工廠林立，且大量雇用女工之現象，與四十多年後關注臺灣勞動力市場變化的學界研究成果互相對照，確可印證此一狀況之真實性；因據陳信行的研究可知，當時在新店地區有許多工廠，其中，以透過政府招商方式進駐臺灣的美商通用器材公司之規模最大，招募工人數目最多，尤其是大量來自臺灣各地之年輕女子；[31]而通用器材公司正式設廠營運始於1964年，次年（1965）萬德華神父即注意到女工住宿問題之迫切性，可見其在致力教堂本身事務、照顧教友團體外，亦未疏忽對堂區附近社會脈動之掌握，並關懷弱勢族群、非教友群體之需要。另據1975、1977年兩次親赴德華女子公寓，對住宿女工展開調查研究的美籍艾琳達博士（Dr. Linda Gail Arrigo）之口訪紀錄、筆者對任職德華女子公寓管理員袁嬤嬤女士之訪談內容，以及當時報紙的相關報導，亦可得知這些住宿女子除部分在其他小型工廠工作外，絕大多數均為通用器材公司所雇用。[32]

大致而言，萬德華神父的樓房式女子公寓興築計畫以1968年為界可分前後兩期，第一期本規劃為容納500人住宿的兩棟四層樓公寓及一座活動中心，分別是位於北方的A棟與位於南方的B棟，而兩棟公寓中間則是一座至少兩層樓高的活動中心，專門提供住宿女子於工

---

30 女子公寓最早規劃之設計藍圖係由林慎白神父（亦稱林昇博神父）負責，然後來有國籍設計師楊卓成（1914-2006）的參與；參見〈興建婦女公寓定卅五日破土〉，《臺灣新生報》，1967.02.22，第3版；〈職業婦女公寓昨行破土禮工程費一千二百萬〉，《徵信新聞報》，1967.02.22，第2版；〈職業婦女公寓落成典禮邀請卡〉，1966.05.25。

31 陳信行，〈打造第一個全球裝配線：臺灣通用器材公司與城鄉移民1964-1990〉，《政大勞動學報》，第20期（臺北，2006.07），頁1-48。

32 艾琳達博士提供的資料中有14份為住在德華女子公寓者的口訪紀錄，均提及在通用器材公司或公寓附近的電子工廠工作；至於筆者與袁嬤嬤女士之訪談日期分別為2014年6月3日及7月21日兩次；而報紙報導可見〈通用工業城員工樂融融〉，《經濟日報》，1976.08.08，第7版。

作之餘從事休閒活動、才藝學習之用。然最早興建的A棟於1967年2月破土動工，至1968年5月完成後，出租情況甚佳，各界反應熱烈，顯見市場需求孔急，令萬德華神父決定擴增計畫到可供1,000人以上住宿之容量，[33] 即除已建好的一棟四層樓公寓（A棟）外，另興築位於南方的B棟、C棟（此二棟樓被萬德華神父稱之為「雙塔」（Twin Tower），及建於B、C兩棟公寓中間的中棟，計有三棟五層樓公寓及一座單層的活動中心；第二期計畫之構思實於1968年10月成形，1969年開始動工，而於1970、1971年陸續完成。

　　整個德華女子公寓計畫進行過程中，最令人困擾者為經費的籌措，按照第一期計畫的規模，萬德華神父估算總金額約為臺幣1,200多萬元（美金約30多萬元），當時他還樂觀地表示：類似計畫在美國要價美金150萬元，而臺灣因物資及人力較為便宜，僅需美國費用的五分之一左右即可完成。[34] 然上千萬元的募款工作進行起來仍甚為吃力，他的作法是：除將個人畢生積蓄全部奉獻外，[35] 亦積極地向內（修會、教會）外（世俗社會）各界尋求支持與援助。

　　就對內而言，1966年1月，萬德華神父所屬的聖言會美國省會即率先支助美金600元；[36] 1967年4月，透過美國省會的積極聯絡與協助解決稅務問題，亦爭取到Philco-Ford Corporation的援助；[37] 而1967年5月，位於義大利羅馬的聖言會總會也提供美金2,000元；[38] 為此，萬德華神父曾於1969年3月致函聖言會中華區會會長彭加德神父（Fr. Ernst Böhm, 1912-1992），請其代為轉達個人對聖言會總會前後兩任會長長期以來之支持女子公寓計畫事及提供相關協助的感謝。[39]

33 "Express News Evening Edition: More Donations Urged," May 25, 1968.

34 "Toward a Better World: Hostels for Factory Girls," *Free China Weekly*, September 4, 1966, p. 2.

35 〈解決女工住宿問題的——職業婦女公寓〉，《中央日報》，1967.02.24，第4版。

36 "Letter from Fr. Francis Kamp to Fr. Edward Wojniak," January 29, 1966.

37 "Letter from B. VanDenburg Hall to Fr. Francis Kamp," April 13, 1967; "Letter from Fr. Francis Kamp to B. VanDenburg Hall," April 18, 1967.

38 "Letter from Fr. Assistant General to Fr. Francis Kamp," May 22, 1967; "Letter from Fr. Edward Wojniak to Fr. Francis Kamp," June 8, 1967.

39 "Letter from Fr. Edward Wojniak to Fr. Ernst Böhm," March 7, 1969.

此外，1966年12月，剛從羅馬返臺的羅光總主教（1911-2004）帶來教宗保祿六世（Pope Paulus VI, 1897-1978）認同並支持女子公寓興築計畫的消息，並經由教廷駐華大使高理耀主教（Baptist Giuseppe Caprio, 1914-2005）捐款美金16,000元。[40] 當然，更多的募款是來自廣大的世俗社會，無論是個人或團體、教友或非教友；尤其，此一計畫乃臺灣首個專為職業婦女，特別是為工廠雇用的女工興建之出租公寓計畫，萬德華神父即以此為號召重點，再透過各式人際網絡及多樣的募款活動，令女子公寓興築計畫得到許多政商名流的參與及中外媒體的廣泛報導，也因而獲得社會大眾的普遍迴響。

當時，該計畫首先受到世俗社會之高度關注，實因1966年2、3月間獲得來自美國好萊塢（Hollywood）一筆高達美金25,000元的大額捐款。該筆款項之捐助者為1965年11月來臺拍攝電影《聖保羅砲艇》（The Sand Pebbles）的美國廿世紀福斯公司（20th Century Fox Company）導演羅勃‧懷斯（Robert Wise, 1914-2005）及該片男主角史提夫‧麥昆（Steve McQueen, 1930-1980）；兩人聯合捐款一事於2月即告知萬德華神父，惟正式的支票捐贈儀式至3月18日才在臺北萬華的拍片現場進行，萬德華神父並將裱好裝框的女子公寓建築藍圖回贈兩人作為紀念品。[41]

1966年3月底至12月間，萬德華神父更是風塵僕僕地遠赴歐美等地、進行長達九個月的巡迴募款工作；其中，4月時曾透過中華民國駐美大使周書楷（1913-1992）之安排，於美國華盛頓獲蔣夫人宋美齡女士（1897-2003）的親自接見，蔣夫人並應萬德華神父之當面邀請，同意擔任女子公寓籌建委員會的名譽主席，[42] 此舉實大為提升該計畫之國際知名度，並號召更多中外支援的挹注。而7月萬德華神父回到曾經服務過的美國著名工業城市匹茲堡時，更大聲呼籲美國企

---

40 羅光總主教致萬德華神父之中英文信件（December 19, 1966）；"Pope VI Blesses Hostel Project," *The China News*, January 11, 1967, p. 8.

41 "NT$1 Million Contributed To Fund For Building Factory Girls' Hostel," *China Post*, March 18, 1966, p. 6.

42 "Toward a Better Word: Hostels for Factory Girls," *Free China Weekly*, September 4, 1966, p. 2.

業對臺灣女工伸出援手。[43] 此外，通用器材公司美國總部亦於8月間致函萬德華神父，表示願意提供未來五年、每年美金5,000元，總額為25,000美元的捐款。[44]

總計至1967年2月止，即女子公寓首期計畫正式破土動工時，來自國內外各式捐贈，除水泥等建築材料外，[45] 現金捐助額度已達臺幣700多萬元，惟與實際需要的總經費相較仍不足臺幣近500萬元。茲將萬德華神父規劃女子公寓首期計畫所需經費與實際募款所得金額明列如下：[46]

（一）規劃所需經費

右棟（北棟、A棟）	臺幣 5,000,000元	（美金 124,300元）
左棟（南棟、B棟）	臺幣 4,500,000元	（美金 113,000元）
社交中心	臺幣 2,800,000元	（美金 70,000元）
（教室、診所、大禮堂）		
總計	臺幣 12,300,000元	（美金 307,300元）

（二）實際募款所得

聖言會美國省會	臺幣 24,000元	（美金 600元）
美國海軍副司令	臺幣 1,000元	（美金 25元）
羅勃‧懷斯與史提夫‧麥昆	臺幣 1,000,000元	（美金 25,000元）
好萊塢演員參與之慈善義演	臺幣 128,000元	（美金 3,200元）
臺灣通用器材公司	臺幣 1,000,000元	（美金 25,000元）
羅馬教廷	臺幣 640,000元	（美金 16,000元）

---

43 "Formosan Factory Girls Aid Sought Here," *The Pittsburgh Press*, July 13, 1966, p. 33.

44 "Letter from Mr. M. Shapiro to Fr. Edward Wojniak," August 15, 1966.

45 〈蔣夫人極關切改善女工生活特在美接見萬德華司鐸垂詢興建女工宿舍計畫〉，《中央日報》，1966.08.25，第2版。

46 相關資料參見〈興建職業婦女公寓蔣夫人任名譽會長該公寓由萬德華神父募款已募七百餘萬現續勸募中〉，《臺灣新生報》，1966.12.14，第3版；《臺灣新聞畫報》，1966.12.16，第4版；"Letter from Fr. Francis Kamp to Fr. Edward Wojniak ," January 29, 1966; "Letter from Mr. Jr. Wm. E. Gentner to Fr. Edward Wojniak," February 11, 1966.

美國與歐洲數個婦女組織	臺幣	136,000元	（美金　3,400元）
萬德華神父	臺幣	452,000元	（美金 11,300元）
臺灣省議會（謝東閔）	臺幣	5,000元	（美金　　125元）
其他各式現金捐款	臺幣	4,120,000元	（美金 103,000元）
總計	臺幣	7,506,000元	（美金 187,650元）

　　至1967年2月25日止，雖然實際募款僅達首期計畫需要金額的六成而已，惟秉持「先興建後付款」之原則，並儘快為需要女子提供住宿協助之想法，萬德華神父仍如期舉行女子公寓的破土儀式，並邀請黨政要人及社會名流參與相關活動，此實大動國內外視聽。[47] 然興築女子公寓的費用支出在首期計畫開工後便經常發生困難，尤其某些捐助款項並未如期到位；再進入到第二期計畫時更是雪上加霜，因二期計畫較前期計畫更為龐大，因此經費需求較以往暴增臺幣500多萬元，令總額高達到臺幣1,750萬元，[48] 且隨著物價逐年波動及高漲，整個女子公寓計畫總額至1970年已逼近臺幣2,000萬元。[49]

　　為此，萬德華神父必須更努力地尋求援助，而據目前可掌握的書信資料，實可見其在經費籌措上之辛勞與經費支付上之窘境；如1967年5月，女子公寓剛開工不到三個月，萬德華神父即寫信給聖言會美國省會會長，要求提供利息在3-4%間、美金50,000元之貸款，以協助他解決美金64,000元的債務問題。[50] 1968年2月，即首期計畫A棟落成前三個月，萬德華神父又致函美國省會會長，說他有「許多、許多帳單要支付」，在三月底前急需美金15,000元。[51] 而1968年11月，當臺灣通用器材公司已允諾美金80,000元之長期低利貸款

47 〈新店大坪林女青年宿舍廿五日行破土禮恭請蔣夫人主持〉，《民族晚報》，1967.02.22，第3版；〈短評──女工宿舍〉，《中央日報》，1967.02.03，第3版。

48 "Architect's Sketch of Proposed Five-Story Addition to Present Building And New Social Center".

49 *Formosa High Lights*, August, 1970.

50 "Letter from Fr. Edward Wojniak to Fr. Francis Kamp", May 1, 1967.

51 "Letter from Fr. Edward Wojniak to Fr. Francis Kamp," February 11, 1968.

時，萬德華神父在給美國省會會長的信函中言，「我知道你會為我得到這一大筆錢而高興，但如果我告訴你，我還需要美金77,000元時，你可以只是為我哭泣，或是貸款給我——省下你的眼淚！貸款給我」，[52] 看似輕鬆幽默、軟硬兼施的語句背後，除顯示彼此間之長期深厚交情外，實隱含肩扛巨額金錢負擔之沉重壓力。又1969年3月，面臨女子公寓二期計畫已開工之迫切經費需求，萬德華神父寫信給中華區會會長彭加德神父，希望能轉達羅馬總會，將其早年在河南新鄉傳教事業的相關經費美金17,800元提供給他目前正在進行的計畫。[53] 而1970年9月，萬德華神父更直接寫信給羅馬總會會長表示：聖言會價值50萬美元的計畫即將完成，但「這快樂的一天，也可能變成悲劇的日子，只有您及您的委員會可以防止這種事情發生在我身上」，因為，「我的經費短缺美金15,000元至20,000元」，[54] 期望羅馬總會能伸出援手協助度過難關。

惟即便如此，萬德華神父仍樂觀面對接踵而至的各式困難，並對女子公寓計畫的日漸完成充滿信心且感恩不已，他曾說興建女子公寓是一個「新的、具真實意義的適切計畫在上主的葡萄園中」，[55] 而他將「利用有生之年，完成這件有意義的社會福利工作」。[56] 又1968年5月女子公寓首期計畫的A棟落成時，他曾對媒體表示：「我很高興，但不滿足；我高興是因為人們現在知道這個計畫是理智的、可行的；但是除非需要住宿的每一個女子均能在此環境下，住得安全、快樂而沒有恐懼，否則我是不會滿足的」；[57] 可見女子公寓計畫在萬德華神父心中的重要地位與深厚意義。

---

52 "Letter from Fr. Edward Wojniak to Fr. Francis Kamp," November 4, 1968.

53 "Letter from Fr. Edward Wojniak to Fr. Ernst Böhm," March 7, 1969; "Letter from Fr. Edward Wojniak to Fr. John Musinsky," April 10, 1969.

54 "Letter from Fr. Edward Wojniak to Fr. John Musinsky," September 4, 1970.

55 *Formosa High Lights*, August, 1969, p. 2.

56 〈興建女工宿舍神父全力以赴演晚會好的開始還要環遊歐美募捐〉，《徵信新聞報》，1966.02.21，第3版。

57 "First Hostel For Working Girls Is Dedicated," *China Post*, June 1, 1968, p. 5.

四、女子公寓的營運成果（1968-1988）

　　德華女子公寓從1968年5月，首期的A棟公寓落成後開始出租，至1988年9月30日正式結束為止，營運時間超過二十年。而營運方式則分住宿與活動中心兩部分，前者是為外出就業或就學之婦女解決住宿問題，並給予適當之生活照顧；後者則是提供其教育學習機會，以增進個人能力與拓展人際關係。

　　首就住宿方面而言，由於萬德華神父觀察到堂區附近女工們原先的租屋環境與品質甚為惡劣；[58] 因此，上下舖的睡床、桌椅合併之家具及桌燈、有熱水器的浴室、有冰箱的廚房、洗衣間等符合人道的居家設施就成為宿舍的必需品；為此，他曾利用聖誕節期間對外募款臺幣5,000元以購置相關物品。[59]

　　除較為現代化的住居設施外，萬德華神父認為女子公寓的興建，不僅提供離家就業或就學婦女一個居住場所，更是給予一個「家」，因此必須擁有家庭的氣氛，為達此目的，女子公寓的空間規劃就不該如軍營般的宿舍模式，而是像家庭似的格局設計；茲以最早落成的A棟為例，其內部隔間如同8人一戶的住家，因8名住宿女子享有兩個具盥洗設備的房間及客廳、廚房、洗衣間等頗為寬敞之空間。事實上，萬德華神父在1970年代女子公寓住宿手冊之首頁，即將女子公寓的家庭特色與氛圍清楚呈現，其言：

> 親愛的小姐：
> 在此我熱切的歡迎著你的光臨，……
> 使我感到慶幸的是，我們的大家庭，將因著你的光臨更加的生氣蓬勃……
> 首先讓我來為你介紹一下，現在你所置身的新環境……。

---

58 "If You Were a Girl of Seventeen – Would You Like to Live Here？" 1966.
59 *Formosa High Lights*, December 8, 1965, p. 2.

這所矗立在東西交通孔道邊的宏偉建築物——德華女子公寓，
他不是旅館也並非學校，而是一座充滿著家庭和樂氣息的好地
方。……

住滿了成千女青年的公寓，他們因生長在不同的生活環境裡，
造成興趣與個性上的懸殊，但朝夕相處彼此都能互相關懷，和
睦相處，這是很好的現象，希望彼此言行之間都要有「愛」，
因為你關心別人，世界才會變得更和諧更可愛。[60]

而女子公寓招租宣傳單上也載明其創建目的在於，「使離鄉的——
您，有一個安全舒適的『家』」；[61]且當時在公寓裡協助服務的韓修
女曾對記者說明：「這幢公寓不是旅館也非學校，而是一座充滿家庭
和樂氣氛的地方，小姐們有心理上或其他切身的問題，都可以請神父
或管理人員協助輔導解決。」[62]由此可見女子公寓長期以來雖提供出
租使用，卻與一般出租房屋在性質上有顯著差距。

當然，數個或十餘個毫無血緣關係者同居一室，上百個彼此陌生
之人共處一樓，為公寓內部之秩序穩定及氣氛和諧，自有必要擬出管
理系統與訂定居住規範。大致而言，女子公寓出現管理組織方案始於
1968年10月，當時僅完成女子公寓的A棟建築，而萬德華神父已構
思好完整之組織系統如下頁表。

其中，總管理人的角色最為重要，其主要工作有四，即：指導與
監督其他宿舍的負責人、在能力範圍內規劃聯繫與提供建言給教會高
層、盡可能將新店宿舍系統推廣至其他區域、維持宿舍財政。此外，
精神導師由神職人員擔任，主要功能是提供宿舍母親及教師的指導與
諮詢；教師與社工是在公寓總管理人指導下，負責活動中心的教育學
習課程；宿舍母親則是提供住宿女子生活上的協助與需要。[63]

---

60 〈德華女子公寓手冊〉。

61 〈德華女子公寓招租宣傳單〉。

62 〈德華女子公寓充滿青春氣息〉，《通用之聲雜誌》，1975.07.15，第3版。

63 "Letter from Fr. Edward Wojniak to Fr. John Musinsky," January 22, 1969.

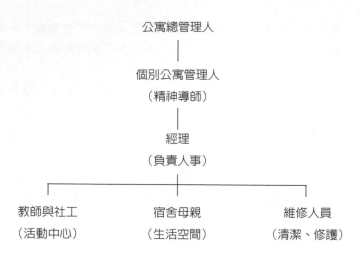

公寓總管理人

個別公寓管理人
（精神導師）

經理
（負責人事）

教師與社工	宿舍母親	維修人員
（活動中心）	（生活空間）	（清潔、修護）

　　惟女子公寓全部建成後的實際營運情形目前所見資料僅知，女子公寓總管理人為萬德華神父，1975 年萬德華神父因病回美就醫後，由柯博識神父接手；而自平房女子宿舍時期即負責照顧住宿女子的李貞德修女則為公寓的經理，以後陸續有瑪麗諾會修女（Maryknoll Sister）Pauline Sticka、自教職退休的教友張陳麗玉女士（Mrs. Mary Chang）、聖家會翁修女及伍修女先後擔任此一工作，[64] 女子公寓另聘有各棟管理員（即宿舍母親、舍監）、維修員及活動中心管理員等人，以共同維持整個女子公寓的運作，而這些隸屬管理組織之雇用人員均具教友背景。

　　至於居住公寓必須遵守之相關規範，則可見於女子公寓的住宿手冊中，最早由萬德華神父具名的手冊裡曾明列九條規定，內容如下：

1. 內務經常保持整潔，每天每人盡好自己的本分工作，使用水電一切設備均應特別愛惜，不可浪費或故意損害。
2. 會客宜在會客室內，必要時先經管理員同意帶往參觀各處，

64 *Formosa High Lights,* August 1970.

不能擅自留宿親友。

3. 每天晚上十一時半以後，嚴守禁默，不要有擾同伴的安寧，十二時正關大門，趕不及回來請打電話通知管理員或事前登記外宿。

4. 每間寢室選派室長一人協助領導各位。

5. 教友應在日常生活中充分表現基督化的精神，樹立好榜樣，守本分，彼此之間要有愛德，好讓別人能在我們身上找到天主的肖像。

6. 來訪客人，請先至傳達室登記。

7. 退宿者應向每棟管理員領取「放行條」方可離去。

8. 三次未請假外宿者或不按規定清掃者，予以退宿。

9. 每月一次慶生會，由各棟小姐彼此慶祝。[65]

1978 年 5 月，女子公寓已產生出經由公寓管理人員會議通過的〈德華女子公寓住宿守則〉，並以單張明載諸條文方式公布實施，其內容如下：[66]

守則	違者處分
01. 凡住宿者必須符合下列資格： （1）有正當職業。 （2）未婚、單身。 （3）身心健康。 （4）未受過刑事處分。	喪失住宿資格時，則失去住宿權利。
02. 遵守公寓之規定；聽從管理人員合理之約束並接受勸導。	不能配合公寓之規定時，其住宿權利即被取消。
03. 照規定辦法辦理住宿與退宿手續。	
04. 照實填寫個人資料表件；如有任何更改，必須通知管理人員予以更改。	

65 〈德華女子公寓手冊〉。
66 〈德華女子公寓住宿守則〉（1978.05.01 公布實施）。

05. 依分配寢室居住；如有特殊理由必須調換，須先徵得管理人員之許可，並以一次為限。	
06. 須以本公寓為主要居所；若非獲得管理人員許可，每月外宿時間不得超過十天。	
07. 每月 1 至 10 日繳納宿費。憑繳費收據住宿。	逾期繳費，每天罰款 5 元。未繳者，迄至押金不足扣繳時即當退宿論。
08. 不得酗酒、吸毒、賭博、毆 、偷竊、或傷害他人身體。	取消住宿權利。
09. 不得造謠生事、損害他人名譽或誘惑別人參加非法組織及不良職業。	
10. 不可帶男賓進入宿舍。	
11. 不可帶客人進宿舍。不可留親友住宿。若母姊自遠方來，亦必須徵得管理人員許可，並繳納宿費每人每天 25 元。	未經許可擅自留宿者雙倍罰款；客人罰款未清付時，由帶客人進來之小姐押金中扣繳。
12. 愛護公物和設備；節約水電，用後順手把開關關閉。	如有破壞照價賠償。無人承認之損壞由公物所在範圍內住宿者共同賠償。
13. 不可擅自用電；熨衣服及吹頭髮須到熨衣室。	電器、爐台、炊具、衣物等由管理人員收去，俟退宿時方可發還；退宿後兩週未來領回者，由公寓自行處理。
14. 除自炊廚房外，公寓內其他地方均不可煮食；暫時不用的爐台須存於倉庫，不可放置寢室內。	
15. 個人衣物，包括皮箱、衣櫥、縫紉機等等，均不可佔放公用地方或空床空櫃，必要時可存於倉庫。	
16. 辦妥退宿手續即須帶走個人全部衣物。	
17. 走廊、欄杆、風扇、電話台、窗口、門口等地方均不得晾晒衣物。	衣物由管理人員收去，每件罰款 5 元方可領回；兩天內未來領回者，由公寓自行處理。
18. 晚上十一時三十分以前回公寓。	逾十二時才回來，取消住宿權利。
19. 早上六時前，晚上十二時熄燈後，均須保持安靜。	無法與多數人合作之小姐請自動退宿，同寢室的小姐亦可聯合向管理人員投訴。經審查屬實，即取消其住宿權利。
20. 搬進與遷出，均以早晚室友在寢室時間為宜。	
21. 寢室內不可吸煙或點燃蠟燭。	
22. 保持個人及環境整潔衛生，輪流值日。	
23. 遵守寢室內多數人通過之合理規定。	

由不同版本之住宿規範可知，女子公寓有如學校宿舍般之嚴格規定，包括門禁、宵禁、愛惜公物、維護個人整潔與公共環境，以及團體生活必要之各式約束等；惟除此外，女子公寓亦存有相當程度之家庭氛圍，並規劃每月一次的慶生會以增進眾人感情，甚至後來有每月一次的宿舍清潔比賽，[67] 以維持如家居般的衛生環境。因此德華女子公寓自落成後風評甚佳、反應熱烈，如1971年5月，即女子公寓全部建築完工後三個月，已有來自全臺灣19個地區，分屬24個不同省籍的400多名女子入住；[68] 再隔一個月，又增至600多人住宿；[69] 另據1980年代報紙刊載，女子公寓最高紀錄曾超過1,200人住宿。[70] 分析該公寓所以如此搶手之因，除具備人道、現代化生活設施之物質條件，及如家庭般之氛圍、管理完善等因素外，平價租金亦是吸引人的重要關鍵。

　　蓋德華女子公寓的房租在規劃之初及首期工程興建期間，均清楚表明為嘉惠附近工廠就業之女工，租金定為臺幣100元左右，然首期工程A棟落成後的實收租金為每人臺幣150元。[71] 惟值得注意的是，整個德華女子公寓共有四棟，其不同空間規劃，實應對不同租金及不同背景之住宿者。大致而言，A棟屬4人或8人房之床位，平均每人享有之空間較為寬敞，租金亦較高，入住者的職業也較為多樣化，除工廠女工外，另有大專學生、教員、護士、銀行職員等社經地位較高者；[72] 而B、C、中棟則屬12人房之床位，平均每人享有的空間頗為狹窄，故租金低廉，投宿者幾乎全為女工或半工半讀之夜校生，特別是臺灣通用器材公司雇用者，當時屬該公司女工入住者之租金往往是

67 吳蕙芳，〈第一部：回首來時路〉，收入《結緣半世紀：傳承‧出發（天主教新店大坪林聖三堂金慶特刊，1962-2012）》（新店：天主教聖三堂，2012），頁32。

68 〈職業婦女公寓〉，《中央日報》，1971.05.10，第3版。

69 *The China News*, January 19, 1971, p. 8.

70 〈公寓易主苦了員工住戶心內恐慌擔憂失業失所〉，《青年日報》（臺北），1988.06.08，第7版。

71 當時報載租金數字有臺幣100元至150元、160元以下等不同紀錄；相關資料參見〈婦女公寓開始出租單身女教師及工讀女生均可申請〉，《經濟日報》，1968.05.26，第5版；〈婦女公寓完成奉獻儀式接受進住申請〉，《聯合報》，1968.05.26，第4版。

72 〈大城市需要女子公寓〉，《經濟日報》，1970.04.02，第8版。

由公司代為支付的。[73]

事實上，德華女子公寓除舒適、安全及平價之住宿部外，另有活動中心之設置，提供住宿女子在工作之餘從事休閒活動以舒緩身心，亦可經由才藝學習課程提升個人能力，並藉此機會改變社會地位。[74]此活動中心之設置在當時為一創新規劃，兼具心靈教育、娛樂與精神培育三方面目的，[75] 其整個區域含室外與室內兩部分，前者有籃球場，亦可充作排球場、羽球場之用，後者包括乒乓球室、圖書室、自習室及各類教室。

當然，萬德華神父如此竭盡心力地創建德華女子公寓，除立基其社會服務之崇高理念外，不可否認亦有一定程度的福傳目的。1965年底，當他決定放棄原先的小學計畫改為創建女子公寓時，曾撰文提及此一改變對福傳工作之重要意義，因為：

> 這個宿舍的主要想法是提供一個「家」給這些女子，並在我們好修女們的指導與監督下，試著提供一個基督教氣氛，我們很確定這些貧窮的好女孩中，許多會不自主地被影響而朝教會來，並最終加入教會，這意謂著這些女子們將來是個基督徒母親，並建立基督教家庭。[76]

1967年他又明白地指出，成功傳教的一個重要原則在於「根基人們的需求並回應他們的需求」，「這些需求有時是物質性的，……但是協助人們解決物質需求，是可以令其接觸教會的，因此應將福音用更有活力的方式傳送出去」，而女子公寓計畫就是一個可以嘗試的作法。[77]

---

73 艾琳達口訪資料：編號3。
74 "Girls Hostel Needs Help," *The China News*, January 19, 1971, p. 8.
75 〈德華女子公寓手冊〉（1970年代）。
76 *Formosa High Light*, December 8, 1965, p. 2.
77 Edward Wojniak, "Taiwan Hostels Inc.," *The Word in the World*, 1967, p. 57.

再至1968年10月，萬德華神父更進一步地闡述女子公寓計畫與當前福傳工作的密切關係與重要性，因為「在快速發展與變化的國家中，社會接觸是僅膽下的一條傳播福音的康莊大道」，而在新店大坪林堂區附近，因工廠林立促成來自臺灣各地之大量年輕女子被僱用：

> 她們離開家庭及父母的指導，被丟到一個工業化複雜及大城市的環境中，這些年輕沒有經驗的女孩，生活在不同的道德與精神之危險及氛圍中，她們需要的，不僅是好的、健康的環境以替代如同家庭的居住條件，同時要有特別的指導及監督以協助她們適應新的生活，於工業化及完全世界化的環境中，……就此神聖任務而言，教會是合格且足以擔當這些年輕女子的督導責任。[78]

　　從前述數則史料可知，德華女子公寓兼具社會服務目的與教會福傳性質之雙重意義；然萬德華神父也明言，他「期望」這些住宿女子最終能成為基督徒，但她們並不「被要求」成為基督徒，[79] 即其並不強調福傳成果之重要性是必須超越社會服務之目的，此可從女子公寓入宿者並不限於教友，活動中心資源享用者不限住宿成員等實際狀況中得到證明。

　　惟1975年萬德華神父回美醫治心臟病，五年後（1980）曾短暫返臺，受到女子公寓住宿者之盛大歡迎，終於1983年11月14日因癌症病逝美國。而1988年6月，聖言會決定將長達二十年的德華女子公寓結束營運，並公告女子公寓住宿者於9月底搬離公寓，即明白宣示德華女子公寓將正式走入歷史。針對此一結果，曾有住宿女子投書報紙，表達不滿；[80] 而當時報紙刊載之世俗輿論認為女子公寓無法維持

---

78 "Letter from Fr. Edward Wojniak to Fr. John Musinsky," January 22, 1969.

79 *Formosa High Lights*, August 1970.

80 〈讀者投書：德華女子公寓不宜停租勿違創建德澤方為上策〉，《民生報》，1988.09.16，第13版。

之原因在於：「經營不善，入不敷出」；[81] 亦有教友向教會陳情，指出「該公寓非為營利事業，若干年來，未有富於經營豐富之專門人員妥善經營」，[82] 乃導致如此結果。而教會所持理由可見於1988年6月9日張貼在女子公寓大門口之公告，內容如下：

> 各位親愛的小姐：
>
> 德華女子公寓本著服務社會的宗旨，已達二十年之久，在這期間，我們一直在努力改進、修理。但由於時代的變遷，二十年前的設備，已不符合現代人的需求，為了達到現代化的標準，唯一的辦法就是拆除重建，使德華的面貌重新改觀，以達到服務人群的目的。因此，我們呼籲，請現住德華的每位小姐，最遲於77年9月30日以前搬離德華，並向愛護德華的諸位小姐，致上十二萬分的歉意。
>
> 願天主降福各位都能找到理想的住處，並祝福各位平安！[83]

即教會認為：二十年前興建完成之德華女子公寓，相關設備等物質條件已因時間因素，無法再經由修理方式予以改善，實難符合二十年後的現代化居住水準與品質，應予拆除改建才是。

其實，世俗輿論、教友陳情與教會考量均有其立論依據，且彼此間相當程度是互為因果的。因德華女子公寓營運至後期，住宿女子人數確實大幅降低，其中原因或與1984年臺灣通用器材公司大規模機械化、自動化生產，雇用女工人數因而大量減少有關；[84] 亦有報紙分析指出：「近年來因為新店市的住宅公寓林立，德華女子公寓的出租

---

81 〈德華女子公寓紅顏已老？經營不善傳要出售五百餘單身女郎何去何從〉，《中國時報》，1988.06.08，第11版；〈德華女子公寓傳將轉售房客員工不知何去何從〉，《青年日報》，1988.06.08，第7版。

82 〈傳德華女子公寓經營不善將予出售謀利應請查明制止〉（教友蘇拯靈致函狄剛總主教，1988.07.07）。

83 〈重要消息〉（德華女子公寓，1988.06.09）。

84 陳信行，〈打造第一個全球裝配線：臺灣通用器材公司與城鄉移民1964-1990〉，頁37-40。

狀況開始走下坡」，[85] 可見德華女子公寓確實面臨主客觀環境之變化。惟可容納千人租用的女子公寓，至結束營運前僅賸 500 多人居住，如此營運之收支狀況自難維持一定水準之居住品質，尤其是老舊公寓必須面臨的龐大維修經費支出。[86] 又據 1988 年記者觀察的報導明言：

> 德華女子公寓開辦初期，庭院花木扶疏，內部設備齊全，工作人員均為清一色的教友，所以都具有高度的服務熱忱，公寓裡面都打掃得乾乾淨淨，堪稱窗明几淨，一塵不染，不像現在，原先的花圃不見了，水泥地、人行道，到處坑洞，一副破瓦殘垣的景氣，置身其間令人不勝惆悵。[87]

可見女子公寓經營二十年後的殘舊景象已不復當年美好盛況。

五、結語

或許是個巧合，萬德華神父出生之時，正是聖言會會祖聖楊生神父過世那年，而萬德華神父之生日又恰為臺灣的教師節。若將此配合其一生作為，他確實傳承並實踐了聖言會會祖所強調的——積極向教外地區宣揚天主信仰之理念，亦如同導師般地率先並竭盡心力照顧需要幫助的廣大群眾——不論是教友或非教友。

事實上，立基於 1930 至 1940 年代在中國河南福傳的十年豐富經驗，而於 1960 年代初自願來臺傳教的萬德華神父，早已細心地觀察到：天主教會面對快速工業發展及環境變遷的臺灣社會，必須以更主

---

85 〈德華女子公寓決改建醫院拆除未事先通知損及一住戶財物〉，《中國時報》，1991.02.03，第 14 版。

86 "'Tehua'Working Girls' Hostel: Dormitories And Social Center – A Report," February 1982. 另據柯博識神父口述可知，女子公寓營運至後期，因時代變遷，觀念改變，住宿女子不願意太多人住在一間宿舍內，因此 12 人房之宿舍不易租出。

87 〈公寓易主苦了員工住戶心內恐慌擔憂失業失所〉，《青年日報》，1988.06.08，第 7 版。

動、更世俗化的福傳方式深入人群，給予社會大眾實質有效的幫助，乃能有所作為並產生影響力。因此，他以不到三年時間完成聖三堂的興築工程後，即全力投入規模更大的女子公寓創建計畫，以嘉惠全臺各地許多離家就學或就業之年輕女子，特別是任職工廠之女工，令這些女子能有安定的生活環境，並因此開展未來的美好人生。而從構思、規劃到付諸行動、全部完工的德華女子公寓耗時約六年，女子公寓從開始營業到正式結束亦超過二十年，其間經歷之困難與艱辛，萬德華神父欣然接受且甘之如飴，其總以樂觀心情、幽默態度應對，並衷心向天主賜福感恩，對教內、教外之協助者致上謝意。

　　若將萬德華神父當時之社會服務作為與日後學界之研究成果互相對照，亦可印證其觀察之細緻、眼光之宏遠，因1980至1990年代，學界曾對1949年以來天主教會遷至臺灣的發展情況予以探究，認為四十年間天主教的發展是逐漸衰退的，此可分為三個階段，即1949至1963年的快速成長時期、1964至1969年的停滯時期，以及1970年以後的衰退時期；其中，快速成長時期每年教友成長率都在10%以上，1963年以後教友人數明顯下降，普遍低於一般人口的成長率，再至1970年以後則呈現負成長局面。[88]也有學者明白指出：1952至1969年間，天主教在臺灣的發展可說是「突飛猛進」，教友人數多達30萬以上，然此後即走下坡，自1984至1989年間，教友人數不會超過30萬人。[89]這些學者曾對天主教教友人數大量流失的情形提出分析與個人見解，綜觀其論述及說明或有相當差異，然重點均強調社會快速變遷下的世俗化問題，故天主教會如何面對世俗化社會並提出因應之道就成為重要課題。而萬德華神父早於1960年代中即已關注此一現象，並身先士卒地積極走入社會，透過對亟需關照的離家年輕

---

88 瞿海源，〈臺灣地區天主教發展趨勢之研究〉，《中央研究院民族研究所集刊》，第51期（臺北，1981春季），頁129-149；瞿海源、姚麗香，〈臺灣地區宗教變遷之探討〉，收入《臺灣社會與文化變遷（下冊）》（臺北：中央研究院民族研究所，1986），頁670-674。

89 宋光宇，〈試論四十年來臺灣宗教的發展〉，收入《臺灣經驗（二）：社會文化篇》（臺北：東大圖書股份有限公司，1994），頁191-192。

婦女，提供人道及安全住居之實質協助以取得信任與支持，並延續教會精神於其世俗生活中，此一前瞻性作為，實可成為教會相關社會服務工作之重要參考範例。

最後，本文將以萬德華神父於其生命終點，致函溫安東神父（Fr. Anton Weber）的一段內容作為結尾，即他認為：應持續將教會的財產安置於社會服務事業中，以聯繫與天主及耶穌基督的心靈。[90] 這句話或許足以代表萬德華神父創建德華女子公寓的最重要理念與終身服膺之信條。

（本文另一較長版本刊登於《國立政治大學歷史學報》，第44期

[2015年11月]，頁223-280）

---

90 Fr. Schmitz Bartley, "Father Edward Wojniak, S. V. D," p. 1.

深度休閒的實踐：
真善美全人關懷協會的「爲成人說故事」系列

蘇友瑞、潘秋郎

摘要

　　現代社會出現大量的休閒活動需求，尤其需要深度休閒的藝文活動，從而期待得到休閒效益。為此一群華人基督徒成立了社團法人真善美全人關懷協會，致力於透過藝文欣賞來迎接尋找深度休閒的人們，並從而得到明顯的社區事工成果。如此研發出「為成人說故事」的社區事工方法，其意涵為：進入職場或家庭而面對各樣繁複生活的成人，不再有過去學生時代充裕的時間找人分享，因而需要專門為他們說故事的人，便可以從故事中重新找回人的意義。這種「找回人」的深度藝文活動，成為基督教社區事工的一個可行策略，並獲得基督教內的支持從而成長茁壯至今。本論文描述「為成人說故事」的基督教社會關懷活動之詳細內容，並提出各種回應與省思，從而提供多元的社會關懷角度。

關鍵詞：社會關懷、社區事工、深度休閒、為成人說故事

一、基督教的社會關懷與現代人的休閒需求

（一）基督教的社會關懷與現代人的休閒活動

游修靜在其〈臺灣教會社區工作模式之探討〉一文中，描述基督教在臺灣社會從早期的興辦教育與醫療社會服務等社會互動，走向近年來著重社區工作的社會互動事工，並舉出大量的相關研究論文為憑據。這些研究皆體現了基督教社會關懷角度的不同面向，然而游修靜文末卻提出：「……基督教會的社區工作可以有再更具積極性的一面。所謂的傳福音，除了口傳與透過提供服務讓人感受到上帝的愛之外，更積極的作為是真正進入社區，協助社區並培力社區。」[1] 從該研究者所列出教會進行的社區服務工作看來，基督教的社會關懷往往傾向慈善活動、急難救助或人際扶持；研究者認為這是基於教會的宣教使命所影響，縱使對「上帝國」的神學觀念各自不同，最後的社區工作取向仍然非常類似。

關於教會的宣教使命的了解，經過數十年宣教學者的持續反省，尤其是「上帝的宣教」（Missio Dei）這個詞彙及其所指涉的觀念廣為流傳之後，已經破除了「傳福音」與「社會關懷」二分思考方式，社會關懷不只是「福音預工」而已，本質上就是傳福音的一環，對教會而言應該看做是神學上的道德訓令：上帝在基督裡對人的心意是一致的，教會應關懷所有鄰舍的身體與心靈、從現在到永遠的真正需要。

吳建明在針對加爾文《基督教要義》的思想探討中，歸納了加爾文對基督徒生活的主張，認為「……基督徒是積極與眾人生活在社群、城邦、國家的群體生活。基督徒不是消極抽離於社會群體之外，也不是單單在教堂內生活；基督徒是積極參與俗世的各個領域，更是在社會群體中榮耀上帝。」[2] 按此加爾文神學的觀點，積極參與世俗

---

1 游修靜，《臺灣教會社區工作模式之探討》（臺南：長榮大學社會工作所碩士論文，2011），頁59。
2 吳建明，《加爾文《基督教要義》中論基督徒生活》（桃園：中原大學宗教研究所碩士論文，2012）。

生活就是關懷人們日常生活中的普遍需要。除了職業、學業或婚姻家庭之外，休閒活動也是現代人非常普遍的生活需要；如果能讓休閒活動具有完善的休閒品質與福音預工或宣教的同時並行，這或許能成為基督教社會關懷的另一種面貌。

國內於2001年實施全面週休二日後，社會出現大量的休閒活動需求。休閒生活雖然逐漸受到重視，但休閒時間的有效利用才是休閒品質提升的重要關鍵。[3] Hutchins 在《學習社會》（*The Learning Society*）一書曾說，休閒時代的來臨，助長人類繼續學習的可能，有益學習社會的形成。[4] 休閒活動已經是現代人生活的重心，其中藝文活動更成為焦點。中國民國在民國70年11月11日成立文化建設委員會（簡稱文建會），並於101年5月20日將文建會改制為文化部，一直把推廣藝文活動視為工作重點，正說明了藝文活動對於現代人休閒生活的重要角色。

根據文化部的統計，民國100年全國舉辦藝文展演活動共59,300次，出席人次為200,634；民國101年舉辦活動共64,534次，出席人次為228,303；民國101年舉辦活動共66,389次，出席人次為254,333。明顯發現國人對於藝文展演活動的需求逐年提高，導致活動次數及參與人次皆明顯成長。馬英華以松山文化創意園區的觀賞人群為例，研究藝文活動參與者的休閒效益，明確發現藝文活動可以在臺灣社會產生明顯的休閒效益，其大小由高而低分別為「紓解壓力」、「腦力激盪」與「促進人際關係」。紓解壓力或其他心理因素的休閒效益成為文創或展演等藝文休閒活動的主要休閒效益，皆得到類似研究的支持。[5]

---

3 周秀華、余嬪，〈深度休閒者學習經驗之研究〉，《教育與心理研究》，第28卷第2期（2005），頁299。

4 劉俊榮，〈從終身學習的觀點談週休二日的意義〉，《社教雜誌》，第250期（2009），頁5。

5 吳慶烜、林怡秀，《六堆客家文化園區遊客休閒效益之初探》（嘉南藥理科技大學：嘉南藥理科技大學文化事業學術研討會，2009）；王儷芬，《枋寮F3藝文特區遊客之目的地意象與休閒效益之研究》（屏東：屏東教育大學生態休閒教育教學碩士學位學程論文，2011）。

（二）藝文休閒活動的「深度休閒」需要

上述研究比較偏向文化展演活動，相對來說，藝術欣賞、電影欣賞或音樂欣賞等藝文活動，似乎與這些文化展演活動有一些本質上的不同。很多人認為藝文休閒活動只要輕鬆、簡單、引人興趣就好，然而從學理上卻發現完全不同的觀念。

阿多諾對資本主義下的社會提出「文化工業」[6]的強烈批判，質疑休閒活動在此文化工業脈絡下的休閒意義。為此許多研究者回應該批判，從Harris所著 *Key Concepts in Leisure Studies* 之條目 "Post-modernism"[7] 與 "Work – Leisure Relationships"[8] 看來，面對文化工業的意義喪失與後現代社會降低的休閒效益，皆有研究者提出「深度休閒」（serious leisure，亦有許多研究者譯為認真休閒）[9] 的觀念來回應，其中以Stebbins[10] 為先驅學者。

Stebbins認為在資訊時代人們有兩種不同的休閒方式：一種是閒逸休閒，[11] 另一種為深度休閒。閒逸休閒指有立即的酬賞特性，並不需要特別訓練技巧，相對之下是較短暫的生活享受。相較於閒逸休閒，深度休閒是目標導向的，指有系統、深度地投入一項業餘、不以此為生的嗜好活動或志願活動，在追求的過程中，休閒投入者會隨生涯階段的發展有不同的目標，因而發展出不同的技能，成為終其一生的興趣。[12]

Stebbins針對多種不同活動的參與者進行研究，他從藝術、運動、科學與娛樂四種領域進行質性研究，包括：1. 藝術領域：古典音樂家、演員。2. 運動領域：棒球選手、足球選手。3. 科學領域：考古

---

6 T. W. Adorno & M. Horkheimer、林宏濤譯，《啟蒙的辯證》（臺北：商周出版社，2009）。

7 T. W. Adorno & M. Horkheimer、林宏濤譯，《啟蒙的辯證》，頁208。

8 T. W. Adorno & M. Horkheimer、林宏濤譯，《啟蒙的辯證》，頁262。

9 劉虹伶，〈深度休閒者之休閒效益〉，《大專體育》，第78期（2005），頁116-122。

10 R. A. Stebbins, "Serious leisure: A conceptual statement," *Pacif Sociological Review*, No. 25, 1982, pp. 251-272.

11 指casual leisure，亦有研究者譯為隨興休閒。卜小蝶、張映涵，〈網路影音休閒之遊歷行為探析〉，《圖書資訊學刊》，第10卷第2期（2012），頁39-74。

12 周秀華、余嬪，〈深度休閒者學習經驗之研究〉，《教育與心理研究》，第28卷第2期（2005），頁300。

學家、天文學家。4. 娛樂領域：魔術師、喜劇演員。[13] Stebbins 並歸納從事自己喜愛的休閒活動者會表現出以下六種特徵：

(1) 遇阻礙時能堅持到底（perseverance）。

(2) 付出努力（effort）。

(3) 經由努力追求而有長時期的生涯發展階段（career）。

(4) 得到持久的利益（durable benefits）：如自我表現、自我實現、增進自我形象與自信心。

(5) 對自己選擇的休閒有強烈的認同（identity）。

(6) 能發展出其休閒團體獨特的特質或精神（unique character or spirit）。[14]

　　從上述「深度休閒」的研究看來，一般人常把休閒活動誤解為只是隨意的「殺時間」活動，其實有系統而深入地持續參與自己所喜歡的活動反而可以得到更大的休閒效益；周秀華與余嬪在地化的質性研究更主張「……深度休閒投入有助於個人、家庭、工作、人際互動與社會的發展。」[15] 因此，藝文活動不應該只是引起參與者的興趣而已；它必須進行深入與持續的主題探討，增加「深度休閒」的特性，才可能得到更有效的休閒效益。

　　從基督教人觀而言：人不是為了工作而存在，也不是為了休閒；工作與休閒，都是為了成全人的存在價值與人的尊嚴，所以是高度宗教性的。從《舊約聖經》對以色列人生活規律，以五十年為一個單位，定下年、節期的細節，歡樂有時、哀哭有時；工作有時、休閒有時，可知人的生活週期是神聖的、是屬於上帝的。休閒，另一個英文字 recreation；按字義是 re-creation，亦即「重新創造」，意味著重造

---

13 T. W. Adorno & M. Horkheimer、林宏濤譯，《啟蒙的辯證》，頁 118。

14 周秀華、余嬪，〈深度休閒者學習經驗之研究〉，《教育與心理研究》，第 28 卷第 2 期（2005），頁 300-301。

15 周秀華、余嬪，〈深度休閒者學習經驗之研究〉，《教育與心理研究》，第 28 卷第 2 期（2005），頁 297。

上帝原先賦予人的人性。在現今與過去過度重視工作的臺灣社會，提倡深度休閒是靈性上的矯正，因為「福音」意味著人性的成全，所以亦是宣教上的應然。

（三）從心靈小憩網站的福音事工探討現代人的休閒需求

1992年開始，臺灣的學術網路興起Internet BBS的風潮；當時以清、交大研究生為主的校園福音團契成員便開始在宗教討論區（以下簡稱宗教板）進行解經與護教的相關文字事工。後來他們帶領當年的校園團契輔導同工陳韻琳上網並使用BBS介面，嘗試採用藝文欣賞與文化分析的文章進行基督教觀點的分享。結果開始吸引對藝文有興趣的非基督徒參與交大網路團契，其中蘇友瑞因而受洗歸主並投身網路福音事工，接受陳韻琳的帶領合作至今。[16]

從1993年至1995年，以交大研究生小組為基本的同工群，在當時學生最常出入的BBS介面，透過各類議題討論而分享信仰或傳講福音信息。很快地發現，直接討論宗教觀念或文化議題，非常容易引起爭議或誘發網路上的鬧場。於是設計「福音月」的觀念，亦即固定每半年一次，事先準備一個藝文議題並且培訓眾多學生寫出相關藝文欣賞的心得分享文章，再以約一個星期的時間密集發表在特定討論區。結果發現，即使在最容易發生針對基督教論戰的宗教板，都會因為這樣的密集藝文相關貼文的資訊攻勢，而出現短暫和平的現象。基於這樣的網路經驗，於1995年在校園福音團契舉辦的第六屆青年宣道大會向基督徒學生講解網路趨勢並傳遞負擔，開始進行文字與網路福音工作人才的培訓計畫。

隨後有感於www型式的網站興起，顯然「深度休閒」的藝文愛好者會轉向使用www介面閱讀完整而深度的圖文資料；故於1997年成立以藝文為主的福音預工網站「心靈小憩」[17]，從1997年到2006

---

16 從1993年到2000年的網路團契歷史與事工可以參考網路上的相關資料：http://life.fhl.net/FHL/history/ntfel.htm。

17 http://life.fhl.net

年持續以心靈小憩藝文網站為基地發展藝文相關的福音預工。透過多元化傳媒 Web，生產跟文學、音樂、電影、藝術、文化趨勢相關的福音預工文字、聲音與影像資料；再將豐富的資料內容轉換為演講與座談會等活動，支援各種藝文福音工作。同時建立專為網路漫遊族成立的虛擬社群（phpbb2 型式的網路討論區），廣泛接觸網友與舉辦網友會，並培訓有負擔透過網路傳福音的 e 世代基督徒以便事工得以永續傳承。

對於需要「深度休閒」的藝文愛好者來說，他們接觸到的是當時華人界最早出現的深度藝文分享網站之一；其資料內容包含以時代、文化、心靈為架構，分別從文學、音樂、電影、藝術、趨勢文化、文藝創作等主題進行具備特色的內容。心靈小憩藝文網站開辦以來，其內容長期被許多研究論文引用為參考文獻，甚至讓沒有任何實體書籍出版的蘇友瑞得以在邱弘毅的論文[18]中被當成關鍵的古典音樂樂評人加以研究，可見其藝文水準的深度是被認可的。

除了資料庫內容的深度水準外，也因應不同情境下成年人或上班族的需要，進行各種藝文節目的設計。以喜愛藝文而無長時間上網的上班族為對象，每週發行藝文電子報；與新竹地區性的 IC 廣播電台合作，不定期製作推出「作家與作品」與「藝文人物專訪」等廣播聲音檔，再以有聲書或唱片的型式傳佈。然後設計種種藝文活動：以「讓科技理工背景的學生對藝文有興趣」為目的，連續六七堂課設計的「通識教育」課程；讓上班族在中午休息一小時的時間中，輕鬆獲取藝文資訊的「辦公室社團」活動；因應學校跟相關單位邀請，針對家長及社區家庭主婦做幫助自我成長的「家長成長團體」課程設計；並於復活節與聖誕節期間配搭教會福音工作。

以上種種藝文節目的規劃，最後都與教會搭配的社區工作緊密結合。教會進行社區工作時，除了直接的福音傳揚外，往往只能進行社

---

18 邱弘毅，《文化工業脈絡下古典音樂樂評的技術性論述》（臺北：世新大學新聞學研究所碩士論文，2013）。

會救助或「閒逸休閒」的活動；如此便無法滿足尚未對福音產生直接興趣的成年人們。因而規劃並舉辦「深度休閒」的藝文活動，補足了教會吸引成年人的需要，便可以得到有力的福音預工果效。多年來陳韻琳與蘇友瑞經常被海內外福音機構邀請進行福音策略的傳授或寫作，並多次在世界華人福音宣教大會擔任分組講員進行分享與異象傳遞，都可以看到這種「深度休閒」的藝文活動被教會機構認可為有效的福音事工。

（四）心靈小憩網站藝文資料的基督教特色

藝文休閒活動與基督教有何關聯，是進行此類社會關懷的一大疑問。本論文認為，豐富的藝文資料或入門的淺顯易懂內容固然是吸引人進入基督教場域的機會，然而內容如果沒有豐富的基督教特色，將很難與基督教信仰進行連結。另一方面，太僵化地制式表達基督教色彩，形同阻隔一般人進入基督教場域的高牆。像托爾金的《魔戒》或路易斯的《納尼亞傳奇》那種充滿基督教色彩的文學作品，會是比較好的福音預工藝文角度。

心靈小憩網站藝文資料有兩大方向：一為「時代趨勢」，從不同的歷史文化時期，看看各種時代背景下藝文作品如何進行回應與省思，這是最容易吸引藝文愛好者的方向。另一是深具基督教色彩的「心靈世界」取向，其意涵為：透過藝文創作者早、中、晚期的代表性作品，分析其人生意義不同時期的體悟；最後發現藝文創作者經常在生命末期出現「心靈躍升」的現象，從各種不同的生活形態，訴諸形而上的心靈需求。從這角度整理非常多藝術家的心靈世界資料，例如音樂類有「貝多芬的心靈世界」、文學類有遠藤周作的作品歷程探討、電影類有柏格曼及塔可夫斯基生命階段不同的作品意義……這些在藝文愛好者看來是深度休閒的藝文欣賞，在基督徒看來幾近是信仰歷程的探索與見證了。

從此可以看出深度休閒的藝文活動不只是藝文同好而已，它可以直接帶出與基督教的豐富連結；無論是福音預工或個人的信仰省思都

能產生深度的探索意義，因而適合成為基督教社會關懷的一個方法。

現代社會重視休閒活動，其中藝文活動理應成為重要的「深度休閒」活動重心。當基督徒嘗試進行社會關懷而走向社區工作時，也發現「深度休閒」的藝文活動可以進行有效的社區事工。同時兼具完善的藝文活動品質與福音預工或宣教的功能，這的確成為基督教社會關懷的另一種面貌。

心靈小憩網站的福音事工發展至此，確立了這種社會關懷的可行性；隨後於2007年成立社團法人中華民國真善美全人關懷協會，並以蘇友瑞為第一任理事長與負責人，陳韻琳為第一任祕書長與執行領導。至今發展出「為成人說故事」的觀念並設計社區活動，於2013年與2014年申請文化部「推廣人文思想活動補助」，皆獲得文化部的補助，創造藝文活動與教會社區工作雙贏的局面。本論文將從「深度休閒」的角度，探討這種基督徒的社會關懷行動被認同為藝文活動的過程，從而提供基督教社會關懷的另一種角度。

二、「為成人說故事」的意涵與活動設計

（一）為何需要「為成人說故事」？

當我們的社會大量推廣替孩子說故事，同時也大量推廣父母受訓進入校園為孩子說故事，並期盼使用故事讓孩子的品格更加完整，也讓親子關係更加增進。但是卻有許多人忽略了，這些長大後的成人也渴望聽故事，也希望有人替他說故事。這些進入職場與家庭，面對各樣繁複生活的成人，不再有過去學生時代充裕的時間，想要好好閱讀一本經典文學，或欣賞藝術及電影，從而遨遊在人文歷史哲學的世界中，顯然已經不大容易接觸到。

這些優質的書籍、電影與藝文內容，包含各種人生的故事；當我們閱讀時，除了能從中提升人文的思想與素養、了解多元文化外；更能從閱讀中，因為深度思考各種人生故事，而得以從故事主角的掙扎與無助中，知道自己並不孤單。從故事敘事的開展、角色與劇情，思

考解決問題的方案；也從故事中人物的成功、失敗與再次挑戰，找到突破困境與人生底蘊的力量，從而找回美好的人生。

如何幫助這些生活中只有破碎時間與身心疲憊的成人、透過這些經典藝文作品提升人文素養從而得到生命向上的力量？需要為他們挑選適合的藝文作品，透過帶領人精闢的導讀和分析；然後能在短短的讀書會時間內，就足以深入探討各樣的人生主題；並透過彼此的討論和交流，獲取其他參與者的人生經驗。

「真善美全人關懷協會」成立於2007年，多年來透過藝文生活化、藝文心靈化的資料創作及編輯彙整，經營「心靈小憩網站」[19]，並主持製作廣播節目（新竹IC之音）、進行「為成人說故事」有聲書製作。近年來，協會更發展出以「社區中心」為概念，經營舉辦各種社區讀書會及帶領人培訓為核心方向，透過組織「為成人說故事」社區故事讀書會及培訓人員，並輔以網站企劃及有聲書的發行，使得參與讀書會的成員獲得支持團體的協助與聆聽，達到社會正向支持的力量與轉化。

（二）從宣教學對「說故事」（Story-Telling）的評估

宣教傳福音的事工中，說故事遠優於「說教」；傳福音不是在「講耶穌」而已，若再加上「決志模式」，形成「權威佈道法」，要求聽者只能聽、不能說，聽完後還要在規定的時間內、回答規定的問題，容易造成聽眾心理的防衛系統升高（因為權力不對等、議題已被預先設定，不夠尊重聽者）。這個年代需要更細膩的作法。

其實宗教信仰不只是a view of life，更是a way of life；既然信仰是一種生活方式，就不只是「一套教理」而已，而如斯馬特所說的，[20]宗教涉及生活的諸多面向，包括實踐與儀式、經驗與情感、敘事與神話、教義與哲學、倫理與律法、社會與制度，以及物質與藝術等七個

---

19 http://life.fhl.net
20 斯馬特，《劍橋世界宗教》（臺北：商周出版社，2004）。

層面。那麼，基督教──一種以基督為中心的「生活方式」──要怎麼傳講？義理的了解與講述是不足的。

說教強調認知，不足以撼動人心裡已根深蒂固的價值體系，相對而言，「故事」的承載力更強大。綜觀各傳統的文化或宗教的價值與義理，是以「故事」形式保存和傳遞的；神聖、規範性的故事，學術上稱為「神話」，包含了宇宙的起源、人之所以為人的意義，用以理解真實、塑造身分與建構意義。那些聆聽盤古開天與黃帝大戰蚩尤的，便成了炎黃子孫；而聆聽亞伯拉罕如何出吾珥、摩西帶領之下出埃及過紅海的，便成了以色列人。不同世代的臺灣人，看四郎真平、史豔文大戰藏鏡人、科學小飛俠、無敵鐵金剛、美少女戰士、火影忍者、海賊王與進擊的巨人，塑造不同的個性，成了不同世界的人。所以，「代溝」不是沒有原因的。

人基本上是看故事長大的，吾人所看的故事會塑造認同與價值感，並形塑世界觀。[21] 聽故事，尤其是入戲於神聖故事時，故事的情節以及其所蘊含的世界觀會逐步「入侵」聆聽者心思，使得聽者心裡的觀念、信念從衝撞、混亂、失序到重整，這個過程隨著聽故事不斷發展演變到某一臨界時刻，或 Peter Stromberg 稱之為 impression point [22]，聽者開始以新的故事來理解世界與建構自我，也就是說，之後，神聖故事從他者故事成了我者的來歷，如此，逐漸建立起基督教式的天地人想像。亞伯拉罕、以撒、雅各，原本是外國人，之後成了祖先，鄰居變成了家人。

另外，說故事的人，以他們的生活同時說了一個故事，說故事的人融入在自己所說的故事裡，這二個故事的信息應該是一致的，一起傳達了那個上帝在基督裡為人受苦的故事。范浩沙教授以舞臺劇作類比，主張《聖經》是上帝救贖戲劇的腳本，主題是上帝國，基督徒是主要演員，在聖靈的引導下，在各地方劇場（教會），同步演出，在

---

21 Salisbury 2009; c.f. Iain H. Murray, *The Undercover Revolution: How Fiction Changed Britain* (Edinburgh: Banner of Truth, 2009).

22 Peter G. Stromberg, "The impression point: Synthesis of symbol and self," *Ethos 13*, No. 1, 1985, pp. 56-74.

不同的時間世代，演出不同幕神聖大戲，而神學是臨場指導，指導各地教會恰當地演出。[23] 也就是說，基督徒信仰群體的生活就是一場實況演出的戲，不能NG，也無法事先排演，觀眾隨時在檢驗他們，是否活出基督。那麼，華人教會既是基督身體的一肢體，承繼了大公教會源遠流長的傳統，觀看了從創世記到先知書；從福音書到使徒行傳，從亞伯拉罕、以撒、雅各以及先知們、使徒們到哥林多、加拉太與以弗所等眾聖徒的生活展演，呈現上帝神聖戲劇的前面幾幕戲之後，那麼，中間失落的，介於使徒行傳第28章與啟示錄21章之間的最終幕，我們是不是會演了？我們活在使徒行傳第29章的時代裡。

（三）「為成人說故事」的活動設計

藉由各樣優質書籍、電影與藝文內容，觸及現代人的內心深處，讓現代人能夠從各樣困境中重新面對挑戰；在高失業率與低就業率的社會環境中，能積極面對生活中的各樣挑戰，滿足心靈需求。透過各種優質故事剖析分享，呈現生命經歷、反映人生，協助面臨多重生命困境之現代人進行生命反思、心靈營造，營造正面積極之價值觀，走向真善美之人生。

「為成人說故事」的活動內容主要有三種，分別為「講座活動」、「社區讀書會」與「師資培訓」，內容設計如下：

1.「為成人說故事」的講座活動

為了讓教會認識從「深度休閒」的藝文活動可以產生的社區工作，同時需要較知名的講員來確保足夠的參與人數，因而讓資深的師資（例如陳韻琳與蘇友瑞）與教會或其他機構合作舉辦「為成人說故事」的講座活動；誘發「深度休閒」的藝文興趣後，可以由社區讀書會接手進行跟進與持續性地連繫。相對的，從社區讀書會被誘發興趣

---

23 Kevin J. Vanhoozer, "One rule to rule them all," in *Globalizing theology: Belief and practice in an era of world Christianity*, edited by Craig Ott and Harold A. Netland (Grand Rapids: Baker Academic, 2006), pp. 85-126.

的成人也可以透過講座活動更深入休閒活動。

（1）時間：每次約2.5小時。

（2）人次：開放宣傳與邀請，以空間為限人數不拘。

（3）內容：

    a. 一則故事想讓我們真正聽見什麼？從《大智若魚》談故事與人生。

    b. 猶豫不決的夏季戀情：從經典導演侯麥《夏天的故事》談男女關係。

    c. 從《點燃生命之海》觀看安樂死倫理議題。

    d. 從音樂劇《悲慘世界》之文學與音樂母題談法律與恩典。

    e. 追尋永恆：梵谷的藝術心靈之歌。

    f. 過去從未曾過去：從電影《扭轉未來》談與自我的和解。

（演講主題可配合當地社區與場地活動需求進行調整）

2.「為成人說故事」社區讀書會的設計

舉辦大型活動必須有資深講員才足以得到號召力，但這不是一般教會能做到的。因此以小型的社區讀書會進行藝文欣賞與分享，不但容易找到師資進行帶領，也容易以較少的資源進行社區的「深度休閒」工作。具體設計如下：

（1）時間：每週一次，每次1.5小時。

（2）人次：採用便於深入討論的小班制，約10～15人。

（3）讀書會主題：

    a. 面對家庭困境與再出發：《蘇西的世界》。

    b. 平凡生活中的生命力量：《聖徒叔叔》。

    c. 兩性關係變奏曲：《男人是不完美的女人》。

    d. 從德國二戰文化後的罪與罰，觀看當代臺灣社會處境：《為愛朗讀》。

e. 理想主義何時能成惡：談格雷安・葛林的《沉靜的美國人》。

f. 大歷史下的女性觀點與側寫：共讀諾貝爾文學獎得主莫言《豐乳肥臀》。

（4）讀書會流程與內容：

第一週 學員彼此熟悉、課程大綱介紹

第二週 書籍背景介紹、作者介紹、讀書會學員認領章節

第三週 章節大綱分析與討論（一）

第四週 章節大綱分析與討論（二）

第五週 人物角色分析與回饋（一）

第六週 人物角色分析與回饋（二）

第七週 總結與成果展演（一）

第八週 總結與成果展演（二）

3. 舉辦「為成人說故事」帶領師資的培訓

大量的小型社區讀書會勢必讓帶領讀書會的師資需求提高，這部分不需要資深師資，只要對藝文有興趣且經過適當的培訓，便足以進行大量的社區讀書會帶領師資。具體設計如下：

（1）時間：以三個月為一期，每週一次，每次1.5小時。

（2）人次：每梯次20～30人次。

（3）培訓流程與內容：

第一週 「為成人說故事」讀書會帶領方法導論

第二週 文本分析要領（一）：起承轉合

第三週 文本分析要領（二）：成書與作者背景

第四週 角色分析要領（一）：平版型與立體型角色塑造

第五週 角色分析要領（二）：文學隱喻與主、配角及劇情轉折之關係

第六週 讀書會問題設計要領（一）：扣題文本、深入淺出

第七週 讀書會問題設計要領（二）：貼近生活、觀看人生

第八週 引導成員回饋技巧要領：隔著距離觀看自己、沉澱

與反思

　　第九週 學員演練與作業（一）

　　第十週 學員演練與作業（二）

　　第十一週 學員演練與作業（三）

　　第十二週 學員演練與作業（四）

　（4）課程講師：真善美全人關懷協會講師群。

（四）「為成人說故事」的延伸設計

　　除了舉辦社區活動之外，生產相關的延伸活動或產物也是加強影響力或永續經營的必要方法。這部分的做法如下：

1.「為成人說故事」有聲書的製作

　　有聲書適合通勤族在車上聆聽或成年人在睡前聆聽；每期有聲書內容可能會是一本書或一部電影，亦可僅是一個畫家或一個音樂家。但不只是提供知識，而是透過說書人／說故事的方式，觸碰聽眾的心靈，提供聽眾另一種清新的聲音，帶出生活中的人文素養與感動。

　　有聲書可作為自我反思之心靈素材，亦可成為家庭、朋友聚會，讀書會及各種文化教育活動運用之教材。目前主要提供社區民眾、參與讀書會／講座活動者免費索取。

2. 心靈小憩藝文網站的相關企劃製作

　　由於實體有聲書數量有限，遠地民眾也不容易索取，因此同時將有聲書剪輯作為網路專輯企劃，透過網路傳媒之力量大量流傳散佈，擴大接觸多數民眾。同時也可以透過網路討論區非同步的線上交流討論，提供學員在課程之外的後續跟進。

三、為成人說故事的實行成果

　　2013年度下半年真善美全人關懷會以「人生美學——為成人說

故事系列活動」為名申請文化部「推廣人文思想活動補助」獲得認可，隨即將上述活動設計具體實踐，得到豐富的實行成果，並據此繼續獲得2014年文化部的補助。

這些實行成果意謂著「為成人說故事」藝文活動的深度休閒成果與社會關懷成果，茲以活動舉辦的數量並進行簡易問卷分析與討論，說明實行成果。

（一）「為成人說故事」的活動舉辦

1. 舉辦「人生美學——為成人說故事」公開講座活動，時間為2013年7月至12月，辦理臺北與新竹共6場，每次約2.5小時。共有609人次（重複參加的同好計入累積）參與臺北與新竹兩地的講座，並回收580份問卷，發出530份「為成人說故事」的有聲書與DM。

2. 舉行「人生美學——為成人說故事」社區讀書會活動，時間為2013年7月至12月，辦理臺北兩梯、新竹三梯共五梯次。每梯次以兩個月為一期，每週進行一次，每次1.5小時。採用便於深入討論的小班制，每次約10～15人。共有489人次（重複參加的同好計入累積）參與五梯次讀書會，回收31份問卷，發出59份「為成人說故事」的有聲書與DM。

3. 舉行「人生美學——為成人說故事」師資培訓活動，時間為2013年7月至12月，辦理臺北、新竹、臺中各一梯總共三梯次。每梯次以三個月為一期，每週進行一次，每次1.5小時。採用便於深入帶領的小班制，每次約20～30人。共有681人次（重複參加的同好計入累積）參與三梯次師資培訓活動，回收67份問卷，發出46份「為成人說故事」的有聲書與DM。

（二）簡易的問卷分析

此次活動當中回收問卷共有706份，以此回收問卷呈現參與活動的社會人士之反應與評價如下：

1. 此次活動的訊息來源

　　在「人生美學——為成人說故事」系列活動裡面的學員與觀眾對於活動的訊息，有51%是來自網路流傳的訊息；由於協會較多與社區當地的教會合作，所以有一大部分的人來自教會禮拜的報告事項或宣傳單張；然而最多的還是來自網路的口耳相傳。

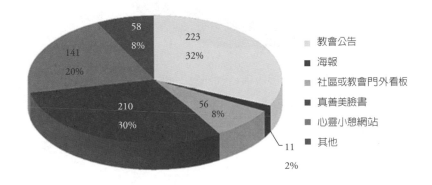

	教會公告	海報	社區或教會門外看板	真善美臉書	心靈小憩網站	其他	總計
有來過	125	7	41	84	58	26	341
沒來過	98	4	15	126	83	32	358
	223	11	56	210	141	58	699

※ 有 7 份未寫有否來過

　　最明顯的是在於表示以前沒有來過，自己前來的人數有將近三成的人，都表明是因為網路訊息而來；若加上「其他」項當中有少部分的人是因為網路搜尋與文化部網站得知的數量，都表示真善美全人關懷協會的「為成人說故事」已經可以透過網際網路的口碑行銷，達到活動的績效，甚至會有大量的人主動參與。

　　另外，在年齡層統計分布的情況，以學生族與社青群組合而成的21～30歲33%為最大宗，其次就是31～40歲的人，佔31%。這個族

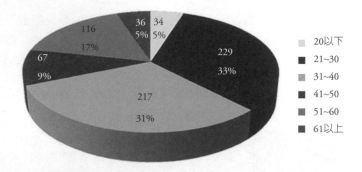

群大多數習慣透過網路接收與傳播訊息，再次印證本活動與網路資訊傳播的緊密關聯。

由以上的資訊可以知道，原本真善美讀書會的群組以已婚的中年婦女為主（約40歲以上），但是逐漸透過網路口耳相傳的影響下，讓大量的社會青年開始投入。

2. 會來參加的原因（複選）

有30%的人次表示對此活動有興趣，有趣的是，這些對此活動有興趣的人們，許多是因為網路觀看後而對此活動有興趣的；當然也有人是因為親友推薦後，自己再主動到真善美全人關懷協會的官方臉

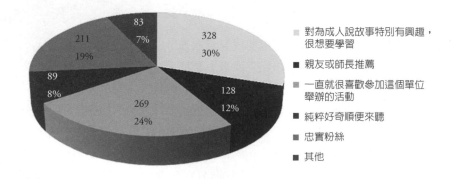

書與網站了解情況的。當然將近一半以上的人本來就是協會或心靈小憩網站的忠實愛護者。

對為成人說故事特別有興趣，很想要學習	親友或師長推薦	一直就很喜歡參加這個單位舉辦的活動	純粹好奇順便來聽	忠實粉絲	其他	總數
328	128	269	89	211	83	1,108

3. 滿意度調查

有 94% 以上的人對此次活動整體安排表示滿意，以滿意度來看是頗高的。

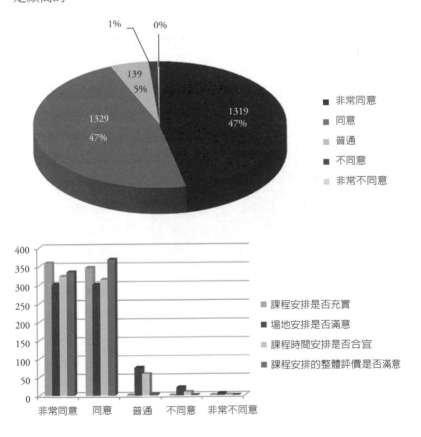

而針對單項場地與時間安排上則呈兩極化的意見，有學員反應很喜歡這些場地，但也有學員反應因為場地有限而在後面的人比較看不到講員與投影片。此項可能是未來將要注意的主要地方。至於時間安排上會盡量有常日梯次與晚上梯次，期待可以滿足不同族群時間要求。

4. 開放性意見回饋的意見歸納

　　針對開放性回饋當中的意見反應歸納如下：

　　a. 希望可以有階梯教室，讓所有參與的學員可以較為清楚地觀看到講員的投影片或是聽到講課。

　　b. 可能因為來參加的人大都是以有家庭的人為主，所以有近三成以上的人表示希望可以探討親子互動等相關問題。

　　c. 另外在期待的項目部分，是希望電影相關的讀書會可以較多，有37%表示希望可以繼續參加電影相關的活動。

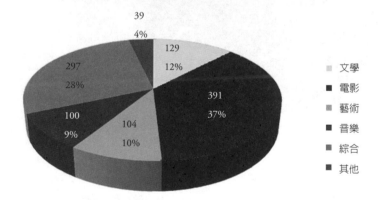

5. 小結

　　從簡易的問卷分析看來，藝文活動的確吸引大量藝文愛好者參與；這活動大多與教會或福音機構合作，亦即帶領大量非基督徒或離開教會的基督徒重新回到教會的場域；可以說創造了藝文活動與教會社區工作雙贏的局面。

有趣的一點是，聽眾固然關心且偏好親子互動相關議題，但是他們沒有選擇輔導或教育的相關課程，反而尋求從藝文活動（尤其偏好電影）尋找親子互動相關議題的省思。本論文認為這是「深度休閒」強大的心理支持效果，正如同周秀華與余嬪主張「⋯⋯深度休閒投入有助於個人、家庭、工作、人際互動與社會的發展。」[24] 無形中透過藝文活動得到自我省思與主動學習的動力，從而勇於解決面對的親子問題。這部分應該可以日後深入研究，獲得「深度休閒」更多的研究成果。

四、基督教社會關懷的回應與省思

　　從網路福音團契的發展，到真善美全人關懷協會的成立，以迄文化部計畫的申請與執行，充分提供一個教會與社區緊密結合的事工模式，並且得到相關的成果。據此經驗，本文提出幾點省思如下：

（一）更貼近真實生活的基督教社會關懷

　　真善美全人關懷協會之所以走向藝文活動，正因為發覺現代人無論生活多麼辛勞與苦悶，總是有大量的藝文活動需求，從而得到心靈與心理的滿足。本論文不認為藝文活動是唯一貼近真實生活的方法，許多「深度休閒」的研究發現各式各樣的休閒活動皆有類似效果，例如慢跑者[25]、足球迷[26]、游泳者[27]、運動舞蹈參與者與插花[28]、單車活

---

24 周秀華、余嬪，〈深度休閒者學習經驗之研究〉，《教育與心理研究》，第28卷第2期（2005），頁299。

25 W. F. Major, "Serious running: An interpretive analysis," Unpublished doctoral dissertation (University of Georgia, Athens, Georgia, 1994).

26 I. Jones, "A model of serious leisure identification: The case of football fandom," *Leisure Studies*, No. 19 (4), 2000, pp. 283-298.

27 D. W. Hastings, S. B. Kurth, M. Schloder & D. Cyr, "Reasons for participating in a serious leisure career: Comparison of Canadian and U.S. masters swimmers," *International Review for the Sociology of Sport*, No. 30 (1), 1995, pp. 101-122.

28 周秀華、余嬪，〈深度休閒者學習經驗之研究〉，《教育與心理研究》，第28卷第2期（2005），頁299。

動參與者[29]、以女性為主的研究[30]、大英國協導覽志工[31] 等。[32]

因此基督教進行社會關懷從而走入現實社會，必須提供更多現代人深度休閒的活動，才能從中與教會進行緊密結合，吸引人重新回到教會。真善美全人關懷協會限於人力與宗旨只適合發展藝文活動，期待其他基督教機構也能提供更多元的深度休閒活動，共同進行更貼近真實生活的社會關懷。

（二）深度休閒活動需要神學支持與教會支持

過去總認為休閒活動只要輕薄短小即可，但是從「深度休閒」的研究看來卻出現不同觀點。若是再結合心理學上對「靈性」的研究結果，便可以發現深度藝文活動對於現代人心靈的滿足成效，非常容易與教會系統進行結合。

然而若要提高藝文分析與文化研究的所謂的「屬世」生活，這需要更多的神學支持。若說加爾文最大的突破即是將「屬靈」和「屬世」的生活連結在一起（吳建明，2012），那麼「鑽研藝文作品（或其他休閒活動）足以榮耀上帝」的觀點能不能被抱持傳統屬靈觀點的教會系統接受，仍是華人基督教社會的一大難題。若是缺乏相關的深度的神學素養，很難產生與福音貼近的深度藝文人才，自然不可能產生深度休閒的領導者，這就無法產生相對應的社會關懷果效了。

（三）師資培訓是永續經營之道
1. 社區讀書會師資代表的文化意義

似乎在本地找不到關於師資培訓這一領域的相關研究，比較多的是對於「文化工業」 造成文化與藝文欣賞能力危機的批判研究。在

---

29 余玥林、陳其昌，〈深度休閒的意涵及效益〉，《雲科大體育》，第6期（2003），頁59-64。

30 J. Raisborough, "Research note: the concept of serious leisure and women's experiences of the Sea Cadet Corps," *Leisure Studies*, No. 18, pp. 67-71.

31 G. Nichols & L. King, "Redefining the recruitment niche for the guide association in the United Kingdom," *Leisure Sciences*, No. 21 (4), 1999, pp. 307-320.

32 T. W. Adorno & M. Horkheimer、林宏濤譯，《啟蒙的辯證》，頁118。

「深度休閒」觀念下，許多非專業相關領域的素人（意指自學而非相關領域的學術專家）反而成為影響深度休閒的重要角色。邱弘毅研究文化工業脈絡下古典音樂樂評現象，便發現「……素人樂評或許更容易跳脫科技的框架，達到海德格所謂的轉機，從而對樂評中的技術性論述進行反思。」[33] 意謂著透過深度休閒所培育出來的素人專家，反而能避免文化工業造成的惡性循環。有可能一個真正能滿足一般人們深層心靈需要的藝文環境，更是需要素人專家的領導，因此素人專家如何能代代相傳，才是文化藝術傳承的重要議題。

據此而論，社區讀書會所需要的師資不見得是專家，更不需要文化工業下知名且高人氣的名人。如果藝文欣賞本身的深度便足以滿足現代人的心靈需要，那麼真誠坦露的藝文分享其影響力將會超越文化工業下的明星，這正是研究者寄望素人樂評家背後的文化思考。因此對於師資的品質要求不見得是本職學能的水準，反而應該是熱誠投入的動機，這也是深度休閒研究中發現重要的參與者特質之一。[34] 如何透過傳承師資讓深度休閒的人們免於文化工業的破壞力量，這是一個很好的研究方向，日後有待加以發展。

2. 師資培訓對基督教社會關懷的意義

認識到深度藝文活動對教會社區工作的幫助後，最大的問題一向是師資。師資培訓是最貼近基督教社會關懷與深度藝文休閒如何並行的一群人，這些師資各自將培訓結果落實在自己的教會或團契中，主動地將學習成果回饋給真善美全人關懷協會。例如培訓師資之一分享：「……因此，在這堂課中，最大的收穫應該是如何在電影中找到那感人的地方，並且學習如何向人說一個感動的故事。這堂課其實最大的挑戰，就是如何用電影講故事的方式將不信主的朋友帶進思考信

---

33 邱弘毅，《文化工業脈絡下古典音樂樂評的技術性論述》（臺北：世新大學新聞學研究所碩士論文，2013），頁113。

34 周秀華、余嬪，〈深度休閒者學習經驗之研究〉，《教育與心理研究》，第28卷第2期（2005），頁299。

仰的過程，真的好難，我們基本上是在學方法，但那信仰的核心及基要真理的基礎，卻是支持我們完成此一服事的重要根基，少了這一塊，可能就只會成為一個好的導聆人。」[35] 這說明許多基督徒需要透過深度藝文活動來與非基督徒進行交流的現象。同時他們也發現真的需要訓練，不是光有熱心與敬虔就可以得到傳講福音的果效。因而透過培訓，讓他們重新找到服事的方法，從而成為進行社會關懷的一份子。

真善美全人關懷協會秉持一個積極入世的基督教神學立場，因而把素人專家的能力主動積極傳承給下一代的有志之士；據此舉辦大量的師資培訓班，並把許多高難度的藝文素材轉化成開辦社區讀書會的必要基礎。進行小規模的長期社區讀書會，需要的藝文水準較容易培訓而得；因此重視師資培訓成為真善美全人關懷協會的事工重點，也期盼這種永續經營之道可以成為進行社會關懷的幫助力量。

同樣的，休閒活動領域中擁有精深專業能力的基督徒，不應以表現自身的高明能力為主，而應致力於培養激發深度休閒興趣的接班人為要務。從文化工業的相關討論可以看出一個危機：如果真善美全人關懷協會的資深師資被社會稱許為專業的休閒文化領導者，將極可能受到文化工業的收編，從而失去真正的力量。如果致力於培養激發深度休閒興趣的接班人，面對的將不是文化工業的收編，而是純粹對深度藝文休閒活動的喜好，或許可以維護原始初衷產生更大的社會關懷力量。

---

35 引自真善美全人關懷協會 2013 禱告信。

【時代考驗】

歐柏林學院與從政前的孔祥熙

陳能治

摘要

　　十九世紀末，以歐柏林神學院校友為主的差團，至山西太谷開闢山西公理會，幼年孔祥熙接受該會醫療診治，進入教會學校就學，並成為基督徒，受歐柏林神學院校友影響甚深。拳變中，孔因山西公理會歐柏林師友死之，身心受創，拳變後，乃由教會安排赴歐柏林學院留學，接受歐柏林校園文化的洗禮。學成返國，承歐柏林學生志願宣教團之聘，返回太谷成立山西銘賢學校，以紀念拳變中死難的歐柏林校友。孔在1926年進入廣州國民政府擔任公職之前，雖有各種教會外發展機會，但仍維持與歐柏林學院之間的緊密關係，續任歐柏林在山西的代表，參與中國教會組織的各種公眾事務；其間雖與山西公理會有所扞格，仍持續主掌銘賢學校，維持歐柏林在銘賢的主導地位。1926年歐柏林學院頒贈孔祥熙榮譽法學博士學位，以彰顯其以「歐柏林山西」代表身分參與社會事工之表現。孔做為基督徒，「歐柏林認同」可謂為其一生基督信仰、公共參與之起始與依歸。

關鍵詞：孔祥熙、歐柏林學院、山西銘賢學校、民國基督徒

一、前言

　　1880年孔祥熙生於山西太谷，具孔子世家與票號商人的家族背景，極早（十九世紀末）進入教會學校，並受洗為基督徒；青年時期經歷拳變，其後由教會安排赴美，於歐柏林學院與耶魯大學留學，返國後以基督徒身分投入公共事工並獲得個人聲望，其經歷在近代中國基督徒中確屬少見。[1] 十九世紀末，由歐柏林神學院畢業生所建立的歐柏林中華團（Oberlin China Band）在山西太谷開啟的福音、醫療及教育事工，為孔祥熙創造了這個機會。

　　從政前的孔祥熙，自幼童時期信仰啟蒙、青少年接受現代教育，留美獲得學位，學成返國後投入公共事工，受歐柏林學院出身的牧師、拳變經歷及歐柏林學院校園氛圍影響甚大。對歐柏林學院而言，孔祥熙以基督徒及「歐柏林山西」（Oberlin-in-Shansi）代表身分，積極參與中國公眾事務，儼然成為中國基督徒領袖之一，其成就也被歐柏林學院視為在華事工開花結果的表徵。[2] 1926年歐柏林學院授與孔祥熙榮譽法學博士學位，表彰其對中國社會及「歐柏林山西」的貢獻，其時孔尚未涉入政壇。

　　學界對近代中國教會領袖人物的研究，從過去「政治」面向，逐漸轉向教會、福音、神學及信仰等「屬靈」面向，如本色教會、本色神學、政教觀等，也就是傾向將基督教視為「中國宗教之一種」；[3] 從「文化史」層面，轉向「社會史」層面的研究，如基督徒的社會流動、婚姻網絡、政商關係等，亦即將中國基督徒的活動視為「中國社

1　陳能治，〈早期的孔祥熙：一位基督徒的教會歷練與公共參與（1890-1922）〉，《國史館館刊》，第48期（2016年6月），頁1-52。

2　Campfield Mary Tarpley , *Oberlin-in-China, 1881-1951* (Ph. D. Thesis-University of Virginia, 1974, Ann Arbor, Mich.: University Microfilms International, 1985), p. 26. 孔祥熙對歐柏林學院的價值，該文認為是憂喜參半（a mixed blessing），是最大的資產，也是最大的負債。

3　劉家峰編，《離異與融會：中國基督徒與本色教會的興起》（上海：上海人民出版社，2005），頁183-350。該書收錄王成勉、劉家峰、吳和興以及朱峰等學者論文，討論余日章之政教觀、誠靜怡的本色教會思想、韋卓民與周聯華的本色神學等。

會現象之一」。[4] 對西方在華宣教師活動的研究，也從單向輸入，逐漸轉向西方宣教師個人在中國文化處境中的「文化涵化」現象，亦即將中國視為一個「文化體系」。[5]

　　本文嘗試將基督教視為在中國的一種宗教，在此前提下，透過孔祥熙的個案，討論近代中國基督徒領袖人物「改宗」（conversion）的機緣，出於信仰的屬世活動，討論西方在華宣教的主客體在兩個文化體系中「施與受」的關係，以及最後在信仰中合一的可能性。[6] 本文主要利用歐柏林學院檔案館（Oberlin College Archives, O.C.A.）所藏資料，包括書信、會議記錄、校園刊物等。

二、受洗與生命轉折

　　1881 年歐柏林神學院畢業生組織差團，在美部會（American Board of Commissioners for Foreign Missions）派任下來華，次年開創山西公理會（Shansi Mission），先後於太谷及汾陽建立兩所基督教會，進行福音、醫務與有限的教育事工，史稱歐柏林中華團，駐地宣教師及眷屬多歐柏林學院校友。[7]

　　1889 年 2 月歐柏林中華團於太谷基督教會試辦男子寄宿學校

---

4 查時傑，〈同負一軛──中國近代基督教家族的婚姻網絡初探〉，收入黃文江等編，《法流十道──近代中國基督教區域史研究》，頁 71-95。吳梓明，〈中華聖公會家族史研究芻議〉，李金強，〈基督徒商人──呂明才（1888-1956）父子及其貢獻〉，收入黃文江、張雲開、陳智衡主編，《變局下的西潮──基督教與中國的現代性》（香港：建道神學院，2015），頁 671-683，頁 685-697。Denice A. Austin, *"Kingdom – Minded" People: Christian Identity and Contributions of Chinese Business Christians* (Leiden, The Netherlands: Koninklijke Brill NV, 2011). 黃文德，〈華洋義賑會與國際社會的互動關係（1921-1938）〉，《近代中國》，第 158/159 期（2014 年 9/12 月），頁 36-37。張志偉，《基督化與世俗化的掙扎──上海基督教青年會研究》（臺北：臺大出版中心，2010），頁 164-172。

5 Xi Lian, *The Conversion of Missionaries: Liberalism in American Protestant Missions in China, 1907-1932* (University Park: Pennsylvania State University Press, 1997).

6 關於中國近代史研究取向之發展，如單向的文化侵略、刺激／反應、傳統／現代、中國中心觀等，學界論述極多，此不贅述。

7 Ellsworth Carlson, *The Oberlin Band: The Christian Mission in Shanxi, 1882-1900* (Oberlin, Ohio: Oberlin Shansi Memorial Association, 2001), pp. 4-5. 拳變前，歐柏林中華團先後共派出 30 名宣教師及眷屬，其中 21 人畢業於歐柏林學院大學部或神學院。

（boarding school），由來浩德（Dwight Howard Clapp）牧師娘 Mary J. Rowland 主持，[8] 女教士貝如意（Rowena Susan Bird）協助校務進行；[9] 8 月正式成立男子寄宿學校，稱明道學堂（Taiku Academy）。[10] 1889 年底孔祥熙罹頸部結核腺瘤（tubercular gland），接受山西公理會醫務宣教師高大夫（James Goldsbury）診治，[11] 因此有機會接觸教會所辦主日學及西式學校訊息，孔病癒後，1890 年 1 月進入明道學堂就讀，不久即受洗為基督徒。[12] 1898 年秋，孔明道學堂畢業後，由山西公理會送至華北公理會潞河書院（North China College）就學。[13]

　　孔因自幼喪母，所以幼時在太谷讀書時，常跟著來浩德太太或貝如意女教士，依戀來浩德太太甚深；[14] 1892 年衛祿義（George Louis Williams）牧師娘 Mary Alice Moon 來太谷後，[15] 對孔尤其照顧，孔暑

8　Ellsworth Carlson, *The Oberlin Band,* pp. 187-188. Dwight Howard Clapp 生於 1845 年，1879 年自歐柏林學院大學部畢業，1884 年自歐柏林神學院畢業，並接受按立成為牧師，與新婚妻子 Mary J. Rowland 出發到中國宣教；Mary J. Rowland 畢業於俄亥俄州 Painesville 的 Lake Erie Seminary，在公立學校教書九年，因此到中國後開啟教育事工，耗十五年時間讓太谷明道學堂逐漸上軌道。Clapp 夫婦從 1884 年到 1900 年殉難，僅返美休假一次；Ellsworth Carlson 認為，他們對山西公理會的貢獻，超過任何一位宣教師。

9　Ellsworth Carlson, *The Oberlin Band,* pp. 190-191. Rowena Susan Bird 生於 1865 年，為美部會派出之單身女教士，其父為長老會牧師，早逝，故其母遷居歐柏林，之後長住歐柏林鎮，畢業於歐柏林高中。Bird 於歐柏林鎮，受歐柏林學生志願宣教團對地方教會活動影響，故有志於海外宣教，因此在歐柏林學院修讀女部學分（Ladies Course），1890 年在美部會派遣下來到太谷。1897 年返美休假，次年再回太谷。Bird 在太谷九年，主要協助 Clapp 太太經理明道學堂，或到里滿庄協助其他宣教師進行夏季福音宣教活動。

10　Mrs. Williams to Corbin, October 20, 1932, p. 3, OSMA Records, Oberlin Band folders, Correspondence, Journals, letters 1900, 1931-1932, 1958 , Box 1, O. C. A.

11　Ellsworth Carlson, *The Oberlin Band,* pp. 194-196. James Goldsbury 為第二位到太谷的醫務宣教師，生於 1860 年愛荷華州 Davenport，1881 年進入位於芝加哥的 Rush Medical College 就讀，在前往中國之前，於多所醫療機構實習，並任職於國際性醫務宣教組織 Medical Missionary Society，汲取豐富的實務經驗，其妻 Mary Grace 畢業於 Boston Normal School。Goldsbury 於 1889 年 9 月來到天津，短暫任職於 London Mission Hospital，其後到太谷及里滿庄開啟戒煙所，1893 年 3 月 23 日因猩紅熱於太谷病逝，留一 3 歲子及一遺腹子，其妻終生關注山西公理會事工。

12　Ellsworth Carlson, *The Oberlin Band,* p. 68, 71.

13　Mrs. Williams to Corbin, October 20, 1932, pp. 1-2, OSMA Records, Oberlin Band folders, Correspondence, Journals, letters 1900, 1931-1932, 1958, Box 1, O. C. A.

14　Mrs. Williams To Corbin, October 20, 1932, pp. 1-2, OSMA Records, Oberlin Band folders; Journals, letters, 1900, 1931-1932, 1958, Box 1, O. C. A.

15　Ellsworth Carlson, *The Oberlin Band,* pp. 193-194. George Louis Williams 生於 1858 年，1887 年左右進入 New England Conservatory of Music 就讀，其後自認需要更深入的音樂教育，因此轉入歐柏林學院，1888 年大學部畢業後進入歐柏林神學院就讀，1891 年畢業。在歐柏林就學期間，Williams 積極推動歐柏林學生志願宣教運動，激發學院及神學院學生志願宣教團的氛圍。1891 年被按立為牧師，並娶 Mary Alice Moon 為

假從潞河書院回太谷，在城內南街福音院幫助教務，都住在衛祿義牧師家；[16] 孔並經常隨宣教師到里滿庄避暑，協助福音宣教，與駐里滿庄的德富士（Francis Ward Davis）牧師娘 Lydia Lord Davis 熟稔。[17]

1900年夏，孔如常返家度暑假，不幸拳變爆發，7月31日太谷基督教會六名教會宣教師及眷屬，包括來浩德牧師夫婦及其子女、衛祿義牧師、德富士牧師、貝如意及露美樂兩位女教士，全部蒙難，僅衛祿義牧師娘與三女，以及德富士牧師娘與三兒，因故返美倖存。[18]

事件最後階段，孔祥熙出入福音堂欲與宣教師共死難，但為貝如意所阻，貝如意將家書交與孔，期望若真死難，請孔將信帶到美國以慰其母。拳變七年後，太谷基督教會女教士賀芳蘭（Flora K. Heebner）傭人在舊書店發現貝如意殉難十天前的手書。從貝如意的日記中，約可了解孔祥熙在其間之經歷：

> 6月30日（貝如意）記載：「我促祥熙為其妹金鳳找個安靜的地方，他卻願與我們同在，不願意把妹子送到家中，恐怕染著拜偶像、纏足的惡俗。」
>
> 7月13日記載：「祥熙勸我們入山，並許幫忙我們；若不逃

妻。其妻 Mary Alice Moon 生於1860年鄰近俄亥俄州 Reedsburg 的 Amish 教區，父親過世後，與其母移居俄亥俄州 Ashland，後在 Brethren College 求學，最後一個學期轉學到歐柏林學院，畢業後在小學教書。Williams 夫婦於1891年來華，先在沿海口岸學習中文，次年到山西。1892至1899年主要在太谷進行福音宣教，1899年 Williams 牧師留太谷監督其房舍施工，其妻則留美國。1900年拳變 Williams 牧師殉難，遺留三名女兒。Mary Alice Moon 於1909年至1912年止，重返太谷明道學校教書，1930年代再回太谷；其女 Gladys 後來返回太谷仁術醫院，擔任護士。

16 Luella Miner, ed., *Two Heroes of Cathay, An Autobiography and a Sketch* (New York, London and Edinburgh: Fleming H. Revel Company, 1903) pp. 179-180.

17 Luella Miner, ed., *Two Heroes of Cathay*, p. 182. Ellsworth Carlson, *The Oberlin Band*, pp. 188-189. Francis Ward Davis 生於1857年威斯康辛州，1886年以29歲之齡進入歐柏林神學院，其妻 Lydia Lord Davis 生於1867年俄亥俄州 Ada，曾任教於家鄉小學。兩人於1889年來華，首先到汾陽，1897年 Lydia Lord Davis 於汾陽成立山西省最早的女子小學。1897年舉家返回歐柏林休假，1899年 Davis 牧師隻身返回太谷，其妻因健康因素未隨行。1900年 Davis 牧師殉難，遺留二子及一遺腹子。Lydia Lord Davis 終其一生奉獻歐柏林山西，曾擔任歐柏林山西紀念社（Oberlin-Shansi Memorial Association, OSMA）祕書及執行祕書，實際參與 OSMA 各種庶務，協助 OSMA 走過二十世紀前半葉動盪的歲月。

18 William E. Strong, *The Story of the American Board: An Account of the First Hundred Years of the American Board of Commissioners for Foreign Missions* (Boston, Mass.: The Pilgrim Press, 1910), p. 377.

走，他就與我們分離。桑劉兩家已逃矣。……祥熙應允亂定之後，送我們到天津，處這夢生醉死之境，議無末（莫？）之何。倘若從此不面，吾亦不後悔來到中華，至於救人與否，惟主知道，萬事由他而成，吾人都安到他那裡去。」

7月14日記載：「今日決定仍舊住在城內。祥熙應許我們，倘若我們遇害，他要替我們發電至美。臨別淚流不止，因活命機會太少。我勸他急（即）早走開，設遇患難，當知是主。走時未曾正式告別。」[19]

1900年大難，孔因被其家人軟禁，得以逃過死劫。[20] 孔家丟棄孔所有教會書籍，僅貝如意贈送之《新約聖經》留存。[21]

拳變之後，1900年12月山西官方埋葬殉道者屍骨，孔與其他年齡較長的學生協助辦屍。次年3月孔回到潞河，身心俱創，有好幾個星期，只要提到山西的事，眼淚就在眼眶打轉，問老師：「為什麼會這樣？」一日，某位老師問他未來想做什麼？他說想到美國，奉養貝如意的母親（按：居Wisconsin州Milwaukee市），還有衛祿義太太，以及其他他所愛的人。此時潞河老師認為必須讓他換個環境，才能療癒他的傷痛，挑起未來重建山西教務的責任。其時潞河教師、歐柏林校友麥美德（Luella Miner）將回美休假，預定8月啟程，遂帶他同行，計畫到俄亥俄州歐柏林學院留學，以為未來重整教會事工做整備。[22]

1901年6月底，孔因須返回太谷徵詢其家族之意見，適浸禮會葉守真（E. Henry Edwards）、公理會文阿德（Iranaeus Atwood）及內地會戴德生（J. Hudson Taylor）等將回山西處理善後賠償及撫恤事宜，

---

19 王學仁編，《山西太谷公理會四十年史》（太谷：山西太谷基督教眾議會，1924），頁29-35。

20 Mrs. Williams to Corbin, October 20, 1932, p. 7, 8, OSMA Records, Oberlin Band folders, Correspondence, Journals, letters 1900, 1931-1932, 1958, Box 1, O. C. A.

21 Luella Miner, ed., *Two Heroes of Cathay*, p. 212.

22 Luella Miner, ed., *Two Heroes of Cathay*, pp. 214-217.

文阿德乃邀孔同行。[23] 8月5日，經文阿德協同前明道學堂學生孔、張振福及劉法成等一一辨視無顱屍骸，其中有被暴民砍首吊於城牆者，亂葬於城牆外土堆、身首異處者，還有從汾陽運來的宣教師遺體，共備30副棺木，其後葬於太谷東關士紳讓渡的宅第「孟家花園」（Flower Garden），即後來銘賢校地所在，其墓地稱「賢士墓」（Martyrs' Graves）。[24] 拳變中，太谷年輕一代基督徒目睹慘案、死裡逃生或協助辨屍的倖存者，受到的創傷或痛失親人的苦痛，都是難以言喻的。9月5日文阿德處理完山西公理會善後事宜後，回到保定，致函衛祿義太太，表示：

> 北京的朋友們認為祥熙受到驚嚇，建議讓他到美國比較好。現在應該已經與麥美德在一起。至於二五（按：應指孔同班同學張振福），感謝妳能讓他在北京繼續學業，但現在任憑我怎麼勸，他都不出發。他也是一樣受驚，很多人都一樣。我嘗試告訴他們，不要將為宣教師死難復仇一事，視為自己的責任；但是沒有用。[25]

孔協助辨屍後，1901年8月7日孔祥熙「蒼白、精疲力盡、瘦弱」的出現在北京，次日清晨，啟程赴美。[26] 另名山西公理會拳變倖存者費起鶴於日本神戶加入，麥美德偕孔、費兩人於9月12日抵美，因美國排華法案衍生入境問題，致遷延時日無法順利至歐柏林鎮就學，麥美德為渠等編撰著名的《華夏兩英雄》一書，該書序言云：「孔的故事讓吾人了解一位來自中國富有且尊貴家族子弟之生活面

---

23 Luella Miner, ed., *Two Heroes of Cathay*, p. 218.

24 E. H. Edwards, "Buried Together," *Ravenna Republican*, n. p., September 13, 1901?, OSMA Records, Oberlin Band folders, General files (printed materials), News, Box 1, O. C. A.

25 Atwood to Mrs. Williams, September 3, 1901, OSMA Records, Oberlin Band folders, Correspondence , Journals, letters 1900, 1931-1932, 1958, Box 1, O. C. A.

26 Luella Miner, ed., *Two Heroes of Cathay*, p. 218.

貌，原本生活平順，但拳變卻在其生命中投下不可抹滅的陰影。」[27]

1903年1月10日，孔與費兩人歷經十六個月的延宕，終於在歐柏林學院及美參議員奔走下，最後由歐柏林鎮鎮產管理處（Property-holders of Oberlin）適時簽署提供兩人在校所有花費的保證書，讓美國海關同意兩人入境，到達歐柏林。[28]

他們沒趕上前一年（1902年）10月美部會在歐柏林學院塔朋廣場（Tappan Square）舉行的（拳變）殉道紀念拱門（Memorial Arch）奠基儀式，但參加了1903年5月14日紀念拱門的揭幕儀式。拱門內側青銅版上鑴刻著拳變中山西與華北公理會13位殉道宣教師及其5名子女的姓名。拱門上書「殉道者的血是教會的種子」（"The Blood of Martyrs – The Seed of the Church"），拱門各面鑴刻以下文字：[29]

> 「靠著愛我們的主，在這一切的事上已經得勝有餘了」
> （" More Than Conquerors through Him that Loved Us"）
> 「我卻不以性命為念」
> （"Neither Count I My Life Dear Unto Myself"）
> 「我們若與基督同死，也必與祂同活」
> （"If We Died with Him We Shall Also Live With Him"）

揭幕儀式中，從主席、拱門捐贈者到參與學生，都是歐柏林人；廣場中，移居歐柏林鎮的殉道者遺族衛祿義太太及德富士太太、曾經等待拳變消息的歐柏林鎮鎮民，以及孔、費兩位歷經萬難初抵歐柏林的中國年輕學子皆在行列裡。[30] 整個廣場瀰漫著為道捨身的氛圍，對參與此一儀式的歐柏林人而言，受到的感召與影響，甚至持續終

---

27 Luella Miner, ed., *Two Heroes of Cathay*, p. 5.

28 Luella Miner, ed., *Two Heroes of Cathay*, p. 237.

29 Natt Brandn, *Massacre in Shansi* (New York: Syracuse University Press, 1994, 1999), p. 291.

30 Oberlin College, *Inaugurations: President Henry Churchill King of Oberlin College* (Oberlin, Ohio: Oberlin College, 1903).

生。[31]

其時，歐柏林學院殉道校友遺留的山西公理會教務亟待重整，在校期間跨越1900年拳變及1903年拱門奠基儀式的歐柏林學生志願宣教團成員，如康保羅（Paul L. Corbin）、賀芳蘭及韶華熙（Albert Staub）等，構成第一批拳變後返回山西的「學生世代」；孔、費在校加入歐柏林學生志願宣教團，該團成員因宣傳所需，經常訪問孔、費兩人，與渠等有深入的交遊。[32] 孔、費兩人也頗融入校園生活，受到兩位殉道遺孀衛祿義太太及德富士太太的照顧，孔與費稱她們為Mother Williams及Mother Davis；1906年孔、費自歐柏林學院畢業，同學在1906級畢業紀念冊上為孔留言：「他將讓異教徒的國度，開出花朵」。[33] 同年兩人再赴耶魯大學進修碩士學位，1907年6月學成，啟程返國。

歐柏林學院校園素具有濃厚的自由派宗教氛圍，十九世紀末二十世紀初，是全美大學校園中，基督徒學生參與校內宗教組織人數比例最高的學校；因校內基督宗教活動極具有活力，因此吸引具堅定基督信仰的學生來校就讀；[34] 其時，歐柏林校園宗教活動取向，正從強調個體救贖的宣教福音主義，逐步轉向強調個體價值及整體社會救贖的進步主義神學之時，1903年著名神學家Henry Churchill King擔任歐柏林校長，更為歐柏林校園帶來社會基督教（Social Christianity）神學，社會福音派的思維成為該校神學思想與課程設計的主流。[35] 正是此時，孔進入歐柏林，很難說，孔不受此一校園氛圍影響。[36]

---

31 陳能治，〈「以山西為名」——拳變後美國歐柏林學院對校友殉道的衍繹〉，《歷史、藝術與臺灣人文論叢（6）》，第6期（2015年1月），頁133-146。

32 *The Hi-o-Hi, 1903* (Oberlin, Ohio: Oberlin College, 1904), p. 117, *The Hi-o-Hi, 1905* (Oberlin, Ohio: Oberlin College, 1906), p. 140, 142. 1904年，康保羅為歐柏林學生志願宣教團宣教研習會（Mission Study Club）主席，賀芳蘭及韶華熙均為成員；1905至1906年，歐柏林學院YMCA主要成員為F. C. Chamberlain及A. W. Staub，皆最初籌備OSMA成員。

33 *The Hi-o-Hi, 1907* (Oberlin, Ohio: Oberlin College, 1907), p. 28, 30.

34 John Barnard, *From Evangelicalism to Progressivism at Oberlin College, 1866-1917* (Columbus: Ohio State University Press, 1969), pp. 29-30.

35 John Barnard, *From Evangelicalism to Progressivism at Oberlin College*, p. 115.

36 H. H. Kung to President of Shansi Memorial Association, "Second Annual Report of the Oberlin-Shansi Academy,

三、參與公共事工

1906年，歐柏林學生會主席兼歐柏林學生志願宣教團主席韶華熙積極籌組歐柏林山西紀念社（Shansi Memorial Association, OSMA），以推動殉道宣教師念茲在茲的教育事工，希望孔、費畢業後，一到太谷，一到汾陽，開辦四年制中學，獲得孔、費首肯。歐柏林學生志願宣教團認為當務之急，就是趕緊募款「綁住」（tie up）他們。[37] 次年韶華熙前往加拿大多倫多參加全美學生志願宣教團年會，途中偶遇一位Allen先生，答應提供孔祥熙之薪津。[38] 韶華熙獲得孔薪資保證後，即刻通知在山西的康保羅，請其在孔抵上海時，告知孔已可返回太谷開啟一所四年制中學。[39]

1907年10月孔自上海登岸，得康保羅函後，花了一個月時間探訪華北相關類型的教會學校，11月間回到太谷，其時太谷四年制中學已經開始運作。孔將學生作適當分班，並正式將此一四年制中學命名為「山西銘賢學校」（Oberlin-Shansi Memorial Schools）。其時，銘賢在四年制中學部分，僅有5位學生。康保羅認為，孔自認有義務繼續殉道者的夙願，他說：

Taiku, Shansi, China, For the Year 1908-1909," OSMA Records, Administrative Records Folders, H. H. Kung 1906-1925, Correspondence, Box 8, O. C. A. 1910年銘賢第二屆畢業典禮，孔以「青年成功的指南」（The Guiding Compass for a Young Man's Success，中文為本文作者譯）為題，指出青年成功的指南，是由四個元素組成的，即仔細觀察、科學思維、祈禱交託（prayerful decision）及果決行動（forceful action），認為青年要與當下之思想革新運動契合，則必須合於時宜，具建設性思維，更需要寬廣、全面性的訓練。以清末之時代背景言，孔強調科學思維與方法，也期望透過禱告交託來符應這個社會的需求，可謂受進步主義理念影響。

37 Staub to Patton, March 19, 1907, OSMA Records, Administrative Records Folders, Correspondence, Founding and Relationship to American Board, Box 1, O. C. A.

38 Allen to Fiske, January 5, 1909, OSMA Administrative Records Folders, Fiske, G. Walter, 1908-1909, Box 6, O. C. A. 根據該函，提供孔薪資者為俄亥俄州Toledo公理基督教會牧師Ernest Bourner Allen（Minister, The Washington Street, Congregational Church, Toledo, Ohio），應是該教會勸募所得；韶華熙因故未募得費起鶴的薪資，費返國後進入YMCA工作。

39 *American Board of Commissioners for Foreign Missions-Reports of Shansi Mission (Oberlin-Shansi Memorial Association, 1908-1909, American Board, 1906-1909),* OSMA Records, Administrative Records Folders, O. C. A., p. 5.

對歐柏林學院而言，能擁有一名當地人擔任校長，而這位校長又是歐柏林之子，殉道者之友，事實上，是殉道者把他帶向基督教，1900年與他們共患難的。因此孔回國後，將其生命中最美好的一段，回到家鄉建立一所為紀念殉道者而設立的學校，這是歐柏林學生志願宣教團宣教事工中最特殊的一件事。[40]

　　康保羅認為孔六年留學生涯，讓他擁有了更敏銳的觀察力，更具備東西文化融通的概念，也更能融合現代科學及基督教的觀點，為太谷基督教會注入了道德元素（moral factor）。[41] 孔在甫整理完成的福音院發表演講，當年度的山西公理會年報寫道，孔的熱情與說服力，見證了其「對殉道友人的忠誠，也驗證其返回太谷教會的目的」。[42]

　　1910年4月16日復活節，孔在銘賢新校園舉辦追思儀式，其時，銘賢甫自太谷南關明道院遷至東關孟家花園，當日早上，銘賢學生由孔引領，在賢士墓前舉行追思儀式，孔於墓前朗讀《約翰福音》20章以及《哥林多前書》15章13節：「若沒有死人復活的事、基督也就沒有復活了。」（"But if it is preached that Christ has been raised from the dead, how can some of you say that there is no resurrection of the dead?"）儀式中受難者遺孤及倖存者都在列，氛圍感傷但莊嚴。[43] 山西公理會短期支援銘賢的宣教師田儉（Wynn C. Fairfield）認為，由孔進行賢士墓證道，特具意義。[44] 此一儀式，日後成為定制。

40　H. H. Kung to President of Shansi Memorial Association, "Second Annual Report of the Oberlin-Shansi Academy, Taiku, Shansi , China, For the Year 1908-1909," OSMA Records, Administrative Records Folders, H. H. Kung 1906-1925, Correspondence, Box 8, O. C. A.

41　Paul L. Corbin, *Ten Years After: A Sketch of the Reconstruction of The Shansi Mission Since 1900 and the Annual Reports for 1911* (Shanghai: Methodist Publishing House, 1911), p. 6.

42　*Annual Report of the Shansi Mission of the ABCFM, 1907* (Tungchou: North China Union College Press, 1907), p. 9.

43　Kung to Bohn, August 26, 1915, p. A-2, OSMA Records, Administrative Records, General Files, Fairfield's Detailed Notes for Writing History of Shansi First Fifty Years, Box 2, O. C. A.

44　Letter from Wynn C. Fairfield, April 17, 1911, p. A-2, OSMA Records, Administrative Records, General Files, Box 2, Fairfield's Detailed Notes for Writing History of Shansi First Fifty Years, O. C. A.

1911年10月辛亥革命爆發後，太谷商會推孔為太谷縣民政長及新軍統制，協助太谷度過革命最混亂的時期，孔組織學生自衛隊防守太谷教會及銘賢校園。[45] 民國建立後，1913年孔主導籌備與創設中美友好協會（Chinese American Association）山西分會，此一組織擴大了教會與上層士紳的關係。[46] 其表現，頗讓宣教師津津樂道。

　　1910年間，歐柏林校長Henry C. King趁安息年休假之便進行環球旅行，接受太谷基督教會之邀到太谷訪問，他稱許孔是一位好的學校行政者，指出就其環遊各地所見類似學校中，當地人當校長，但歐洲人在其底下工作且能順利運作者，只有印度德里（Delphi）的Stephens College案例，可以與之比擬。[47] 1912年King在歐柏林學院理事部年度報告中，特別稱許孔的表現不僅證明其個人價值，而且「OSMA也慶幸得人」。[48]

　　1910、20年代孔以OSMA代表及銘賢校長身分，代表山西公理會參與省內及全國性教會組織及活動，或任事於其衍生之活動，[49] 或為這些組織成立山西分會，如中華基督教教育會（China Christian Educational Association）、晉直魯教育會、[50] 中華基督教青年會全國

---

45 Corbin to Home Folks, December 21, 1911, OSMA Records, Administrative Records Folders, Corbin, Paul, 1904-1916, Correspondence, Box 4, O. C. A.

46 *The Christian Movement in Greatvale: An Abridged Report of the Work of the Taikuhsein Station 1913-1914* (n.p.: Shansi District North China Mission of American Board)（印刷品），p. 7, 9, 14-15.

47 Stephens College位於印度德里，1881年由劍橋大學畢業生組成之劍橋差會（Cambridge Mission）所建，1906年校長衛爾（Hibbert-Ware）牧師將校長職禮讓印度當地人 Susil Kumar Rudra，Rudra 成為第一位掌理印度主要教育機構之本地籍校長。http://www.ststephens.edu/，2015年8月24日點閱。

48 Report of the President,1911-1912, p. 92, OSMA Records, Administrative Records Folders, Oberlin President Report, 1907-1920, Box 2, O. C. A.

49 《中華基督教年鑑》（1915）（臺北市：中國教會研究中心橄欖基金，臺二版，1983），頁壹玖，頁413。《中華基督教年鑑》（1917），頁參。1915年之年鑑孔祥熙簡介為：「曾任日本留學生青年會幹事，1915年為太谷銘賢中學校長、中華續行委辦會會員」；1915年之年鑑所列中華續行委辦會會員名單中，孔列為公理會籍，名銜為「銘賢中學校長」。

50 孫廣勇，《社會變遷中的中國教會會研究》，華中師範大學博士論文（未出版，2006年5月1日），頁137。1912年中華教育會改名中華基督教教育會，每年召開一次12人執委會（通常在上海），1914年5月6日召開改組後之第一次議事會，下含8個區會，其中「直隸、山東、山西、陝西及甘肅」列為一區。

協會、東京中華留日學生青年會、太原基督教青年會、[51] 中華歸主運動（China for Christ Movement）、晉魯直三省公理會聯會、[52] 國際華洋義賑會及國際華洋義賑會山西分會等。[53]

　　首先是，1910年愛丁堡世界宣教大會鼓吹普世教會合一運動，其後，中國各地教會領袖為貫徹愛丁堡會議之合一精神，開始舉行分區會。1913年3月世界宣教大會主席穆德（John Raleigh Mott）來華主持在上海召開的全國基督教大會，為華人列席此一全國性教會領袖會議之始；[54] 孔祥熙先以山西銘賢校長名銜參與北京續行委辦會，受北京續行委辦會之聘，至上海參與穆德主持的全國基督教大會。[55] 在上海，孔趁便參加中華基督教青年會全國組合會議，會中，中華基督教青年會全國協會副總幹事王正廷，提出向歐柏林及山西公理會請求借調孔祥熙到東京中華留日學生青年會服務一年之議案，滿期後仍歸建山西銘賢學校。[56]

　　1913年10月孔赴日本東京中華留日學生青年會履新，次年9月與宋靄齡結婚，1915年5月孔返回山西，偕宋靄齡同行。[57] 1915年11月18日完成山西太原基督教青年會向全國協會登記，以就地籌款，孔擔任副會長。[58] 1918以後，閻錫山戮力改造山西為模範省，孔任其

---

51 （美）邢軍著，趙曉陽譯，《革命之火的洗禮：美國社會福音和中國基督教青年會，1919-1937》（上海：上海古籍出版社，2006），頁36-60。邢軍認為，二十世紀初期，中國基督教青年會本土領導人物承社會福音理念，具備更新的救國方針、社會改革及國際主義概念，而受社會福音思潮影響的青年會美籍人員，強調「本土改革源於本土領導」，也讓中國基督教青年會華籍領導人物成為中國政治社會改革的代言者。

52 〈公理會報告〉，《中華基督教年鑑》（1916），頁續3、7，1914年山西公理會併入華北公理會，稱「晉直魯三省公理會聯會」，分直、晉、魯三區，太谷教會自1915年起歸其管理。

53 陳能治，〈早期的孔祥熙：一位基督徒的教會歷練與公共參與（1890-1922）〉，孔氏返國後所參與的各種公共事務及其活動，詳見該文。

54 羅炳生，〈中國宣教事業最近十年之進步〉，《中華基督教年鑑》（1917），頁11-15。

55 Kung to Watts O. Pye, March 18, 1913, OSMA Records, Administrative Records Folders, H. H. Kung 1906-1925, Correspondence, Box 8, O. C. A.

56 Kung to Watts O. Pye, March 18, 1913, OSMA Records, Administrative Records Folders, H. H. Kung 1906-1925, Correspondence, Box 8, O. C. A.

57 〈銘賢中學校教職員致函歐柏林〉（中文書法，八行書），1915年5月5日，OSMA Records, Administrative Records Folders, General File, Ming-Hsien History Information, Box 2, O. C. A.

58 〈本年中國教會大事紀〉，《中華基督教年鑑》（1916），頁華22。

省政顧問，其間1918年山西旱災，孔與其他公理會宣教師協助閻進行賑濟工作。[59] 1919年在孔的努力下，紅十字會在修築山西主要幹道之外，多興築了幾條支線，其中一條通往銘賢，讓太谷經榆次可接上晉中聯外鐵路。[60]

1919年五四運動之後，12月中華續行委辦會在上海舉行全國大會，討論教會如何有效協助中國，與會人士皆認同必須仰賴基督教的靈性力量，中華歸主運動乃應運而生。[61] 孔被選為大會臨時委員。[62] 1921年11月，中華歸主運動正式在中華續行委辦會內運作，委員中西各半，孔祥熙被選為執委，其名銜為「山西銘賢中學校長」。[63]

1920年華北五省發生大災，中國紅十字會及華洋義賑會委由各省教會組織處理賑災相關事務，孔擔任山西募款之執行祕書，協助處理山西賑災問題，除自行勸募外，也擔任華洋義賑會山西代表，協助賑濟款之發放。[64] 次年9月，北京救災總會司庫蔡廷幹召集北京國際救災會，以及天津、上海、山東、山西、漢口、河南及湖南等華洋義賑會，籌設國際華洋義賑會。[65] 華洋義賑救災總會在北京成立，孔祥熙為中國華洋義賑會創會成員之一，成員皆一時之選。[66]

1922年4月到1923年8月，孔祥熙協助王正廷進行山東問題談判，以及中俄談判之八人代表團代表，說服張作霖脫離俄之牽制，也說服加拉罕（俄代表團）到北京談判等。[67]

---

59 Wynn C. Fairfield, China's Model Province（Shansi Governor Yen Hsi-Shan), OSMA Records, Administrative Records Folders, Box 3, O. C. A.

60 Kung to Bohn, Jan. 17, 1920, OSMA Records, Administrative Records Folders, Correspondence, H. H. Kung 1906-1925, Box 8, O. C. A.

61 查時傑，《民國基督教史論文集》（台北：宇宙光，1994），頁94。

62 Kung to Bohn, May 6, 1920, OSMA Records, Administrative Records Folders, Correspondence, H. H. Kung 1906-1925, Box 8, O. C. A.

63 全紹武，〈中華歸主運動〉，《中華基督教年鑑》（1922），頁44-49。

64 Oberlin-Shansi Memorial Association, 1920-1921, OSMA Records, Administrative Records Folders, Reports, Oberlin College President Report 1907-1920, Box 2, O. C. A.

65 黃文德，《非政府組織與國際合作在中國——華洋義賑會之研究》（臺北：秀威資訊，2004），頁61。

66 Kung to Bohn, March 6, 1921, OSMA Records, Administrative Records Folders, Correspondence, H. H. Kung 1906-1925, Box 8, O. C. A.

67 Kung to Bohn, December 21, 1923, OSMA Records, Administrative Records Folders, Correspondence, H. H. Kung

1925年上海五卅慘案掀起反帝風潮，孔函OSMA報告，他與其他中國教會領袖約集態度較為溫和的基督徒，鼓勵學生領袖及受學生敬重的燕京大學教師們參與學生愛國運動，讓學生及工人的抗爭能走在正確的道路上；孔認為，不能責怪布爾雪維克利用時局發展，而應該責備那些讓布爾雪維克趁勢而動的外國人，呼籲美國應該率先允諾歸還中國該有的利權，他說：「如果美國人民知道這個事實，一定會支持中國所提出的要求。」[68] 孔的呼籲，得到OSMA的認同與支持。[69]

四、公共參與的矛盾與抉擇

1925年為教會學校多事之秋，中國人要求關稅自主及取消治外法權問題，衝擊教會學校。9月，孔向OSMA報告，認為歐柏林的利他精神，是有目共睹的，而銘賢教育的目的，非在增加基督徒，而是訓練「幾百位貢獻國家的年青人，這是普遍被理解的事」，所以請OSMA不必擔心。其間，孔擔任中俄談判幫辦、外交關係委員會委員、中央政府委派調查沙基慘案二位代表之一，以及擔任馮玉祥之鐵道礦務部長等，參與中山陵建築規劃，云：「必盡心而為」，渠也坦言：「政治事務已經讓我無法關切太谷學校的事，甚至我自己私人的企業。」[70]

孔擔任銘賢校長，按銘賢之運作，係在OSMA與山西公理會協作下進行的，山西公理會支援銘賢一至二位宣教師協助校務。自

1906-1925, Box 8, O. C. A.

68 Kung to Bohn, September 25, 1925, OSMA Records, Administrative Records Folders, Correspondence, H. H. Kung 1906-1925, Box 8, O. C. A.

69 Bohn to Kung, October 30, 1925, OSMA Records, Administrative Records Folders, Correspondence, H. H. Kung 1906-1925, Box 8, O. C. A. OSMA執行秘書William Frederick Bohn（1878-1947）提到他剛從華盛頓回來，參加為期十天的全美公理會會議，會中支持中國收回利權運動，並列入OSMA記錄。

70 Kung to Bohn, September 8, 1925, OSMA Records, Administrative Records Folders, Correspondence, H. H. Kung 1906-1925, Box 8, O. C. A.

1909年起，先後有韶華熙、伍樂福（Jesse Wolfe）、田儌及溫爾安（Franklin B. Warner）等；雖然這些宣教師都是歐柏林校友，也是孔在歐柏林參與歐柏林學生志願宣教團前後期同工（或同學），但孔外務日多，讓某些宣教師認真思考孔對歐柏林的價值，兩者關係日漸對峙，孔個人也須認真考慮去留問題。

從政前孔以基督徒身分參與各種公共事務，為何留駐銘賢與西籍宣教師周旋，甚至對抗？以下僅就歐柏林檔案館館藏，說明孔廣泛參與公共事務衍生與外籍宣教師之間的衝突，以及渠心中所堅持的基督信仰與歐柏林認同。

1913年春，孔確定借調東京中華留日學生青年會，其時支援銘賢的山西公理會牧師伍樂福向OSMA抱怨孔外務太多，平均來說，每年約有十二週不在太谷，且孔薪水太高致使銘賢無法改善師資，建議OSMA趁孔借調東京一年不必承擔其薪水之機會，增聘老師，改善學校財務赤字，並進行組織重組。伍樂福坦言，如果在孔主政時進行重組，過程中他可能就會離開了；而他的離開，伍樂福認為：「對歐柏林事工將帶來不幸的結果。」即使伍樂福對孔頗多微詞，但也確信孔對歐柏林忠貞，也對主耶穌忠貞。[71]

1918年以後，孔投入外務的時間更多，山西公理會不得不讓城市佈道宣教師田儌轉至銘賢支援。1919年以後孔留駐銘賢時間更少，因此銘賢進行組織重整，實施科長制。[72] 田儌先後掛名預科主任、副校長，為銘賢的實質領導者。田儌太太抱怨，認為孔在外確實有影響力，這也許對學校有利，但「孔從銘賢得到信譽（credit），再利用此一信譽在其他地方得到好處」。[73] 1922年底孔回太谷，停留

---

71 Wolfe to Bohn, April 1, 1913, OSMA Records, Program Areas Folders, China, Ming Hsien, Taiku Property 1916-1935, Correspondence Wolfe, Jesse B, Box 6, O. C. A.

72 Kung to Bohn, December 12, 1919, OSMA Records, Administrative Records Folders, Correspondence, H. H. Kung 1906-1925, Box 8, O. C. A.

73 Fairfield to Bohn, May 1, 1919, p. B-1, OSMA Records, Administrative Records, General Files, Fairfield's Detailed Notes for Writing History of Shansi First Fifty Years, Box 2, O. C. A.

三週後，再回上海，其後約半年返回銘賢一次。[74] 銘賢副校長田儉對此頗有微詞，認為歐柏林方面根本不介意他個人代替孔為銘賢做了多少事，因為當局喜歡吹噓孔與歐柏林學院的關係。[75]

相對於田儉夫婦對孔之微詞，1918 年年底山西公理會宣教師溫爾安調任銘賢小學部，渠坦言帶著對孔的偏見而來，但來到銘賢之後，才發現自己所認知的完全錯誤。因為與孔逐漸建立較親近的關係，讓他對孔完全改觀，認為孔是一位知識廣博、具有同情心且非常有能力的人，對自己認為對的事非常無畏，是一位堅定的基督徒；孔無論在專業或實務上，都獲得許多華人基督徒的仰慕；他認為，歐柏林如果失去孔，對銘賢，對歐柏林來說，都是不幸的。[76]

溫爾安分析，孔有自己的企業，以他的能力他可以在其他地方獲得很豐厚的收入，他的家人根本不想住在山西，他大可留在上海，可是為什麼留在這裡（銘賢），而且將薪水回饋給這所學校？溫爾安一直感到疑惑，經仔細觀察後，唯一的答案是：「純粹而簡單的，就是他對拳變殉道友人的忠誠。」溫爾安描述一件讓他印象深刻的事，一個晚上，孔來到他家中，坐下來談一些瑣事，然後話題講到那些殉道者，溫爾安寫道：「他無法繼續下去，聲音哽咽，然後崩潰，放聲痛哭。」溫爾安趕快把話題拉到其他地方去。從那次開始，溫爾安確信讓孔待在銘賢的力量。他說：

> 每一種拉力都可能讓他走，但是因為他放不下這個事工（銘賢），對此他有一種特殊情愫，他對那些來到中國的宣教師，將知識帶給他及他的國人卻以身殉之的那些人，有一種特別的承諾（commitment）。我自己看到那些從外面回來的（銘

---

74 Kung to Bohn, September 8, 1925, OSMA Records, Administrative Records Folders, Correspondence, H. H. Kung 1906-1925, Box 8, O. C. A.

75 Fairfield to family, February 18, 1923, B-9, OSMA Records, Administrative Records, General Files, Fairfield's Detailed Notes for Writing History of Shansi First Fifty Years, Box 2, O. C. A.

76 Warner to Bohn, February 14, 1918, OSMA Records, Administrative Records Folders, Correspondence, Warner. Franklin B., 1915-1922, Box 15, O. C. A.

賢）學生──已經在外地獲得更多見識的學生，仍然不斷自我追尋，這就是一種見證。[77]

溫爾安謂，歐柏林應該慶幸有這樣一位「忠誠而真摯的兒子」（son, loyal and true）。他願意放棄個人利益，留在內地這麼一個小教會與其他夥伴一起工作。那些批評他的人，是因為沒有了解孔最深沉的情感；溫爾安呼籲，為了銘賢，希望美國 OSMA 朋友們，可以給孔充裕的經費，給他真正的鼓勵，讓他繼續留在這裡。[78]

五、公共參與下的歐柏林認同

　　1919 年前後，孔夾於外務與銘賢校長職之間難以兼顧，有曠廢校務之虞，因此向 OSMA 提出說明。他承認由於其個人身兼基督徒、山西省民及國家公民的多重角色，在當前中國及世界劇變的時代中，有其當下必須承擔的責任（duty），這是責無旁貸的。孔自認他個人在所有教會事工中，是嘗試「作為一位忠實的歐柏林事工代表，以及山西省基督徒之忠實代表」。即使他不常在銘賢，但對整個學校並不完全是個損失，因為他抓緊每一個機會介紹銘賢及銘賢的需要──利用各種接觸貴賓的機會，邀請他們來銘賢參訪，也設法主動接觸對銘賢有興趣或認同銘賢精神的人。對於他與銘賢的關係，孔堅定表示，要紀念那些為耶穌基督獻出生命的人，他必盡其所能與銘賢連繫在一起。他說：

> 當前中國事情多，但領導者少，所以只要能掌握力量，個人就會奮力去完成，以不負他人的期待，如果可以擇一而為，那當

---

77 Warner to Bohn, February 14, 1918, OSMA Records, Administrative Records Folders, Correspondence, Warner. Franklin B., 1915-1922, Box 15, O. C. A.

78 Warner to Bohn, February 14, 1918, OSMA Records, Administrative Records Folders, Correspondence, Warner. Franklin B., 1915-1922, Box 15, O. C. A.

然更容易一些，但是銘賢是我不能放棄的。雖然投入銘賢的時間很少，但是我想要建立一個永續發展的具體紀念物，以紀念那些為耶穌基督獻出生命的人，驅使我必須盡其所能與銘賢維繫在一起。[79]

　　孔的基督徒信仰，對拳變殉道者的忠誠，以及埋於心中的基督信仰與歐柏林認同，根據兩位到銘賢擔任短期英文老師的殉道宣教師遺孤 Lewis Davis 及 John Davis 兄弟，以及溫爾安的陳述，可見其一二。

　　1918 年清明節，孔在銘賢主持了一場動人的賢士墓前紀念儀式，當時孔已廣泛涉入公共事務。[80] 溫爾安詳細描述儀式細節，他寫道，當日學生在榆樹及松樹下，在中、外殉道者墓前，由孔校長主持儀式，溫爾安說：「孔個人已經為此做了很大的犧牲，他鼓勵中國年青人，必須對新生命的意義有所領會。」孔要學生脫帽以示敬意，最後他唸出《希伯來書》11 章 36 節、37 節、38 節、39 節、40 節，關於保有信仰，以及信眾所受苦難的章節：

36 節：又有人忍受戲弄、鞭打、捆鎖、監禁、各等的磨煉。

37 節：被石頭打死，被鋸鋸死，受試探，被刀殺，披著綿羊山羊的皮各處奔跑，受窮乏、患難、苦害。

38 節：在曠野、山嶺、山洞、地穴，飄流無定，本是世界不配有的人。

39 節：這些人都是因信得了美好的證據，卻仍未得著所應許的。

40 節：因為神給我們預備了更美的事，叫他們若不與我們同得，就不能完全。

---

79 Kung to Bohn, December 12, 1919, OSMA Records, Administrative Records Folders, Correspondence, H. H. Kung 1906-1925, Box 8, O. C. A.

80 陳能治，〈1900 年拳變的死亡與轉化——記一位西方殉道宣教師遺族的見證〉，收入《歷史、藝術與臺灣人文論叢（5）》，第 5 期（2014 年 7 月），頁 317-334。

溫爾安描述當時的情形，當孔唸出這些句子時，他的聲音哽咽，眼淚從他臉頰滑落下來，溫爾安感受到：

> 他自己就是經歷過這些苦難的人，所以他知道它的意義。死難者埋骨在此，過去及現在的基督徒讓學生領會生命的新視野，然後依使徒的生命行事。犧牲是新生命最大的理路，為了讓中國得救，所以他們來到這裡；在此寧靜且感性的時刻，學生站在那裡。[81]

接下來是 Lewis 簡短致詞，他站在父親的墳前，懇求學生接受耶穌基督做他們的主，他說：「基督是我的主，也請你們接受主的領導。那些埋在地下、死難的人們，並沒有白死，在他們死去的肉體之旁，已樹立銘賢此一偉大事工，上帝國度將要到來，他們沒有死亡。」Lewis 致詞結束後，學生聚在矮樹周圍，然後孔校長逐一介紹每一位埋身在此宣教師的生前事跡，以及當時屠殺的情形；溫爾安以為，這些小軼事讓這些男孩如親炙殉道者的生命。儀式結束後，學生排成兩列，慢慢前進，唱著〈效聖徒盡忠〉（"The son of God goes forth to war"）及 "Who follows in their train" 等，唱著：「我離世的時候到了。 那美好的仗我已經打過了。當跑的路我已經跑盡了。所信的道我已經守住了。」[82] 經檔案比對，1903 年 5 月 14 日孔初抵歐柏林不久參與的紀念拱門揭幕儀式當日，歐柏林神學院教授 Henry M. Tenney 領禱，所採用的聖歌就是希伯（Reginald Heber, 1783-1826）的〈效聖徒盡忠〉。[83]

---

81 "A Discussions Relative to the Location of the Oberlin-Shansi Memorial School, 1919," OSMA Records, Administrative Records Folders, Correspondence, Warner. Franklin B., 1915-1922, Box 15, O. C. A.

82 "A Discussions Relative to the Location of the Oberlin-Shansi Memorial School, 1919," OSMA Records, Administrative Records Folders, Correspondence, Warner. Franklin B., 1915-1922, Box 15, O. C. A.

83 Oberlin College, *Inaugurations: President Henry Churchill King of Oberlin College* (Ohio: The College, 1903), p. 17. 歌詞為："The Son of God goes forth to war, A kingly crown to gain; His blood-red banner streams afar: Who follows in his train?"

溫爾安對此一儀式的感性描繪，整個儀式所彰顯的服事與犧牲精神，孔對殉道者深刻的情感及見證，尤其是 Lewis 在自己父親的墳前，為銘賢學生講述耶穌基督的恩典，這動人的一幕，感動很多人，包括在現場的孔，以及閱讀報導的美國歐柏林 OSMA 諸公。儀式結束後，孔致函 OSMA，寫道：「看到 Lewis 這位年青人站在距離自己父親埋身的地方不到一呎的距離，對學生述說信仰的重要時，我的心從來沒有這麼被觸動過」；[84] 溫爾安也說：「這是我一生所參加的各種紀念儀式中，最令我感動的一次。」[85]

溫爾安針對 OSMA「我們究竟要辦理怎麼樣的學校」的徵詢，提到銘賢所有特殊元素中最特別的是，銘賢有一位中國籍的校長。溫爾安分析，孔已逐漸成為中國最被熟知的公民之一，他的交遊，他進入中國領導階層，了解中國及國際事務，他穩健並中肯的觀點，以及傑出的見解，歐柏林只有透過孔才有機會讓銘賢真正走向本色化，成為中國的一部分，而且也比那些單獨由差會經營的學校，更具有協和的本質，也更能實踐「歐柏林」所代表的一切理想。溫爾安認為，OSMA 比雅禮（Yale-in-China）更大的利基在於，從一開始就是中國人當領導者，他說：「當我們思及這些獨一無二的優勢，我們就會感受到，這些優勢就是歐柏林海外宣教事業中最炫目的一顆寶石」，建議 OSMA：「我們不要放棄這樣的校長。」[86] 溫爾安轉述孔與他的談話：

> 我是靠著信仰堅持下去，當我想到 OSMA 幾位特定人士對我
> 的信任，以及那些來中國發展基督教而付出生命的人，我覺得

---

84 Kung to Bohn, June 28, 1920, OSMA Records, Administrative Records Folders, Correspondence, H. H. Kung 1906-1925, Box 8, O. C. A.

85 "A Discussions Relative to the Location of the Oberlin-Shansi Memorial School, 1919," OSMA Records, Administrative Records Folders, Correspondence, Warner. Franklin B., 1915-1922, Box 15, O. C. A.

86 Warner to Mrs. Davis, February 7, 1919, "Extracts from Letters," "What types of works which OSMA should undertake," OSMA Records, Administrative Records Folders, Correspondence, Box 15, Warner. Franklin B., 1915-1922, O. C. A.

我必須竭盡心力去完成這些任務。那就是我留下來的原因。我不相信歐柏林的朋友會背棄這所學校。他們完全不了解我們代表什麼，以及我們完成了些什麼。對此，我深感愧疚，我沒能盡全力寫更多信件去告訴他們。[87]

溫爾安表示，孔在其他地方有很多機會，「這一點都不誇大」，孔有很多管道可以貢獻他的國家，但是，「他放棄，而到銘賢來。他已把他人生最好的時光奉獻給這所學校，這是他真正在乎的工作，是一生工作的一部分。他確信美國的朋友會站在他的旁邊。」[88] 溫爾安此信在OSMA廣為傳閱，許多人都非常感動， Davis太太隨後致函OSMA，表示：「我們必須保住孔。」[89]

1922年底孔回太谷，停留三週後，再回上海，其後約半年返回銘賢一次，有時甚至沒有回來，銘賢校務均由副校長田儆主持。根據歐柏林駐銘賢學生代表穆懿爾（Raymond T. Moyer）觀察，認為孔已經投入商場和政治事業，因此不可能妥善扮演校長的角色，渠轉述宋靄齡對此事的態度：「若孔回銘賢，絕對不是兩個人主政，不是孔，就是田儆，必須是其中之一。」[90] 田儆與孔諸多齟齬，此類中、西行政掌控權的問題，在1929年田儆離開銘賢之前，一直困擾著銘賢與OSMA。

1926年銘賢面臨立案後必須面對的諸多問題，4月OSMA為釐清銘賢未來發展方向，也為爭取霍爾教育基金（Hall Educational Fund），因此趁田儆返美休假之際，邀孔至美國共同商議，故以電報通知孔，歐柏林學院將在孔畢業二十週年的畢業典禮上，頒贈榮譽法學博

87 Warner to Mrs. Davis, July 17, 1919, "Extracts from Letters," "What types of works which OSMA should undertake," OSMA Records, Administrative Records Folders, Correspondence, Warner. Franklin B., 1915-1922, Box 15, O. C. A.

88 Warner to Mrs. Davis, July 17, 1919, "Extracts from Letters," "What types of works which OSMA should undertake," OSMA Records, Administrative Records Folders, Correspondence, Warner. Franklin B., 1915-1922, Box 15, O. C. A.

89 Davis to Bohn, September 17, 1919, OSMA Records, Administrative Records Folders, Correspondence, Davis, Lydia Lord 1918-1938, Box 5, O. C. A.

90 Moyer to Bohn, April 16,1924, OSMA Records, Administrative Records Folders, Correspondence, Moyer, Raymond 1928-1932, Box 10, O. C. A.

士學位，請孔親自出席。[91] 孔於5月20日啟程赴美，家人未同行。

孔在美停留將近半年，自1926年5月至同年10月，與OSMA討論銘賢未來，也為銘賢爭取霍爾基金，以當時孔公私兩忙的情況來看，這是非常難能的。1926年歐柏林學院頒與孔榮譽法學博士的證詞，先由美國著名圖書館學家Azariah Smith Root 介紹孔，Azariah稱渠為「偉大民族果敢的領袖，可託付的學校行政首長，銘賢校長」。歐柏林學院著名古典文學家Louis Eleazer Lord教授代表校長King致詞，說明頒贈的理由：

> 我們居住在以十年為度的土地上，今天頒授孔祥熙榮譽博士學位。他來自歷史悠久的中國，當哥倫布啟航之時──他的祖先已任巡撫，其家族可以回溯的是四至五代的歷史，是至聖先師、儒家思想創建者孔子的後代；今天我們美國這個年輕的國家向古老的中國致敬，因此我們授與這位歐柏林之子，我們在山西銘賢的校長，以及偉大孔夫子的後代，榮譽博士學位。他承擔各種政府職位，被賦與崇高的責任及權力，凡事竭盡心力且成效卓著。他潔身自愛，不讓自己被任何派系貼上標籤，在政治上，他堅拒任何公職。他的人民對他處理國事的智慧、對權力的自制以及各方面的才智，已加諸榮耀；今天在王萬王之前，歐柏林學院很榮幸能授與1906級的畢業生，孔祥熙，法學博士學位。[92]

10月初「孔博士」回到上海，幾天後，廣東國民政府催其南下，他拒絕所提外交顧問之職，但允暫代中央銀行總裁及財政部長之

---

91 Bohn to Corbin (telegraph), April 14, 1926, OSMA Records, Administrative Records Folders, Corbin, Paul, 1904-1916, Correspondence, Box 4, O. C. A.

92 Citation of HSIANG-SHI K'UNG for the honorary degree of Doctor of Laws at the Oberlin College Commencement of 1926 (The presentation by Professor Lord'), p. 74, OSMA Records, Administrative Records, General Files, Fairfield's Detailed Notes for Writing History of Shansi First Fifty Years, Box 2, O. C. A.

職，其後也接受蔣中正之邀到漢口處理漢口事件，同時兼任農業部部長。[93]

1926年以後，孔可以說完全以政府公職生涯為重，開啟另一段生命歷程，雖然仍擔任名義上的銘賢校長，直至1950年。[94]

六、小結

從政前的孔祥熙，自信仰啟蒙、接受現代教育，到留美返國後投入公共事工，受歐柏林學院影響甚大。對歐柏林學院而言，孔祥熙以基督徒身分積極參與中國教會公共事務，儼然成為中國基督徒領袖人物之一，也被歐柏林學院視為在華事工開花結果的表徵，否則不會在1926年頒與榮譽法學博士學位——當然其後孔於政治上的浮沉，歐柏林如何看待，又是另一段故事。

1926年從政前的孔祥熙基督徒角色的公共參與，其代表性來自山西公理會與OSMA。他以「歐柏林山西」代表、銘賢校長、太谷教會華人基督徒領袖身分，參與晉省及全國性教會組織，自承「承繼」了歐柏林殉道校友的遺志。其間，孔因外務分身乏術，引發與山西公理會美籍宣教師之間的各種衝突，既包括了人力分工、經費承擔及政策方向等，也涉及組織效忠及個人利益問題。但是，從歐柏林學院檔案館藏資料中，可以看到從政前的孔祥熙之基督信仰、公共參與成就及歐柏林認同，是被多數西方宣教師及其母會肯定的。

1928年2月、3月間，孔因外務過多，無法兼顧銘賢校務，兩度向OSMA提出辭呈，此讓OSMA深感挫敗。其時，OSMA祕書Davis

---

93 Kung to Bohn, October 16,1926, OSMA Records, Administrative Records Folders, Correspondence, H. H. Kung 1926-1930, Box 8, O. C. A.

94 1926年後，孔祥熙進入南方政府，擔任中央政治會議廣東政治分會委員、廣東財政廳廳長、武漢國民政府實業部部長，其後進入南京國民政府，擔任國民政府委員及工商部長、中央銀行總裁及行政院副院長兼財政部長等職。1939年擔任中央、中國、交通、中國農民四銀行聯合辦事處總處常務理事，後任行政院長，旋改任副院長，仍兼財政部長及中央銀行總裁。1945年春夏間先後辭去各職。1947年因病赴美療養；1962年來臺；1966年再赴美療疾，1967年8月16日，病逝紐約，享年88歲。

太太致函孔，告訴孔，當她到上海拜訪孔家時，宋靄齡告訴她，在山西辦理的學院（college in Shansi），與在美國的歐柏林學院（Oberlin in America），兩者的精神價值是完全相符的，「值得孔一生的努力」，宋靄齡個人完全理解這一點；而孔也一再向Davis太太表述同樣的想法。因此Davis太太說服孔，將銘賢辦理學院的責任放在OSMA手上，OSMA將盡力而為，但必須有「孔個人人格特質的動能在後支撐（dynamic personality behind it），在神的庇佑下，才能完成」。[95] 從孔擔任銘賢校長至1950年止，並與OSMA維持終生的關係，吾人毋寧相信其基督信仰與歐柏林認同，在其人生中是具有意義的。

自1900年拳變至1920年代，西方在華宣教進入「改革與進步」的階段，教會外在環境有利於宣教事工的發展。此間宣教範圍擴大、教會人才增長、教會生活進步，中國基督徒領袖人數增長，渠等對全國教會事務的參與，化被動為主動，這是「鼓舞人心」的發展。[96] 隨著新史料的開發，學界對這些中國基督徒領袖人物的研究，從個案、微觀的角度切入，將可呈現更清楚的歷史脈絡，以及單一歷史事件（如1900年拳變）在宣教史上的連續性效應。[97]

本文透過孔祥熙的個案研究，討論近代中國基督徒領袖人物「改宗」的機緣，出於信仰的屬世活動，西方在華宣教的主客體在兩個文化體系中「施與受」的關係，以及最後在信仰中合一的可能性，亦即將基督教視為在中國的一種宗教，將教會史研究帶入信仰層次的討論，此有待未來發展，本文僅為一種嘗試。

---

95 Mrs. Davis to Kung, April 7, 1928, p. 112, OSMA Records, Administrative Records, General Files, Fairfield's Detailed Notes for Writing History of Shansi First Fifty Years, Box 2, O. C. A.

96 中華續行委辦會調查特委會編，蔡詠春、文庸、段琦、楊周懷譯，《中國基督教調查資料（上卷），1901-1920》（北京：中國社會科學出版社，1987年11月第一版，2007年9月第二版印刷），頁128-143。

97 王立新，〈近代基督教在華傳教史研究主要範式評述〉，收入《東亞基督教再詮釋》（香港：香港中文大學崇基學院與中國社會研究中心，2004），頁107-136。

從協進會幹事到國府專員：
張福良與鄉村建設（1927-1939）[*]

劉家峰

摘要

　　張福良（1889-1984）是一位基督徒，是近代中國鄉村建設運動
中的一位重要領袖，但其功業卻少為世人所知。1927-1934年他擔任
中華全國基督教協進會的農村幹事，從「鄉村牧區」入手，以「基督
化鄉村社會」為最終目標。之後應國民政府之邀，作為政府工作人員
赴江西創辦農村服務區，強調恰當「運用政治」，以「救亡圖存」、
「民族復興」為標的。張福良在前後兩個時期的鄉建理念與實踐方法
差異固然有其身分轉變的緣由，但也反映出基督教信仰與社會關懷之
間的緊張關係，社會關懷是福音的自然結果，但社會關懷卻未必是通
向福音的直接橋樑。

關鍵詞：張福良、基督化鄉村社會、黎川試驗區、社會關懷

---

[*] 作者在論文修訂中參考了匿名評審專家的批評與具體建議，但囿於時間和條件，部分建議未能付諸實
　　施，特此說明並向評審專家致謝。

一、前言

　　鄉村建設（以下簡稱「鄉建」）稱得上抗戰前中國規模宏大的一場社會運動，有700餘個公私團體參與，各類實驗區多達1,000餘處，可謂盛極一時。其中最著名的民間團體莫過於平民教育促進會、山東鄒平鄉村建設研究院、南京曉莊師範學校、江蘇無錫省立民眾教育院、中華職業教育改進社等。值得注意的是，中國鄉村建設運動的先驅並非國人，而是如平教會領袖晏陽初所稱讚的「那一班篳路藍縷，開創基督教道的初期宣教士」。[1] 因此，鄉建領袖中不少人有基督教的背景亦不足為奇了。平教會除晏陽初是基督徒，大部分核心工作人員如傅葆琛、李景漢、陳志潛等都是。創辦曉莊學校的著名教育家陶行知、在北京創辦清河實驗區的燕京大學教授許仕廉等也都是基督徒。中外基督徒秉承耶穌「非以役人，乃役於人」的精神，致力於改善中國農民生活，由此可見基督教對近代中國的貢獻。[2]

　　張福良（1889-1984）是鄉建運動中的一位重要領袖。他曾擔任中華全國基督教協進會（National Christian Council of China）的農村幹事，之後應國民政府之邀赴江西創辦農村服務區，抗戰快結束時擔任中國工業合作社總幹事，後又擔任中美合作農村復興委員會鄉村工業幹事等。1950年後到美國肯塔基州的伯里亞學院（Berea College）擔任校長助理和社會學教授。1972年他出版了一本自傳性的著作《東方遇見西方：中國鄉村建設的個人史》，他的好友賽珍珠（Pear S. Buck）撰寫了序言，稱讚該書「不僅是一部個人的歷史記錄，也是一個民族、國家的時代記錄，以及為那個偉大國家而獻身、非凡卓越的一群人的記錄」。[3] 作為一名長期工作在一線的鄉建領袖，他在當

---

1 孫恩三，〈中國鄉村建設運動在吶喊〉，《中華歸主》，第138期，識字運動專號（1933年9月1日），頁3。

2 筆者曾以此為題在2001年撰寫了博士論文，《中國基督教鄉村建設運動研究（1907-1950）》，後同名由天津人民出版社2008年出版，本文有部分資料出自該文。

3 Pear S. Buck, "Forward," in Chang Fu-liang, *When East Met West: A Personal Story of Rural Reconstruction in China* (New Haven: Yale University Press, 1972). 為節省篇幅，以下該書簡寫為 *WEMW*。

時也算得上基督教界、政界以及社會上的一位知名人士，但其聲譽從來都無法與他的連襟晏陽初相提並論。張福良去美之後在華人世界更幾乎被人遺忘，就連當今研究中國鄉村建設的著作中都甚少提及他的名字，專門研究張福良的論著就更不多見。[4] 一位美國學者在1970年代的文章以「沉默的英雄」來評價張福良，[5] 可謂一語中的。

但如果仔細爬梳與張福良相關的歷史資料，就會發現他在中國鄉建史上應有一席之地，值得史家去發掘、書寫，尤其是關於他在中國鄉村建設中不同一般人的經歷，他從基督教協進會的幹事轉任國府專員，不僅僅是身分和地位的轉換，也帶來了其鄉建理念及實踐方法的變革。無論這些實踐最終成效如何，包括張福良在內各家各派的鄉建經歷都在在體現了近代中國鄉村問題的複雜性和艱巨性。因此，筆者不揣淺陋，擬在以前研究基督教鄉村建設的基礎上，對張福良進行專題研究，不是要為他爭地位，也不是為了拯救大眾的遺忘，而是要理清其鄉建理念與實踐的變遷歷程。筆者亦希望通過張福良的鄉建思想，再思福音與社會關懷以及社會服務中的宗教與政治關係等複雜而敏感的議題。

二、從耶魯（Yale）到雅禮（Yali）：張福良的早期經歷

關於張福良早期生平的資料並不多，本文所述主要來自他的自傳。1889年張福良生於上海，母親來自無錫，為逃避太平天國之亂，只十歲的母親和鄰居一起到了上海的外國租界，後跟做生意的父親在這裡結婚，生下了五個孩子，張福良是家中老么，上面有兩個哥哥兩個姐姐。張福良和哥哥姐姐得以幸運地在中國最現代、最國際化

---

4 除本人著作曾提及張福良外，美國學者 Stacey Bieler 在其著作 *"Patriots" or "Traitors": A History of American Edu-cated Chinese Students* (New York: M. E. Sharpe, 2004) 中有一章簡要描述了張福良的一生。該書有中文版《中國留美學生史》（北京：三聯出版社，2010）。

5 Ann William, "Chang Fu-liang: The Quite Hero", 未刊列印稿，見 RG 8, "Chang Fuliang's Paper"，耶魯神學院圖書館藏。

的都市中長大，並接受了西式教育。大哥讀到高中，能講流利英語，繼承他父親的鋼材煤炭生意。二哥讀美國聖公會創辦的聖約翰大學，1900年畢業後去了長沙，成為湖南省第一位教英語的中國人。二哥拒絕了父母安排的婚姻，堅持跟上海中西女中（McTyeire School，美國監理會創辦）的畢業生結婚，父母最終支持了他的選擇，這讓當時年輕的張福良感受了什麼是「個人自由」。[6] 1903年張福良進了聖約翰大學附中，就像走進了「一個做夢都沒想到的新世界」。自由和民主的思想吸引了他，但他做了一番實驗後很快得到了「自由」的教訓。張福良的家庭並無基督教背景，父母、祖父母一生都篤信觀音，在聖約翰讀了六年書（四年中學和兩年大學）的張福良並沒有成為基督徒，但也不得不按照基督教學校的規矩參加早禱和晚禱。一次他在禱告時單膝跪地，學校要求雙膝，學監發現後報告給校長。校長問他為何如此，張福良施展了他的小聰明，反問校長學監是如何發現他單膝跪地，因為按要求禱告時所有人必須閉上雙眼，但他還是被記過處分。[7]

1909年8月，中國首次庚款留學生選拔考試在北京舉行。雖有1,000餘人競爭，但這對已在聖約翰受過西學與中學良好訓練的張福良以及他的五位同窗來說不是難題，他們全部通過。首批47名留學生同年10月12日從上海啟程，11月6日抵達三藩市，然後經芝加哥最後到達麻塞諸塞州的春田（Springfield）。張福良和三位同伴被安排在波士頓附近的勞倫斯中學（Lawrence Academy），住在校長家裡，開始學習、適應美國的生活。第二年，張福良進入耶魯大學的謝菲爾德學院（Sheffield Scientific School）。大學時代有兩件事讓他在五十五年後仍記憶深刻，其中一件就是他皈依基督教。1912年中國留美學生青年會會議在麻省的北田（Northfield）舉行。他和兩位同學梅貽琦（後任清華大學校長）及唐悅良（後來任北京政府外交部次

---

6 *WEMW*, p. 7.
7 *WEMW*, p. 8.

長）都決志信教，但直到他1915年歸國後才告知父母已受洗。他跟母親講述了基督怎麼幫助像他這樣的年輕人獨身在外，如何抵禦酒、女人、歌舞和賭博的誘惑，還告訴母親他在過去五年裡，在紐黑文（New Haven）的浸禮會教堂主日學校教中國洗衣工學習英語。母親雖然篤信觀音，但仍為兒子找到信仰而高興，因為「你就多一個神——基督神來看護你」。[8] 這是張福良生命中至為重要的一步，直接影響到他以後的工作、婚姻及家庭。

1913年，張福良因為美國總統希歐多爾・羅斯福的一段話而決定去耶魯林學院讀研究生。羅斯福總統希望美國人民注意自然資源的保護，特別是森林保護，並以中國為例，說明森林植被被毀，大面積水土流失，黃河成為「中國之痛」，在過去幾百年裡奪去數萬人生命。張福良聽後大受感動，決定進林學院讀研究生，希望回國後能為國效力。[9] 在耶魯期間，他未免感到孤獨，幸好有中國留美學生組成的團體，他還和其他林業專業的學生組成了「中國森林人」俱樂部。他皈依基督教後更參與了中國留美基督徒學生聯合會，擔任過美束分部的記錄幹事和司庫。真正不再讓他感到孤獨的是他遇見了以後相伴一生的伴侶，即紐約長老會華埠教會首任牧師許芹（Huie Kin）的長女許海麗（Louise）。許牧師有六個女兒，二女兒許雅麗（Alice）嫁給了晏陽初。[10]

1915年夏天張福良從林學院畢業，帶著新婚夫人回到中國。他也許還記得他出國前在聖約翰的獲獎講演稿《改良風俗》，其中寫道：「故為今日中國計，不求自強則已，若求自強，非改良風俗不為功」；「誰是改良風俗者，則曰有我學生在，問誰是製造新中國者，則亦曰有我學生在」。[11] 言語之間，豪情萬丈。現在他學成歸國，「充滿了希望，也準備冒險」。然而，他回到中國時正是國家四分五

---

8 *WEMW*, pp. 22-23

9 *WEMW*, p. 23.

10 後面四位女兒分別嫁給了朱友漁、桂質廷、周學章、王義暉，都是當時中國教育界、知識界的翹楚。

11 張福良，〈改良風俗〉，《約翰聲》，第20卷第2期（1909），頁11-13。

裂、軍閥割據時代，北京的中央政府軟弱無力，正面臨著與日本簽署「二十一條」的壓力，人民也朝不保夕，誰顧得上保護自然資源呢？這時的張福良形容自己就像「從水裡跳出來的魚」。很顯然，保持水土、植樹造林需要一個長期的規劃，需要一個穩定的政府逐步來實施，當時條件下顯然是不可能的目標。他認為他學的林學在中國超前了五十年。[12]

　　既然不能用林學「製造新中國」，他就到了二哥所在的長沙，在這歷史上「最排外」的地方成了雅禮大學的一位教師。雅禮大學是1906年由耶魯大學畢業生創辦。受過「耶魯精神」薰陶的張福良深受雅禮大學的歡迎，他熟悉雅禮的文化，除了教授科學，他還擔任足球教練，讓足球成為當時最流行的校園運動。他跟夫人一起發起很多社會活動，邀請各階層的男女人士參加。1922-1926年他被聘為雅禮中學的校長，同時仍在大學教課。他通過雅禮試圖建立一個理解東方和西方的橋樑，老人與年輕人及保守與自由之間的橋樑。

　　然而，張福良這時已不太滿足於校園的教書生涯。二十年代初開始，晏陽初、陶行知等推行的平民教育和農村改良已經引起國人關注，作為與晏陽初交往甚密的張福良自然也不會不關注。當時已有不少專門的美國農業傳教士來到中國，和教會學校、教會等幫助發展農業和鄉村教育。受此觸動，1926年夏天張福良決定返回美國，到喬治亞大學（University of Georgia）研究生院學習棉花培育、農藝、園藝和鄉村教育。他學習這些課程，跟一位來自密西根Ann Arbor的教育傳教士Harold S. Gray不無關係。他們商定了一個計畫，準備在1927年秋天全家都搬到華中的漢江平原，先是幫助當地農民改良棉花品種，使之適應當地條件，再幫助農民組織紡紗、織布、印染等合作社。通過規模生產的方法，把布匹剪裁成標準大小的布料、床單等。這個農產品工業計畫是建立在合作的原則上，農民和工人他們共用產權、管理、勞工及利潤。這個夢很美，但因為當時政治變化，他

---

12 *WEMW*, p. 24.

們被迫放棄了這個項目。[13]

　　1927年秋天，張福良從喬治亞學成回國，雖然上述計畫流產，但他碰上了新機遇，終於可以學以致用，不僅可以在中國基督教鄉村建設運動中大展身手，而且還領導了國民政府在江西的農村服務實驗區，從而在中國鄉建史上留下了濃重的一筆。

三、「基督化鄉村社會」：作爲協進會幹事的張福良（1927-1934）

　　二十世紀初期美國興起了一場頗有聲勢的「農業傳教」（Agricultural Mission）運動。這場運動的核心人物是著名農業專家包德斐（Kenyon L. Butterfield, 1868-1936）。他先後擔任三家農學院院長，為推動美國農業進步做出了很大貢獻，被譽為「美國農業之父」。包德斐作為一名平信徒，對美國乃至世界基督教會最大的影響就是推動了教會廣泛參與鄉村生活建設。早在1911年他就出版了《鄉村教會與鄉村問題》，[14] 提出神學院、教會應和農林學院一道合作培訓鄉村教會人才，讓鄉村牧師不僅僅醫治靈魂，還能成為當地社區領袖，在建設「神的國」或「新的鄉村文明」中扮演更重要的角色。1914年，他擔任麻州農學院的院長，邀請出席第十屆留美中國學生總會會議的同學到阿姆赫斯特（Amherst）參觀校園，並為他們做講演。筆者現在無法確證，當時還在耶魯林學院讀研究生的張福良是否出席並聆聽了包德斐的講演，但出席的可能性很大，因為兩地相距不遠，交通還算方便。不管怎樣，包德斐與世界上農業人口最多的中國從此結下不解之緣，1921-1922年他來華考察農業教育，1930-1931年再次來華。

　　農業傳教士作為一類新型的傳教士在二十世紀初期到了中國，其

13　*WEMW*, pp. 35-36.

14　Kenyon L. Butterfield, *The Country Church and the Rural Problem* (Chicago, Illinois, The University of Chicago Press, 1911).

對中國的最大貢獻之一是創辦、發展了兩所著名的農科，即金陵大學農林科和嶺南大學農科，他們把美國農業高等院校教學、科研、推廣體制率先引進中國，不僅為中國農業高等教育發展、人才培育、科技推廣做出傑出貢獻，而且也推動了基督教會參與農村服務，成為近代中國鄉村建設的先驅。金陵大學農林科科長芮思婁和其他傳教士通過對教會現狀的反思和批評，根據中國國情，提出了「教會鄉村化」的主張。所謂教會鄉村化（Ruralize the Christian Church），就是要求教會把工作重心從城市轉向農村，運用農業傳教方法，使鄉村教會成為為農民服務的教會，從而贏得農民的信仰，並建立本土化的中國教會，最終實現「中華歸主」的目標。[15]

「教會鄉村化」的主張在1922年第一次全國基督教大會上得到重視。中華全國基督教協進會馬上成立了「鄉村問題及鄉村教會委員會」，負責調查、研究鄉村教會如何轉變職能，推進農業教育和鄉村服務。但1926年協進會針對鄉村教會所作的一份調查報告顯示，鄉村工作進展不大，其原因部分來自基層教會對福音仍持狹隘的理解，只注重拯救靈魂，而不注重拯救肉體；而有些教會領袖卻因為思想不解放，不能大膽地實施挽救計畫，滿足鄉村經濟、社會生活的需要。[16] 而協進會缺乏一位強有力的鄉村工作推手也是重要原因。

恰在此時，張福良在1927年秋學成歸國，由於其農業計畫受挫，遂應邀去上海擔任協進會鄉村工作幹事，協進會幸運地擁有一位幹才。這一時期也正是世界農業傳教運動大發展的時候，作為世界基督教協進會主席和青年會世界協會總幹事的穆德博士（John R. Mott），在1928年與印度的38名農業傳教士集會，號召教會發起一場世界性的鄉村運動。在同年3月24日至4月8日，世界基督教協進會在耶路撒冷召開大會，農村問題成為會議的一個熱門話題，因為參加這次大會的很多代表都是來自亞洲、非洲的後起教會，而這些地區的人民大

---

15 詳細內容請參閱拙著《中國基督教鄉村建設運動研究（1907-1950）》，第二章第二節。

16 Heng-chiu Chang, *The Rural Church of China Today: A Report of the Special Secretaries of the Committee on the Country Church and Rural Problems* (Shanghai, National Christian Council, 1926).

部分是農民。中華全國基督教協進會對這次會議非常重視，派出旅行幹事到各地教會徵求意見，就鄉村教會和鄉村工作問題還專門準備了大小兩份報告。[17]

耶路撒冷大會安排包德斐做了「基督教與鄉村文明」的演講，對鄉村事業的意義、指導原則、方法和手段等都做了闡述。他指出村莊和社區作為一個社會單位是頭等重要的，鄉村文明要在經濟和社會方面基督化，只有這些本地組織的人民以基督教的精神來工作和生活，要基督化鄉村，「不能單靠勸東一個西一個的個人歸主，也不是在社區裡建個教會就可以的，除非教會努力使整個社區過上基督化的生活。」[18] 這次大會關於鄉村工作的討論取得了很多成效，明確了教會對鄉村建設的責任，認為基督教應對此做出特別的貢獻，即「無論是在東方還是西方，鄉村工作都是傳教事業中的一個組成部分——領導建設一個鄉村文明，基督是其核心……使鄉村人民朝著有理性、有文化、高效率的方向發展，組織並領導他們，使他們分享經濟、政治和社會的解放。」[19] 耶路撒冷會議之後，鄉村建設工作就成為傳教事業的一個組成部分，大會提出的「建造基督教的鄉村文明」也成為世界各地基督教鄉村工作的哲學。

張福良雖未能親往耶路撒冷感受會議的氣氛，但該會所宣導的鄉村工作精神與他的理想不謀而合。作為新上任的鄉村幹事，從1929年1月，他奔赴南北各地，先是陪同協進會幹事羅炳生（E. C. Loben-stine），到南方參加地區退休會，目的是要喚起南方鄉村教會對鄉村工作的興趣。2月去濟南參加齊魯神學院組織的鄉村牧師會議，3月又去南方參加鄉村生活委員會準備會議，4月和5月去華中幫助當地研究鄉村教會問題。[20] 通過他對鄉村教會、神學院、教會大、中學

---

17 張坊，〈在耶路撒冷舉行之世界基督教會議〉，《中華基督教會年鑑》，第10期（1928），壹，頁15-20；*National Christian Council (NCC) Report 1927-1928*, p. 73.

18 Kenyon L. Butterfield etc. *The Christian Mission in Relation to Rural Problem*, The Jerusalem Meeting of the International Missionary Council, Vol. VI. (New York and London, 1928), pp. 9-10.

19 *The World Mission of Christianity: Message and Recommendations* (International Missionary Council, 1928), p. 55.

20 *NCC Report 1928-29*, p. 70.

校、職業學校、醫院、各類實驗區、推廣中心以及領袖訓練所的廣泛調查，他大致摸清中國基督教會在鄉村的情況。他發現儘管中國整個基督教運動的領袖和資源還算豐富，但過於分散而且沒有有效利用，「事實上，每個地區的每個宗派都或多或少是一個獨立王國」。[21] 因此，他的工作重點就是尋求一個共同的工作理念，並以此實現各教會及基督教組織在鄉建工作領域的大聯合。

為了將久未起色的基督教鄉村工作打開局面，張福良在傳教士界影響很大的《教務雜誌》發表多篇文章，一方面號召教會要敢於迎接「中國鄉村生活的挑戰」，另一方面教會界更要考慮「為鄉村工作做些什麼、如何去做」的問題。[22] 張福良從各地調查中深切地體會到鄉村牧師地位之低。一位牧師曾對張福良說他如何安排三個兒子前途：最聰明的兒子去學醫，差一點的去當老師，最不聰明的去做牧師，理由是「當牧師不需要動腦筋，至少可以做個鄉村牧師」。但張福良所期望的鄉村牧師是全才式的人物，既要在靈性方面提供持續的資源，而且還是豐富農民日常生活的仲介：「他還是一個中心點，讓基督教的表現形式鄉村化，讓鄉村生活基督化。」[23] 但究竟如何「鄉村化、基督化」呢？張福良感受到各地教會雖然對全方位的基督化農村生活抱有興趣，但卻沒有多少經驗，關鍵是缺乏這方面訓練有素的人才。因此，張福良又在《教務雜誌》發表文章，開列了經濟、社會、教育、宗教四個方面的具體工作，並希望跟「任何願意考慮一個綜合鄉村服務計畫的教會合作」。[24]

耶路撒冷會議後不久，包德斐將作為世界基督教協進會鄉村工作顧問到世界各地巡視，這時中華全國基督教協進會迅速向他發出了邀請。在張福良的周密安排下，包德斐於 1930 年 11 月開始了他的第二次中國之行。11 月 13 日包德斐經朝鮮到達瀋陽，然後從北向南，依

---

21 *WEMW*, p. 37.

22 Chang Fu-Liang, "The Challenge of China's Rural Life," *The Chinese Recorder*, Vol. 59 (April 1928), p. 210.

23 Chang Fu-Liang, "The Challenge of China's Rural Life," *The Chinese Recorder*, Vol. 59 (April 1928), pp. 205-206.

24 Chang Fu-Liang, "Program for a Rural Church," *The Chinese Recorder*, Vol. 59 (August 1928), pp. 504-505.

次到達昌黎、天津、保定、華北的一些鄉村、北平、定縣、濟南齊魯大學、南京金陵大學、上海、香港和廣州嶺南大學，1931年1月16日離開中國前往馬尼拉，2月26日返回上海，接著分別在北平、濟南、杭州參加一系列教會鄉村工作會議，直到4月23日離開中國前往日本。[25] 包德斐來華訪問期間，參加了各地大大小小的會議，發表了大量演講，向中國教會介紹了他的「鄉村牧區」的建設理念。所謂「鄉村牧區」，在包德斐看來，就是一個擁有自立教會的鄉村牧區，用本土化的方法，在一位受過訓練的牧師（不僅是個佈道者，也是社區的領袖和建造者）領導下，在平信徒和農村專家支持下，最大可能地服務社區，他認為這是把中國鄉村生活建立在基督教基礎上唯一的方法。[26] 鄉村牧區的理念引起中國教會的重視，特別是在1931年被稱為「包德斐會議」的協進會杭州大會上，鄉村牧區得到了教會廣泛的認可。

在張福良看來，耶路撒冷會議還標誌著另外一個進步，即更強調鄉村社區的「基督化」（Christianization），而不是「福音化」（Evangelization）。從詞義上講，這兩個詞並無本質區別，是同一件事情，一方自然會引起另一方。但他發現基督教在中國一百多年來的歷史說明實際並非如此。很多鄉村教會有著二十年甚至七十年的歷史，只擁有20～70位的會友，這樣的團體本應成為他們社區的「酵母」，但在某種程度上，他們卻失去了酵母的作用，對社區建設「無關痛癢」，根本起不到「基督化」當地社區的作用，他認為鄉村牧區的計畫可以解決這個弊端。他稱讚鄉村牧區是「各方面都令人滿意的教會組織」，理想的教會應該能夠吸引受過良好訓練的牧師，把全部的生命投入到服務社區的教會，並在自立的基礎上建造社區，使之成為天國在中國鄉村的一個細胞。[27] 但即便如此，張福良也提醒各教

25 Kenyon L. Butterfield, *The Rural Mission of the Church in East Asia: Report and Recommendation* (International Missionary Council, 1931), pp. 2-3.

26 Ibid, p. 344.

27 Fu Liang Chang, "Christian Leaven in Rural China," *The Chinese Recorder*, Vol. 64 (May 1933), p. 274.

會，鄉村牧區只是教會組織的一種形式，雖然是最有希望的一種，但仍需根據實踐結果進行修正。[28]

在包德斐訪華之後，很多教會特別是華北的教會，已開始按照鄉村牧區的模式開展鄉建工作，如華北公理會在通縣（潞河）成立「潞河鄉村服務部」，河北美以美會在昌黎教區的安各莊、中華基督教會在南京附近的淳化鎮等多達幾十處。在張福良等教會領袖的積極籌畫下，華北公理會、長老會、美以美會等根據鄉村牧區的理念組成了華北基督教農村事業促進會，隨後華東、華中、江西也都成立類似的聯合組織，極大地改善了過去教會各自為政的局面。張福良根據這些實踐的結果，也修正了自己過去對牧師「全才式」的不合理要求，他強調在一個或幾個牧區內合作的必要性：「鄉村教會雖有領袖專家為之指導，然實際推行某項工作時，或試辦某項工作時，非賴全體教會領袖充分彼此了解之同情，及分工合作之制度，無以見功！」因此，他提倡不但教會與學校，即教會與教會之間，各專家對於進行方法，都應採取分工合作制度，各展所長，在經驗上彼此交換意見，在程式上有一致推進之效，而免重複之弊。[29] 正是在各地鄉村牧區實踐的基礎上，教會發現包德斐的鄉村牧區以「市鎮教會」為中心的做法並不符合中國農民的習慣，因此在1935年潞河鄉村服務部召開的鄉村工作領袖訓練會議上把它修改為以「村莊教會」為中心，「牧區」也不是市鎮為中心的地區，而是一個範圍更大的區域。[30]

1930年基督教協進會發起的「五年奮興佈道運動」（簡稱「五運」），又為張福良推進教會的鄉建運動提供了前所未有的契機，使之逐漸達到鼎盛時期。「五運」主要目標在於基督徒「量的增加和質的加深」，希望在五年之內，使現有信徒人數至少增加一倍，以宗教

28　Ibid, p. 278.

29　張福良，〈一年來的鄉村建設運動概觀〉，《金陵神學志》，第14卷第7、8期合刊（鄉村教會專號，1932年9-10月），頁18。

30　具體見 *A Report of the North China Institute for Supervisors of Rural Work*, held under the auspices of the North China Christian Rural Service Union, at the Lu Ho Rural Service Center, Tunghsien, Hopei, China, March 20-April 3, 1935, p. 1.

教育、基督化家庭、識字運動、擴大佈道、受託主義、青年事業為六大工作計畫。「五運」原定於1930年1月開始,後因種種原因,展期舉行。[31]「五運」的六大計畫並不分城市和農村,也沒有針對廣大農村地區的工作計畫,但由於大部分信徒都在農村,農村理所當然成為工作的重點區域。負責「五運」的幹事中有兩位對鄉村工作興趣濃厚,即張福良與孫恩三,在他們的宣導和努力下,鄉村建設工作也就成為五運的重要內容。張福良認為,「五運」就是對教牧人員「到鄉村去」的偉大呼召;解決中國鄉村問題,對青年人,不論是基督徒還是非基督徒,都是極好的「挑戰」,是「冒險、愛國主義和中國基督化的青年運動」,因此,「五運」應該接受中國鄉村生活的挑戰,「應該對全國的鄉村建設運動做出基督教的貢獻」。[32] 協進會總幹事誠靜怡認為,全國農村需要改革的地方千頭萬緒,這正好造就了教會鄉村工作的「絕好機會」。[33] 於是「五運」六大工作計畫中的識字運動就成為「五運」的重要突破口,而且成績顯著。

對教會而言,識字不僅是人們增加知識的一種工具,也有宗教教育的目的,教會希望教友都能閱讀《聖經》。據1922年《中華歸主》調查的結果,男性基督徒文盲率為40%,女性文盲率為60%,基督徒的識字情況要比全國平均好些,但仍有一半的信徒是文盲,農村信徒文盲率還要高些。因此,在張福良看來,「基督徒一天不識字,就一天不易在宗教生活上求進步,也不易對外為基督發光,結出領人信主的善果。」這樣就不可能完成「五運」基督徒人數倍增的目標。另外,張福良從保定公理會和其他辦理平教的實驗中,許多非基督徒因為進教會所辦的平民學校,與基督徒多有來往,也漸漸明白基督教的內容,因此加入教會;而這些人意志和才力大半高出常人一等,進教時對於基督教的意義又認識的比較明確,對宗教的知識又能一天比

---

31 朱立德,〈兩年來的中華全國基督教協進會〉,《中華基督教會年鑑》,第11期(1929-1930),壹,頁11-12。

32 F. L. Chang, "Go to the Country," *The Chinese Recorder*, Vol. 61 (January 1930), pp. 17-18.

33 誠靜怡,〈第九屆大會隨感錄〉,《中華歸主》,第137期(1933年6月1日),頁4。

一天進步，因而也就能領到別人信基督教，所以，教友識字運動不但
是「一種教導信徒服務社會的運動，也是一種最好的領人信主的運
動」。[34] 因此，張福良把「一個識字並能閱讀聖經的教會應當成為
五年奮興運動中的首要目標」。[35] 當時平教會以及出版界編寫了不少
適合農民閱讀的識字課本，但其內容並非基於信仰耶穌的立場。為了
適合教會識字運動的需要，張福良不僅組織了「宗教讀物委員會」，
還親自編寫了兩種宗教讀物，一是《為什麼做基督徒》，還有一本
《為什麼加入教會》，都是用淺顯的文字寫成的小故事，採用農村中
有普遍性的事實作為背景，蘊藏著改進鄉村生活的願望，引導讀者探
求基督真理。[36] 這兩本書從1930年發行，一直到1938年仍不斷再
版，可見極受歡迎。

為加強各教會識字運動經驗的交流推廣，在張福良的提議下，協
進會1930年4月在定縣召集全國基督教識字運動研究會。這次會議本
預定30人與會，但到達者多達90餘人，來自11個省、9個宗派的教
會。[37] 到1933年4月，在定縣又召開了全國第二次識字運動，主題是
「基督教對鄉村建設應當有何貢獻」，會議原擬代表以80人為限，
但實際到會人數186名，來自14個省份、18個教會團體，其中有150
名中國人，36名外國傳教士，很多代表都是教會的高層領導。[38] 會議
代表的高層次和廣泛性充分說明這時教會對鄉村建設的熱情和重視，
加上當時政府與社會都予以提倡，國人興趣也很濃厚，識字運動要比
「五運」其他五項工作的推行順利得多，參與教會之多、範圍之廣、
規模之大、影響之深，是教會以往任何運動所不及的。雖然張福良對
識字運動的成效表示「差堪告慰」，[39] 實際上成績最顯著。就像晏陽

---

34 張福良，〈教友識字運動的初步工作〉，《興華》，第27期（1930），頁12-16。

35 F. L. Chang, "Religious Education and the Rural Church," *The Chinese Recorder*, Vol. 61 (January 1930), pp. 21-22.

36 張福良，《為什麼做基督徒》（上海：廣學會，1938年10月），第9版。

37 張福良，〈民國十九年的識字運動〉，《中華基督教會年鑑》，第11期（1929-1930），肆，頁87。

38 詳見 *The Church and Rural Reconstruction: A Symposium on the Tinghsien Rural Institute 1933* (Shanghai, Christian Literature Society, 1933)。

39 張福良，〈民國十九年的識字運動〉，《中華基督教會年鑑》，第11期（1929-1930），肆，頁86。

初領導的平教會的發展軌跡一樣，基督教會大規模的鄉建工作也是從識字－鄉村教育入手，逐漸擴展到生計、合作、衛生、娛樂等方面，成為綜合性的鄉村建設。

這次會議一年之後，也正是在基督教鄉村建設漸趨達到頂峰時，張福良辭去協進會鄉村幹事，被國民政府經濟委員會聘到江西，負責全省的農村服務實驗區。縱觀他擔任幹事的七年，他以熱情、視野與才幹為協進會增添了活力，恰當地運用了世界農業傳教運動的理念與資源，抓住「五運」所帶來的前所未有的機會，終於讓基督教鄉建從涓涓溪流匯成大河，在全國鄉村建設潮流中佔有一席之地。「基督化鄉村社會」雖然不是他首先提出，但卻是他擔任協進會幹事期間堅信且努力去踐行的目標，這些都讓基督教鄉建成為中國當時鄉建運動中的一個富有特色的一部分。如果把他在協進會的鄉建工作與他後來在江西的工作相比，前者就顯得更與眾不同了。

四、從宗教界到政治界：張福良在江西的實踐

中國基督教的鄉建運動不僅注重教會、教會團體之間的合作，而且還特別注重與政府、教會外鄉建團體的合作，因為他們意識到自己的力量總歸有限，而鄉村需要無限，必須聯合一切力量來發展鄉村，這是基督教鄉建實踐中非常強調的一個原則。在教會與政府合作的案例中，江西黎川是基督教鄉村建設數個實驗區中影響最大的一個，它是全國基督教協進會與中央、地方政府直接合作的產物。張福良正是因為黎川實驗區的突出表現，才被國民政府經濟委員會借調到江西，負責省政府舉辦的鄉村建設，他的身分也從基督教會的鄉村幹事一躍變為政府專員。身分轉變也影響到他對鄉村建設理念的思考。本節結合他在江西的鄉建經歷對此做一考察。

1931年11月，中共在江西瑞金成立了蘇維埃共和國，對閩贛交界地區的教會而言，共產主義成為實實在在的「挑戰」，一些傳教士被迫離開。在國民政府先後發動了五次圍剿中共的戰鬥後，1933年

中共從江西撤出。這時，無論是政府還是教會，都在想把飽受戰火摧殘的江西鄉村進行徹底的變革復興。當時蔣介石的行營設在南昌，並在牯嶺租了南昌美以美會的房子。蔣氏夫婦都是美以美會的教友，宋美齡和美國傳教士長孫維廉（William Richard Johnson）尤為熟悉，宋希望長孫維廉能為江西籌畫一個大規模的鄉村建設計畫。後來，宋美齡得知政府正準備撥款實施這樣一個計畫，她就希望教會的計畫做得小一些，她可以從經費上資助。[40] 長孫維廉很快把這個消息傳達給美以美會在上海的主教，建議教會儘快做出反應。[41] 之後不久，他又收到宋美齡信，宋對他有興趣改善江西農業表示讚賞，並說「蔣委員長和我對鄉村建設都很感興趣，如果您能仔細研究教會如何才能幫助政府這項工作，我們將會非常高興，因為我們都相信，教會一定能對江西的鄉村建設有明確的貢獻。」[42]

此消息通過漢口聖公會吳德施主教（Logan Roots）很快傳到中華全國基督教協進會，協進會立即開會商討如何回應。先由吳德施和協進主席給宋美齡回信表示對此有興趣，然後派張福良到南京諮詢金陵大學農學院院長謝家聲及洛夫（Harry H. Love），後去南昌和牯嶺諮詢長孫維廉和其他傳教士。在牯嶺期間張福良拜訪了宋美齡、宋子文、孫科。張福良一開始對基督徒能對政府做點什麼並不熱心，等他見了宋美齡等人後，才感受到「宋的誠意，認為我們必須要做點什麼」。協進會為慎重起見，在隨後兩週裡又派副總幹事羅炳生北上濟南和北平，同那裡的教會團體協商。羅發現濟南和北平的意見一致，都認為「此邀請是一個不能忽視的挑戰」，同時也考慮了兩個隨之而來的危險：一是基督教團體可能會和政府關係太密切；第二，教會可能會表現為南京政府經濟理論的代表。華北各代表中，燕京大學司徒雷登和齊魯大學張伯懷最熱心，而華北基督教農村事業促進會的核心

---

40 *William R. Johnson to Bishop Herbert Welch* (June 9, 1933), pp. 3-4.

41 Ibid, p. 6.

42 *Mme. Chiang Kai-shek to W. R. Johnson* (June 10, 1933), pp. 1. RG06-14-241.

人物，也是富有鄉村建設經驗的胡本德卻極為審慎。[43]

　　到9月19日，協進會臨時委員會討論了宋的建議和長孫維廉的計畫，最後形成八條意見：應該做這件事；應由獨立的機構來實施；應保持濃厚的基督教氣氛；如有可能，不用政府的補貼；要有確定的人員；要事先籌募經費；嚴格限定範圍；計畫一開始不要太大。[44] 但仍有一個主要問題沒有解決，即如何處理教會與政府的關係，似乎讓協進會感到頗為棘手：如果教會接受政府的資助，福音工作是否會受到影響；如果不接受資助，教會能否有能力支持這個項目。而且更有趣的是，協進會還非常擔心另外一個問題，「用什麼樣的方法，才能防止人們把教會的立場與共產主義的經濟理論聯繫起來呢？」最後，吳德施提出教會與政府之間應實行「合作式的獨立」（cooperative independence）政策，在和諧的工作關係中教會應保持主動權和行動自由。[45] 臨時委員會派張福良和富有鄉村工作經驗的福建公理會傳教士牧恩波（G. W. Shepherd）到江西進行為期兩週的調查，為制定工作計畫做準備。

　　10月31日，協進會在南昌開會，會議成立「江西基督教農村服務聯合會」，蔣介石夫婦和一些省府官員都參加了。聯合會成員有美以美會、聖公會、青年會、美以美女部會、中華基督教會閩北大會，由長孫維廉擔任聯合會主席，聘牧恩波任總幹事，張福良協助主持。會議要求協進會支持新成立的聯合會，發起一個鄉村建設項目，如果可能，可以安排在曾由共產黨統治過的地區，範圍不要太大，可能只在一個縣的一個區進行。蔣和宋在這次會上答應認捐一半經費。[46] 此後，牧恩波跟著國民黨軍隊終於到達江西內陸，他認為閩贛交界處、靠近邵武的黎川正是合適的地點，實驗村莊定在第四區。他通過在

43　James C. Thomson Jr., *While China Faced West: American Reformers in Nationalist China, 1928-1937* (Cambridge: Harvard University Press, 1969), p. 67. 後面簡稱 *WCFW*。

44　*WCFW*, p. 68.

45　*WCFW*, p. 69.

46　"Christian Rural Project in Kiangsi," *Chinese Recorder* (Vol. 65, No. 1, January 1934), pp. 61-62.

《教務雜誌》做宣傳，招募受過農業、醫藥衛生、鄉村工業、組織和宗教教育方面的基督徒人才。[47] 但招聘到合適的人員並非容易。1934年9月，人員基本到齊，各公私機構包括省、縣政府也給予密切合作。國民政府經濟委員會給予5,000元用於購置基本設備，平教會派四人幫助啟動教育事業，黎川基督教鄉建工作正式開始。[48]

　　至此，從宋美齡對長孫維廉的請求開始，協進會費了將近四個月的時間才做出明確的回應，開始具體的組織運作，教會反應的時間不可謂不長。究其原因，主要是政府的邀請對教會而言是不曾預料到的。協進會對如何擺正教會和政府關係頗費斟酌，雖然從一開始就不可避免和政治沾邊，但教會還是覺得遠離政治為好，採取所謂「合作式的獨立」模式，盡可能保持它是基督教的事業。另外，教會對自己是否有能力發起這樣一個規模的專案有很多保留。教會從事鄉建工作雖然至少已有十年歷史，但也體會到工作的艱巨性。羅炳生就說，如果認為教會現在可以從事一項大規模的鄉建工作是非常愚蠢的。[49] 很顯然，教會非常清楚自己的局限，但政府的熱情邀請也是不可拒絕的，因為這將影響到將來兩者之間的關係，更何況這個邀請也給了教會一個難得的機遇，如同張福良在1933年的一封聖誕信中所說：「對這個挑戰的成功回應將振興我們的基督宗教，而且也為充滿理想、冒險和愛國精神的年輕人指明了服務國家的方向，同時希望在鄉村建設中，教會能找到應對共產主義挑戰的明確具體的答案。」[50]

　　與此同時，宋子文所領導的國民政府經濟委員會在江西的鄉村建設計畫也正在緊鑼密鼓地進行。1933年11月，國聯三名技術專家應經濟委員會之邀到江西調查研究，隨後提出了建議報告。經委會除了對土地問題的建議表示尚需研究外，其餘全部採納。國民政府決定從

---

47 "Christian Rural Project in Kiangsi," *The Chinese Recorder* (Vol. 65, No. 1, January 1934), p. 62.

48 Hugh W. Hubbard, "Kiangsi Christian Rural Service Union", *NCC Report, 1933-1935*, pp. 113-114.

49 *Lobenstine to Shepherd* (August 28, 1933), 引自 *James C. Thomson Jr.*, p. 70.

50 Chang Fu-liang, *Christmas letter* (Nov. 23, 1933), 引自 *WCMW.*, p. 74.

美國棉麥貸款中拿出190萬元用於這一建設計畫。[51] 1934年4月，根據這個計畫，江西省政府為此專門成立省衛生委員會和農業研究院，聘請專家主持工作。另外，經濟委員會準備在江西建設十個農村服務中心，成立江西農村服務區管理處，請求協進會借調張福良來擔任專員。張福良作為協進會的鄉村工作幹事，其能力與成績有目共睹，對整個教會來說，他們肯定不願意失去這樣一名傑出的領袖，對江西基督教鄉村建設而言也是重大損失，牧恩波失去了一個能幹的同事。但協進會更看重與政府的友好合作，最後批准張的調動。張福良似乎也沒有選擇，只能走馬上任，從教會工作人員轉身成為政府工作人員。他在多年後的自傳中寫道，江西省衛生委員會和農業研究院的設立和職能都有省政府的法律根據，而江西農村服務處則是中央政府全國經濟委員會的一個臨時機構，其組織很大程度上都取決於當時負責人的想法。[52] 言下之意，他或許認為自己不過是臨時客串一下政府人員的身分。但無論是否臨時機構，他現在是為政府服務，已踏上政治之路，無論是具體建設方法還是最終目標，跟他過去領導教會鄉建相比有很大不同。

張福良首先在江西全省選了十處鄉村來設立服務中心，其標準是人口多的鄉村地區，遠離土匪、交通方便、有廟宇家祠等公共建築，還有比較開明的地方領袖。為更有效發揮服務中心的功能，他們以「區」為單位，大概是一個縣的四分或五分之一。[53] 工作的內容跟當時流行的鄉建工作並無區別，大致是教育、農業、衛生、合作和家庭手工業，包括棉花工業。農村服務工作的標的就是針對貧愚弱散四種病態，實施「管教養衛」措施：以「管」理其「散」，而求其能自治，以「教」啟其「愚」，而求其能自覺，以「養」救其貧，而求其能自給，以「衛」扶其弱，而求其能自衛，以達到自強不息之境地。

---

51 詳見 Head Office of Kiangsi Rural Welfare Centers of National Economy Council: *Rural Reconstruction in Kiangsi* (Nanchang, June 1935), pp. 1-2.

52 *WEMW*, p. 43.

53 *WEMW*, p. 47.

張福良在前兩年所使用的工作方法主要是教育與引導，用他自己的話說就是「順從農民興趣之自然傾向，委婉引導農民自助互助之精神，使能自力更生，自謀解決農村各問題，避免賑濟與包辦式消極方法」。但這種以友愛、溫和的路線因為「農民之保守心理以及地方惡勢力之阻礙，一切改進工作，推行仍多困難，而進度亦見迂緩」。[54] 因此，服務中心從一開始也適當地運用政治力量去推行工作。

張福良強調創設服務區的旨趣是「協助政府，服務農民，使政治與服務打成一片」。[55] 他認為管理處雖然是個中央機關，但是在江西的農村工作，並不是寄生在政府之外的一種事業，其要旨是輔助當地的政府，推行「管教養衛」的政策，只有「政治與服務相輔相行，相得益彰，農村建設才有光明燦爛的前途」。[56] 張福良在江西農村服務管理處的兩年從政經歷中體會到，有些事情單靠教育、勸說是做不成的，政治上的威權是必須的。他以政府在控制鴉片、種痘和義務教育方面為例，說明政治已顯示出它的效率。[57] 曾擔任江浙基督教鄉村服務聯合會幹事的施中一也應邀來到服務區工作，根據他一年的經驗，也認為在江西用政治的力量來推進建設工作，可以免許多圈子，原因是雖然有許多事業確與大多數人有福利相關，但因為風俗習慣及自私觀念所阻撓，因此無法推行，如種痘可防天花，卻去迷信天花姑娘，修堤原為保全大家的生命財產，卻互相推諉。倘使全用政治力量來推進，則一定可以減少若干時間達到相當的階段。[58]

當然，這裡張福良所談的「政治」，不過是指運用強制性的行政手段，並非涉及到「政黨理念」、「政治改造」或「政治手段」等通常意義上的政治行為。當時張福良面臨的真正的政治問題是土地所有權，而國民政府並不想從根本上觸動這個問題。一位西方觀察家喬

---

54 張福良，〈江西農村服務區概況及其改進方針〉，《地方政治》，第 5 卷第 2 期（1941），頁 17-19。

55 張福良，〈求仁得仁〉，《農村服務通訊》，第 4 期（1935），頁 2。

56 張福良，〈政治與服務〉，《農村服務通訊》，第 2 期（1935），頁 2。

57 Fu-liang Chang, "Reconstruction Rural Life in China," *The Christian Rural Fellowship Bulletin* (Number 23, June 1937), p. 3.

58 施中一，〈江西農村工作的第一年〉，《消息》，第 9 卷第 1 期（1936 年 1 月），頁 47-48。

治‧泰勒（George E. Taylor）在1935年訪問江西後，警告國民政府在土地問題上的不作為，「這樣的忽視意味著引起共產主義的真正原因還沒有觸及」，他認為國民政府害怕土地改革會疏離士紳階層。泰勒認為這樣做是很危險的，「一個農業國家如果不為千百萬食不果腹的農民提供土地，那麼，共產主義雖然可能沒有希望，但引起共產主義的原因卻很難消失。」[59] 張福良當然在這方面也無能為力，他還從技術層面解釋了政府無法進行土改的原因。他認為土地改革之前必須先進行測量，而這需要一筆很大的經費，全省需要1,100萬，而這在當時是無法支付的。[60] 僅此一點，這意味著江西乃至全國性的鄉建運動都不能有根本性的突破。

到1936年7月，江西省政府和農村服務管理處決定實施三年計畫，其核心內容就是服務區幹事兼區長。張福良認為這是一個很理想的安排，因為服務區幹事就可以成為服務區與當地縣政府的橋樑，用服務區的技術知識來服務政府。但他發現縣政府對此態度不一，有的認為服務區是協助縣政府推行政令，表示充分好感；有的誤認為服務區奪取或割裂政府權益，以致步調不同而生摩擦；也有以冷靜態度、漠不相關，似非其事者。第一種似乎無須兼區政府，第二種即使兼了區政府也無效，第三者兼猶未兼。總之，張福良認為這是一把雙刃劍，服務區幹事兼秉區政，有時能幫助工作、排除障礙，有時亦難貫徹，易起糾紛，這樣的政治路線也不能保證暢行無阻。但張福良還是認為這種安排是利大於弊，其功效要取決於省長與縣長合作的意願、態度。[61]

但是，由基督教在黎川推行的農村服務實驗區對是否利用政治卻一直猶豫不決。燕京大學徐寶謙在接手黎川實驗區一開始對此很謹

---

59 George E. Tailor, "Reconstruction after Revolution: Kiangsi Province and the Chinese Nation," *Pacific Affairs* (Sept. 1935), p. 311. 引自 *WCFW*, p. 113.

60 Chang Fu-liang, *New Life Centers in Rural Kiangsi*, Special Bulletin Number Two (Head Office of Kiangsi Rural Welfare Centers, National Economic Council, May 1936), p. 19.

61 *WEMW*, pp. 65-66. 張福良，〈江西農村服務區概況及其改進方針〉，《地方政治》，第5卷第2期（1941），頁17-19。

慎，因為他看到利用政治帶來的流弊也很多。他認為要利用政治力量改造農村，必須要有兩個先決條件：運用政治者必須得人；政治本身必須先經徹底改革。[62] 然而，黎川所得的經驗逐漸讓他改變了想法，感到沒有政治力量，工作不易推廣，種種困難使他最終改變了對政治和利用政治的看法。他認為基督教既「以改造整個生活相號召，則政治當然包括在內。不但如此，政治對於人生，處處有關係。設政治不清，則整個人生的改善，殆將成為不可能。根據基督的精神，去澄清政治，並使政治成為建設的勢力，正是吾儕基督徒的責任。」[63] 徐寶謙強調黎川實驗區的最後目的是在縣單位的建設，走入政治途徑，是「當然的步驟，應有的手續，決不是什麼宗旨的改變。」[64] 作為基督教黎川實驗區董事會成員的張福良對教會參與政治也持肯定的態度，主張教會與政府合作，因為「政治的目的也是謀人民的福利，政府正需要大批熱心服務的人到鄉間去從事下層工作，以發揮政治的效能，所以教會應該切實與政府合作。」「以政治的力量，去推動各種事業，以宗教的熱忱去感化農民。兩者互相為用，工作進行就得事半功倍了。」[65] 因此，徐寶謙最終所確定的實驗區工作方法就是宗教、科學、教育與政治的結合。但實際操作中卻又難度極大，尤其是黎川作為基督教會支持的實驗區，其宗教建設方面一直很薄弱，飽受協進會及教會的批評。[66]

張福良在江西領導鄉建的幾年，也正是國難日重、民族存亡危機之秋，因此，他對鄉建目標的定位不僅僅是復興農村，更要復興民族。他在服務區創辦的《農村服務通訊》發表了多篇文章或講話，直接把鄉村服務事業看成是「建國大業」，[67] 並反覆敘說他對鄉建最終

---

62 徐寶謙，〈黎川服務日記〉，《真理與生命》，第9卷第5期（1935年10月），頁289-290。

63 徐寶謙，〈黎川實驗區的理論與實際〉，《中國基督教會年鑑》，第13期（1934-1936），頁101。

64 徐寶謙，〈黎川實驗區的理論與實際〉，《中國基督教會年鑑》，第13期（1934-1936），頁102。

65 張福良，〈目前教會從事農村工作應取的方針〉，《中華歸主》，第160期（1935年11月1日），頁4。

66 NCC Minutes, Ad-Interim, Jan. 19, 1937. *WCFW*, p. 119.

67 張福良，〈卷首語〉，《農村服務通訊》，第1期（1935），頁2。

目標的理解「當然是復興民族」。[68] 抗戰期間他曾如此表述鄉村服務的目標是：「實現農民富足、高尚、健康、安樂之生活，從農民本身生活之改善，進而謀社會之改進，民族之復興」。[69]

無論是復興農村還是復興民族，都不是一蹴而就。不幸的是，江西農村服務區的「三年計畫」僅僅實施一年之後，中日戰爭就全面爆發，不僅華北的鄉村建設工作受到很大影響，到 1939 年，由於人員、經費等條件所限，江西的鄉建工作也限於停頓狀態，張福良和服務區的工作重點轉向難民救護，一直到 1945 年早期，張福良離開江西去重慶，擔任聯合救濟會副會長，後又於 1945 年 2 月接任工合總幹事。張福良在江西的鄉建工作就這樣結束了。

五、結語：再思信仰、福音與社會關懷的關係

以上大致勾勒了張福良在基督教協進會和江西的鄉建實踐經歷。他在這前後兩個時期對鄉建的最終目標以及路線方法的表述有明顯差異：前者從「鄉村牧區」入手，以「基督化鄉村社會」為最終目標，後者強調恰當「運用政治」，即以行政手段推動鄉村建設，以「救亡圖存」、「民族復興」為標的。這些表述差異，在張福良的身分轉換中可以得到合理的解釋：他擔任協進會幹事自然會以基督教的發展為最終目標，而在江西他作為政府專員，秉承政教分離，不宜再提教會建設，加之當時國難日重，應當以國家、民族復興為最高目標。前者代表了中國基督教界鄉建的特別追求，有神聖性、宗教的一面，當然也包括了救國救民、世俗的一面，但強調以「基督化」為最後目標，無可厚非；而後者則是當時日本侵華背景下參與鄉建的當時公私各家各派的共同心聲，省略宗教目標是理所當然。當然，雖然張福良在前後兩個階段對最高目標的表述有所差異，但建設新農村、改善民生的

---

68 張福良，〈農村工作的大聯合〉，《農村服務通訊》，第 9 期（1936），頁 2。
69 張福良，〈江西農村服務區概況及其改進方針〉，《地方政治》，第 5 卷第 2 期（1941），頁 17-19。

基本目標卻從未改變。

有意思的是，作為基督徒張福良在領導基督教鄉建時，處處以《聖經》為依據，以耶穌為模範，作為其信仰和力量的源泉；而他在領導江西鄉建時，亦多次談及鄉建所需要的精神信仰，卻不再提及耶穌，偶爾提及，也是把耶穌跟大禹、伊尹、釋迦牟尼、甘地等歷史人物相提並論，他讚賞這些大人物勇於去「救人類、救世界」，能為「愛」和「善」而犧牲自己，這就是他理解的「宗教的精神」。[70]他曾給江西的同工們解釋他對信仰的理解：「有人認為信仰是指宗教而說的，實則每個人對任何事都一定要有信仰，沒有信仰就沒有熱力，沒有熱力，就不能有成功。從事農村事業，須有信仰，才能有建樹。」他坦誠他的五條信仰（相信人生是樂觀；相信中華民族能復興；相信農村服務是需要的；相信同工人格高尚；相信農村工作前途），[71]唯獨不再像以前那樣談其堅信的基督教信仰。

張福良一生信仰虔誠。他曾在自傳中寫道：「我經常感到有一隻看不見的手指示一個人的命運。我承認我的生命中有這種看不見的力量或意識，我願意將他歸於上帝。」[72]但為何江西時期的張福良不再像以前把他從事鄉建工作的動力歸於耶穌基督呢？同為基督徒的晏陽初等也有類似的表現，他們只有在面對教會、基督徒講話時才談及教會立場、耶穌精神。這其中固然有不同聽眾需要有不同的講演策略問題，但後面是否也暗含了基督教信仰、福音與社會關懷之間存在緊張關係的問題呢？

張福良從事鄉建的最初動機當然是因為他是基督徒，他認為他應該以耶穌為榜樣，以他的犧牲、服務精神來關懷社會。他說，「與其說耶穌是個傳佈福音的人，不如說他是個實際的社會改造家。我們要發揚基督的精神、主義，就非以基督一生的言行為標準，非實行農村

---

70 張福良，〈宗教的精神〉，《農村服務通訊》，第14期（1936），頁3。
71 張福良，〈信仰〉，《農村服務通訊》，第17期（1936），頁3-4。
72 *WEMW*, Preface.

服務不可。」[73] 但反過來，由此而發生的社會關懷是否必須體現出基督教的福音特徵呢？就鄉建運動而言，它是否應該成為一場引人信主、教會自立的運動呢？對這個問題，教會內有不同的回答。基要派認為只有傳福音才是基督徒的使命，根本就不相信通過社會服務或改良就能實現天國，因此也反對任何表達社會關懷的世俗性改良。而即使支援鄉建工作的教會人士，以三十年代來華的平信徒調查團為例，他們認為「因為是基督徒，所以才去做農村工作」完全合乎耶穌的精神，但反過來說，「農村事業可以成為引人入教的工具，或成為使教會自養的方法」，如果因為這個理由而去從事農村事業，他們認為這就失去了意義，因為這類動機根本上與耶穌所說的「你既然將這些事做在我兄弟中最小的一個身上——那就是在我的身上了」不合。[74] 因此，他們極力反對在鄉建工作上附加直接傳福音的功能。

　　事實上，張福良、徐寶謙等發現鄉建實踐也很難直接實現其傳福音的價值。這一點連最早在中國提倡鄉村建設的前金陵大學農林科科長芮思婁在1947年遠東之行後，也感到是個難題：「我們怎樣才能把農村改良和宗教意識的培育、禮拜統合在一起呢？很多農民是基督徒，但有多少基督徒農民能夠理解，他們的農耕生活都是上帝之手在做工呢？又有多少農民在日常生活中的經驗能把他們引向理解、體驗上帝的存在呢？」[75] 在基督教鄉建運動中，除識字運動直接帶來信徒效果較為明顯外，整體上看不出基督教鄉建運動在推進「鄉村歸主」方面有何明顯貢獻。而身為基督徒的晏陽初從事平教運動，從來都是以社會為立場，而不標榜其福音的意義，然而，這在張福良看來，他的努力卻「處處表現出基督精神」，反而獲得社會的讚賞。[76] 從張福良、晏陽初等基督徒豐富多姿的鄉建經歷中可以發現，雖然他們從事

---

73 張福良，〈目前教會從事鄉村工作應取的方針〉，《中華歸主》，第160期（1935年11月1日）。

74 美國平信徒調查團編，徐寶謙、繆秋笙、范定九譯，《宣教事業平議》（商務印書館1933年版），頁191。

75 Frank Wilson Price, *The Rural Church in China: A Survey* (New York, Agricultural Missions, Inc., 1948), p. 241.

76 張福良，〈農村教會〉，《中華基督教會年鑑》，第12期（1933），頁63。

鄉建的最終目標可能不太一樣，但他們所表現出的社會關懷卻都是信仰基督教的自然結果。而社會關懷實踐卻未必是通向基督教信仰的直接橋樑，或者說使人皈依基督教，並非是社會關懷所追求的唯一目標。當然，兩者之間並非是完全對立的關係，社會關懷與基督教信仰在理念上存在很多共通性。但在類似鄉建的社會關懷中，兩者之間究竟應該是怎樣的一個平衡關係？這不僅是個神學理論問題，更是一個實踐的問題，不僅在當時，即使是現在仍是值得教會和社會關注的話題。

大米與信仰：戰後中華基督教會汕頭區會的重建及困境（1945-1949）[*]

胡衛清

摘要

抗戰勝利後，在面臨國家經濟瀕於崩潰、潮汕地方自然災害不斷的情況下，中華基督教會汕頭區會開始修復受損教堂、恢復相關教會和相關機構的正常運作。儘管汕頭區會自身也作出不少努力，力圖逐步實現自養，不過很明顯，區會財政工作的重點是爭取來自海外的資源，尤其是宣道會的撥款，表現出對宣道會的高度依賴。從基層堂會的情況看，汕頭區會不僅面臨嚴重的財政危機，更面臨深刻的精神危機。隨著各種救濟和補助管道的不斷開闢，在戰時及戰後，基層堂會向教會中樞中請款項成為常態，在各堂會普遍「哭窮」聲音的背後，實際包含鮮明的利益企圖。與此同時，教牧人員為了獲取職位，獲得更多的米薪而不擇手段，教牧之間、教牧與教友之間、教牧與教會中樞之間關係惡化，明顯表現出離心離德的趨向，教牧職位的神聖性被大大弱化。精神層面的危機不僅削弱了教會重建的基礎，也深刻影響到潮汕以後教會的發展。

關鍵詞：英國長老會、中華基督教會汕頭區會、戰後重建、財政危機

---

[*] 本文研究得到汕頭大學文學院基督教研究中心的項目資助（專案編號CCSRF1315-C），謹此致謝。

抗戰勝利後中華基督教會嶺東大會汕頭區會開始恢復和重建進程。因僻處華南一隅，該會受國共內戰的直接影響並不大，但國家整體經濟狀況的惡化和潮汕地區持續不斷的自然災害還是對該會的戰後重建產生了很大的影響。不過，更深刻的危機來自教會內部，儘管該會一直標榜自立，但是此時教會重建的動力和資源究竟是源出自身，還是基本仰賴差會支援，這個問題成為困擾嶺東大會發展的難題。本文主要從財政方面考察戰後該會的恢復、重建及其所遭遇的困境。

一、恢復與重建

　　英國長老會（Presbyterian Church of England）1843年組織大會（Synod），決定成立海外宣道委員會（Foreign Mission Committee）。1847年，英國長老會海外宣道委員會派遣教士進入中國，1856年進入潮汕地區。英國長老會海外宣道委員會（以下簡稱宣道會）在海外宣教區通稱英國長老會差會（English Presbyterian Mission，簡稱EPM），教士會為英國長老會差會在傳教總站設立的傳教管理機構，參加者為英國長老會差會傳教士，英國長老會差會在廣東潮汕地區先後設有汕頭教士會（Swatow Mission Council）、客家教士會（Hakka Mission Council）。1881年英國長老會差會在潮汕成立本土教會「潮惠長老大會」。1900年，五經富成立長老大會，與汕頭大會並立，潮惠長老大會遂改名為潮惠長老總會，1914年，該會參加長老宗合一運動，改名嶺東長老大會，下設汕頭中會和五經富中會。1927年，該會參加中華全國基督教會，改名為中華基督教會嶺東大會，前述兩中會分別改名為汕頭區會、五經富區會。區會下設多個機構，其中財政部專門負責區會的財政預算、收支等事項。1943年上述汕頭教士會和客家教士會合併為嶺東教士會（Lingtung Mission Council）。

　　1945年8月日本投降後，汕頭區會的幹事林之純由五經富趕回汕

頭，查報損失，接收教產，巡慰教友，開始復員準備工作。[1] 稍後，傳教士也陸續從英倫和澳洲等地返回汕頭和五經富。最早重返汕頭的傳教士是華河力（H. F. Wallace）和歐陽德（R. A. Elder），[2] 後來兩人又到府城等地巡視。[3] 從華河力等人考察的情況看，在所有傳教站中，只有揭陽的五經富基本沒有遭受損失，其他各站包括汕尾在內都有程度不同的損失。汕頭區會88個堂會中有85個曾遭遇過時間長短不一的淪陷之苦，其中有8間教堂完全被毀，8間嚴重受損。[4] 汕頭作為嶺東大會的中樞所在，該會所屬聿懷中學受損嚴重，[5] 福音醫院也要花費鉅款修復才能使用。[6] 潮安傳教站和汕尾傳教站也都受到程度不同的損毀。[7] 恢復各種損毀的教會建築耗資巨大，這自然會對戰後的教會自立產生巨大的影響。

當時宣道會對於包括中國在內的各教區的恢復重建有整體的考慮和計畫，它通過聯合呼籲基金（United Appeal Fund）首次作出的有關差會的損失預算是71,000英鎊，後來被削減為60,000英鎊。最初包括撥給中國教會的10,000英鎊重建費用和20,000英鎊房產的修復費用。按照當時1英鎊兌換港幣16元的匯率，英國長老會在華（臺灣不包括在內）的重建和房屋修理費應為港幣48萬元。其中傳教士的住屋每座配置費400英鎊，學校每座配置費400英鎊，醫院每座配置費750英鎊。在當時，宣道會還需要平衡考慮各個傳教中心撥款的總要求。[8] 到1945年12月，聯合呼籲基金實際分配65,000英鎊來應對宣道會的需要，具體的資助標準則沒變。[9]

---

1 《中華基督教會汕頭區會伍拾年史略》（1950年10月汕頭區會辦事處印），頁6。

2 Wm. Short to H. F. Wallace, 30th October, 1945, No. 928, H-10, Presbyterian Church of England, Foreign Mission's Committee in Missionary（以下簡寫為 PCEFM），Archives Microfiche.

3 H. F. Wallace to Wm. Short, 1st November, 1945, No. 928, H-10, PCEFM, Archives Microfiche.

4 H. F. Wallace to Wm. Short, 9th December, 1945, No. 929, H-10, PCEFM, Archives Microfiche.

5 H. F. Wallace to Wm. Short, 1st November, 1945, No. 928, H-10, PCEFM, Archives Microfiche.

6 H. F. Wallace to Wm. Short and Miss Galt, 1st November, 1945, No. 928, H-10, PCEFM, Archives Microfiche.

7 H. F. Wallace to Wm. Short and Miss Galt, 27th February, 1946, No. 929, H-10, PCEFM, Archives Microfiche.

8 Wm. Short to H. F. Wallace,15th November, 1945, No. 928, H-10, PCEFM, Archives Microfiche.

9 Wm. Short to H. F. Wallace, 21rd December, 1945, No. 929, H-10, PCEFM, Archives Microfiche.

汕頭區會雖然也重視恢復和重建，不過在募集款項方面並沒有作出有成效的努力，只是把希望寄託在英國長老會海外宣道會的撥款上。1945年10月16日，汕頭區會召開區議會，全面籌畫復員事工，決定由區會產業部通告各堂，「從速填報損失」，同時委派專人接管「在汕被佔敵產」，籌備恢復貝理神學院或開辦聖經學院，並由傳道部擬定培養高級人才的章程。區會還決定向宣道會請求教會復原費法幣120萬元，並代聿懷中學申請復原費法幣200萬元。由於上一年度整個區會的財政支出才法幣97萬6千餘元，區會對宣道會期望之重從此可見一斑。應當指出的是，上述款項是宣道會常規撥款之外的專款，當時宣道會還承擔區會牧師每人每月法幣9,000元，傳道教師6,000元的補助款項。[10] 10月31日，汕頭區會在給宣道會的公函中詳述自身的損失，並指出在此期間「貴會處同樣窘況之中，仍本大無畏精神，高舉十架向前衝鋒，欽佩莫可言喻，尤其是身在窘難之中還能抱舍己愛人之道，迭蒙惠來巨款，救濟敝會同工」，區會對此表示感謝，不過對於1946年的常規請幫款問題區會當時沒有作出決定，準備將來由該會財政部與教士會按季酌請。[11]

　　無論是宣道會還是本地教會，它們首先要做的工作是評估各項具體的損失情況以及恢復建設所需要的費用，但是在戰後初期這成為一項困難的工作，嶺東教士會甚至不能給宣道會提供下一年度完整的支出預估，或者一個大體的預算。在當時形勢下，這種情況幾乎無法避免。許多實際依靠差會人力和財力的工作尚未開展，已經開展工作的傳教士也不能預判未來的發展結果，五經富和潮州府等傳教站都要等傳教士返回後才能決定開展什麼工作。根據華河力在1946年5月17日的說法，汕頭區會產業部當時已收到各堂會關於戰爭期間教產損失的報告，決定不提出明確的幫助重建的金額，而是報告總的情況，請

---

10 民國資料C295：〈汕頭區會議事簿〉，《汕頭市檔案館藏》（以下簡稱《汕檔》），汕頭區會第132次會議記錄（1945年10月16-20日）。

11 中華基督教會汕頭區會公函（汕字第14號，1945年10月31日），No. 763, H-10, PCEFM, Archives Microfiche.

求宣道會盡可能幫助他們。汕頭區會產業部只能提出粗略的數目，因為它無法對堂會報上來的數目進行仔細審查，也很難了解這些堂會依據什麼標準來確定損失的金額，而飛速上漲的物價也使得無人能夠預測教堂重建時的建築價格和法幣價值。[12] 事實上就在同一天，區會會長王超英、幹事林之純在致英蘭宣道會會長幹事的信中寫道：

> 去歲戰事結束，舉世歡騰之際，敝會方慶進入佳境，滿冀從此會務日興，以副貴會之厚望。不料物價飛漲，較戰時尤甚，且入春以來久旱成災，田園龜裂，早造無望，人心岌岌不可終日。敝會所屬八十八堂會，大多務農為業，值茲災情嚴重，自身生活尚待救濟，對於堂會之捐獻，教牧之供給自屬力不從心，表示無法。緬想敝會前途，除托賴上帝外實難設想。同人等目擊心傷，除分函向僑外同道報告災況，請求救濟外，爰於第十四次常務委員會會議表決，將災況報告貴會，請求再撥巨款，以濟急需。
>
> 敝會每季請幫款項，係依據預算指定數目請求幫撥，但自本年七、八、九等月以情形特殊，需要甚多，慚愧之下未敢指定數目，惟有敬請體念敝會特別需要，准予格外說明而已。
>
> 敝會於九年戰爭中教堂損失慘重，經遵命調查統計，照目前物價，擬請貴會准幫修建費港幣陸拾萬元，敬乞貴會一本過去提攜初衷，竭力援助。[13]

1946年9月汕頭區會召開年度會議，根據各堂會上報的戰事損失進行統計，報告中華基督教會總會和英國長老會海外宣道會，並確定請求宣道會撥款「港幣陸拾萬元」。[14] 對照華河力和王超英等人的說

12 H. F. Wallace to Wm. Short, 17th May, 1946, No. 930, H-10, PCEFM, Archives Microfiche.

13 汕頭區會會長王超英、幹事林之純致英蘭宣道會會長幹事函（1946年5月17日），No. 763, H-10, PCEFM, Archives Microfiche.

14 民國資料C295：〈汕頭區會議事簿〉，汕頭區會第133次會議記錄（1946年9月3-6日），《汕檔》。

法以及汕頭區會的決議，可以看出，區會的目的實際是希望獲得最大額度的撥款，並不一定是要求撥款港幣 60 萬元。可是港幣 60 萬元的數額畢竟太大，當時宣道會對中國宣教區的恢復重建預算不過港幣 48 萬元，而這是初步分配給閩南大會和嶺東大會的總額，並且不是一次就撥款到位，而是多年的重建費用。當時英國也面臨十分困難的經濟形勢，政府嚴格限制英鎊輸出國外，[15] 對海外匯款實行額度控制，1946 年宣道會對華匯款的總額是 23,000 英鎊，[16] 這是包括傳教士薪資在內的全部款項。可能是港幣 60 萬元的數額實在太大了，所以上述區會信件被翻譯成為英文時被改成了港幣 6 萬元。[17] 由於翻譯信件是列印件，無法從筆跡上判定是華河力還是其他傳教士翻譯。但有一點可以肯定，該譯文內容至少得到了傳教士的認可，譯者不希望提出一個宣道會根本不可能撥付的金額，以免給本地教會帶來負面的印象。大約同時期的教士會報告也說汕頭區會教產部估計整個區會恢復重建的費用是港幣 6 萬元。[18] 這的確是一種十分有趣的現象，兩條英文史料均說是港幣 6 萬元，而兩條中文史料均是港幣 60 萬元，由於中文信件和會議記錄均是用漢字大寫，且按照長老會的章程，區會會議記錄須經嚴格審核校對，才能登錄正式的會議記錄簿，所以不存在誤寫的可能性。由於在汕傳教士直接參加區會的會議，所以這裡只有一種解釋，那就是傳教士非常清楚區會在常規撥款上的含糊其辭，在爭取重建和修理費用方面獅子大開口的真實心態，他們在翻譯時故意採取了策略性的做法。

事實上，宣道會很快就通過與華河力等傳教士的通信，了解到汕頭區會的真實態度。宣道會幹事蘇為霖（William Short）在給胡德（George A. Hood）的信中就表達了對汕頭區會做法的不滿：

15 Wm. Short to Sheffield Cheng, 5th December, 1947, No. 764, H-10, PCEFM, Archives Microfiche.

16 Wm. Short to H. F. Wallace, 21rd December, 1945, No. 929, H-10, PCEFM, Archives Microfiche.

17 Heng Thiau Eng and Lim Tsu Sun to the Couvener and Secretary of the Foreign Mission Committee of the Presbyterian Church of England, 24th June, 1946, No. 763, H-10, PCEFM, Archives Microfiche.

18 Lingtung Mission Council, 10-11 may, 1946, No. 755, H-10, PCEFM, Archives Microfiche.

我收到林之純8月3日寫的信，信中既沒有談及受損教會的修理費，也沒有提到區會自身為傳道人員所做的努力。我從華河力信中得知，他對每季度宣道會是否應當撥付港幣10,000元作為教牧傳道人員的薪水是有些懷疑的。誠然，由於匯率好，你得到20,000英鎊對於區會的基金來說是十分慷慨的捐助，這遠遠多於我們給其他傳教中心的款項。不過，如果我們要求英國教會慷慨捐助的話，那麼我們應從林之純那裡看到當地教會自身的努力。[19]

在本地教會提出請款要求後，傳教士只能轉達給宣道會，由宣道會決定是否撥款。戰後到1946年初一段時間，嶺東長老會使用的是「英國傳教團體和救濟機構聯合帳號」，通過重慶結匯轉寄。[20] 1946年1月宣道會匯入聯合帳號1,000英鎊，嶺東和閩南各一半。[21] 3月份聯合帳號關閉，改匯上海。[22] 之後，宣道會可以通過香港滙豐銀行匯款。[23]

在教士會提出撥款要求後，宣道會感到很為難。如果拒絕這類要求，可能會使教牧傳道人員陷入困難的境地，如果不拒絕，宣道會一個季度就要給汕頭區會撥付港幣10,000元（約628英鎊），[24] 一年要撥付汕頭教牧傳道人員約2,400英鎊。在宣道會的財政收支中這筆撥款佔了很大的比例，它比閩南大會任何一筆款項的數額都要大。宣道會提出的方法是讓傳教士來決定能夠削減多少。[25] 實際上，宣道會的撥款大都來自英國國內的教友捐款，但英國長老會在戰後也面臨嚴峻的困難，[26] 宣道會幹事蘇為霖指出：

19 Wm. Short to George A. Hood, 12th September, 1946, No. 887, H-10, PCEFM, Archives Microfiche.

20 Wm. Short to H. F. Wallace, 11th January, 1946, No. 929, H-10, PCEFM, Archives Microfiche.

21 Wm. Short to H. F. Wallace, 28th January, 1946, No. 929, H-10, PCEFM, Archives Microfiche.

22 Wm. Short to H. F. Wallace, 22nd March, 1946, No. 930, H-10, PCEFM, Archives Microfiche.

23 George A. Hood to Wm. Short, 31st July, 1946, No. 887, H-10, PCEFM, Archives Microfiche.

24 Wm. Short to H. F. Wallace, 30th April, 1946, No. 930, H-10, PCEFM, Archives Microfiche.

25 Wm. Short to H. F. Wallace, 18th April, 1946, No. 930, H-10, PCEFM, Archives Microfiche.

26 Wm. Short to Mr. Lim, 3rd July, 1946, No. 764, H-10, PCEFM, Archives Microfiche.

剛剛結束的世界大戰比任何之前的戰爭的影響都嚴重，不僅戰敗國遭受痛苦，我們自己的國家也更窮了。如果我們要恢復繁榮的話，我們人民的生活不得不更簡樸，工作更努力。我們負擔沉重，投資利潤很低，所有的投資利潤現在都減少了很多，稅收很重。所以我們要求會友慷慨捐贈。[27]

　　儘管明知宣道會對本地教會的過度要求不滿，傳教士本人對此也頗有微詞，但在申請撥款時傳教士還不得不與本地教會人士保持一致。華河力就明確表示，可能有人希望減少要求撥款的數額，但是當時形勢非但沒有改善，反而迅速地惡化。日本人的佔領和自然災害毀壞了潮汕地區的經濟生活。1945年12月1斤大米法幣60元，1946年1月份是法幣150元，到4月份漲到法幣900元，之後下降到法幣650元和600元，在同期，港幣兌換法幣從1比200元變為1比700元。[28] 1946年春季收成的前景非常不好，已種植的作物主要依靠河流管道和水塘裡的水來灌溉，即使在水情最好地方的周邊地區也有不少土地荒蕪裸露，那些缺水的地方土地荒蕪的情況更為嚴重，當時「局勢非常令人不安，人民對未來非常憂心」。在世界不景氣的條件下，人們也很難指望有大量資源從國外輸入進來。[29]

　　汕頭區會盡一切可能來滿足牧師和傳道人員的需求，當時基本薪水是以大米分發的，在1946年汕頭區會每月要募集3,000斤大米，這並非易事，按現金來算，約合法幣200萬元，也就是一個季度法幣600萬元。[30] 儘管有宣道會的支持，本地教會也在努力籌集經費，希望在支付教牧人員的薪資津貼方面分擔一部分。1946年本地捐款約計港幣37,500元，宣道會的撥款約港幣30,000元，[31] 本地教會在負擔

---

27 Wm. Short to Mr. Lim, 17th February, 1947, No. 764, H-10, PCEFM, Archives Microfiche.

28 George A. Hood to Wm. Short, 24th August, 1946, No. 887, H-10, PCEFM, Archives Microfiche.

29 H. F. Wallace to Wm. Short, 19th April, 1946, No. 930, H-10, PCEFM, Archives Microfiche.

30 George A. Hood to Wm. Short, 1st August, 1946, No. 887, H-10, PCEFM, Archives Microfiche.

31 H. H .Wallace, The Church in the Swatow Field, 1946, 6th Jannuary 1947, No. 754, H-10, PCEFM, Archives Microfiche.

教牧人員薪資方面似佔多數，不過，考慮到宣道會還不時追加特別款項，用於救濟和補助，所以本地教會的薪資負擔實際應在一半左右。

在爭取款項的過程中，本地教會明顯表現出希望將戰後初期宣道會撥付的帶有救濟和補助性質的款項變成固定撥款的企圖。1946年4月1日林之純致蘇為霖牧師信中提出：「多謝貴會的厚愛，允照我們的請求，准撥本年一、二、三月幫款及聿懷中學幫款。敝區會仍請求貴會續幫四、五、六月幫款港幣一萬元，因復員種種問題發生，困難較甚，而需要亦必前增多，敬請允准」，林在信中還表示，「我們的教會已屆百年，但尚如此虛弱，仍然需要貴會過去與未來的巨款幫助，無論在受款或請款的時候我們的情緒上總是帶著感激和慚愧，甚盼望在最近期內我們能夠照著計畫，統籌自立基金，以減輕貴會的負擔。」[32] 不過這些話表達的究竟是真的有「慚愧」之意，或者只是一種客氣的套話，旁人很難分辨清楚。值得注意的是，到4月底林之純在寫信給宣道會時重申了上述要求，並表示「是所切盼」。[33]

在嶺東長老會恢復重建的關鍵時刻，傳教士華河力病倒了。華河力是繼汲約翰（John C. Gibson）之後嶺東大會的又一位精神導師，也是當時嶺東教士會最資深的牧師，在嶺東大會的恢復重建中居於核心地位。華河力自返回中國後，以近70歲的高齡往來奔波於潮汕各地[34]，身體和心理一直處於緊張狀態，最終積勞成疾，在1946年5月心臟病發作，[35] 當月底被解除顧問職責。[36] 華河力先在潮州府城休養，後被轉送到汕頭，病情雖然有所緩解，但一直沒有康復。嶺東長老會對於華河力突然病倒，感到「極其難過」，認為這對於嶺東長老會的前程來說是「空前問題」，並提出請宣道會調派在新加坡傳教的汲多瑪來負責。[37] 華河力在汕頭停留一年後於第二年夏季抱病回

---

32 林之純致蘇為霖牧師函（1946年4月1日），No. 763, H-10, PCEFM, Archives Microfiche.

33 林之純致蘇為霖牧師函（1946年4月29日），No. 763, H-10, PCEFM, Archives Microfiche.

34 按：華河力生於1877年。

35 Harold R. Worth to Wm. Short, 28th May, 1946, No. 930, H-10, PCEFM, Archives Microfiche.

36 H. F .Wallace to Wm. Short, 11th August, 1946, No. 755, H-10, PCEFM, Archives Microfiche.

37 林之純致蘇為霖牧師函（1946年6月14日），No. 764, H-10, PCEFM, Archives Microfiche.

國，³⁸ 兩年後去世。³⁹ 華河力突然生病使汕頭區會的事情一度陷入混亂，特別是在財政方面。教士會方面只能派缺乏經驗的胡德代理總幹事，以應對困難。⁴⁰ 華河力離開後，本地教會尤其是汕頭區會與教士會之間的聯繫和溝通出現一些問題，汕頭區會幹事林之純在致蘇為霖的信中提到：

> 自華牧師回國後，感覺教士會與教會缺聯絡，在合作精神有些阻礙，以華牧師在汕頭時，雖住潮安，他常到汕頭，談及會事，有時我等亦到潮安，請教一切。可是現在教士除醫生外，不住汕市，較老輩者竟居汕尾，往來須較長時間，每有事件發生起來，無從可以面談會商。如長此，誠恐各事其事，殊為憾事。雖然華牧師計畫今後汕市或可免有教士牧師住汕，鄙人前亦同情此舉，然現在之教士不如華牧師，而且較老輩可商會事者居去汕市太遠，為是，鄙人迫切請求貴會，再派教士住汕，以聯絡一切。大會、汕頭區會中心在汕市，自然有許多政工急需常時座談故也。⁴¹

顯然，雙方的關係不再像之前那麼密切，教會內部已出現公開抱怨傳教士的聲音。

1947年後嶺東大會的總體形勢更加困難。麥端仁（Miss Gwen Burt）、黎節（Miss Agnes Richards）、段恩華（Miss Cecilia Downward）等女傳教士返回汕頭，固然對加強教會中樞有所幫助，在青年活動、義工以及教會經濟等方面都有進步，但另一方面嶺東大會組織不健全，幹部人員太少，總幹事鄭少懷患肺病，教會行政進展遲緩，教會尤其是鄉村教會呈現衰敗的趨向，這從嶺東大會的年度報告可以

---

38 Sheffield Cheng to Mr. Short and Miss Galt, 10th June, 1947, No. 764, H-10, PCEFM, Archives Microfiche.

39 〈華河力博士傳略〉，《奮進》，卷5第6、7期合刊（1950年6月），頁21。

40 George A. Hood to Wm. Short, 6th June, 1946, No. 886, H-10, PCEFM, Archives Microfiche.

41 林之純致蘇為霖牧師函（1947年12月27日），No. 764, H-10, PCEFM, Archives Microfiche.

明顯地感受到：

> 對於中國人民來說，1947年是令人失望的一年，政治、經濟
> 和軍事形勢惡化，人民對國家不再抱有八年抗戰期間那樣高的
> 期望。儘管政府希望通過制定新憲法，並進行歷史上的第一次
> 選舉來開創國家發展的新階段，如果未來的歷史學對這些活動
> 過於看重，高估它們的意義那就是錯的。嶺東教會的工作已經
> 間接受到了北方的政治和軍事形勢的影響，而直接受到了整個
> 國家的經濟形勢的影響。政府的軍事需要意味著從南方抽取資
> 源物質，而在嶺東地區增加了大量的盜匪和小偷，這增加了誠
> 實生活的困難。越來越多的人進入城市而不是冒險地留在偏僻
> 的鄉村，這和抗戰期間的趨勢正好相反，那時很多人都逃到鄉
> 村。在嶺東教會以鄉村教會為主，這種趨勢意味著削弱鄉村教
> 會，而兩個城市教會錫安堂和伯特利堂因戰爭造成的會友流失
> 則借此得以恢復。生活在鄉村比城市更艱難，通常要遭遇到洪
> 水和颱風以及海潮的襲擊。在6月到7月，韓江水位猛漲，為
> 過去十年來最高，我們的教會多在韓江三角洲，江堤在日本佔
> 領期間完全失修，結果有兩處決口，洪水吞沒沿岸地區，毀壞
> 了很快就要成熟的莊稼。下半年，10月7日，颱風和海潮造成
> 了更大範圍的災害，損失為近二十年來最大。整個嶺東地區第
> 二季收成因風災受損，而沿海地區則被海潮淹沒，直接影響到
> 35個堂會，損失總額約在7,000英鎊。除了這兩次災害外，五
> 經富地區的湯坑鎮遭受洪水襲擊，三名會友被淹死，財產損失
> 很大。在汕頭和汕尾沿海地區，海盜也不時偷襲鄉村，綁架教
> 會會友，勒索贖金，這使得旅行不再安全。[42]

---

[42] The Lingtung Synod of Church of Christ in China, Annual Report, 1947, No. 758, H-10, PCEFM, Archives Microfiche.

客家地區的情況也不樂觀，「中共武裝在白天襲擊市鎮，使當地一些人陷入某種緊張狀態之中」。不過，更不穩定的是法幣，因為持續內戰，不可能恢復和平，這會導致法幣持續不穩，時常迅速下落。當然，即使在時局不寧的環境下客家教會也在努力維繫各項事工，五經富青年團契十周年的活動就比較成功。對中部和北部客家地區的堂會，蔡融牧師一年兩次進行巡視訪問，春季由穆華德（G. F. Mobbs）陪同，秋季是歐陽德。[43]

　　應當指出的是，嶺東長老會90%是鄉村教會，大體與英國長老會所屬的120個鄉村教會情形類似，比如諾森伯蘭郡等地，儘管有相當數量的堂會沒能達到自養的程度，[44] 但嶺東大會採用米薪加現金津貼的發放方式，米價的高漲使其在嶺東大會的收入中比例得到提升，本地實際擔負大半以上的教牧人員薪資，以汕頭區會為例，1947年這部分的比例達到了66%左右，整體上教會仍維持了一定的自養水準。[45] 客家教會在1948年更「面臨共產黨游擊隊的壓力，後者強制徵收大米稅，這使大部分鄉村教會更加困難」，[46] 不過客家教會仍然完成了它之前承諾的教牧薪金數額的90%。[47]

　　華河力病倒後，嶺東教士會的財務由年輕的傳教士胡德具體負責，從胡德與宣道會的通信中可以看到，當時宣道會是持續不斷的撥付各種款項給嶺東長老會。[48]

　　此時宣道會給嶺東大會的撥款是與教士會分開的。1948年6月20日，宣道會執委會開會討論嶺東大會的撥款問題，同意下一年度撥付嶺東大會2,375英鎊。宣道會要求教士會向嶺東大會解釋宣道會面臨的經費短缺問題，說明除非英國國內教會的捐贈有大幅提升，否則緊

43 G. F. Mobbs, "Hakka Church Work Report,1947," No. 757, H-10, PCEFM, Archives Microfiche.

44 Freda Starkey etc., to Friends, August, 1947, No. 757, H-10, PCEFM, Archives Microfiche.

45 Sheffield Cheng to Mr. Short and Miss Galt, 10th June, 1947, No. 764, H-10, PCEFM, Archives Microfiche.

46 E. J. Edler, "Report on Tao-chi Middle School, Wukingfu, 1947-8," No. 760, H-10, PCEFM, Archives Microfiche.

47 R. A. Elder, "Hakka Church Work Report, 1947-1948," No. 761, H-10, PCEFM, Archives Microfiche.

48 Wm. Short to George A. Hood, 16th July, 1946, No. 887, H-10, PCEFM, Archives Microfiche.

縮開支不可避免。[49] 1948年度嶺東教士會年收入總額為15,420英鎊。[50]另外，宣道會還撥有教會重建撥款4,000英鎊，用於未來二到三年的建設。[51]

宣道會既要考慮嶺東傳教士的要求，更要考慮各宣教區的整體財政支出。從1949-1950年宣道會預算看，英國長老會海外宣道會和女宣道會每年的結餘數都是負數，也就是每年都是財政赤字，而在該會的五個海外傳教區中，無論是嶺東教士會還是嶺東女宣道會所獲得的款項都是最多，[52] 這也不難理解為什麼宣道會總是對嶺東教士會和女宣道會的請款要求有所保留，甚至有時會提出批評。

二、請款、救濟與生計

儘管英國長老會宣道會在戰後一直給予嶺東大會正常的財政撥款，同時嶺東大會也通過各種管道獲得海外潮人有力的經濟支持，[53]但本地教牧人員的生活卻遭遇到極大的困難，處境似乎十分悲慘，他們紛紛向教會中樞請求幫助。改善教牧待遇，維繫教牧生計已成為牧師和傳道教師共同的呼聲與要求，在這種情況下有人提出保障教牧生活的明確要求：

> 呈為通貨膨脹，物價飛騰，教牧待遇亟須調整補助，以維生活而利會務。竊思中樞去年冬季函著各堂增教牧薪金一倍以上，故調派教牧最高參拾陸萬元，自理堂亦僅伍拾萬元，而不及者尚不知凡幾，但自去年十月份起物價繼續增加，殆大幣出籠，日用必需品莫不漲高五至十倍以上，尤以米價飛升更可駭怕！

---

49 Wm. Short to George A. Hood, 23rd July, 1948, No. 764, H-10, PCEFM, Archives Microfiche.

50 George A. Hood to Mr. Short and Mr. Brown, 9th June, 1948, No. 889, H-10, PCEFM, Archives Microfiche.

51 Jas. Waddell to Wm. Short, 21st February, 1948, No. 759, H-10, PCEFM, Archives Microfiche.

52 Extracts from the Minutes of the F. M. Executive Committee Meeting on July 21st 1949, No. 761, H-10, PCEFM, Archives Microfiche.

53 參拙文〈英國長老會在華慈善事業研究〉，《近代史研究》，第1期（2014）。

中樞例定教牧食米斤數，信徒因物價增長，致不能按數供給者比比皆是。所得薪金一季為一月之用，仍感不足，為此教牧生活均陷於極度困難中，況中樞之補給數年來均在季末撥發，於是教牧告貸無門，變賣乏物，皇皇汲汲，惟充饑之是慮，影響聖工，在所不免，瞻顧前途，惶恐曷已。為教會前途計，為教牧生活憂，亟應請求中樞對教牧生活謀改善之道，試陳管見，聊當拋引。

查政府及機關、學校，對工作人員之待遇除實物外，薪金均改按月調整辦法，且依人口為比例，或改全部以實物為本位，故中樞今後亦應改按月調整，廢止季末撥補辦法，以免教牧生活無法維持，此其一也。我會工作人員除服務中樞外，分為自理堂及未自理堂，且以在此普遍民難關頭，一切教牧不論在任何場合所受待遇，皆不足應付直系親屬生活，昭然若揭，況中樞又有七口之規定，過七口之家，中樞及聯堂皆置不理，為是全部教牧不論人口多寡，皆同罹困厄，竊以今後中樞對工作人員一方提高待遇，另方對過七口者應酌量撥補，庶咸受其惠，此其二也。當此農村破產，百業凋零之際，除一、二富有資源之堂會外，莫不同歌巧婦無米之調，所謂自理堂目前勢難維持原狀矣，為此教牧無聘、派，均遭同等困厄，固非危言聳人也。今後中樞應事先籌畫，庶足減少當前之大難，在新才未成，舊員宜保情勢中，安定教牧生活，即所以為教會留元氣。[54]

從呈文可以看出，當時教牧人員的生計狀況已經非常窘困。教會中樞為了保障教會的運行，只有答應教牧的要求，全部以大米為本位發放薪資，[55] 避免因物價波動造成教牧實際收入的下降。不過，這樣一來勢必對嶺東大會的財政運作機制作重要的調整，這又牽涉到複雜

---

54 12-11-41：中華基督教會汕頭區會檔，《汕檔》，胡若霖致汕頭區會財政部函（1948年1月28日）。
55 民國資料C212：中華基督教會汕頭區會財政部會議記錄，《汕檔》，財政部第14次會議記錄（1948年7月13日）。

的技術問題，尤其是宣道會對嶺東大會的財政撥款體制以及外匯市場的匯率問題，而這些問題嶺東大會本身是難以解決的。

不僅如此，從現有的檔案文獻看，汕頭區會的許多堂會在戰後似乎都遭遇到嚴重的財政危機，各種請求幫款的函件紛紛飛向區會財政部、產業部以及其他相關部門個人。根據筆者的初步統計，僅僅提出教牧薪資撥款要求的就有30多個堂會，幾乎佔到汕頭區會堂會總數的一半，如果再加上申請其他補助和救濟的堂會，則超過半數以上的堂會都提出了增加撥款的要求，這表明伴隨國家整體經濟形勢的惡化和潮汕當地接連不斷的水旱災害，汕頭區會的大部分基層堂會在駐堂教牧的米津和薪金的捐納都非常不理想，教牧及其家屬的生活面臨嚴重困難。應當指出的是，汕頭區會的堂會多數屬於沿海集鎮性堂會，經濟實力遠遠超過同屬嶺東大會的五經富區會，汕頭區會的情況如此，則五經富區會的境況必定更加艱困，惜因資料缺乏，這一時期五經富區會各堂會的具體情況並不清楚。從相關資料看，普通信徒本身的生計也面臨困難，有的信徒當時「賴以度生者惟藉高利貸，此種生活實無異飲鴆止渴」，[56] 有的信徒生活幾乎陷入絕境，[57] 他們不僅缺乏穀物供應教牧，自己本身也是艱難度日。[58]

不過，對於這些撥款要求還必須作深入的分析。

首先，上述請款函件多數是以堂會名義向中樞發出，少部分以教牧個人名義提出，但實際上反映的也是堂會的集體意見，其中必然有堂會本身的利益考慮在內。雖然當時潮汕各地普遍遭遇到經濟的困難，但是否都到了無法保證教牧基本薪資的程度其實是值得懷疑的。上述堂會中有的是城市集鎮堂會如揭陽聯堂、惠來堂，還有不少是信徒人數較多的集鎮型堂會等，經濟實力一直較為強勁。事實上，當時

---

56 12-11-40：中華基督教會汕頭區會文件，《汕檔》，中華基督教汕頭區會遮浪堂會執事黃奎書等至汕頭區會財政部長吳國維函（1948年4月3日）。

57 12-11-41：中華基督教會汕頭區會文件，《汕檔》，京岡堂議會致區會慈善部長函（1946年7月7日）；
12-11-41：中華基督教會汕頭區會文件，《汕檔》，京岡堂議會致區會傳道部函（1946年7月7日）。

58 12-11-40：中華基督教會汕頭區會文件，《汕檔》，碣石堂執事黃宜之等致財政部長吳國維函（1948年11月7日）。

有不少堂會故意隱瞞經濟實力，希望多獲得一些中樞的撥款，否則就以不聘請教牧相威脅。如波頭堂會本有力量供養傳道教師，可以「減輕中樞之負擔」，但卻故意「隱瞞」實力，直到1948年舊曆年底仍不鬆口，聲稱不準備繼續聘請原傳道教師，目的是以此迫使該聯牧師為該堂爭取更多的撥款。牧師自然清楚其中的內幕，所以直接報請區會主裁，而區會裁定下來不派傳道教師駐堂，則該堂今後就會「難覓傳道教師主持」。在聯牧報請區會後，堂會只能聘請原駐堂傳道教師。[59] 黃岡堂向中樞宣稱自己「經濟力量素稱薄弱」，但實際情況是多位教牧竟然激烈競爭堂會的傳道職位，進而引發激烈的衝突，[60] 揆諸常理，實在難以說得通。而貴嶼堂發生的多名傳道教師互爭職位事件表明，堂會向中樞「哭窮」，實際是一種慣常使用的手段，哭窮訴苦固然包含爭取中樞財政資助的考慮，也包含有壓低駐堂教牧薪資標準，使教牧之間相互競爭，以期「低價求售」的明顯意圖。[61] 有的堂會公開要求區會派遣「賢明」且「價廉」的傳道教師，否則就負擔不起。[62] 在當時從節省雜費的角度看聘請本鄉教牧人員是最經濟合算的，所以本鄉或臨近地區教牧人員成為部分堂會聘請的首選，而對教牧的靈性、品德的要求自然有所降低。如隆江堂會在得知中樞調派外地傳道教師到其堂任職後，馬上給傳道部去信，要求聘請本鄉的一位傳道教師，[63] 這種做法居然也得到該聯聯牧的認可，[64] 而被派的外地

---

59 12-11-41：中華基督教會汕頭區會文件，《汕檔》，聯牧林憲文致汕頭區會傳道部特委會函（1949年2月4日）。

60 詳參拙文〈基層教會與鄉村政治：嶺東長老會黃岡堂驅逐教牧事件〉，載吳義雄主編，《地方社會文化與中西文化交流》（上海人民出版社，2010），頁140-174。

61 12-11-41：中華基督教會汕頭區會文件，《汕檔》，蔡家彥致汕頭區會傳道部長郭啟瑞函（1946年9月27日）。

62 12-11-41：中華基督教會汕頭區會文件，《汕檔》，新亨堂鄒鎮標致林之純函（1948年3月9日。原件只有月份及日期，並無年度，該年度係筆者根據函件內容推定）。

63 12-11-43：中華基督教會汕頭區會文件，《汕檔》，隆江堂會林騰漢等致汕頭區會傳道部函（1946年5月30日）。

64 12-11-43：中華基督教會汕頭區會文件，《汕檔》，中華基督教汕頭區會第十四聯堂牧師陳述經致汕頭區會傳道部長函（1946年6月5日）。

傳道教師也不願意前往該堂上任。[65]

其次，既然1945年後潮汕各地普遍遭受災害，那麼受其影響的並非只有教牧，普通信徒尤其是鄉村信徒受影響應當更大，更應得到較多的救濟和幫助。可是相關資料表明，當時只有極少數堂會提出對教友進行救濟，絕大部分堂會都沒有提及教友的救濟問題，這說明1945年後潮汕各堂會雖遭遇到災害，但其程度並不嚴重，多數堂會的教友維持生活應不成問題。堂會和教牧向教會中樞哭窮，主要是為了爭取更多的財政資源。事實上，當時以哭窮的方式爭取資源在嶺東大會內部已成為一種習慣和風氣。堂會向教會中樞伸手要錢，教會中樞則向英國長老會宣道會提出各種名目的追加撥款的要求。對此，曾經負責汕頭區會財政的華河力深感不安，他指出：

> 我將區會的撥款要求附在信中。對目前的趨勢我感到不安。關於撥款之事我已非常清晰地告訴區會各部，不過他們似乎並不是按照我建議的那樣去做，在宣道會看來特別的交流可能有理想的效果。我認為，中國在目前基本上像一個乞丐，伸出她的雙手接受一切東西，任何人都會向她施捨東西。她認為整個世界都有義務去彌補她在戰爭中所遭受的損失，她已被鼓勵在這方面做得太多。大量的錢和物已經給她或正在給她，使她認為還會有更多的錢和物會給予她。我相信，教會應當被告知要有一個限度，那就是英國長老會能夠為她做什麼，他們已經做了什麼，如果她的要求被拒絕的話。[66]

在爭取救濟資源方面，嶺東大會所屬的汕頭區會和五經富區會各顯神通，競相向海外教友募捐。當時汕頭區會的海外教友無論就人力和物力資源都遠遠超過五經富區會。從現存資料看，當時汕頭區會能

---

65 12-11-43：中華基督教會汕頭區會文件，《汕檔》，張雪澄致汕頭區會傳道部長函（1946年5月28日）。

66 H. F. Wallace to Wm. Shor1945t, 21ˢᵗ May, 1946, No. 930, H-10, PCEFM, Archives Microfiche.

夠募集到大筆的救濟資源，其中1945年10月至1946年12月該會收到澳洲潮人教會、香港潮人生命堂、南洋長老大會、新加坡長老會、暹羅黃橋堂以及劉業基、鄭謙受等海外教友個人的各項多批次捐款，合計法幣1,042萬元，佔當時該區會的全部收入的24%，如果加上該會慈善部直接募集以及各種國際救濟款項法幣378萬元，合計1,420萬元，佔到總收入的33%。[67] 1947年3月，該會委託暹羅監賑團訂購運來的180包賑米除撥給鹽灶孤兒院36包外，其餘全部發給該會教牧，人均4包。[68] 從支出的情況看，這些都用於汕頭區會本身的救濟補助，並無對五經富區會的任何幫助。

由於汕頭區會在爭取各種款項和救濟補助方面只顧自身利益，基本不給予經濟更為困難的五經富區會任何幫助，1946年7月1日，英國長老會宣道會幹事蘇為霖（William Short）在寫給汕頭區會幹事林之純的信中直接提出了批評：

> 或許我可以大膽地建議，嶺東大會應當被認為是一個整體，在考慮大會的需要時，汕頭和客家兩區會的要求都應被考慮。我們可能會感到，歷史更久也更為富裕的汕頭區會應當經常把客家地區的中國弟兄們的要求牢記在心，把相互幫助的準則牢記在心。[69]

兩天後，蘇為霖在回復汕頭區會請求宣道會幫款的信件時再次明確指出：

> 我建議請求幫款的要求應當由整個嶺東大會而非區會提出，我

---

67 民國資料C313：中華基督教會汕頭區會帳簿，《汕檔》，1945年10月至1946年12月31日汕頭區會進支總報告。

68 12-11-33：中華基督教會汕頭區會文件，《汕檔》，汕頭區會教牧、孤兒院托運賑米姓名表（1947年3月11日）。

69 Wm. Short to Mr. Lim, 1st July, 1946, No. 764, H-10, PCEFM, Archives Microfiche.

們都希望從教會中看到福音的果實，不論是我們英國教會還是你們中國教會，教會團結的意義和必要性就在於力量強大的教會幫助力量弱小的教會。我們會考慮整個嶺東地區即客家話地區和福佬話地區的需要。[70]

　　不過，宣道會當時所能做的只是在年度撥款時適當照顧五經富區會，至於汕頭區會從海外潮人募集的款項宣道會則無法施加有效的影響。當時汕頭區會對於募集的海外款項基本上是按堂會信徒人數進行分配，其結果是城市堂會和沿海集鎮性堂會分得的錢款最多，而真正需要救濟的貧弱堂會反而很少。[71]

　　在區會的示範下，當時各堂會也是各行其是，通過各種途徑從海外募集款項。汕頭錫安堂是汕頭區會經濟實力最強的城市堂會之一，該會擁有極為廣泛的海外人脈關係。1947年該堂募集的救濟款項達法幣384.2萬元，實際支出為70.8萬元，結餘313.4萬元。[72] 實際上，汕頭區會不少堂會都有海外人脈關係，其中不少人經商，給予堂會很多經濟支援。實力不強的潮陽新寮堂「經商南洋、港、滬、汕」者為數不少，[73] 汕尾品清堂也有不少人在香港等地經商。[74] 普寧流沙堂稱旅外教友對「母會捐款尤為熱誠努力，凡本堂物質建設，多賴旅外同道之捐助」。[75] 潮陽仙城堂「經濟方面原極薄弱，幸有旅居外地之信徒趙資光長老、趙廣恩執事不忘母會，時刻關懷，比年以來屢捐巨款」，該「會之得以維持，二君與有力焉」。[76] 田心堂經濟力量薄

70　Wm. Short to Mr. Lim, 3rd July, 1946, No. 764, H-10, PCEFM, Archives Microfiche.

71　12-11-33：中華基督教會汕頭區會文件，《汕檔》，汕頭區會各堂簽領第3次教友賑款登記表（實叻款1948年9月）。

72　民國資料C302：錫安堂長執會議案簿，《汕檔》，錫安堂堂議會第28次會議記錄（1948年3月11日）。

73　12-11-14：中華基督教會汕頭區會文件，《汕檔》，新寮堂史略（1949年）。

74　12-11-14：中華基督教會汕頭區會文件，《汕檔》，品清堂史略（1949年）。

75　12-11-14：中華基督教會汕頭區會文件，《汕檔》，流沙堂史略（1949年）。

76　12-11-14：中華基督教會汕頭區會文件，《汕檔》，仙城堂史略（1949年）。

弱，「旅外同道年有捐獻」。[77] 揭陽廣美堂「旅外教友關心母會，每年捐款尚足聘師之用」。[78] 京岡堂旅外教友人數竟然佔到堂會信徒總數的三分之一。[79] 即使實力薄弱的蔡口堂會也有旅外教友百名左右。[80] 這些堂會從海外教友募集的經費自然都用於本堂。部分由汕頭區會從海外募集的賑濟款項，其中也有部分款項明確指定給特定的堂會和個人使用。

由於缺乏必要的內部制約，各堂動用各種關係競相向海外募款，結果有教牧私自募集，並將得來的款項中飽私囊。1949年初，新寮堂會以自傳為名，不再續聘原駐堂傳道教師林振德。[81] 汕頭區會決定林振德改調新亨堂，但是林振德卻認為新寮堂拖欠自己應得的薪津，為此遲遲不赴任。[82] 他還以此為藉口自行向新寮堂旅外會友募捐款項，曾經一次就募得港幣50元，除去貼水實得港幣46元，折合白米113斤，[83] 同時一直堅持要求區會補發薪津。[84] 新寮堂會則對林振德以該堂「欠薪為幌，四出招搖」，向該堂會教友「私捐巨款」表示強烈不滿，認為這不僅敗壞該堂的聲譽，而且妨礙了該堂的財政計畫。新寮堂職員將收集到的林振德私自募捐款項的相關證據呈送區會，要求區會質問林振德本人。[85]

在汕頭區會內部不同的堂會經濟實力差距甚遠，同一堂會內部教友自然也是貧富有異。在面臨經濟困難的情況下，堂會之間、堂會內部的教友之間本應相互幫助，但是他們卻把爭取救濟資源的努力都主

---

77 12-11-14：中華基督教會汕頭區會文件，《汕檔》，田心堂史略（1949年）。

78 12-11-14：中華基督教會汕頭區會文件，《汕檔》，廣美堂史略（1949年）。

79 12-11-14：中華基督教會汕頭區會文件，《汕檔》，京岡堂史略（1949年）。

80 12-11-14：中華基督教會汕頭區會文件，《汕檔》，蔡口堂史略（1949年）。

81 12-11-41：中華基督教會汕頭區會文件，《汕檔》，京灶聯會聯牧林憲文致區會傳道部長函（1949年1月7日）。

82 12-11-23：中華基督教會嶺東大會文件，《汕檔》，傳道部長蔡愷真批復林振德函（1949年3月24日）。

83 12-11-36：中華基督教會汕頭區會文件，《汕檔》，林銘修致林振德函（1949年3月30日）。

84 12-11-36：中華基督教會汕頭區會文件，《汕檔》，林振德致□□□函（1949年9月6日）。

85 12-11-36：中華基督教會汕頭區會文件，《汕檔》，新寮堂議會致區會傳道部長蔡愷真函（1949年8月30日）。

要放在了教會外部。儘管按照區會的要求，各堂均設有「賑濟捐」的專門捐項，但從各堂上報區會的1948年度統計資料看，各堂實際所收的賑濟捐款非常之少。如經濟狀況良好的潮安堂會，1948年總收入法幣104,247萬元，賑濟捐款竟然只有法幣55萬元，只佔總收入的萬分之五。[86] 登塘堂總收入法幣115,354萬元，賑濟捐款50萬元，[87] 佔總收入的萬分之四。實力強勁的鹽灶堂會該堂現金總收入3,710元，賑濟捐款530元（從數目上看，應為金圓券），賑濟捐款佔到現金收入的14%，不過收入在當時堂會只佔極少部分，而該堂乾穀收入為82石，而統計時金圓券125元才能買到1斤大米，[88] 實際賑濟捐款只能購米4斤2兩。經濟實力最強的錫安堂會賑濟捐款合港幣120元，當年總收入合計港幣42,567元，[89] 賑濟捐款也只佔總額的千分之三。此外，約一半左右堂會統計表中「賑濟捐」這一欄為空白。

事實上，當時嶺東大會重要慈善機構鹽灶孤兒院的經費也主要依靠社會捐助，1948年該院收容孤兒102名，聘院長1名，教員5名，工人3名，該院加入美華兒童福利會，成為該組織的會員單位，因此「經費源源不絕」，同時該院還得到暹羅華僑回國監賑團以及廣東國際救濟會的食物、布匹等實物捐助。嶺東大會的百齡安老院以收養教會內孤寡無依的老人為主，該院的開辦雖然得到汕頭市內錫安堂、伯特利堂、新中華堂等堂的婦女團契的支持，但主要經費是依靠林重三牧師娘在上海的募捐，另外也得到暹羅華僑回國監賑團供應的大米。[90]

第三，從基層堂會的報告看汕頭區會所有的教牧人員生活似乎都陷入了嚴重困境，但實際情況應是教牧人員的生活確實受到了很大影響，而被派往貧弱的鄉村堂會的教牧受到影響更大。但情況遠非堂會

---

86 12-11-28：中華基督教會汕頭區會文件，《汕檔》，潮安堂會統計表（1948年11月15日）。

87 12-11-28：中華基督教會汕頭區會文件，《汕檔》，登塘堂會統計表（1949年2月）。

88 12-11-28：中華基督教會汕頭區會文件，《汕檔》，鹽灶堂會統計表（1949年2月28日）。

89 12-11-28：中華基督教會汕頭區會文件，《汕檔》，錫安堂會統計表（1949年4月20日）。

90 民國資料 C295：《汕頭區會議事簿》，《汕檔》，汕頭區會第135次會議記錄（1948年11月18-22日）。

和教牧聲稱的那樣悲慘，因為這個時期英國長老會宣道會的撥款一直都能按期匯到，而汕頭區會80多個堂會中大部分都是不能自立的堂會，它們主要依靠宣道會的經濟支持。[91] 宣道會正常的撥款已經初步保障了這部分教牧人員的基本生活。至於堂會供應的米薪是按正常的薪資標準捐題，即便沒有這部分收入，教牧人員生活水準會受到較大影響，但也不致有凍餒之虞，因為宣道會為應對各種緊急情況而臨時增加的特別救濟和補助款項能及時緩解這種局面，這一點從區會對部分教牧哭窮函件的回覆中可以清晰地看出。[92] 與抗戰時期部分教牧為了生計辭去教職形成鮮明對照的是，戰後基本沒有汕頭區會的教牧辭職，而那些在戰爭時期辭職的教牧也通過各種方式，積極爭取復職。而一些教牧為了爭奪貧弱堂會的職位而不擇手段，不顧聲譽，也說明這一時期即使是擔任那些真正貧弱堂會的傳道教師也能保障基本生活。

在戰後嶺東大會的教牧人員為了維持家庭家計，增加個人收入，採取各種方式賺錢已經成為較為普遍的現象。有的傳道教師在本職之外兼任他職為此荒廢聖工，引起堂會的不滿。[93] 有的堂會教師在傳道之餘，開設抽紗業和布業，但因經營不善，與堂會教會發生經濟糾紛，被教友在教堂內當眾痛毆。[94]

為了賺錢，有的教牧甚至從事與其身分完全不相符合的事業，以獲取金錢。這種情況不僅中華基督教會嶺東大會存在，在同一地區傳教的嶺東浸信會也不鮮見。如嶺東浸信會汕頭堂傳道主任鄭則經牧師在任期間居然開花會，共請三班月蘭會，分別於1日、15日，5日、20日以及10日、25日開標，實際上每五天即開一次標，參加者共49

---

91 關於英國長老會宣道會對嶺東大會教牧人員的財政支持，筆者擬專文探討。

92 12-11-36：中華基督教會汕頭區會文件，《汕檔》，汕頭區會傳道部長蔡愷真致林景波函（1949年5月19日）。

93 12-11-41：中華基督教會汕頭區會文件，《汕檔》，貴嶼堂長老歐陽基致汕頭區會傳道部長函（1946年11月24日）。

94 12-11-36：中華基督教會汕頭區會文件，《汕檔》，吳裕寬呈汕頭區會會長楊作新文（1949年10月28日）。

人次，鄭則經獲利法幣1,000萬元，購買汕頭市內房產一座。[95] 此外，烏橋堂的傳道主任黃邦基也請有月蘭會一班，每月初一、十五開標。[96] 參加者不僅有浸信會教友，也有不少長老會教友。這種利用教牧聲望公開召請堂會之教友賭博的現象，實在是匪夷所思的事情。

根據筆者的統計，在戰後嶺東大會汕頭區會至少三分之一的堂會因為人事和財務問題發生風波。有的教師為爭傳道職位，在教堂內「狂罵區會要員」，並鼓動會友來堂恫嚇、驅趕駐堂傳道教師，最終得償所願。[97] 有的牧師任期屆滿，賴著不走，居然盜用他人名義杜撰所謂的「挽留函」，欺騙教會中樞，實際上是自己挽留自己。[98] 還有的傳道人員公然造假，冒領米薪，[99] 其道德人格之卑下，令人不齒。至於普通教友道心減弱，禮拜日教堂人數寥寥，對於教會不願給予支援，所謂「有心者無力，有力者無心」。[100] 教友與教牧之間，教牧與教會中樞之間的齟齬和衝突不斷。有的堂會職員和教友對教會中樞、駐堂傳道和聯牧都非常失望，他們在信函中表示「求神使教會領袖有主能力，治會嚴正，不看情面，顧全教會威信，避免苟且因循態度」，「求神給我們有一位真正屬靈的牧者，領導久已失散的群羊，使會務得進展，主道得發揚」，「對於聯牧方面，求神使其尊重人格，保守信譽，盡忠職守，勿為錢財奔趨」。[101]

毫無疑問，經濟上的困境使得部分堂會無力聘請駐堂傳道，當時有少數堂會被迫關閉，如葵潭堂會將本來是崇拜場所的教堂租給俗人

---

95 12-11-47：嶺東浸信會文件，《汕檔》，韋約瑟呈嶺東浸信會執行委員會主席洪文（約1947年底）。

96 12-11-36：中華基督教會汕頭區會文件，《汕檔》，浸信會汕頭堂執事林希舜報告（1947年9月24日）。

97 12-11-41：中華基督教會汕頭區會文件，《汕檔》，楊作新、餘秉堅致林之純函（1946年8月28日）。

98 12-11-39：中華基督教會汕頭區會文件，《汕檔》，黃岡堂友鄭仁惠呈汕頭區會常委會會長楊作新文（1947年6月4日）。

99 12-11-36：中華基督教會汕頭區會文件，《汕檔》，長美堂執事陳希榮等致汕頭區會傳道部長函（1949年1月10日）。

100 12-11-40：中華基督教會汕頭區會文件，《汕檔》，捷勝堂會施明謙致林之純牧師函（1947年11月28日）。

101 12-11-23：中華基督教會汕頭區會文件，《汕檔》，鄭為華、鄭義恩致汕頭區會幹事林之純函（1948年9月9日）。

居住，而且不肯將租金上繳區會。[102] 不過，更多的則是放棄聘請教牧，由義工暫時維繫，或由聯堂內部的傳道教師兼攝，如德里堂會，[103] 洪洲堂會，[104] 海豐堂會等。[105] 信眾由於缺乏牧養，自然信仰更加淡漠。「道心」成為當時反覆被提及的一個詞。潮陽鳳山堂提及「復員之後，教友生活猶在窘蹙中」，該「堂領餐友三十餘名，皆屬鄉民，道心未固，急待誨治」。[106] 桑田堂「國難期間，堂宇毀於兵燹，地方荒亂，會務乏人主持，教友殍于饑饉，所存數名，道心渙散，目前尚在停頓中，無法恢復」。[107] 玉浦堂「連年以來，無師駐堂，以致一暴十寒，形式精神，大非昔比」。[108] 海豐捷勝堂「久乏牧治，以致道心冷落」，「復員以來，因會友生活艱困，會務阻滯」。[109] 品清堂自抗戰後區會就「未派教師駐堂，以致道心不固者離道從俗」。[110] 靖海堂在戰後信徒雖然「如常聚會，但因生活困難，致道心日淡」。[111] 沙港堂「際此災難頻仍，農村破產，信徒不明受託主義，加以信心冷落，生活艱辛」。[112] 公平堂自「抗戰軍興，信徒道心冷落」，此後一直元氣未復。[113] 陸豐東山堂「連年迭遭戰亂，道根淺薄者多退縮冷淡」。[114] 惠來堂也因「乏常川誨治教牧，又欠崇拜場所，教友道心未免日淡」。[115] 饒平長美堂「惜經濟

---

102 12-11-43：中華基督教會汕頭區會文件，《汕檔》，陳述經致汕頭區會常委會主席楊作新、幹事林之純函（1948年5月22日）。

103 12-11-41：中華基督教會汕頭區會文件，《汕檔》，德里堂議會長老陳名晏等致傳道部長郭啟瑞函（1947年12月29日）。

104 12-11-39：中華基督教會汕頭區會文件，《汕檔》，第二聯牧師王超英致傳道部函（1949年1月14日）。

105 12-11-40：中華基督教會汕頭區會文件，《汕檔》，胡若霖等致區會傳道部函（1948年5月21日）。

106 12-11-14：中華基督教會汕頭區會文件，《汕檔》，鳳山堂史略（1949年）。

107 12-11-14：中華基督教會汕頭區會文件，《汕檔》，桑田堂史略（1949年）。

108 12-11-14：中華基督教會汕頭區會文件，《汕檔》，玉浦堂史略（1949年）。

109 12-11-14：中華基督教會汕頭區會文件，《汕檔》，捷勝堂史略（1949年）。

110 12-11-14：中華基督教會汕頭區會文件，《汕檔》，品清堂史略（1949年）。

111 12-11-14：中華基督教會汕頭區會文件，《汕檔》，靖海堂史略（1949年）。

112 12-11-14：中華基督教會汕頭區會文件，《汕檔》，沙港堂史略（1949年）。

113 12-11-14：中華基督教會汕頭區會文件，《汕檔》，公平堂史略（1949年）。

114 12-11-14：中華基督教會汕頭區會文件，《汕檔》，東山堂史略（1949年）。

115 12-11-14：中華基督教會汕頭區會文件，《汕檔》，惠來堂史略（1949年）。

力量微弱，會友守道不專，主日崇拜寥寥無幾」。[116] 柘林堂「自抗戰七七事變後，地方荒涼，教會銳退」，戰後存教友僅數家，信徒十幾人而已。[117] 顯然，對於這些弱小堂會而言，經濟危機已演化為深刻的精神和信仰危機。

三、結語

戰爭對教會造成的影響不僅反映在物質層面，更表現在精神方面。儘管中華基督教會嶺東大會對教牧人員和普通信徒高度重視物質利益的態度感到憂慮，對於形成「米飯基督徒」（rice Christians）的危險保持一定的警惕，[118] 不過，當時普遍的情況是教友的注意力越來越集中在如何掙錢，而非精神方面的進步。戰後，在面臨國家經濟瀕於崩潰、而潮汕地方自然災害不斷的情況下，嶺東大會將重建的重點主要放在修復受損教堂、恢復相關教會和相關機構的正常運作上，並將重建的希望主要放在爭取宣道會的撥款上，表現出對宣道會的高度依賴。至於精神方面的重建，儘管有人提出「提倡本色化」和「基督化生活」的構想，[119] 但並未見有效的具體措施。從基層堂會的情況看，嶺東大會不僅面臨嚴重的財政危機，更面臨深刻的精神危機。隨著各種救濟和補助管道的不斷開闢，在戰時及戰後，基層堂會向教會中樞申請款項成為常態，在各堂會普遍「哭窮」聲音的背後，實際包含非常鮮明的利益企圖。與此同時，教牧人員為了獲取職位，獲得更多的米薪而不擇手段，教牧之間、教牧與教友之間、教牧與教會中樞之間關係惡化，明顯表現出離心離德的趨向，教牧職位的神聖性被大大弱化。精神層面的危機不僅削弱了教會重建的基礎，也深刻影響到潮汕以後教會的發展。

---

116 12-11-14：中華基督教會汕頭區會文件，《汕檔》，長美堂史略（1949年）。

117 12-11-14：中華基督教會汕頭區會文件，《汕檔》，柘林堂史略（1949年）。

118 George A. Hood to Wm. Short, 24th August, 1946, No. 887, H-10, PCEFM, Archives Microfiche.

119 民國資料C222：〈常務委員會記錄〉，《汕檔》，汕頭區會常務委員會第十四次會議記錄（1946年5月8日）。

國家圖書館出版品預行編目（CIP）資料

華人情境下的基督宗教與社會關懷 / 王成勉主編 . --
初版 . -- 桃園市：中央大學出版中心；臺北市：遠流，
2016.12
面；　公分 . --
部份內容為英文
ISBN 978-986-5659-12-7（平裝）

1. 基督教　2. 宗教與社會　3. 文集

240.16　　　　　　　　　　　　　　105023876

華人情境下的基督宗教與社會關懷

主編：王成勉
執行編輯：許家泰
編輯協力：簡玉欣

出版單位：國立中央大學出版中心
　　　　　桃園市中壢區中大路 300 號 國鼎圖書資料館 3 樓

　　　　　遠流出版事業股份有限公司
　　　　　台北市南昌路二段 81 號 6 樓

發行單位／展售處：遠流出版事業股份有限公司
地址：台北市南昌路二段 81 號 6 樓
電話：(02) 23926899　傳真：(02) 23926658
劃撥帳號：0189456-1

著作權顧問：蕭雄淋律師
2016 年 12 月 初版一刷
售價：新台幣 480 元